THE LANGUAGE OF TRAGEDY

THE
LANGUAGE
OF
TRAGEDY

By Moody E. Prior

COLUMBIA UNIVERSITY PRESS
New York • 1947

Published in Great Britain and India by Geoffrey Cumberlege,
Oxford University Press, London and Bombay

MANUFACTURED IN THE UNITED STATES OF AMERICA

ACKNOWLEDGMENTS

IN THE PREPARATION of this book I have received valuable aid from various persons. To my wife and to my sister, Miss Sophia Prior, I am indebted for material assistance in matters of detail and in the preparation of the manuscript. Mrs. Wilda Stuart was helpful in securing bibliographical information for the final chapter. Professors Bergen Evans, Lyndon Shanley, and Walter Scott each read particular portions of the manuscript and made useful suggestions. Professor Arthur Nethercot read the entire manuscript, and to his good judgment and meticulous care I owe a number of improvements. To Professor Ronald Crane I am indebted for a searching criticism of the method. To all these persons I wish to make public acknowledgment of my gratitude. They did their generous best to help make the book better than it is.

Permission to quote from copyrighted works has been obtained from the publishers in the following instances: Anderson House for Maxwell Anderson's *The Essence of Tragedy* and *Winterset;* Thomas Y. Crowell for Allardyce Nicoll's *British Drama;* Mr. Thomas Dickinson for his *Playwrights of the New American Theater;* Dodd, Mead and Company for William Archer's *The Old Drama and the New;* Harcourt, Brace and Company for T. S. Eliot's *Murder in the Cathedral* and *The Family Reunion;* Harvard University Press for T. S. Eliot's *The Use of Poetry;* Houghton Mifflin Company for Stephen Spender's *The Destructive Element;* John Lane, The Bodley Head for John Davidson's *Godfrida;* The Macmillan Company for Thomas Hardy's *The Dynasts,* John Masefield's *The Tragedy of Nan,* Stephen Phillip's *Ulysses,* and W. B. Yeats's *Cutting of an Agate, Wheels and Butterflies, Plays and Controversies, Calvary,* and *Purgatory;* Oxford University Press for Louis MacNeice's *Modern Poetry* and Bonamy Dobrée's *Restoration Tragedy;* Random House for Stephen Spender's *The Trial of a Judge,* C. Day Lewis' *A Hope for Poetry,* and W. H. Auden and Christopher Isherwood's *The Dog beneath the Skin* and *On the Frontier;* Charles Scribner's Sons for Edmund Wilson's *Axel's Castle.* The London *Times* has granted permission for quotation from a leading article in its *Literary Supple-*

ment for May 26, 1921, and the *New Republic* for an article by Stephen Spender, "The Artistic Future of Poetry." Permission to use modern editions of old authors as a basis for reference has been granted by the publishers in the following instances: G. Bell and Sons for P. A. Daniel's edition of *The Maid's Tragedy;* Dial Press for U. M. Ellis-Fermor's edition of *Tamburlaine;* E. P. Dutton and Company for T. M. Parrott's edition of *Bussy d'Ambois;* Ginn and Company for David Stevens's edition of *Aureng-Zebe* in *Types of English Drama;* D. C. Heath and Company for Katherine Bates's edition of *A Woman Killed with Kindness* and S. P. Sherman's edition of *The Broken Heart;* Oxford University Press for F. L. Lucas's edition of *The Duchess of Malfi,* J. W. Cunliffe's edition of *Gorboduc* in *Early English Classical Tragedies,* F. S. Boas' edition of *The Spanish Tragedy,* C. H. Herford and P. Simpson's edition of *Sejanus,* and Bonamy Dobrée's edition of *All for Love* in *Five Restoration Tragedies;* Charles Scribner's Sons for E. H. Coleridge's edition of the plays of Byron. I regret that I have been unable to trace the present owners of the copyright in the case of John Davidson's *The Theatrocrat* and Allardyce Nicoll's edition of the works of Tourneur.

It is also a pleasure to make grateful acknowledgment for the assistance granted by Northwestern University toward the publication of this book.

M.E.P.

PREFACE

THE PRESENT WORK is an exploration into the nature of verse tragedy. Specifically, it attempts to discover the relationship between the language of plays written in verse and the dramatic nature of the form. The first chapter consists of an analysis of verse drama from this point of view, directed toward establishing certain essential general principles. The subsequent chapters are centered in the analysis of selected plays. These chapters follow a chronological order, and the discussion of individual works is preceded by a consideration of the circumstances which in any given period of dramatic development, from the Elizabethan age to the present time, helped to shape the various styles of poetic drama. The aim is primarily critical rather than historical, however, and therefore many plays which deserve a place in a systematic and exhaustive survey of poetic drama are not included or find only passing mention.

This study is confined largely to tragedy. The principles developed cannot be applied without modification to other types of dramatic composition—comedy, for instance—which presumably demand a separate inquiry. It has been found necessary, however, to take into account certain plays which are not in any strict sense tragedies, either because of the bearing which they have had in the development of particular dramatic styles, or because of some special insight which they afford into the nature of poetic tragedy itself. This is particularly the case in the last chapter, which is concerned with the modern age; for the characteristic features of the important dramatic traditions of our times have had the effect of breaking down or obscuring the distinction between dramatic genres, which in former times was more strictly observed. The study is confined, further, to English drama for the most part. Theoretically, there is no reason why other tragedy, notably Greek and French, should not have been included. The chief practical consideration which dictated the limitation was that the method of analysis employed requires something more than a working familiarity with the language. However, to the extent that they are supported by the English plays considered, the general conclusions about diction and form in verse tragedy are not invalidated by the limitation.

The method employed is based in part on a study of the diction of individual plays, and is dictated by the principles considered in the first chapter. It may be likened to the effect of a slow-motion camera, which can produce revealing results, provided deliberate distortion is not introduced through lens and angle. If the appropriateness of the method be granted, the results should help to enlarge our understanding of the art of poetic tragedy. Indirectly, therefore, they might even contribute toward answering those general questions about the form which have occupied critics since Aristotle and which take on a new interest and meaning in every period of dramatic activity. The results are restricted, however, by the limits which the principles themselves define and within which their application is legitimate and useful. This is only another way of saying that like any other work of criticism this one is limited to partial insights. No single procedure can reveal all we would like to know about works of art. It is possible to ask a variety of questions about them, and each question will demand its own special answer.

M.E.P.

Evanston, Illinois

May, 1946

CONTENTS

CONTENTS

CHAPTER I

THE NATURE OF THE PROBLEM

THE GENERAL ACCEPTANCE of prose as the appropriate medium for most drama, including tragedy, is relatively recent. Until the later years of the nineteenth century, it was taken for granted that plays of a serious nature would normally be written in verse and that prose would be the exception. With the revolutionary success, however, of Ibsen, Tchekov, and the playwrights of the realistic school in England and America, verse drama has everywhere become the exception and its composition is regarded with uncertainty and even suspicion. The term "poetic drama," which criticism in recent years has applied to older verse drama, is an indication of the special category to which the once standard form of serious drama has now been relegated, and implies in some cases that verse is a somewhat specialized and perhaps dispensable accessory.

These recent developments have not, however, had the effect of making verse drama a dead issue. On the contrary, they have given it a new importance, since for the first time it has become a matter of explicit critical concern whether for the serious dramatist verse is better than prose. For in spite of the remarkable vitality of modern drama, the tragedies about whose unquestioned greatness there is general agreement are in verse, and it has therefore been suggested that with the general abandonment of verse, modern drama may have lost something—whatever it might be—that enabled the Greek tragedians and Shakespeare to do greatly what later writers seem able only to do well. Partisan enthusiasts of the modern drama have been inclined to question whether verse was an essential element in the success of the older drama—whether, in fact, it was not a handicap. Though at times their discussions show traces of the rough and ready improvisations of controversy, they have served to bring the issue into prominence and to encourage more philosophic and dispassionate excursions into the problem. Some of these have sustained the apologists of the modern prose play to the extent of maintaining that the use of verse in drama is now an anachronism and that the dramatist of today must find his way to greatness without it. On the other hand, there have been a number of attempts to explore the nature of poetic drama, to discover the special function of verse and the advantages, if any, which accompany its use, and to consider the possibilities of its continued use in the modern play. And there have not been wanting attempts to make a trial of these possibilities. Verse drama continues to be written. For the most part, the dramatists in verse in recent years have written tentatively and experimentally and not with the requirements of the popular stage primarily in mind. Yet even in the commercial theatre, the efforts of Maxwell Anderson to find a verse form suitable for the drama of our times illustrate that at least one kind of poetic drama can still enjoy considerable popular success. Both in theory and practice, the question of verse drama is still an open one.

A good approach to the problem would appear to be the thorough understanding of the great classics of tragedy. On the particular questions involved in this study, however, most of the critical writings about these plays do not prove very helpful. There are many illuminating studies of origins and development, and analyses of action, character, themes, and other related matters. There are also admirable appreciations of their "poetry," style, and particular felicities of expression. But scarcely any rigorous efforts have been made to bring these characteristics of expression into distinct and close relationship with other aspects of these plays. We learn, for example, a great deal about Shakespeare the dramatist, and we are shown much to admire about Shakespeare the poet, but the precise relationship which exists between these two aspects of that comprehensive genius has not often been seriously and painstakingly studied.

Yet one of the distinctive qualities of great tragedy is its wholeness—the impression it leaves of being undivided and fused, of being the product of genius under the directing impulse of one impressive dramatic idea. If we are to understand the special virtues and peculiar possibilities of the use of verse as the conditioning factor in the style, we must start with the assumption that there is an essential relationship between the particular way in which words are used in these plays and the order in which they are used, and the totality of the final product. Complete artistic wholeness could not have been achieved if the poetry had been added to a dramatic design as a kind of final adornment. Since the form is dramatic, then all the means used had to be ordered to dramatic ends. Under no other circumstances could artistic success have been possible.

The results of any inquiry into this matter are hardly likely to be very rewarding, however, if what is involved in the idea of the dramatic is reduced, as it often is in loose and popular usage, to exciting intrigue, movement and bustle on the stage, or those moments of maximum force and excitement which any good play will afford. It is with the idea of the dramatic in its most comprehensive formal sense that the problem must be approached.

This will involve repetition of familiar and elementary concepts, but it is best to start building from simple, even if commonplace, assumptions. As a first premise, drama—and more particularly tragedy—as an art form may be defined as the representation of a complete action of some sort.[1] There are many to whom this will appear a limited and old-fashioned notion. There are those who agree wholeheartedly that, as one writer puts it, "Everything in the drama of these days indicates the passing of the importance of plot";[2] there are those who have criticized Aristotle for making the action the soul of tragedy since character is by far the most interesting and memorable feature of any good play; and there are those who believe that stressing the importance of plot and action confuses the serious dramatist since it interferes with his primary purpose of giving expression to his ideas about man and society. Nearly all such objections arise from at least partial misapprehension of what is involved in the definition. To say that action is the primary formal principle in a serious play is not the same as saying that the plot is the supremely interesting thing about it, or the feature which fascinated the dramatist most and provided the main inspiration to his efforts, or the aspect which provides the chief grounds for gratification and reflection: what is meant is that in a serious play, action is the principle of order and selection. It determines what is to be included, since the relevance of any given speech or episode may be judged by what it contributes to the progression of events as part of a beginning, middle, and end continuum; it determines the order of the speeches and episodes, since they must be introduced in such a way as not to confuse the progression. In this sense, action is the "soul" of the play.

The significance of this principle for the art of the drama can be further appreciated if, for the moment, character or thought is considered in the same way as the end of drama. Character as a principle of organization is looser and less exacting than action. If what may be included in a play is determined only by its appropriateness in illustrating or defining character, the possibilities in the way of what may be relevantly introduced become very great. In addition, if character is regarded as the end of the play, no clear scheme of order is implicit in the formal principle: as Johnson said of the descriptions in *Windsor Forest*, "Of many appearances subsisting all at once, no rule can be given why one should be mentioned before another." In consequence, the effect of finality or inevitability characteristic of good drama is less likely to result. Where thought becomes the primary end, character tends to become a point of view or an attitude toward the issues being discussed, further development being in the way of additional touches or flourishes to add interest and variety to the persons of the play and thus to arouse sympathy or antipathy to particular views. Action in such a case assumes the role of providing theatrical stimulation to keep one interested and awake to the ideas. In the first instance (character), the action would serve merely as a loose narrative scheme to provide a practical check on the extensive possibilities for inclusion. In the second (thought), action would function merely as a rhetorical device.

The idea of action as the end of drama is not, however, by itself, sufficiently comprehensive unless account is further taken of the principle that a dramatic action must be probable and necessary. Character, for instance, is an important factor in any scheme of probability and necessity in a play; what we know about a character gives us grounds for comprehending his actions and also restricts the way in which he will meet the contingencies of the situation. Moreover, though the character becomes more fully understood as the number of episodes in which he functions is multiplied, that very enlargement of our knowledge actually limits the probable ways in which the character can behave. For instance, the behavior of Othello when he dismisses Cassio for unbecoming conduct while on duty anticipates his judgment and murder of Desdemona, and so, once we take into account the intervening differences in circumstance between the two events, his horrible act of perverted justice and honor becomes a matter of necessity. Moreover, in any given dramatic situation there are only a finite number of possibilities within which the play may properly move, any one of which may be probably determinant in the outcome. As the progress of the action eliminates one or more of the possibilities, the others become increasingly probable. The importance of these considerations may be emphasized by raising the question of what distinguishes a thin and shallow play from one that is rich and profound, or what distinguishes two different plays based on precisely the same plot. It is in large part a matter of differences in the kinds of probabilities which are determinant in the action—differences of character, differences in the bearing which some particular factor has on the outcome, and the like. If broadly enough considered, the principle of necessary and probable action will be found to define the formal basis of most good plays.

It is unwise, however, to be dogmatic about this. Not everything which is capable of being put on the stage, not every work which uses the conventions of act and scene division and characters in dialogue is ordered by action, and failure to conform to this formal principle is not necessarily a mark of artistic error. Many excellent one-act plays, for instance, are not thus ordered, nor are certain modern expressionistic plays. Every work of art is in one sense *sui generis*, and must be approached in terms of the principles appropriate to it. Dogmatic insistence on a narrow definition or undeviating application of a single, restricted critical technique is not, however, the only danger: at the other extreme is the incorporation into the idea of drama of anything from the Catholic Mass to dancing. Two characters dressed as shepherds reciting in turn the stanzas from an eighteenth-century pastoral do not constitute a play. Neither does a dialogue of Plato, since, in spite of the characterization, setting, and movement of persons, the work is primarily a dialectical exploration. Aristotle's principle of action as the formal basis of tragedy is useful in establishing a category of works which are, in a formal sense, dramatic, and thus in affording a convenient instrument of analysis for works which come properly within its province.

Before seeking to establish the connection between language poetically used and a dramatic action as just defined, it is further necessary to consider what is involved in the use of verse as the normal conditioning feature of dialogue. A good deal of attention has been paid to the metrical nature of such dialogue. Rhythm of itself must certainly play an important part in the large currents of a poetic play. In *Othello*, for instance, the measured and orderly cadences of Othello's defense before the senate are a mark of his honesty and complete self-assurance; the broken and unbalanced rhythms of his speeches during the undermining assaults of Iago indicate not only the destruction of his peace of mind but also the temporary disorganization of his noblest faculties; the forced calmness of his speech before killing Desdemona reflects the reluctant resolution of his mind; and the fine cadences of his last speech mark a return to the Othello of the opening scenes.

But the use of verse has also the most important consequences on diction. The regularity of metrical language, even though the rhythms are freely manipulated, imposes a discipline on the order of words such as is not encountered in ordinary discourse, and represents a break, therefore, with the characteristics of informal speech. Verse establishes a condition which eliminates the standard of strict verisimilitude as the criterion of appropriateness for any given speech, and hence opens the way to exploitation of all the resources of language for whatever artistic needs may arise. This is a matter of fundamental importance: it has immediate consequences which affect everything about the play in an essential way. It is misleading to contend, therefore, that "The use of verse instead of prose because of its emotional effect is . . . resorting to an extraneous aid for doing what the plot itself should accomplish; but it is not as dispensable a device as the spectacle because the medium of the drama is language."[3] Since words are, in a sense, the material with which a play is created, what happens to language is of primary importance and in no way comparable to the spectacle, which in most conventional plays is theoretically dispensable. And in the last analysis, it is not the verse that is important but the consequences in the diction which are important. The use of verse may be regarded as a sign that the criterion of appropriateness in diction is not reportorial exactness, or even a freely interpreted concern with faithfulness to the actual circumstances governing dialogue in life, but the needs of an art; it represents an intention of using all possible means to gain appropriate artistic ends without being hampered by the demands of verisimilitude.

There are several difficulties in the way of becoming reconciled at once to this attitude toward the language of a verse play. One of these is inherent in the nature of drama itself. A play represents characters speaking and acting, and the performance gives us these characters as actual persons. To the extent that the stage illusion is successful, the audience will tend to construe itself as an interested spectator of other people's lives. Hence the opportunity is constantly present to relate the dramatist's account of these persons' experiences with one's own, and in the process to eliminate, and perhaps even to resent as extraneous and confusing, whatever features of the play interfere with the ready formation of judgments on this basis. This attitude is particularly common at the present time as a result of the prevalence for several decades of realistic methods in playwriting. Not only have these accustomed spectators to look for minute resemblances in the life being portrayed, but they have made the standard of "truth to life" a major criterion of excellence. It is, of course, quite natural to look in a play for anything which the author's experiences might contribute to one's own knowledge, to find illumination about life in it, and to despise an author who is evasive or guilty of falsehood and misrepresentation. Truth to life in a play might raise one's respect for the matter, and indirectly might be responsible for good artistry, since honesty and sincerity must be presupposed for any great creative effort as distinct from clever writing or competent craftsmanship. Yet of two plays each equally praiseworthy in the respect of truth to life—however the phrase is understood in any given context—the one which is a better play will be preferred. This is another way of saying that truth is not—of itself—an artistic merit. It is a condition of intelligibility and acceptability. The dramatist needs the experiences of life to write at all. To the extent that he knows what he is talking about and that he presents his material in a way which makes us recognize his competence as an observer, he has established a rapport between himself and his audience. The question of whether the play is good or bad, however, still remains to be decided. That is an artistic question.

It is necessary to labor this point because poetic drama has been brought into question as a result of the confusion about it. William Archer argued against the appropriateness of verse in drama at all, and regarded verse dialogue as, at best, an accomplishment inferior in kind to excellent management of normal discourse. His views illustrate how far critics had gone toward assuming that drama acquires excellence as it approaches observed behavior in detail. Even professed admirers of the older dramatists—to whom, incidentally, the term "poetic tragedy" would have seemed a redundancy—occasionally reveal in their literary judgments a tacit acceptance of principles made current by the dramatic traditions of the last half century. Levin Schücking, for example, finds fault with a figure of speech used by Laertes to Ophelia because "This comparison of the tender feelings of a girlish heart with the artillery fire of an army in battle seems to us almost absurdly artificial."[4] Not all the figures of speech in the older tragedies are unexceptionable by any means, but judgment of their merits cannot be made in isolation from the larger context of the whole play or in terms of the realistic ideal of verisimilitude, simply because in the best sense they are "artificial."

Even when it is recognized that the condition of diction in a poetic play requires a different kind of appreciation from that appropriate to a style purporting to reproduce informal speech, the various methods of analysis which can be used are not all equally successful in revealing the dramatic function of language poetically ordered. Artifices of expression may be regarded, for instance, as serving the needs either of decoration or of rhetoric. It is not possible in practice to preserve a sharp line of demarcation between these theoretical extremes, but distinction between them is not wholly arbitrary. If we can consider language being manipulated chiefly for its possibilities as ornament, the ultimate criterion of excellence would be conspicuous technical expertness in the formulation of devices of speech and pronounced pattern and design in phrasing. Euphuism, though not wholly the freak suggested by our hypothetical case, has the marks of a style for which such criteria of excellence are clearly in place. When criticism of poetical works is guided primarily by the search for patterns as patterns, the results are chiefly valuable only as they provide understanding of the mechanical organization of the means. Consideration of the rhetorical approach to language represents a more involved problem, since the term "rhetoric" has acquired many shades of meaning and is used with both complimentary and pejorative force. Rhetorical use does not imply any one particular style; under certain circumstances, for instance, the cultivation of ornament may indicate a special instance of rhetorical intention. In its classic sense, rhetoric is the art of persuasion, and rhetorical usage is seen as governed in any given instance by the difficulties of subject matter and circumstance which stand in the way of securing approval or conviction. From this point of view, the nature of the audience is an essential consideration in determining rhetorical appropriateness and excellence. It is easy to appreciate this fact in oratory and pamphleteering; it is less obvious, perhaps, that the same criteria may be applied to such forms as satire, whose end is to secure disapproval and ridicule for the objects satirized, to particular speeches of certain plays where the dramatist makes a partisan plea for sympathy, or even to special artistic devices designed to suggest the preservation of artistic proprieties. The cultivation of sententiousness in some Elizabethan tragedies illustrates one consequence of thinking of the problem of expression in rhetorical terms. Where the critic relies primarily on rhetorical principles, the result usually takes the form of demonstrating the special effectiveness of individual passages.

The most familiar method of dealing with the poetical aspects of verse drama takes the form of appreciative comment on individual lines or passages conspicuous for beauty and power and expressive of intense feeling or depth of reflection. The two modes of analysis just considered often play a part in such comment. The fine effects of emphasis which rhythmic phrasing produces, of richness of suggestion and strength of statement which result from figurative expression and heightened diction, are so pronounced in these specially brilliant lines that, though isolated from their context, they seem complete and almost final acts of composition in themselves. A great deal can be learned from viewing these great moments in detail, but the widespread use of the method has bred aberrations of critical view; for instance, that the proper function of poetry in drama is simply the expression of passion, or that the great speeches are lyrical interludes or "extra-dramatic moments." It seems unlikely, however, that a sensitive dramatist could write a play wholly or largely in verse only so that he might be ready for a few special utterances of fine frenzy, particularly if these moments represent an indulgence in fine writing distinct in function from other speeches. There are many magnificent lines in the best verse tragedies which one wishes to recall by themselves, and there are mediocre and poorly managed verse plays which are saved only by a few speeches of great splendor. But these considerations should not get in the way of the main critical problem. Isolation of the notable passages, special consideration of devices of expression by themselves, leaves the main question of relationship to the whole still unanswered, if indeed it does not definitely stand in the way of its solution.

For this reason, it is necessary to regard the work as a whole in order to understand the artistic role which the constituent elements must play in it. Where the diction of a play is poetically conceived, a dramatic understanding of its function, in the most comprehensive sense, must be arrived at through a consideration of the relevance of any given speeches, words, images, or figures to the work considered as a developing form.

The circumstances of a lyric make it altogether simpler to illustrate this way of looking at the problem of diction and form. By way of analogy, consider, for instance, Keats's use of "requiem" in "Ode to a Nightingale":

> Now more than ever seems it rich to die,
>   To cease upon the midnight with no pain,
>   While thou art pouring forth thy soul abroad
>   In such an ecstasy!
>   Still wouldst thou sing, and I have ears in vain—
>   To thy high requiem become a sod.

The word "requiem" is appropriate here because it fits in with suggestions of death and at the same time of music. But to realize the artistry in the use of "requiem" it is necessary to recall the poet's desire at the outset to be free of the sorrow and mutability of life and to identify himself somehow with the song of the nightingale, which is established as the symbol of joy and permanence. The poet's desire to resolve the discrepancy between these two planes is conveyed through the interplay of images which oppose and balance suggestions of sorrow, pain, death, and mutability against those of joy, beauty, life, and permanence. Even when the poet, on the "viewless wings of poesy," finally imagines himself at one with the nightingale in the forest, the description of the beauty of the setting is still haunted by suggestions of death, change, and opiate oblivion—"embalmed darkness," "fast fading violets," "murmurous haunt of flies." These suggestions lead directly to the reflections of the next stanza: death is the appropriate ending of this moment, a permanent, though imperfect, avenue of escape. This momentary resolution in the development of the poem is preceded by the extreme contrast between "rich to die" and "ecstasy" and it is effected in the word "requiem"—the one word which could at once sustain the symbolic significance of the nightingale's song and the poet's preoccupation with death, and thus bring to a focus the tragic paradox of his most hopeful solution. The word demands the whole preceding development, just as the whole preceding development demands the word.

The extraordinary concentration of lyric poetry makes such demonstrations a comparatively easy matter. In tragedy, however, such effects and associations may appear to be more difficult to uncover—one may justifiably wonder if they are possible at all, since tragedies are so often based on violent and even brutal plots and are generally intended to endure the harsh test of performance before a miscellaneous audience. Yet a principal consequence of writing drama in verse is precisely that it opens the same resources of language to the dramatist as to the lyric poet. Because words are freed from the limitations of verisimilitude, all these resources become available for supporting, illuminating, and magnifying the action. Imagery of all kinds, ambivalences of meaning and suggestion, words made uniquely potent and momentous by the circumstances of the context, figures of speech, in particular metaphors—all these become available to the dramatist to be used as his artistic needs require. And if one of the distinctive qualities of great tragedy is its wholeness, then it is permissible to assume that when poetic tragedy approaches perfection in the proper adaptation of means to ends, the question of propriety in diction may be determined by asking whether a given word or image has been put to use in such a way as to contribute to the development of a dramatic form. In the light of our definition of tragedy as a necessary and probable action of a particular sort, diction in poetic tragedy may be regarded as essentially related to the factors of necessity and probability which determine the form as an action.

Though detailed illustration of the nature of such relations must be reserved for the discussion of individual plays to follow, some of the general conditions governing them may be briefly stated. If we can imagine, for a moment, establishing a hierarchy of the devices of speech and special ways of using words available to the poet, metaphor would be at the apex as the type-form which the diction of poetry might be said to approach as a limit. The language of poetry is generally directed away from the literal and toward the symbolic, and it functions so as to increase the relevant implications and suggestions at any given point and to establish associations and correspondences between analogous or unlike things. Metaphor performs such functions with the most concentration. Aristotle regarded the ability to create illuminating metaphors as the one thing the poet could not learn but must have from nature. The importance of metaphor and of the other devices of language which imitate or approximate its function lies in the fact that poetry begins where the possibility or likelihood of literal exactness ceases. "Metaphorical language," says Shelley, "marks the before unapprehended relations of things and perpetuates their apprehension." The poetic functioning of language is in itself a symptom of and a contribution to an extension of our experience: it is, in a sense, a form of discovery, a pushing of the bounds of apprehension beyond the limits of exact observation and into areas where literal certainty and systematic knowledge do not provide the appropriate answers. This may be Shakespeare's meaning in a well-known passage from *A Midsummer Night's Dream:*

> And as imagination bodies forth
> The forms of things unknown, the poet's pen
> Turns them to shapes . . .

There need not be anything mystical about this, though some writers have not hesitated to approach metaphor as the key which might unlock the mysteries and show us what God and man is. Insights into aspects of experience which because of their obscurity or complexity cannot be readily reduced to explicit propositions can be expressed analogically or symbolically in such a way as to reveal an imaginative grasp of their nature and their emotional weight and moment. Things hitherto unrelated can be brought into association and disparate things shown in relationship.

For the dramatist, the advantages of such an instrument of expression and exploration are evident. Motives, conflicts of will, and emotional responses to events are in their nature too involved, even too little understood, to be reduced to plain and self-evident clarity without destroying their essential nature or giving them a narrow and false simplicity. Had the tragedies of Shakespeare and of the ancients not been poetic tragedies, the impression of depth and vividness which their characters convey would have been impossible. Another quality to which critics have repeatedly called attention, particularly in the case of Shakespeare's tragedies, is their largeness and grandeur and the sense they convey of having somehow touched on great and obscure truths about life. In part this impression is the result of the extension of the implications of a limited and unique action through the operation of figurative diction. Figures of speech, ambivalent words, and the like involve a reference to at least two aspects of reality or experience seen in relation to one another. In a richly poetical play the dramatist draws from so wide a range of impressions for his figures and gives to individual words so many special and intensified accents that by the accumulation of association and implication the simple action of the play seems to reach out to the most remote boundaries of human experience. The effect is, on the one hand, to endow the limited story with great generality (universality is a common term for expressing this quality), and, on the other, to endow the action with great magnitude.

Undisciplined use of these devices of speech could well lead to inflation, bombast, and diffuseness. It is, therefore, only when they operate within the restricted scheme of probabilities which govern the action and thus exert a directive force on the determinant elements of the play that they assume their most effective role in a dramatic form. Since character is one of the most important of such determinant elements, figures and images which apply to character can be made to enlarge our understanding of it or give additional force and expectation to what we know. When Bosola, in *The Duchess of Malfi*, says of the Duke and the Cardinal,

> You have a pair of hearts are hollow graves
> Rotten and rotting others,

he has illuminated them and their role in the play and the life of the court of which they are the center, and done so with a concentration and economy unattainable by any attempt to disclose the same things explicitly. Where the language of a play is through and through poetic, it can stay within the restricted scheme of the play and yet develop great complexity of reference. Enobarbus' description of Cleopatra's barge which "burned on the water" is something more than a highly decorative piece of reporting. The paradoxical phrase not only calls attention to the splendor of the barge, but it glances also at the queen, and the whole vivid picture is part of the contrast between Rome and Egypt which occupies an important place in the play and is an aspect of the dilemma in which Antony is caught.

Such effects, moreover, occur not only in the notable passages: where poetic language is integral to the play, the whole fabric of the work becomes affected, and the most inconspicuous speech may perhaps contribute to the probabilities of character and situation. In a relatively unimportant speech in *Macbeth*, Ross says,

> . . . by the clock 'tis day,
> And yet dark night strangles the travelling lamp.

The use of the word "strangles" to suggest the diminution of the light in the dense and unnatural darkness is part of an elaborate scheme in the diction which continuously reinforces the impression of the unnaturally violent world of the play. And, finally, since a play is an action, a progressive movement of events, the diction can properly reveal something of this dynamic development. When Cassius dies in *Julius Caesar*, Titinius says:

> O setting sun,
> As in thy red rays thou dost sink tonight,
> So in his red blood Cassius' day is set;
> The sun of Rome is set. Our day is gone;
> Clouds, dews and dangers come; our deeds are done.

The action continues briefly from this point until Brutus, defeated and left with only a handful of friends, takes his own life. Just before he runs on his sword, Brutus says:

> So fare you well at once; for Brutus' tongue
> Hath almost ended his life's history.
> Night hangs upon my eyes; my bones would rest
> That have but labored to attain this hour.

The night image has relevance to the final completion of the action as the sunset image has to the partial completion of it in the death of Cassius. The two images derive additional significance, moreover, from other developments within the play. The reader of *Julius Caesar* will recall the passionate nature of Cassius, who in the storm, for instance, had bared his bosom to the lightning "in the aim and very flash of it," who had a heart "dearer than Pluto's mine, richer than gold." He will recall, too, that it is Brutus who broods disquietly over each issue and who, from the time that Cassius urged him against Caesar, could not sleep. The images thus have relevance both to character and to the status of the play at the moment they appear.

These few illustrations are merely suggestive of the way in which the resources of diction available to poetic tragedy can be made to cooperate with those determinant elements which direct the action in a necessary and probable way. It is almost inevitable that most of them should be drawn from Shakespearean tragedy. To assume, however, that all poetic tragedy must do things in precisely the same way would be dogmatic and incorrect. Any alteration in the conditioning elements which operate to shape a given drama, whether in the nature of the materials used, or even in the construction and mechanics of the theatre for which the play is intended, will demand some modification in the manipulation of the means and in the conventions employed, and will produce a reorganization of the whole structure which will affect every detail, diction included. And since the devices and methods employed by Shakespeare can not be expected to function without change in the tragedy of any other age, the precise critical technique useful in discovering relations of diction and form in Elizabethan tragedy must not be assumed to be applicable in every detail and without modification to all verse drama whatsoever. Nevertheless, critical study of the great poetic tragedy of the past, as well as theoretical consideration of the potentialities of the form, seems to point to the general conclusion that, whatever material differences may exist between individual plays or types of plays, artistic success in the use of verse in tragedy, or of any style which attempts to approximate verse or take advantage of the effects possible through it, is contingent on an essential formal relationship between a diction poetically conceived and ordered and the dramatic character of the work. A play is, of course, not a lyric; and the language of a play —a verse play as much as any other—must conform to all of the practical and artistic requirements of the form: it must be adapted to the exigencies of performance, since drama is determined in many respects by the limits and conventions of a given playing stage; and it must be properly adjusted to the emotional demands of crucial moments—it must satisfy many conditions and demands which may, in one sense or another, be thought of as dramatic.[5] But in the most comprehensive sense, the diction of poetic tragedy becomes dramatic only when, after satisfying all other necessary demands, it contributes to the form as a necessary and probable action.

CHAPTER II

THE ELIZABETHAN TRADITION

THE EIGHTY YEARS between 1562, the date of *Gorboduc* and the conventional starting point for the history of English tragedy, and 1642, the date of the closing of the theatres by Parliament, are the great era of English verse drama. The age would be noteworthy for its drama if only because of the vigor of the dramatic activity which characterized it—because of the great number, the variety, the scope, and the energy of the plays it produced. Many of these, it is true, are negligible, many of them contemptible; nevertheless, some of them have commanded serious critical attention to the present time. This whole drama, moreover, acquires a special significance from the circumstance of having been the vehicle through which Shakespeare gave expression to his extraordinary and manifold genius. And in the shifting history of English drama, the drama of this age has been a kind of lodestar; either through emulation, adaptation, or repudiation, each age has, consciously or not, regarded its plays critically from a perspective determined by the relation of its drama to that of the age of Shakespeare. Particularly where verse drama is concerned, these plays have never been far from the mind of the playwright or critic, and any remaining hope that the distinction between plays and poetry may be once more resolved largely nourishes on the phenomenon of the plays of the late sixteenth and early seventeenth centuries.

I

Elizabethan tragedy, beginning in *Gorboduc* under elegant academic auspices, developed into one of the principal features of an energetic and successful commercial theatre. As the product of a popular art, it reveals qualities of vigor and excitement; as the product of an age which is distinguished for the variety and splendor of its poetry, it is frequently marked by beauty and even magnificance of expression. The merits of this tragedy have become the commonplaces of the literary historian. Yet, though its superficial characteristics are readily discernible and the conventional admiration seems understandable enough, definition of its essential nature and assessment of its final artistic accomplishment are another matter. Criticism of Elizabethan tragedy in modern times shows, in fact, a divergence of opinion on these matters sharp enough to amount to controversy. All important literatures stimulate differences of opinion, but the divergence of views in this case raises basically the problem of the nature and the artistic accomplishment of Elizabethan tragedy. For this reason, some familiarity with the trend in recent criticism of this drama is a useful preparation for an understanding of its art.

A convenient starting point for viewing the modern controversy over the nature and the merits of Elizabethan drama is the criticism of Lamb and Swinburne. These two are commonly regarded as being responsible for a separation of the purely dramatic aspects of this drama, in the sense of plot and theatrical effectiveness, from the purely literary aspects, in the sense of the imaginative realization of situations and episodes and beauty of language. This is not a wholly accurate interpretation of their critical work on the Elizabethans, but the method of Lamb's *Specimens*, in the effect which it has of isolating particular beauties, and his special insistence, as well as Swinburne's, on the quality of striking imaginative force which he repeatedly noticed in these plays makes this view of their criticism plausible. The two are generally regarded as having stressed poetry at the expense of drama, of having, as T. S. Eliot put it in the preface to his *Elizabethan Essays*, treated the plays as literature. At the opposite extreme from this view is William Archer, who sharpened the cleavage between what he called the "exaggerative or lyrical element" and the dramatic, and, rejecting the poetic elements as irrelevant to drama, condemned Elizabethan drama as artistically confused: "The modern realistic drama is a pure and logical art-form. The other elements of primitive drama, the lyrical and the saltatory, have been sloughed off and have taken independent form in music-drama, commonly known as opera, and in ballet."[1] Elizabethan drama emerges from his pages as impure, illogical, and primitive, and a principal point of his objection is its use of verse and its adoption of conventions which permit eloquence and diction that escape the limits of verisimilitude.

Archer precipitated something of a crisis in dramatic criticism. It was clear that much in his protest was common sense, and that the excitement of the nineteenth-century enthusiasts had glossed over a good deal of confusion and ineptitude in this older drama. But it was also clear that the evolutionary logic on which he founded much of his analysis rested on questionable assumptions and that he had missed much of the excellence of Elizabethan drama at its best by his determination to establish the importance of modern drama. He excepted Shakespeare from the common attack on the grounds that a genius is exempt from ordinary critical methods, and by this unwarranted procedure oversimplified the whole problem, though Archer has by no means been the only one to use the evasion. It might be stated categorically that any exemption of Shakespeare from consideration of Elizabethan drama as a particular art form is basically illogical since it was not by the repudiation of the style or its conventions that Shakespeare succeeded, but by superior artistic use of them, and consequently the attack cannot be directed at Elizabethan drama as illogical and confused, but at specific Elizabethan dramatists as bad workmen with the materials at their disposal. Archer performed the service, however, of making uncritical enthusiasm untenable and of stating the absurdities of Elizabethan drama so radically that those who felt otherwise about its merits were forced to look for a solid basis for their taste. Essentially, however, he pointed up precisely the same kind of separation of the "poetic" aspects from the "dramatic" which the nineteenth century had encouraged, and by using the dichotomy to the discredit of this drama he made strikingly manifest the necessity of looking for a principle of reconciliation.

Theoretically, there are various ways of coming to terms with Archer's problem. One is to attack the premise that in drama complete verisimilitude is the ideal goal, and to reject the inference that conventions which destroy the possibility of realism are in themselves bad. This is T. S. Eliot's position in an argument directed at Archer; but Eliot does not therefore come to the defense of Elizabethan drama as an integrated art. Though he objects that Archer has failed to distinguish faults from the conventions which these dramatists used, he nevertheless finds the Elizabethans deficient for having failed to work consistently within these conventions, because they succumbed to the same desire for realism which Archer admires and which Eliot believes to be the fault of modern drama as well as Elizabethan: "The great vice of English drama from Kyd to Galsworthy," he maintains, "has been that its aim of realism was unlimited." The failure of the Elizabethans was not that they adopted unrealistic conventions, but that they did not preserve them as a self-consistent schematism of art: "Their great weakness is the same weakness as that of modern drama, it is the lack of a convention. Mr. Archer facilitates his own task of destruction, and avoids offending popular opinion, by making an exception of Shakespeare; but Shakespeare, like all his contemporaries, was aiming in more than one direction. In a play of Aeschylus, we do not find that certain passages are literature and other passages drama; every style of utterance in the play bears a relation to the whole and because of this relation is dramatic in itself."[2] In short, Eliot, though repudiating Archer's principles, arrives precisely at the same conclusion: that Elizabethan drama is a confused and unintegrated art. Only he has the courage and consistency to include Shakespeare in the generalization.

It is possible, however, that both Eliot and Archer, though for wholly different reasons, have failed to come to a sympathetic grasp of the nature of the Elizabethan dramatic conventions. A prominent line of development in modern Elizabethan studies has been directed toward discovering and understanding the nature of these conventions. The most elaborate attempt in this direction has been Muriel Bradbrook's *Themes and Conventions in Elizabethan Drama*. The premise on which this work rests is that all preconceptions drawn from Aristotle or Ibsen, Shaw or Dryden, must be abandoned if we are to discover the secret of the unity of Elizabethan drama, especially its tragedy.[3] Miss Bradbrook raises suspicion, however, by insisting that "the plays of Shakespeare should be, as far as possible, excluded from the mind when the lesser Elizabethans are being considered."[4] Did Shakespeare not use these conventions? And, in fact, it does not appear in the end that Bradbrook, except for the thoroughness of her study, has gotten very far from Archer, whom she condemns; what Archer called faults, she resolves into conventions, but having done so she is inclined to approve of them as a legitimate scheme of operation. The danger of her method, which she does not escape, is that often merely the stock in trade of the artisan, the dodges and shifts of a hack, find themselves enshrined as conventions with a peculiar dignity and sanction. In consequence, there is nothing to distinguish a good artist from a bad one, and the effect is not so much of helping to raise a second-rate artist to a proper level of comparison with a good one, as of bringing the great artist down to the level of a hack. Moreover, driven by the pressure of consistency, Bradbrook is occasionally forced into generalizations that are unacceptable; for instance, that because in many Elizabethan plays "causal succession of events is not of first importance," therefore "the Elizabethan dramatist *could not* rely on this causal sequence of events,"[5] or that "If the Elizabethan audience were told that a man was honest, they did not alter their mind because he happened to be caught picking a pocket"[6] (what a nightmare of incomprehension *Othello* must have seemed to this ingenuous audience!). To enter the Elizabethan heaven, we are advised to become as little children. Bradbrook is forced, in reality, to beg the whole question of the unity of this drama: "The unity of a good Elizabethan tragedy cannot be imitated, because it is the personal possession of the dramatist and depends on his power as a poet."[7]

A logical outcome of such a view is to abandon dramatic aspects as trivial and concentrate on qualities of another sort. This is the method of Miss U. M. Ellis-Fermor's *Jacobean Drama*. The confusion of a play like *The Duchess of Malfi* when regarded in the conventional way, "Is balanced by a surprising shapeliness which appears when we look at the play as a two-dimensional map of moods and personalities in their relation to each other rather than as a single-dimensional line of progression from event to event."[8] This "spatial" way of regarding a play, which derives somewhat from G. Wilson Knight's methods as applied to Shakespeare, leads to a frequent resort to analogies with other arts, particularly music; in fact, Ellis-Fermor finds it difficult to talk about the conclusion of *The Duchess of Malfi* without systematic application of the analogy with music, conductor's baton and all.[9] The Elizabethan dramatist, in short, was good at "serving two masters," one the audience and the other his own serious vision of human experience, and all his incongruous sub-plots, inconsistencies, and the like are merely "Concessions to the needs of the theatre," and have "no valid part in the main business of his plays which is . . . . the illumination of character and thought by aid of event."[10] It is difficult to see how

this can be interpreted to mean anything other than that Elizabethan drama was a mixed kind of art, in which certain very crude
and quite inappropriate devices were resorted to which never could,
and consequently never did, become an integral part of what is best
in this drama; and that lyrical rather than dramatic methods can
best be applied to it. Archer somehow seems to have come off the
winner, and the separation of the dramatic and poetic aspects of
these plays which Lamb and Swinburne were accused of perpe-
trating has not, seemingly, been rectified.

The problem, however, is not an easy one; criticism may well be
perplexed at the frequency with which amorphous narrative pattern, childish ineptitude, and mixture of appeals coexist in the
same play with moments of insight or of extraordinary beauty,
depth of suggestion, and sophistication of language. The critical
difficulties lie in the nature of Elizabethan drama itself.

Two of the most prominent features of Elizabethan drama are,
in general, a tendency toward wide narrative sweep and multiplicity of episodes, and a tendency toward richness and copiousness
of language. Both were partly encouraged by the conditioning elements of the theatre and the style of staging. If we regard for a
moment the way in which imaginative dramatists of our age depend
on the technical facilities of scene, lighting, and the like, particularly
in expressionistic forms, it may be conjectured what the effect
would be on an imaginative dramatist of the stage of the Elizabethan public theatre, relatively barren of any such resources, or
at best possessing resources of so primitive a nature that sophisticated writers like Jonson despised them. The emphasis necessarily
fell wholly on the spoken line, which had to sustain nearly the entire
burden of whatever effects needed to be made. This was an extraordinarily lucky contingency. In any except highly individual or
experimental plays, the ultimate unit, the essential instrument
among the means, is the line of dialogue. In Elizabethan drama it
was raised to the highest possible importance. Had there been no
other influence at work, the resources of the dramatist in the matter
of diction would have been strained to the utmost if only because of
this technical fact itself. At the same time, these very conditions
encouraged extravagant emphasis on the speeches, so that the circumstance which made for one of the excellencies of this drama
made also for one of its principal evils—verbal virtuosity and lux-

uriant copiousness. On the side of structure, the conditioning elements of the stage had an analogous effect. There was no very strict delimitation of locale on the large outer, or apron, stage, and this, combined with the possibility of using the alcove stage and balcony as playing areas, gave a fluidity to this drama somewhat like that of the motion picture with its merging of one scene into the next in a continuous pattern undisturbed by the introduction of sudden or remote changes in locale. This too was an extraordinary advantage, permitting amplitude and scope in the action and allowing extended and complex narratives to become amenable to the restricted compass of the drama. But this very fluidity, with its accompanying multiplicity of episodes and amplitude of range, enormously complicated the problem of structure. It also encouraged a tendency to multiple narratives not always even remotely connected or appropriate, and, even where the worst of these ills are absent, it encouraged a tendency toward diffuseness or lack of proportion.

On the purely technical side, such a drama offered the opportunity for a popular entertainment combining all the allurements of vaudeville and the double-feature picture. But these features of construction, coupled with the tendency toward richness of expression, posed great difficulties to the serious artist. It required stern artistic conscience to master these possibilities and not be seduced by them; and it required no less than comprehensive genius to exhaust their possibilities while subduing them within an appropriate and cohesive formal pattern. This is an important consideration to bear in mind in any attempt to evaluate Elizabethan tragedy. There was less likelihood of complete integration and formal unity in this drama than in almost any other dramatic style before or since.

Other factors, general in their nature and not directly connected with the theatre, helped to shape the character of Elizabethan drama, particularly in the matter of style and diction. A tendency toward ornateness and lavishness characterized the fine and useful arts of the age, which literature in some respects shared.[11] There was a good deal of interest in allegorical schemes, emblems, witty devices, and the like.[12] Poetry, moreover—both its composition and appreciation—played a large part in the general notion of the accomplishments appropriate to a cultivated person. More specifically, two factors may be isolated for the deep and permanent mark which they left on this drama—the general acceptance of the principle of the didactic function of poetry, and the great interest in the technicalities of rhetoric.

The second of these is sufficiently well recognized to pass without elaborate illustration.[13] Training in rhetoric was an important feature both of elementary and advanced education. Such a style as that of Lyly, to mention the most notorious example, could hardly have attained notice among readers unsophisticated in the lore of rhetorical figures; and the banter with rhetorical terms and expressions in the early plays of Shakespeare argues familiarity with such matters on the part of the audience.[14] That rhetorical virtuosity was esthetically gratifying to the Elizabethans seems apparent. But rhetoric was generally regarded officially as a handmaiden to the various sciences of instruction, and poetry was regarded by Elizabethan critical theorists as the queen among instructors. The importance of eloquence was bound up with this demand placed upon poetry to be instructive: ornament was an allurement, wit a servant of the "sentence." Sidney's conception of poetry as the best teacher is well known. For the drama the connection between rhetoric and instruction is explicitly made by one of the most authoritative of Renaissance critics, Scaliger: "Now is there not one end, and one only, in philosophical exposition, in oratory, and in the drama? Assuredly such is the case. All have one and the same end—persuasion."[15] Significantly, nearly all of the early attempts at serious drama state explicitly a didactic aim.[16] And in many of the comments by later dramatists bearing on the nature and function of tragedy, didactic function and rhetorical appeal appear together. For Chapman, writing in the dedication to *The Revenge of Bussy D'Ambois*, "Material instruction, elegant and sententious excitation to virtue, and deflection from her contrary" are "the soul, limbs, and limits of an authentical tragedy." Jonson admits, in his address to the reader in *Sejanus*, that he has violated some of the forms of classical tragedy, but apparently does not regard this as fatal "if in truth of argument, dignity of persons, gravity and height of elocution, I have discharged the other offices of a tragic writer." Webster similarly admits his failure to observe the proprieties of true tragedy in his address to the reader in *The White Devil*, but observes that "Should a man present to such an auditory, the most sententious tragedy that ever was written, observing all the critical laws, as height of style, and gravity of persons, inrich it with the sententious chorus, and as it were liven death in the passionate and weighty Nuntius, yet after all this divine rapture . . . . the breath that comes from the incapable multitude is able to poison it . . . ." The common point in all of these is the emphasis, as primary desiderata of tragedy, on eloquence and on instruction. The insistence on sententiousness is particularly interesting, since both notions of instruction and rhetorical elegance are implicit in the term. It is likely that one of the reasons why Seneca became an admired model for tragedy was that he fitted so completely into these presuppositions. In the early days of English tragedy, "climbing to the heighth of Seneca his style"—in Sidney's phrase—was high praise.

As a consequence, therefore, of one of the commonplace assumptions about literature, tragedy was encouraged from the start in the direction of artifice and elevation of expression. One insidious effect, however, was that, eloquence being thus related to instruction, it bore on the element of thought ("elegant and sententious excitation to virtue," for example); theoretically, this involves a subordination of purely poetic relations to devices of persuasion, and the elegant and pointed expression of commonplaces is given an improper appropriateness. Such a theory, in practice, can encourage exploitation of a common stock of tragic embroidery and reflections, aptly phrased, on such general matters as fortune, death, the corruption of courts, and other edifying topics suggested by the occurrences of the play but not necessarily intimately involved in it, or involved in that particular way. Such practices sometimes interrupt the harmonious integration of essentially related sentiments or figures. Webster is a case in point: he can finish off a beautifully modulated speech with such a stock cliché as, "Tell my son to fly the courts of princes," and end his somber masterpiece, *The Duchess of Malfi*, with the lines,

> Integrity of life is fame's best friend,
> Which nobly, beyond death, shall crown the end.

—a sentiment pointed by a couplet rhyme and set off by quotation marks so that no one will miss the fact that it is a "sentence," but a sentiment woefully beside the mark and utterly out of harmony with the play. Elizabethan tragedy is full of traces of this original and persistent association of rhetoric with instruction and of instruction with poetry.

Stylistically, the effect of the preoccupation with rhetoric was the cultivation of point, of patterned artifice, and of figurative ornament. In the eighties and nineties of the sixteenth century, when such effects are most marked in the drama, these qualities had general critical approval. Thus, William Webbe, in a prefatory note "To his friend R. W." in Wilmot's revision of *Tancred and Gismunda* in 1591, refers to the original (1567) version "as a work, either in stateliness of shew, depth of conceit, or true ornaments of art, inferior to none of the best in that kind: no, were the Roman Seneca the censurer," and though he commends Wilmot for having shaped the new version in conformity to the stylistic fashions of later times, he compliments him for having more than preserved the original merits by adorning the play "With the approved guise of our stateliest English terms (not diminishing, but more augmenting his artificial colors of absolute poesie, derived from his first parents) [which] cannot but be grateful to most men's appetites, who upon our experience we know highly to esteem such lofty measures of sententiously composed Tragedies." The emphasis on ornamentation is even plainer in the more general context of Puttenham's *Arte of English Poesie*: "Even so cannot our vulgar Poesie shew itself either gallant or gorgeous, if any limb be left naked and bare and not clad in his kindly clothes and coulors, such as may convey them somewhat out of sight, that is from the common course of ordinary speech and capacity of the vulgar judgment, and yet being artifically handled must needs yield it much more beauty and commendation. This ornament we speak of is given to it by figures and figurative speeches, which be the flowers as it were and coulors that a Poet setteth upon his language of art . . . ."[17]

Supplementing these demands of the critics for ornateness of expression was the growing feeling of confidence that the English language was rich and copious, offering the poet unlimited resources for whatever needs he might have.[18] Stanyhurst, having translated Virgil after Phaer had already done so, was undisturbed by any fear of duplication since he felt in no need of repeating any of Phaer's phrases: "I would not run on the score with M. Phaer or any other, by borrowing his terms in so copious and fluent a language as our English tongue is."[19] The sometimes extraordinary results of his effort to avoid using Phaer's terms is not as much in point at the moment as his belief in the resources of the vernacular. Much the same conviction animates Richard Carew in *The Excellency of the English Tongue* (composed about 1595), who expatiates on the topic of "our tongue's copiousness," and who affirms that in the matter of metaphors, "the English is very fruitful and forcible."[20] It is, in fact, the case that something in the tremendous growth and development which the English language underwent during the sixteenth century rendered the language not only amenable to experiment of all sorts, but fruitful in striking ambivalences of meaning and implication and in sustained trains of analogy and suggestion which are common in Elizabethan tragedy during the years when it flourished.

If, however, we regard the general interest in ornament and the conditions which encouraged metaphor, not to mention the more studied artifices of rhetoric, in relation to the structural freedom which these plays enjoyed, it will be seen that inducements were not lacking to indulge in bravura passages and in isolated moments of eloquent and extravagant speech that had something of the character either of lyrical interlude or impassioned aria. It is one thing, however, to recognize that conditions commonly encouraged such practices, and another to regard them as the chief merit of this drama or as the inevitable consequences of its nature. However splendid some of these passages may be in themselves, the modern critic needs to discriminate between the dramatist who indulged himself indiscriminately and the dramatist who, like Shakespeare, did these things with a difference. It required a stronger catalyst than the talent of the average Elizabethan playwright to effect a fusion. Yet although these conditions all conspired to make it difficult for the dramatist to integrate his materials and achieve formal unity in this complex medium, the same conditions enabled the dramatist to turn to verse easily without the strain which the modern playwright suffers in his self-conscious effort to bridge the gap between the artifice of his means and the claims of verisimilitude.

In this all-important particular, the Elizabethan dramatist enjoyed a further advantage from the fact that, in large part, tragedy dealt with persons of exalted station. This may have developed partly out of the common misreading of Aristotle by which tragedy was assigned persons of high station and comedy persons of low station. The practice was also no doubt influenced by the medieval idea of tragedy as exemplified in such works as *The Falls of Princes* and *The Mirror for Magistrates*.[21] In any event, whatever the reasons which made such material the popular choice for tragedy, it was a fortunate one under the circumstances since it offered possibilities for dramatic treatment on an impressive scale and facilitated the use of verse.

Not all materials which can be effectively developed into plays are amenable to poetic treatment. Since one of the principal effects of verse is that it frees diction from conformity to a literal realism of expression, a primary condition of verse plays must be the elimination of conditions in the nature of the plot, the setting, the sentiments, and the like, which would interfere with freeing the diction from the limitations of verisimilitude. It has consequently become a popular notion that poetic tragedy must deal with circumstances which are presumed to occur at a time remote from that of the time of composition. This, however, is to raise a convenient device to the level of an axiom. Chapman's tragedies—to cite but one instance—deal with events almost contemporary with their author. The removal of the story to a remote period in time is merely the simplest way of eliminating the temptation or necessity of giving to local features of setting, custom, habit, and fashion so preponderant a place that verse dialogue and all that goes with it are rendered incompatible with the material used. For Greek tragedy, the problem was conveniently taken care of by the use of myths of the heroic age as material for plots, and the myth element is not wholly lacking in Elizabethan tragedy—for instance, in *King Lear*.

The general use of persons of high station in Elizabethan tragedy offered an artistic solution for somewhat different reasons. In the "courtier" and the "governour" the highest ideals of the Elizabethan age had their focus; and in the person of a monarch with great endowments, the political thought of the age centered its hopes and aspirations. The literature on the courtier and governor during the Tudor years gives ample evidence that the court was regarded as the center of cultural and political life, and that the full flowering of man's capabilities was expected to be achieved, if at all, among those whose life moved in its orbit. It was natural, therefore, that dramatists working in a form that required characters capable of great action, and at the same time not deficient in intensity and refinement of feeling and depth of reflection, should have selected plots in which persons embodying the highest personal ideals and aspirations of the age could be used as principals. Because they saw the courtier, the warrior, and the king in the light of these ideals, their use of such persons in tragedy made possible the high generality of treatment which they were able to give their materials and at the same time rendered these materials effective for the poetic language which they believed appropriate to tragedy. The changes which these ideals underwent under the Stuarts exerted a subtle influence on the character of later tragedy, but what has been said will apply in general to Elizabethan tragedy during its formative years and for the most part during the period of its great fulfillment.

In one additional respect the use of persons in high station for tragedy facilitated the use of verse and figurative diction. It is difficult to say how far a tacitly applied feeling for decorum—something akin to the more naïve medieval practice of dressing Mary in rich robes and decorating the manger with carvings in the nativity paintings, or making God and important dignitaries talk scraps of Latin in the vernacular Biblical plays—operated to encourage an artificial heightening of the language in plays dealing with characters in high station. Certainly the dramatists were not bound by inhibitions imposed by a desire for complete verisimilitude. But there was an even more compelling consideration. The language of formal court address was apparently full of artifice and elegance. It is, of course, not possible to find any reports of courtly speech which can be regarded as free from embellishment, but even the act of embellishment itself on the part of the person reporting might be construed as evidence that courtly address was regarded as an elegant affair. Since all dramatic dialogue of whatever sort necessitates a certain amount of editing and embellishment, the step involved in raising the discourse of such characters to artful rhetoric or exalted verse was not a violent one. The dialogue which occurs in an actual drawing-room bears something of the same relation to the dialogue of a drawing-room play as the formal speech of Elizabethan court life does to the speeches of the important characters in Elizabethan tragedy. This analogy involves some stretching perhaps, but not too much. In his double play, *Conspiracy and Tragedy of*

Byron, Chapman represents a courtier reporting Queen Elizabeth's remarks to Byron on the occasion of his leaving England after a visit. This speech is closely modeled on the source, Grimestone's *General Inventory of the History of France*, which reads as follows: "She could not say that a courage which feared nothing but the falling of the Pillars of Heaven, should fear the sea, or not trust unto it for a passage of seven or eight hours, blaming them rather which had not instructed him as well to contemn the waves of the sea, as the designs of his enemies uppon the land."[22] There is not a great deal which even Chapman felt compelled to do to raise this report of a historian to the almost epic stateliness of the speech in which it appears. Granted that Grimestone and his French original had done some touching up of their own; nevertheless, what is reported by the historian as the actual words of the queen approaches in style and diction the final product of the poet. The kind of material which Elizabethan tragedy found suitable for its plots was but one more circumstance which made a poetic drama not only possible, but well-nigh inevitable.

A further condition, finally, which made for successful composition of poetic tragedy was the development of a verse form suitable both to the exigencies of drama and to the materials with which Elizabethan tragedy dealt. By a fortunate coincidence, the play recognized as the first English tragedy, *Gorboduc* (1562), was also the first play in which blank verse was used. The few examples of blank verse before *Gorboduc*, beginning with Surrey's original experiment in the translation of Virgil, appear all to have had the epic in mind, and, in fact, English dramatic blank verse shows occasional marks of its epic origin for some time.[23] The blank verse of Gorboduc, however, seems to have been designed as an adaptation to the characteristics of the English language of the tragic meter and style of Seneca, and Sidney's compliment—"climbing to the heighth of Seneca his style"—should be sufficient to dispel doubts on this point. If the choice of this meter for Elizabethan tragedy has come to seem natural, a few specimens of what the translators of Seneca thought an appropriate equivalent for classic tragic style should make clear the wisdom which Sackville and Norton showed in their choice. None of the translations of Seneca up to 1581, when all the previous separate translations were collected by Thomas Newton and printed in one volume along with a few new ones, are in blank verse. Most of them are in "fourteeners," hepta-meter couplets. The following lines from a speech of Oedipus in the *Thebais* are from Newton's own translation:

And lo, dost thou not plainly see, how he my panting Ghost
With raking paws doth hale and pull, which grieves my conscience most?
Dost thou not see how he my face bescratcheth tyrant wise?
Tell me (my Daughter) hast thou seen Ghosts in such griesly guise?

Twenty years after *Gorboduc*, Newton still regarded this awkward meter as the proper English equivalent for the Latin tragic style. Preston's popular *Cambises* (1569?) had been written in this meter, the author apparently concluding that a verse form selected for translation of Seneca was the proper one for English tragedy also. But several academic tragedies followed the lead of *Gorboduc*, and the die was finally cast for blank verse when, almost simultaneously, Marlowe used it in *Tamburlaine* and Kyd used it in *The Spanish Tragedy* in plays intended for the popular theatre.

The blank verse which finally became the accepted verse medium of Elizabethan drama combined at its best a degree of formality which is preserved by the metrical scheme of the blank verse line, with sufficient flexibility to permit its use either for the easy inter-change of dramatic dialogue or for the demands of impassioned eloquence. The maximum point of usefulness and adaptability was not, however, reached without much experiment and effort. In the history of this drama there is a marked shift involving a decrease in formality and increase in flexibility, and in some of the later drama-tists—Fletcher, for instance—the shift is carried to an extreme that suggests an effort to escape from the formality altogether. The development of dramatic blank verse in the direction of increasing adaptability to its ultimate perfection in the hands of Shakespeare is usually explained as the natural result of increase in technical mastery. This explanation is, of course, only partial. Increase, for example, in the number of run-on lines is not necessarily, per se, an improvement; *Gorboduc* would not be "improved" by such a change. Technical changes are determined in part by the needs which they serve. The original formality of blank verse was in part due to its having been made subject to the ends of rhetoric. The infrequency of run-on lines and the general regularity of the iambic meter in early dramatic blank verse merely rendered it more suitable as a mould for such devices as balance accentuated by assonance and

alliteration, patterned antithesis within the line and between separate lines, stychomythia, and the like. The increase in metrical
variety and flexibility was not only the result of defter mechanical
handling of metrics, or even of closer approximation to ordinary
speech; it was a function also of a change from rhetorical, patterned
ordering of the diction to what might be called, in contrast, a
poetic ordering.

II

What such a change meant can be appreciated by a glance at
Gorboduc. Aside from the stiffness of the verse commonly complained
of by critics, the noticeable feature of the style in this play is the
deliberate formality of pattern which is the principal adornment
of the language:

> Your *age* in quiet shall the *longer last;*
> Your *lasting age* shall be their *longer* stay;
> For *c*ares of *k*ings that *r*ule, as you have *r*uled,
> For *p*ublic wealth and not for *p*rivate joy,
> Do waste man's life and hasten crooked age,
> With *f*urrowed *f*ace and with en*f*eebled limbs. (1.2.99–104)*

The repetitions in the first two lines are not only ingenious manipulations of similar words, but of similar sounds. The last line is built
on the *f* alliteration. There is a further pattern in the occasional
balancing of an adjective plus a noun in the first half of the line with
a similar combination in the second. These are common devices to
be found throughout the play:

> The *silent night*, that brings the *quiet pause*
> From *painful travails* of the *weary day*.   (1.1.1–2)
>
> Guiding so *g*reat estate with *g*reat renoun   (1.2.4)
>
> But this *unhap*, among so many *heaps*   (4.2.52)
>
> To see the *h*ugy *h*eaps of these *unhaps*   (5.2.109)

Sometimes the alliteration accents a play on words:

> In kind a father, not in kindliness?   (1.1.18)

There are also occasional "sentences" set off on some occasions by
quotation marks, though usually these pithy generalizations do not

*Line references are to J. W. Cunliffe's edition of *Gorboduc* in *Early English Tragedies*
(Oxford, 1912).

rely on any very pronounced devices of appeal to the ear or eye to
carry their point:

> "O most unhappy state of counselors,
> That light on so unhappy lords and times
> That neither can their good advice be heard,
> Yet must they bear the blames of ill success."   (2.2.69–72)

Even here, however, the repetition of "unhappy" pointing up the
contrast between "counselors" and "lords and times," and the antithesis of the last two lines with their air of paradox, are certainly
noticeable. Though the verse form is clearly an improvement over
the fourteeners used by many of the translators of Seneca and
others, its most noticeable feature is its formality, both in the regularity of its metrical pattern and, especially, in the prevalence of
rhetorical schemes of order and arrangement.

In organization, the play gives ample scope for such treatment.
It is unmistakably designed to emphasize the moral that danger
lurks in a kingdom which does not provide for a clear succession or
which makes possible a divided rule. The scenes are constructed
either as debates (the king and his counselors, each of the two
brothers accompanied by advisors representing opposing counsel,
etc.) or as elaborate reports of dire events by a messenger followed
by comments on these events by various characters, or as high-
strung passioning by some individual character. This pretty nearly
sums up the play. Any of these scenes lends itself to the sort of
rhetorical treatment illustrated above. Where speeches are not
characterized by such patterned embellishments as have been noted,
they have simply the qualities of prosy assertion:

> And this is much, and asketh great advice.
> But for my part, my sovereign lord and king,
> This do I think: your majesty doth know
> How under you, in justice and in peace
> Great wealth and honor long we have enjoyed,
> So as we cannot seem with greedy minds
> To wish for change of prince or governance.   (1.2.77–83)

What is especially surprising about this play in view of what became an invariable feature of the diction of Elizabethan tragedy, is
the almost complete absence of metaphor. There are, also, very few
similes, and some comparisons that suggest the device are not
strictly similes:

Too soon he clamb into the flaming car,
Whose want of skill did set the earth on fire.
Time and example of your noble grace
Shall teach your sons both to obey and rule.   (1.2.330–33)

The story of Phaeton is alluded to here in a condensed form of a
favorite Elizabethan device, the "history," to illustrate a point, and
is not strictly a similitude in the technical sense of the term. To
glance ahead momentarily at *King Lear* at this juncture would seem
at first a preposterous procedure, but the suggestion of such a comparison is useful to show how essentially different in kind the poetic
drama which developed out of this really was. The two plays deal
with the same situation: a king of legendary British history divides
his realm among his children, latent hatreds develop, and the
family and the state suffer tragically. Both plays are preoccupied
with the law of nature which binds families together and with the
chaos which succeeds the breaking of the laws of "kind." This
similarity in subject matter brings out in sharp relief not so much
the difference in talent between the two authors, which is another
matter, but the wholly different technical organization of all the
parts, and especially the wholly different way of seeing the function
of style and diction in a verse tragedy.

The critical turning point in the development which is marked
by these two polar opposites is the year 1587/8, the year to which
the appearance of Marlowe's *Tamburlaine* and Kyd's *Spanish Tragedy*
is generally assigned. Each play represents in its own way a radical
reorganization in the matter of diction. *Tamburlaine* has enjoyed a
greater fame, probably because in this play the celebrated "mighty
line" of Marlowe made its first appearance. Yet there are many
features of the style of this play which recall *Gorboduc* and its immediate progeny rather than later tragedies. There is the same
regularity in the metrical treatment of the individual line, and even
though some interesting irregularities appear, it is not the variety
but the regularity of the line which stands out on examination.
End-stopping is the rule rather than otherwise; in fact, comparative
sampling from the two plays seems to indicate that the proportion
of run-on lines is no greater in *Tamburlaine* than in *Gorboduc*. Schemes
of arrangement built on alliteration and assonance, on balance of
adjectives in both halves of the lines, and the like, are also not uncommon in Marlowe's play. The opening lines of the Prologue in

which Marlowe repudiates the rhyme and silliness of earlier plays
are a typical example:

> From *jigging* veins of *riming* mother wits
> And *s*uch *c*onceits as *c*lownage keeps in pay. •

The possibility of parody here is excluded by the number of other
occasions when lines like

> Now will I *g*ratify your former *g*ood
> And *g*race your calling with a *g*reater sway   (2.5.30–31)*

appear. It has been on occasion pointed out that Marlowe's most
original accomplishment in style in this play is the construction of
the sustained verse paragraph, yet it is to an established trick of
rhetorical balance that he resorts to bring to a conclusion one of the
most famous of these, the speech on aspiration:

> That *perfect bliss* and *sole felicity*,
> The *sweet fruition* of an *earthly crown*.   (2.7.28–29)

The *f* and *s* alliteration should also be noticed in these lines. But
however common these tricks may be in this play, they represent
but an interesting survival. In such a play as *Gorboduc* their appearance is expected, in *Tamburlaine* the large number of instances one
can find of them comes as a surprise even though they are not
necessarily felt to be wholly out of place. It is simply that in any
final accounting, the distinctive feature of Marlowe's verse is seen
to lie elsewhere.[24]

On the surface, the language of the play gives the impression of
almost prodigal richness and sometimes of strained elevation
amounting on occasion to rant and bombast. The bombast, it must
be admitted, is certainly there. The language is highly metaphorical, and there are numerous similes, some of them extended to the
epic formula. In part, the effect of ornateness is the result of hyper-
bolical statement:

> And sooner shall the sun fall from his sphere
> Than Tamburlaine be slain or overcome.   (1.2.175–76)

More often it depends on the introduction of items of an unusual
or striking sort, as in Tamburlaine's picture to Zenocrate of what
rare things he will provide for her:

*Line references are to U. M. Ellis-Fermor's edition of *Tamburlaine the Great* (London
1930).

Thy garments shall be made of Median silk
Enchased with precious jewels of mine own.

With milk-white harts upon an ivory sled
Thou shalt be drawn amidst the frozen pools,
And scale the icy mountains' lofty tops.   (1.2.95ff)

To these must be added the unusual place names, and the recurrence of striking words in critical positions. The effect of extravagance in the combination of all these is undeniable, but there is more to the style than profusion of ornament. There is, in fact, a close and essential relationship between the impressions and associations thus set up and the other features of the play, notably character and action and thought, and their absence would fundamentally alter the nature of the play.

The play opens in the court of the feeble Persian king Mycetes, where Tamburlaine is reported as a daring thief who is said to have foolish dreams of empire. Tamburlaine appears first in the next scene, accompanied by Zenocrate and her attendants whom he has captured, and by his lieutenants. He is confident of his powers and his future conquests. When Zenocrate addresses him hesitantly, "My lord—for so you do import," he replies, "I am a lord, for so my deeds shall prove," thus announcing his conviction that nobility is a matter of attainments and not of birth. The whole speech expresses vaguely Tamburlaine's sense of the grandeur and dignity of his ambitions. Toward the end of the first act he demonstrates his growing sense of personal power by triumphing over Theridamas, not by battle, as his lieutenants prefer, but by so overawing Theridamas with his majestic bearing and confidence that the latter, disregarding the punitive expedition against Tamburlaine on which he had been sent, deserts Mycetes and with his thousand horse joins the Scythian shepherd. Tamburlaine now allies himself with the Persian usurper Cosroe, and together they defeat the unworthy Mycetes. For the moment, Tamburlaine seems happy in being given the general lieutenancy of the Persian armies for his part in the victory, until, as Cosroe sets off to be crowned, an officer says,

Your majesty shall shortly have your wish
And ride in triumph through Persepolis.   (2.5.48–49)

This phrase stirs Tamburlaine deeply, and he catches at the refrain:

And ride in triumph through Persepolis!
Is it not brave to be a king, Techelles?

> Usumcasane and Theridamas,
> Is it not passing brave to be a king,
> And ride in triumph through Persepolis? (2.5.50–54)

And so, before Cosroe has a chance to enjoy the crown snatched from his brother, he is overtaken by Tamburlaine, defeated, and killed. When the dying Cosroe reproaches Tamburlaine for his treachery, Tamburlaine's reply reveals the large meaning that power and conquest have assumed for him: his act is no more treachery than heavenly Jove's overthrow of his Titan father; it is the expression of the aspiration natural to man:

> Nature, that framed us of four elements,
> Warring within our breasts for regiment,
> Doth teach us all to have aspiring minds. (2.7.18–20)

This is now what gives meaning to kingship; Nature

> Wills us to wear ourselves and never rest
> Until we reach the ripest fruit of all.
> That perfect bliss and sole felicity,
> The sweet fruition of an earthly crown. (2.7.26–29)

Thus against the ineptitude of the born king Mycetes is seen Tamburlaine's conception of nobility as a matter of attainments; against the capacity for intriguing and practical politics of Cosroe is seen his imposing conception of power and kingship.

From this point on, the play shows Tamburlaine the conqueror, successful beyond the caprices of fortune, cruel, and resistless as a force of nature. Not even the tears of Zenocrate will dissuade him from killing the supplicating virgins of her native city and putting the town to sword. But the beauty of Zenocrate in her grief troubles him more than opposing armies, and arouses a new train of reflection. He ponders the question, "What is beauty, saith my sufferings, then?" The greatest spirits are necessarily aspiring, he had said—"always moving as the restless spheres"; his theme is now that such spirits are stirred equally by an instinct for beauty. Poets, who are purely the apostles of beauty, have in common with the greatest of men that same urge for some ultimate expression of themselves, yet if poets ever could distill their search for beauty in some single line,

> Yet should there hover in their restless heads
> One thought, one grace, one wonder, at the least,
> Which into words no virtue can digest. (5.2.108–10)

Tamburlaine expresses a momentary shame at harboring such effeminate thoughts, but he carries them to their conclusion nonetheless:

> . . . every warrior that is rapt with love
> Of fame, of valor and of victory,
> Must needs have beauty beat on his conceits. (5.2.117–19)

The lines which conclude this notable passage are something of a puzzle even when emended, but there is no doubt concerning the main drift of his statement nor the meaning of the concluding lines:

> That virtue solely is the sum of glory
> And fashions men with true nobility. (5.2.128–29)

Low birth, as he had earlier told his lieutenants, is no blemish, "for virtue is the fount whence honor springs"; virtue expresses itself in aspiring, and it involves an instinct for beauty as well as exertion for power. The marriage of Tamburlaine to Zenocrate which concludes the play bears the same relation to this passage on beauty as the seizure of crowns and empires does to the earlier speech on aspiration. Viewed in this way, the play is not simply a series of military victories and acts of inhuman cruelty; it is the progressive unfolding of Tamburlaine as a heroic figure, as a man of "virtue."

From this view of the action it becomes clear why the enhancing of Tamburlaine necessarily becomes one of the principal functions of the imagery. Though there is an impression of copiousness in the diction, the figures of speech which appear most frequently and which are used with most consistency are drawn from a limited and fairly definite range of categories—the gods of classical mythology, principally Jove; jewels, treasure, and precious stones and metals; stars, planets, and other heavenly bodies. Dozens of instances of these are dispersed throughout the play. In addition to these principal ones, considerable use is made of references to and analogies drawn from elemental forces of nature and features of the classical underworld, and of historical and geographical references. In their interplay, these images intensify markedly the impression of magnitude and are more responsible for the heroic character of the play than the increasingly glorious military triumphs of the hero. Scarcely a single act or accessory of Tamburlaine's is unadorned with one of the characteristic associations. His army will be vaster than the force of Xerxes, which was said "to drink the mighty

Parthian Araris" (2.3.13–17). His host is like Caesar's "that never fought but had the victory" (3.3.152–53). The movements of his army's weapons "fill all the air with fiery meteors" (4.2.51–52). Their bullets, "like Jove's dreadful thunderbolts," "shall threat the gods more than Cyclopian wars" (2.3.17–21). His meanest soldier cannot be bought with "all the gold in India's wealthy arms" (1.2.84–86). Tamburlaine's sword will fly "As doth the lightning or the breath of heaven" (2.3.58). His favor, Zenocrate thinks, would content the "Queen of Heaven" (3.2.11). His exploits will be spoken of until "Plato's wondrous year" (4.2.96). The heightening produced by the accumulation of such expressions is in direct proportion to the associations carried by the allusions involved: the meanest act of Tamburlaine is equated with those of the heroes of myth or history, and is attached to ideas that convey strength and majesty. Thus is produced that elevation above the common order of human events which the play requires, and without which it would be nothing more than a monotonous account of savage butchery and an insane lust for power. The images and allusions render Tamburlaine congruous with the general conceptions about man of which he becomes the focus and, in a way, the symbol.

Most of these devices of language, however, have at least a double aspect. They not only give magnitude to Tamburlaine and to his motives and sentiments, but at the same time they help bring the various parts of the play into closer relationship and underscore the various features that introduce probability and unity into the play. As he is the center of the action, Tamburlaine is also the center for this development. The images underline features of his character and establish the scale on which it is drawn, and they reflect on the motives which inspire his actions and on the growth of his capacities and vision. As an invincible warrior, he strikes terror in his enemies who,

> . . . like flocks of fearful roes
> Pursued by hunters, fly his angry looks.   (3.3.192–93)

Techelles likens him to

> . . . princely lions, when they rouse themselves,
> Stretching their paws, and threatening herds of beasts.
>   (1.2.52–53)

The combination "princely lions," though conventional enough, brings into association the notions of ruthless valor and kingship which characterize Tamburlaine's conduct and sentiments. To his foes, Tamburlaine is "bloody and insatiate" and is deficient in the prescribed and generally recognized code of honor to which they resentfully and helplessly appeal, but he regards his conduct as the manifestation of an aspiration that is compact of all that is most divine and natural to man. It is partly in this connection that Jove "who overthrew the Titans" is so frequently used as an analogue to Tamburlaine, and that Tamburlaine's deeds and bearing are so often allied to notions of divinity. On his first view of him Theridamas remarks that "his looks do menace heaven and dare the gods" (1.2.157), and Tamburlaine assures him that

> Jove himself will stretch his hand from heaven
> To ward the blow, and shield me safe from harm.
>   (1.2.179–80)

His humble station and his high hopes suggest to him the similarity between himself and the leader among the immortals:

> Jove sometimes masked in a shepherd's weed;
> And by those steps that he hath scaled the heavens,
> May we become immortal like the gods! (1.2.199–201)

These allusions are reflected in Menaphon's report to Cosroe:

> Of stature tall, and straightly fashioned,
> Like his desire, lift upwards and divine. (2.1.7–8)

And the analogy, with its combination of the ideas of divinity and aspiring assertion of power, reaches its full development in Tamburlaine's speech to the dying Cosroe:

> The thirst of reign and sweetness of a crown
> That caused the eldest son of heavenly Ops
> To thrust his doting father from his chair,
> And place himself in the imperial heaven,
> Moved me to manage arms against thy state.
> What better precedent than mighty Jove? (2.7.12–17)

Later references to the gods often reflect the implications of this comparison. It is not as the "defenders of the innocent," appealed to at first by the captured Zenocrate, nor as the guardians of honor and anointed majesty prayed to by his impotent enemies that Tamburlaine sees the gods, but as the archetypes of the restless passion for achievement which he embodies, and it is this implication which these images sustain.

Such aspiration, Tamburlaine believes, is imposed on man by his very constitution:

> Nature that framed us of four elements
> Warring within our breasts for regiment,
> Doth teach us all to have aspiring minds.   (2.7.18–20)

The elements are in strife in man, and it may be in relation to this notion that allusions to the forces of nature represent them in violent conflict. The inference of such images seems to be, as in the speech just quoted, that in his heroic, if violent, agitations, man conforms to the order of nature; note, for instance, Tamburlaine's description of the action of his army:

> Even as when windy exhalations,
> Fighting for passage, tilt within the earth.
>   (1.2.50–51. See also
>   4.2.41–46, 3.2.75–80)

In many such cases, the use of such words as "warring," "fighting," "tilt," and the like to describe the behavior of natural forces turns these images directly toward the characteristic incidents of the play.

Of the images most frequently employed, those derived from the heavenly bodies play a diversified role, but one quality they almost invariably suggest is splendor—the sun-bright armor of his armies will "chase the stars from heaven"; their weapons will "fill the air with fiery meteors." But they shade off in different directions. Often they are bound up with Tamburlaine's belief that he is beyond the influence of fortune—"For Will and Shall best fitteth Tamburlaine" (3.3.41)—and holds "the fates bound fast in iron chains," since the astrological notion about the stars can be combined with the other inferences in order to reinforce figuratively Tamburlaine's conviction (for example, 1.2.92, 2.1.33, 3.3.42, 4.2.33–34). Sometimes the notion of menacing violence is suggested by meteors and comets (for example, 3.2.74–75, 5.2.65). At times such associations are subordinated to the notion of the inevitable and systematic movement of the heavenly bodies, as for instance in Menaphon's description of his eyes, which suggests Tamburlaine's undeviating progression toward his goal:

> Whose fiery circles bear encompassed
> A heaven of heavenly bodies in their spheres,
> That guide his steps and actions to the throne
> Where honor sits invested royally.   (2.1.13–16)

The most elaborate of such treatments is to be found in the concluding lines of the speech to Cosroe, in which the exercise of man's
highest faculties is endowed with suggestions of infinitude and restless motion through reference to the movements of the heavenly
bodies:

> Our souls, whose faculties can comprehend
> The wondrous architecture of the world,
> And measure every wandering planet's course,
> Still climbing after knowledge infinite,
> And always moving as the restless spheres,
> Wills us to wear ourselves and never rest
> Until we reach the ripest fruit of all,
> That perfect bliss and sole felicity,
> The sweet fruition of an earthly crown.   (2.7.21–29)

Since the earthly crown is the physical goal of Tamburlaine's
aspiration, the idea of kingship and empire is elaborately embellished with figures and images involving precious stones and metals.
Crowns themselves play a singular part in the play; they are frequently referred to as symbols of royal powers, as in Theridamas'
description of the pleasures of wearing a crown

> . . . enchased with pearl and gold,
> Whose virtues carry with it life and death.   (2.5.60–61)

The occasions when Tamburlaine takes crowns away from defeated
kings, or gives them to his lieutenants, and his crowning of Zenocrate at the end, all have a kind of high ceremonial quality about
them. More generally, however, there are numerous allusions to
the wealth of cities and of far-flung empires and the riches derived
from spoils and ransoms, and such phrases descriptive of the proper
setting for kingly power as "roofs of gold and sun-bright palaces."

There are two attainments on which Tamburlaine concentrates
his activity: the achievement of his empire, and marriage with
Zenocrate. His intention to achieve both he asserts in his first appearance, and in the course of the play he is represented as seeing
the two as complementary aspects of his aspiration. The use of the
same category of images both for Zenocrate and for thrones and
empires has the effect of keeping these two in a close relationship
from the beginning, anticipating, as it were, the explicit recognition of their connection in the last act. In his first dialogue with her,
Tamburlaine pictures her as his future queen,

Enchased with precious jewels of mine own
More rich and valurous than Zenocrate's. (1.2.96–97)

In his sight she is "fairer than rocks of pearl and precious stone"
(3.3.118). And during the speech in which he identifies his feelings
for her with the need for beauty, he uses similar images as he thinks
of her weeping over the destruction of her native city:

Shaking her silver tresses in the air,
Rain'st on the earth resolved pearl in showers;
And sprinklest sapphires on thy shining face
Where beauty, mother to the Muses, sits. (5.2.78–81)

The heavenly bodies are also used as the source of images in connection with Zenocrate. Her eyes are "brighter than the lamps of
heaven"; her looks can "clear the darkened sky" (3.3.120, 122).
Her eyes make

. . . the mantle of the richest night,
The moon, the planets, and the meteors, light. (5.2.86–87)

And just as Tamburlaine is likened to Jove, Zenocrate is "lovelier
than the love of Jove"; her looks can "calm the rage of thundering
Jupiter"; when she is crowned queen, she is likened to

Juno, when the giants were suppressed
That darted mountains on her brother Jove. (5.2.458–59)

The double application of these categories of images brings
Zenocrate into close relation with Tamburlaine's ambition for
empire; certain other types of images, however, set her in a sense
apart. Tamburlaine the warrior is sanguinary and dark, spreading
his black and red colors to warn the enemy of his bloody purposes.
Zenocrate is not associated in the imagery with these ideas, but
rather exclusively with suggestions of brightness and purity. Such
impressions are suggested in the jewel and star images, and in such
phrases as that her looks can "clear the darkened sky." White and
silver are associated with her: she is

Brighter than is the silver Rhodope,
Fairer than whitest snow on Scythian hills. (1.2.88–89)

Of her future equipage and attendants Tamburlaine tells her,

With milk-white harts upon an ivory sled
Thou shalt be drawn amidst the frozen pools,
And scale the icy mountains' lofty tops. (1.2.97–100)

In one or two instances, suggestions of whiteness are used in connection with military actions, notably in the reference to "Brave horses bred on the white Tartarian hills" that trample the bowels of his enemies (3.3.148–51), or, in the same speech, the allusion to victory "resting herself upon my milk-white tent" (3.3.161). But the only consistent use of the impression of whiteness in relation to the warfare is in connection with the white tents which Tamburlaine displays on the first day as a sign of mercy for peaceful surrender, before the ominous red and black colors are displayed on successive days. The messenger reports to the Soldan of Egypt:

> The first day when he pitcheth down his tents,
> White is their hue, and on his silver crest,
> A snowy feather spangled white he bears,
> To signify the mildness of his mind,
> That, satiate with spoil, refuseth blood.   (4.1.50–53)

It seems not stretching the point too far to see a connection between the white colors of mercy and Zenocrate, whom Tamburlaine names at the end as "She that hath calmed the fury of my sword" (5.2.375).

The dark and cruel aspects of Tamburlaine are fully developed in the imagery. The red colors displayed on the second day, when his "kindled wrath must be quenched with blood," and the black colors of the third day which "menace death and hell" are mentioned frequently as symbolic of his terrible purposes. Early in the play Cosroe's lieutenant says of Tamburlaine,

> Some powers divine, or else infernal, mixed
> Their angry seeds at his conception.   (2.6.9–10)

The "infernal" imagery is projected largely through the speeches of Tamburlaine's opponents, especially Bajazeth, who more than any one else suffers brutal and inhuman treatment. His laments and curses compress all the dark and violent acts and emotions of the play into imagery which draws frequently from features of the classical underworld. He prays that the "dread god of hell" may "with ebon sceptre strike this hateful earth" (4.2.27–28); he implores the furies to "dive to the bottom of Avernus' pool" to bring up "hellish poison" for Tamburlaine (4.4.18–23). His life becomes more loathsome to him

> Than noisome parbreak of the Stygian snakes
> Which fills the nooks of hell with standing air.   (5.2.193–94)

Images of this sort, which appear frequently, especially during the fourth act in which Bajazeth is brutally humiliated and baited, accent the darker aspects of Tamburlaine's character and actions. They correspond to the "coal-black colors" displayed on the third day, which "menace death and hell." Not all the "infernal" images are pejorative, however. Theridamas, in his first astonished admiration for Tamburlaine, describes his looks as

> . . . meant to pierce Avernus' darksome vaults,
> To pull the triple-headed dog from hell. (1.2.159–60)

And just before the crowning of Zenocrate, Tamburlaine exults in his military invincibility in a long speech full of blood and agony and references to Styx, Charon's boat, the fatal sisters, and grisly death.

It is, as we have seen, a feature of the diction of the play that characteristic images are used in more than one way and that by this means relations are more closely established and important resolutions in the action are prepared for and accented. But no similar explanation on the same basis offers itself concerning the "dark" images. The excessive cruelty of Tamburlaine, especially toward Bajazeth and Zabina, appears nowhere to be fully accounted for or brought into explicit relation to those aspects of character and thought which affect the main development; in a similar fashion the "infernal" images are never woven very closely into the threads of the figurative texture of the play, but maintain a more distinct and independent line. The concentration of most of these images during the central portion of the play when Tamburlaine's acts are cruelest, and Zenocrate's revulsion on seeing the dead bodies of the emperor and his wife, might be regarded as an indication that Tamburlaine's studied cruelty is only an incidental expression of his lust for self-fulfillment and not essential to his nature, which is energetically ruthless but not sadistic; but the return of these images in full force just before the crowning of Zenocrate renders such an interpretation questionable. It may well be that a consistent explanation of this play is out of the question, and that the conflicting interpretations of it result from Marlowe's failure to effect a final integration of all its elements. In the relative isolation of the dark and infernal images may be found perhaps a symptom of his failure.

In most other respects there is close harmony. It is not possible, by a selective and necessarily discrete isolation of the leading images, to show in more than a limited way their interpenetration and their contribution to the formal development of the play. There are long speeches, for instance, in which the introduction of one type of image is the preparation for a series of mutations, in the course of which several of the dominant images are brought into play in a sustained pattern (for instance, 4.2.30–55). The repetition of key words in different speeches has the effect of acting as a clue to their close relation; for example, the word "restless" occurring in the speech on aspiration and in the one on beauty—"and always moving as the restless spheres" paralleled by "still would there hover in their restless heads." Cosroe angrily calling Tamburlaine a "fiery thirster after sovereignty" recalls the phrase in Menaphon's description of him as "thirsting with sovereignty" and prepares for the opening of the speech, "The thirst of reign and sweetness of a crown."

That this harmony is not always apparent is the result, in part, of a still somewhat incomplete solution of the problem, of a failure to distinguish between dramatic and lyrical methods. For one thing, the sequence of episodes that might be called the plot of *Tamburlaine* consists so largely of a series of increasingly great military triumphs, each one involving more kings and more troops, that it conceals the line of development on which the imaginative treatment of the diction appears to be centered and hence throws into prominence the boasting and the rant. And it makes not for a schematic unfolding of an action, but for a repetitious sequence of analogous episodes in which the central figure is seen in a familiar role; and with these repetitions in situation occur repetitions in the sentiments and hence in the images, so that there is loss of power which a cumulative development would have produced. A related difficulty arises from the fact that as Tamburlaine rises in stature and dignity he also becomes generalized into a symbol and an abstraction. The Tamburlaine who speaks the lines about aspiration and beauty is not so much a character representing a man aspiring to virtue, as, rather, the embodiment of the philosophical ideal of virtue; and so, too, the union of Zenocrate and Tamburlaine is not simply the marriage of a warrior and a beautiful princess, but the dramatic counterpart of Tamburlaine's assertion that an instinct for beauty is inherent in the man who aspires to virtue. The extravagant and lofty suggestions, the balanced and opposed relations in the imagery would have been appropriate to no other treatment; but there is, as a result, an incongruity in some of Tamburlaine's acts when seen against this scale which complicates any attempt at a comprehensive interpretation.

Nevertheless, the importance of *Tamburlaine* can hardly be exaggerated. Though it has superficial stylistic resemblances with the early experiments in tragedy, essentially the language is not ordered by rhetorical ideals of pattern, wit, sententiousness, and the like, but is managed poetically. It reveals a concern for that intimate union between diction and dramatic form which became the common property of the poetic tragedy of the best Elizabethan dramatists.[25]

The Spanish Tragedy also occupies an intermediate position between the academic experiments of the middle years of the sixteenth century and the fully developed Elizabethan tragedy. Its contribution to this development was very great, though it was different from that of *Tamburlaine*. In comparison with that play, it is distinguished by a scheme of construction conventionally described as an intrigue plot. The principal action is set in motion by the love of Bel-Imperia for Horatio, shortly after Horatio returns victorious from battle bringing home captive the Portuguese prince, Balthazar, who had slain her former lover in the combat. This love ends in the murder of Horatio by Lorenzo, Bel-Imperia's brother, who is promoting the suit of Balthazar for his sister's favor. From this point on, the principal episodes are taken up with the attempts of Hieronimo, Horatio's father, to discover the murderers and obtain justice and revenge. But the thread which started the play is not neglected. Bel-Imperia comes eventually to Hieronimo's aid, partly to secure her own vengeance and partly to forestall the plans to have her marry the Portuguese prince in a politically advantageous match. The revenge is not accomplished until the offending persons are killed during the performance of a tragedy staged by Hieronimo as part of the celebrations for the forthcoming state wedding. If the play fails at times to maintain a close progression of events through a systematic dovetailing of the episodes it is not through any weakness in the nature of the design as such, but through faults in craftsmanship—for example, the introduction of the story of the treacherous noble in the Portuguese court, which has no bearing on the main action, and the disproportionate amount of preliminary preparation necessary before Hieronimo is introduced as the avenging agent. Nevertheless, close integration of episodes is inherent in the design of *The Spanish Tragedy*. The play provides for continuous excitement on the stage within a restricted and progressive narrative framework. It was not too bad a model for other dramatists to learn from.

The distinctive feature which later dramatists borrowed from *The Spanish Tragedy* was the use of revenge as a motive for the principal character. Whatever the merits of this formula as a basis for tragedy, it had the advantage of imposing a fairly strict pattern on the play. It thus assisted in discouraging multiple narratives and irrelevant episodes, and, in general, acted as a check on the tendency toward diffuseness and digression which was a common defect of popular Elizabethan drama. Comparison might be made with the influence toward concentration which the detective story and the "western" have had on the wayward tendencies of the motion picture. The revenge formula, however, possessed another advantage in the fact that through the practical and moral dilemmas which it forced on the main character, it was not incompatible with serious and exhaustive exploration of character, as *Hamlet* alone will indicate. In Hieronimo, Kyd made a brilliant choice. Hieronimo is a marshal, the principal officer of justice, with a highly developed sense of right and a reputation for humanity and integrity. Great probability is thus established, on the one hand, for the delay of the revenge—his suspicion of Bel-Imperia's secret letter, his attempts to get justice through the king, and his belief that the heavens are just and will not permit cruelty to go unpunished, a point reiterated throughout the play. Probability is also established for Hieronimo's madness or near-madness: he is appalled at the wanton injustice of the murder and inveighs against the "monstrous times" and a world which is a "mass of public wrongs"; he is driven to frenzy at the calculating way in which the avenues to justice are blocked to him and concludes finally that there can be none for him, "for justice is exiled from the earth." He is thus forced to rely on himself, and when Bel-Imperia joins with him as a confederate, he concludes

> . . . that heaven applies our drift,
> And all the saints do sit soliciting
> For vengeance on those cursed murderers.   (4.1.32–34)*

*Line references are to F. S. Boas's edition of *The Spanish Tragedy* in *The Works of Thomas Kyd* (Oxford, 1901).

That Hieronimo is not one of the great dramatic figures is chiefly
due to the technical immaturity of Kyd; the brilliance of the conception, not wholly apparent in Kyd's early play, is to be seen in its
progeny.

In view of the remarkable originality of so much of this play, the
presence of the conventional rhetoric of the older tragedies seems
surprising. The appearance of balanced and alliterative lines recalls again the early experiments in blank verse:

> To *gracious fortune* of my *tender youth*
> For there in *p*rime and *p*ride of all my years,
> By *d*uteous service and *d*eserving love . . . . (1.1.7–9)

But the rhetorical artifice of the style of *The Spanish Tragedy* has
variety and complexity beyond these devices. The repeated line-
pattern is very common, the following lines being the most notorious
because Jonson subjected them to ridicule in *Every Man in His
Humour:*

> O eyes, no eyes, but fountains fraught with tears;
> O life, no life, but lively form of death;
> O world, no world, but mass of public wrongs. (3.2.1–3)

Kyd uses stychomythia, and the variant of it in which the statement and reply occur within the same speech, as in the following
lines of Balthazar:

> Yet might she love me for my valiancy—
> Ay, but that's slandered by captivity.
> Yet might she love me to content her sire—
> Ay, but her reason masters his desire. (2.1.19–22)

And so on for almost ten lines. Another device is the telescoping of
one line into the next by the use of the last word of one line to introduce the idea in the succeeding one:

> First, in his hand he brandished a sword,
> And with that sword he fiercely waged war,
> And in that war he gave me dangerous wounds,
> And by those wounds he forced me to yield . . . . (2.1.118–22)

In this particular instance the device is sustained for eleven lines.
In addition to the common appearance of such artifices of style the
effect of studied eloquence is conspicuous in sustained speeches
like the Induction spoken by the ghost of Andrea, or the General's
description of the battle, or Horatio's report of the death of Andrea.

A comparison of Bel-Imperia's soliloquy about her new love (1.4.58ff.) with soliloquies in later plays will also show some of the pervasive effects of the rhetorical style: it is constructed more like a formal debate or brief of the issues than a reflection on an emotional crisis.

What is not at once apparent is that in spite of his preoccupation with such elegances of expression, Kyd did a great deal in this play to liberate dramatic blank verse from the patterns of the fashionable rhetoric. While still within the discipline of a fairly regular meter, many lines have the flexibility that suggests ordinary speech:

> Then shalt thou find that I am liberal.
> Thou know'st that I can more advance thy state
> Than she; be therefore wise, and fail me not.
> Go and attend her as thy custom is,
> Lest absence makes her think thou dost amiss.   (2.1.102–6)

More striking is the use of varied and flexible rhythms to suggest Hieronimo's distraction and antic disposition before Lorenzo (3.2.61–63). Such a shift in the handling of the verse and in the phrasing necessarily implies an equally radical shift in the diction, and, in fact, the play proves on examination to have accomplished some remarkable developments in that respect. Kyd could not have come to anything like satisfactory terms with his plot structure and characters otherwise. The transitional nature of the play is therefore to be seen in the retention of the older style in spite of the original advances. The older features were retained, no doubt, because such formalized enhancements of language had become established through the academic tragedies fostered by *Gorboduc* as the traditional signs of the tragic art, just as in a similar way the reflections on Fortune in the irrelevant Portuguese episodes presumably acknowledge the expectation of sententious or eloquent expression of certain conventional themes, though the idea of fickle Fortune has no essential bearing on anything involved in the main action. The survivals appear, however, not merely as vestigial remains. The variations in style seem to conform to some vague principle of appropriateness to the speaker or the kind of situation involved. Thus, the Induction, spoken by the Ghost, is done in the style of the imitations of the Virgilian descent to hell common to the metrical tragedy, of which Sackville's Induction to *The Mirror for Magistrates* is the best known example.[26] The reports of battles are ren-

dered with an epic stateliness combined with the turgid sensation-
alism of reference to broken bodies and bloodshed which had
become the characteristic manner of the conventional Nuntius, and
was retained for such accounts in later plays—for instance, in
Chapman's plays where they are conspicuous, and less obviously
in the report of the battle by the Sergeant in the second scene of
Macbeth. The speeches of Balthazar are almost invariably marked
by greater artifice than those, for instance, of his Machiavellian
companion Lorenzo. Certain of the speeches in which a character
is represented as probing for himself the personal aspects of some
situation are, as we have already noted, marked by a patterned
formality. It appears as though Kyd, confronted by the need of
introducing a wholly new style to satisfy the special demands of his
plot and characters, and at the same time of retaining the established artifices of manner which were features of the tragic pieces
up to his time, solved the problem by admitting a variety of styles
through a kind of principle of decorum which suited the style to
person or occasion.

The solution, though ingenious, is not, however, wholly satisfactory, for, the two methods being essentially incompatible, one
must sometimes succeed at the expense of the other. Those passages
in which both methods appear distinctively in the same speech
demonstrate at once the technical skill with which Kyd effected
his compromise, and the extent to which it weakened his originality:

> Alas, it is Horatio, my sweet son.
> O, no, but he that whilom was my son.
> O, was it thou that call'dst me from my bed?
> O, speak, if any spark of life remain.
> I am thy father. Who hath slain my son?
> What savage monster, not of human kind,
> Hath here been glutted with thy harmless blood,
> And left thy bloody corpse dishonored here,
> For me, amidst these dark and deathful shades,
> To drown thee with an ocean of my tears?
> O heavens, why made you night to cover sin?
> By day this deed of darkness had not been.
> O earth, why didst thou not in time devour
> The vile profaner of this sacred bower?
> O poor Horatio, what hadst thou misdone,
> To leese thy life ere life was new begun?

O wicked butcher, whatsoe'er thou wert,
How could thou strangle virtue and desert?
Ay me most wretched, that have lost my joy,
In losing my Horatio, my sweet boy! (2.5.14-33)

The opening lines are patterned, as though in formal introduction of the emotional outburst; the central portion is more flexible in its rhythms and more rich in its imagery; the closing lines, a sort of miniature peroration, return to a formalized pattern again, emphasized not only by the systematic repetition in phrasing, but by the couplet rhymes. The immediate effect of the patterned sections is to bring this speech in stylistic conformity with the rest of the play. In a sense, the presence of these artifices tends to soften the raw physical impression of blood, violence and death, and of wild grief; and it might be argued for these professed formalities of style—in this as in certain other Elizabethan plays of violence—that in the absence of other means to that end, they tend to give to the expression of horror and outrage a semblance of art. But ostentatiously rhetorical art of any sort endows almost any sentiments with an academic, generalized quality. Consequently, where, as in the passage just quoted, other means are also used, such devices tend to undercut their effect and limit their operation. It becomes necessary in *The Spanish Tragedy* to isolate them from their rhetorical environment, as it were, in order to understand their function. Omission of the first four and last eight lines will show to what extent they weaken the most effective part of the speech.

The necessity for effecting such an isolation for purposes of analysis in the case of this play can be illustrated by means of the allusions to classical mythology with which it abounds. Such typical lines as "Ere Sol had slept three nights in Thetis' lap," "Now while Bellona rageth here and there," and "Till Phoebus waving to the western deep," are obviously devices of ornament and stylistic elevation. They come early in the play, the first in the Induction, the others in the General's report of the battle; they appear, that is, in set speeches which by convention are formal and deliberately elevated in manner. There are others like them, and they establish the expectation that all the mythological references will be of the same sort. The fact is that they are not. In the love scenes and in the speeches of Hieronimo following his son's death they occupy quite a different role. Indeed, with the declaration of affection between

Horatio and Bel-Imperia, the love episodes become for a moment the focus of the play and a new manner of handling the diction is introduced; with the discovery of the body of his son by Hieronimo, the focus of the play shifts to the Marshal and the diction once more enters a new phase. The mythological references become a feature of the new treatment and there is a consistency in each instance in the way they are selected: in the love scenes appear Vesper, Flora, Cupid, Venus and Mars; the mythological allusions in Hieronimo's speeches almost without exception are to characters and features of the underworld or to persons who were associated at some time with it—Furies, Orpheus, Aeacus, Proserpine, Pluto, and the like. Particularly in the latter case, these are a part of a sustained and homogeneous development of images.

The first scene in which Bel-Imperia and Horatio acknowledge their love is complicated by the presence of the spies, Lorenzo and Balthazar, whose asides are worked into the main dialogue with due consideration for the artifices of phrasing in the whole development. It contains Bel-Imperia's extended similitude of the storm-tossed bark and the harbor, and the likening of love to war. The latter figure plays a part in the next love episode, but it is only in the closing line of the scene that the poetical development of the subsequent scene is suggested as in miniature:

> Then be thy father's pleasant bower the field,
> Where first we vowed a mutual amity.
> The court were dangerous; that place is safe.
> Our hour shall be when Vesper gins to rise,
> That summons home distressful travelers.
> There none shall hear us but the harmless birds;
> Haply the gentle nightingale
> Shall carol us asleep, ere we be ware,
> And, singing with the prickle at her breast,
> Tell our delight and mirthful dalliance.   (2.2.42–51)

The scene in which the lovers next meet is little more than an amplification of this speech—the darkness that brings pleasure to lovers, the beauty and safety of the bower, the singing of the nightingale, and the allusions to Venus and Mars which introduce the artful playing with the similitude of war and love. These elements are fairly skillfully blended into a kind of idyll to suggest the beauty and happiness of the lovers, and provide a moment of tense quiet before the murderers burst in. The tenseness is introduced not merely in

the passing apprehension of Bel-Imperia, but in the infusion of
irony in the symbols; the darkness brings not happiness but sorrow
and the bower holds not safety but death, and since we are aware
of the plot against the lovers, we know this from the start and the
images take on a double aspect. For instance, in the opening speech
of Horatio—

> Now that the night begins with sable wings
> To overcloud the brightness of the sun,
> And that in darkness pleasures may be done,
> Come, Bel-Imperia, let us to the bower
> And there in safety pass a pleasant hour   (2.4.1–5)

—it is the words "sable wings," "overcloud," and "darkness" which
take on a sinister prominence, and all the later references to Flora
decking the arbor with flowers and the birds which "record by
night" for Bel-Imperia are insufficient wholly to remove these suggestions and other similar ones lurking in the speeches. It is through
this ironic strain that the language of this scene is tied in to what
follows. When Hieronimo runs out in response to the cries for help,
he exclaims, "This place was made for pleasure, not for death,"
and in his first outburst of grief at discovering the body to be
Horatio's,

> O heavens, why made you night to cover sin?
> By day this deed of darkness had not been.   (2.5.24–25)

There is thus a complete reversal in direction of the imagery used
in the arbor scene. The ironic overtones in Horatio's line, "The
more will Flora deck it with her flowers," are brought out in full
in the scene during which Isabella tears down the arbor:

> Fruitless forever may this garden be,
> Barren the earth, and blissless whosoever
> Imagines not to keep it unmanured.
> An eastern wind, conmixed with noisome airs,
> Shall blast the plants and the young saplings;
> The earth with serpents shall be pestered,
> And passengers, for fear to be infect,
> Shall stand aloof, and, looking at it, tell:
> "There, murdered, died the son of Isabel."   (4.2.14–22)

In the speeches of Hieronimo, darkness and night become central
sources for the imagery of sorrow, indignation, and madness. Combined in a supplementary relationship with the mythology of the
underworld, and touched up with reiteration of the violence of the

murder and the pity of Horatio's death and of the sighs and tears of the parents, these images become important means through which we are enabled to follow the tortured disorder of Hieronimo's mind.

In their simplest function the "dark" suggestions project the horror of the deed and the gloom of death. They make their appearance, heightened by the sanguinary references to the corpse, in Hieronimo's first outcry on discovering the dead Horatio (quoted above). The "dark and deathful shades," the "deed of darkness," "the night to cover sin," mingle with the other impressions to underscore the horror of the murder. There is an elaborate extension of this later when Hieronimo in his madness imagines an old man to be his son:

> Sweet boy, how art thou changed in death's black shade!
> Had Proserpine no pity on thy youth,
> But suffered thy fair crimson-colored spring
> With withered winter to be blasted thus? (3.13.145–48)

The same images are used to impress the wanton cruelty of the murder in Hieronimo's long speech of explanation following the accomplishment of his revenge in the play-within-the-play:

> But night, the coverer of accursed crimes,
> With pitchy silence hushed these traitors' harms. (4.4.101–2)

> There merciless they butchered up my boy,
> In black, dark night, to pale, dim, cruel death. (4.4.106–7)

This entire speech is singular in the direct forcefulness of its expression, and in its relative freedom from ornament; moreover, with the exception of the two excerpts quoted, some references to wounds, and sanguinary expressions accompanying the display of the bloody handkerchief which Hieronimo has carried with him as a token of his duty to revenge, there is very little in the way of the characteristic figures which are prominent in the middle portions of the play. The directness of the speech may be considered a sign of Hieronimo's calm of mind with the completion of his task and of freedom from the "brainsick lunacy" which he had to struggle against while he was working toward his goal. The presence in these lines of such figures of speech as are concerned only with the expression of the horror of the crime is a hint, however, that the fuller development of the principal images in the central portion of the play serves another function than to underline the physical violence of the events, and that from the moment Hieronimo resolves on his revenge they are no longer needed.

After the first shock of realization, the force of the images shifts and is focused on the turmoil in Hieronimo's mind. They become expressive of his inability to reconcile the violence of the act with the innocence of his son, of his gloomy conviction that the world is a "mass of public wrongs," of his growing doubts whether the justice of men or of heaven can be depended upon, and of his increasing turmoil and harassment of mind verging upon madness. As these conflicts come to occupy his mind, the opposition of dark and light imagery becomes involved with other suggestions:

> O sacred heavens, if this unhallowed deed,
> If this inhuman and barbarous attempt,
> If this incomparable murder thus
> Of mine, but now no more my son, ·
> Shall unrevealed and unrevenged pass,
> How should we term your dealings to be just,
> If you unjustly deal with those that in your justice trust?
> The night, sad secretary to my moans,
> With direful visions wake my vexed soul,
> And with the wounds of my distressful son
> Solicit me for notice of his death.
> The ugly fiends do sally forth of hell,
> And frame my steps to unfrequented paths,
> And fear my heart with fierce inflamed thoughts.
> And cloudy day my discontents records,
> Early begins to register my dreams,
> And drive me forth to seek the murderer.   (3.2.5–21)

There will be noticed implied here a new opposition between heaven and hell. As Hieronimo's frustration grows, as he becomes increasingly skeptical of finding justice, as his mind becomes more disordered, this opposition is more elaborately phrased and "the fierce inflamed thoughts" are reflected in imagery derived from the classical underworld. Such imagery is first introduced into the play in the Induction, spoken by the Ghost, but whereas its presence in the Induction is clearly for the purpose of describing the horrors of Hades, in the speeches of Hieronimo it is symbolic of horrors within. His fierce lamentations, he complains, have blasted the trees and meadows and "broken through the brazen gates of hell"—

> Yet still tormented is my tortured soul
> With broken sighs and restless passions,

> That winged mount, and, hovering in the air,
> Beat at the windows of the brightest heavens,
> Soliciting for justice and revenge.
> But they are placed in those empyreal heights,
> Where, countermured with walls of diamond,
> I find the place impregnable; and they
> Resist my woes, and give my words no way. (3.7.10–18)

Nevertheless, though he subsequently finds indisputable evidence of who the murderers are, he reflects that heaven cannot be denied and has its own ways. It is this idea which forms the basis for the elaborate description of a guilty conscience which Hieronimo gives to the Portuguese who ask him to direct them to Lorenzo's house; in a mad conceit, he directs them to the path that leads from a guilty conscience through darksome forests to despair and death—

> Whose rocky cliffs when you have once beheld,
> Within a hugy dale of lasting night,
> That, kindled with the world's iniquities,
> Doth cast up filthy and detested fumes—
> Not far from thence, where murderers have built
> A habitation for their cursed souls,
> There in a brazen caldron, fixed by Jove
> In his fell wrath, upon a sulphur flame,
> Yourselves shall find Lorenzo bathing him
> In boiling lead and blood of innocents. (3.11.69–78)

This effort to find satisfaction in the thought of punishment for the murderer through the terrors of a guilty conscience, symbolically represented by the shifting of the infernal images to Lorenzo with a change in emphasis, is momentary: it is not justice and revenge, and in the next scene Hieronimo, with rope and poniard in hand, contemplates suicide, and the infernal images focus again on him:

> Hieronimo, 'tis time for thee to trudge.
> Down by the dale that flows with purple gore
> Standeth a fiery tower. There sits a judge
> Upon a seat of steel and molten brass,
> And twixt his teeth he holds a fire-brand,
> That leads unto the lake where hell doth stand.
> Away, Hieronimo! To him be gone;
> He'll do thee justice for Horatio's death. (3.12.6–13)

The absence of heavenly images reveals the implicit rejection of the justice of heaven. The piling up of the infernal images from this point on reflects the full bitterness of Hieronimo's mind and his growing resolution that he must secure justice through vengeance. Thus in the next scene:

> Though on this earth justice will not be found,
> I'll down to hell, and in this passion
> Knock at the dismal gates of Pluto's court,
> Getting by force, as once Alcides did,
> A troop of furies and tormenting hags
> To torture Don Lorenzo and the rest.   (3.13.108–13)

To the old man whom in his madness he mistakes for his son, he says,

> Go back, my son; complain to Aeacus,
> For here's no justice. Gentle boy, begone,
> For justice is exiled from the earth.   (3.13.137–39)

> What, not my son? Thou then a Fury art,
> Sent from the empty kingdom of black night
> To summon me to make appearance
> Before grim Minos and just Rhadamanth,
> To plague Hieronimo that is remiss,
> And seeks not vengeance for Horatio's death.   (3.13.152–57)

Only when he discovers a spur and an ally in Bel-Imperia and determines on the one course left him do these infernal images leave the play:

> But may it be that Bel-Imperia
> Vows such revenge as she hath deigned to say?
> Why, then I see that heaven applies our drift,
> And all the saints do sit soliciting
> For vengeance on those cursed murderers.   (4.1.30–34)

Private vengeance is now identified with the justice of heaven, and the torment of his mind is over. In the episodes which follow he is calculating and self-possessed. In his speech of explanation, images of blood and darkness return, but here they are clearly distinct from those which were the index of a troubled mind and are a repetition in kind of those initial images which gave emphasis to the recognition of the horror and violence of the crime. The bloody handkerchief is the symbol of the determination to secure justice which had kept him from final despair and death.[27]

Since the action of the play is centered in Hieronimo's attempt to secure justice and in his final success through private vengeance, and since the probability of the delay and the final execution of the revenge thus resides chiefly in the character of Hieronimo, the diction of the play is quite properly ordered to cooperate with the exploration of Hieronimo's mind, which occupies the central portion of the play. The imagery is in this way brought into intimate relationship with the action. The means Kyd used are less complex and less subtle than those of certain later dramatists, and his compromise with the precedents in style established by such plays as *Gorboduc* helps to conceal the originality with which he freed the blank verse line from its dependence on rhetorical design and made it answerable to his purposes. Nevertheless, *The Spanish Tragedy* greatly advanced the art of verse drama and represents a genuine break with Kyd's immediate dramatic past; it was still a long way from the tragedies of Shakespeare, but it was essentially like them in kind.

The contributions to the art of verse tragedy made by the immediate contemporaries of Kyd and Marlowe were not of the same order. It is true these men were very much interested in style and in the problem of the language of poetry and of drama. The variety of verse forms in Peele's *Arraignment of Paris* is alone evidence of technical interest in such problems. Greene's criticism of exaggerated vigor in blank verse and his annoyance at those who "had it in derision for me that I could not make my verses jet upon the stage" indicates the fastidious craftsman who knows what he wants. Similarly, Nash, who has much to say about style and language, attacks, in his Preface to Greene's *Menaphon*, those "alcumists of eloquence" who "think to outbrave better pens with the swelling bombast of a bragging blank verse," and he also praises Peele as the "primus verborum artifex." All this, aside from its relationship to private literary feuds, shows a preoccupation with the refinement of the instruments of expression, certainly a valuable concern at a time when the drama was just beginning to find its way. Moreover, these men, with their pride in their university learning and their resentment of the crudity of unlettered popular dramatic hacks, regarded themselves as custodians of the art of letters, and thus brought to drama, even at their worst moments, some sort of artistic conscience. It is not to disregard their influence in this and in other matters to consider them primarily as men of talent who brought greater refinement and flexibility to dramatic verse, so that later writers were spared the labor of having to overcome their own awkwardness. Nor should any inferences be drawn from the absence in this discussion of the rest of Marlowe's plays, which are perhaps more remarkable and more effective dramatically than his first and which must have had a considerable influence. The importance of the two plays discussed arises from the fact that they are, in the strict sense, poetic dramas, and that in comparison to the tragedies which preceded them they are, in a manner of speaking, mutations. It is not an exaggeration to say that, with *Tamburlaine* and *The Spanish Tragedy*, English tragedy had been clearly started in the direction of its artistic destiny—toward that final integration of proper means to proper ends without which no art can realize its possibilities.

III

It was Shakespeare's important accomplishment to bring to complete and plenteous fruition the dramatic art of his times. The possibilities latent in the drama of his age he realized to their last measure. In comedy, perhaps, the work of such dramatists as Ben Jonson, Middleton, Fletcher, Massinger, and Shirley developed in directions which he left relatively unexplored, but his complete mastery over tragedy and his extensive development of it left no room for any of his fellow dramatists to extend its limits. Without sacrificing any of the amplitude and variety which were characteristic of the tragedy of his day, without denying himself any available resources of matter or technique, without repudiating or scorning any established practices or devices, he brought the intransigent elements of contemporary tragedy under the discipline of an integrated art. Of none of the writers of tragedy contemporary with him is it possible to say this. One mark of Shakespeare's superiority is the copiousness and felicity of his diction. No English dramatist equals him in the virtuosity and imagination with which he uses language. This is a commonplace, but it is a commonplace which becomes startling once the plays are searched methodically and critically to illustrate it. It is not, moreover, only in the felicity of particular words, or in the brilliance or depth of individual images that Shakespeare's artistry is finally to be seen, but in the thoroughness with which he made use of these resources of language for his dramatic needs.[28]

Shakespeare began writing plays about 1590 when the first generation of professional dramatists just discussed was leading the field, and it was from their plays necessarily that he must have learned his craft. Between this date and the end of his career, the remarkable development which is apparent in all other aspects of his art is traceable also in his diction and in his use of figures. It is necessary to take this fact into account in any general treatment of his use of language. For example, his early plays, notably the histories, show a conspicuous use of stately rhetoric and occasional adaptation of the design of the line and of the imagery to the end of giving brightness and variety to a truism or adding dignity or point to argument. Figures are deliberately and extensively developed, and often explicitly introduced with "like" or "as." There is a tendency, too, in these earlier plays toward virtuosity of invention that shows itself in images which stand out by themselves, as it were, for their ingenuity and intricacy; for instance, "unthread the rude eye of rebellion" (*King John*, 5.4.11),* or

> . . . my cloud of dignity
> Is held from falling with so weak a wind
> That it will quickly drop.
> (*Henry IV, Part II*, 4.5.99–101)

Distinction must also be made, however, between kinds of plays; for instance, there are fewer sententious or studied images in *Romeo and Juliet* than in the history plays written almost contemporaneously with it, where the notion of the dignity of statecraft or feeling for the rhetorical moment in the council chamber and the like left its mark. The general development is clearly, however, in the direction of a less explicit presentation of imagery and a more metaphorical language, reaching its culmination in the great tragedies where often the thought and image become one. It is therefore extremely difficult to discuss the imagery in some of these tragedies in which isolation of the images becomes almost an impossibility when every other word is a figure of speech or functions very much like one—"unkennel itself," "rough hew them," for instance—and where one figure of speech is left half finished and plunges on into a new one. Yet in these tragedies the language of poetry is most completely dramatic in its use, that is, it most closely

*Line references are to *The Complete Works of William Shakespeare* in the one-volume Student's Cambridge edition.

cooperates with those elements of necessity and probability which shape the form of the play, and it in fact becomes one of those elements.

An exhaustive analysis of the Shakespearean tragedies from this point of view is out of the question here; the problem under discussion demands merely adequate illustrations. Furthermore, a precise demonstration of the relationship which exists between the action of any given play and every important image, figure, or crucial word, though extremely illuminating, would call for a small volume. The needs of the present study can be met by the analysis of a few examples, carried sufficiently far to suggest, with some reason, such conclusions as might be drawn from a more exhaustive study. The plays to be discussed are *Romeo and Juliet* and *King Lear*—the first, because, though still showing traces of the earlier manner, it illustrates the relationship of diction to action in a poetical tragedy with greater clarity and simplicity than do some of the later plays; and *King Lear*, because of its recognized greatness in point of magnitude among the Shakespearean tragedies.

Romeo and Juliet is characterized by a wide variety of styles. At one extreme, it reveals some of the studied artifices which are so common a feature of early tragedy; at the other, it has the colloquial rhythms and diction of the speeches of servants, and the urbane ease of the conversations of Mercutio with Benvolio and Romeo. Figures like "the shady curtains from Aurora's bed" are thus balanced by speeches like "Where's Potpan, that he helps not to take away? He shift a trencher! He scrape a trencher!" That such extremes can appear without great violence of harmony in this play seems owing to the absence of the most obvious tricks of balance, alliteration, repetition, and the like and to the application of much the same principle of decorum in styles which we have already observed in the case of Kyd, only in this instance the variety is greater and the skill with which appropriateness to person and situation is worked out is also greater. The speeches of Friar Laurence are often in couplets and have a sententious flavor. The decree of the Prince ordering banishment is also in couplets. The speeches of old Montague and of Capulet at times are florid, and the imagery on these occasions has an explicitness of presentation not usual with the talk of the young people. There is, however, the studied development of the image of the pilgrim and the shrine in sonnet form at the first meeting of Romeo with Juliet, to suggest the arch formality of the two infatuated strangers and to associate their love at its inception with the lofty devotion of the sonnet sequences. There is a good deal of wordplay, and several sustained efforts at paradox, like Romeo's definition of love and Juliet's remarks about Romeo on first hearing of the death of Tybalt. In the conversations of the young men there is considerable alternation. The first scene with Mercutio—the one containing the Queen Mab speech—is in verse with richness of language, particularly in Romeo's opening and closing speeches in which he describes the heaviness of his mood and presages an ill outcome of their visit to the Capulets. The scene with Mercutio and Benvolio before the appearance of the nurse is in prose, urbane and conversational, and so too is the scene preceding the duel with Tybalt; but with the death of Mercutio it becomes verse again, and Benvolio's report of the duels to the Prince is quite formal, having the flavor of the reports of the conventional Nuntius. The sense of variety of treatment, however, is not the primary impression which this play leaves. It is the great brilliance and beauty of the speeches of the lovers and all that pertains to them which stands out most conspicuously. Moreover, in the diction of these speeches is to be found one of the principal features of order in the play.

Prominent among the figures of speech in *Romeo and Juliet* are those which suggest light, usually against a background of darkness, and from the outset these images become associated with the two main characters.[29] The appropriateness of this is apparent: two young people find themselves overwhelmingly in love—an infatuation that has become synonymous with young romantic love—against a background of family hatred and fighting. But the importance of this feature of the diction goes far beyond this simple relationship to the general situation. At their first appearance, words suggestive of light and darkness appear to be indifferently introduced. Benvolio tells Romeo's parents what he has observed of the young man's behaviour in his first infatuation with Rosaline:

> Madam, an hour before the worshipped sun
> Peered forth the golden window of the east,
> A troubled mind drave me to walk abroad;
> Where, underneath the grove of sycamore
> That westward rooteth from the city's side,
> So early walking did I see your son. (1.1.125–30.)

The ideas introduced by sun and darkness are applied more directly
to Romeo, however, in the speech of Montague which follows:

> Many a morning hath he there been seen
> With tears augmenting the fresh morning's dew,
> Adding to clouds more clouds with his deep sighs;
> But all so soon as the all-cheering sun
> Should in the farthest east begin to draw
> The shady curtains from Aurora's bed,
> Away from light steals home my heavy son,
> And private in his chamber pens himself,
> Shuts up his windows, locks fair daylight out,
> And makes himself an artificial night. (1.1.137–46)

In its florid language, this speech still seems primarily descriptive
in its force, with the emphasis on suggestions connoting darkness
glancing at Romeo. They are primarily designed to impress his
mood, the dark melancholy of unreturned love, as the next line of
Montague's speech indicates—"Black and portentous must this
humor prove." And this seems to be the main function of Montague's description of Romeo a few lines further:

> As is the bud bit with an envious worm
> Ere he can spread his sweet leaves to the air
> Or dedicate his beauty to the sun. (1.1.157–59)

Already, however, the last phrase foreshadows the imagery of the
balcony scene.

In a similar manner, images are pointed in the direction of
Juliet. The first of these is again somewhat general in its import;
Montague, delaying Paris' suit to Juliet, asks him to come to the
banquet and view her among others:

> At my poor house look to behold this night
> Earth-treading stars that make dark heaven light. (1.2.24–25)

Benvolio urges Romeo to attend the Capulet banquet so that he
might weigh his love for Rosaline

> . . . against some other maid
> That I will show you shining at this feast. (1.2.102–3)

From the first moment when Romeo sees Juliet, however, the images
take on a precise association:

> O, she doth teach the torches to burn bright!
> It seems she hangs upon the cheek of night
> As a rich jewel in an Ethiop's ear. (1.5.46–48)

Benvolio's speech after Romeo has leaped the orchard wall—

> Blind is his love and best befits the dark   (2.1.32)

—seems to recall the earlier use of the "dark" images, for Benvolio is still speaking in ignorance of Romeo's change of heart, but the line has that double meaning, so effective a feature of Elizabethan poetry, which comes from the enlargement, and hence intensification, of significance which words take on in the progress of a poem, and appears here to presage vaguely the sequent action; almost the identical phrase appears in a speech of Juliet's somewhat later (3.2.9–10).

With the appearance of Juliet on the balcony, the dominant images introduced at Romeo's first view of Juliet appear in a veritable torrent:

> But, soft! what light through yonder window breaks?
> It is the east, and Juliet is the sun.
> Arise, fair sun, and kill the envious moon,
> Who is already sick and pale with grief
> That thou, her maid, art far more fair than she.
> Be not her maid, since she is envious;
> Her vestal livery is but sick and green,
> And none but fools do wear it; cast it off.   (2.2.1–9)

The moon introduces the idea of chastity, but the suggestion is only momentary, and is at once replaced by another, the allusion to the stars, with which Juliet had been vaguely associated in Capulet's speech to Paris:

> Two of the fairest stars in all the heaven,
> Having some business, do entreat her eyes
> To twinkle in their spheres till they return.
> What if her eyes were there, they in her head?
> The brightness of her cheek would shame those stars,
> As daylight doth a lamp; her eyes in heaven
> Would through the airy region stream so bright
> That birds would sing and think it were not night.   (2.2.15–22)

The last line anticipates the imagery of the scene in the chamber. The images change again, but the contrast of light against darkness is preserved:

> O, speak again, bright angel! for thou art
> As glorious to this night, being o'er my head,
> As is a winged messenger of heaven
> Unto the white-upturned wond'ring eyes

> Of mortals that fall back to gaze on him
> When he bestrides the lazy-pacing clouds
> And sails upon the bosom of the air.   (2.2.26–32)

This speech concludes this line of figurative development in the scene. Scattered allusions to darkness take its place. The night is their ally and it has been gracious to them: "night's cloak" hides Romeo from his enemies, "the mask of night" prevents Juliet's blushes, and "the dark night" had revealed her love unawares. As Juliet leaves the balcony for a moment, Romeo exclaims,

> O blessed, blessed night! I am afeard,
> Being in night, all this is but a dream,
> Too flattering sweet to be substantial.   (2.2.139–41)

The light images are recalled once again in their substantial reality in the faint echo of them which occurs in Juliet's reply to Romeo's, "A thousand times good-night":

> A thousand times the worse, to want thy light.   (2.2.156)

The light-dark images continue to play a significant role in the play, but nowhere again do the impressions of light appear with the same predominant brilliance, or convey the same unmarred exaltation of mood as in the opening of the balcony scene. Romeo's address to night seems to shift the emphasis, and his fear that the whole experience might be a dream seems to cast over the opening development an air of brilliant unreality, and Juliet's "to want thy light" is scarcely sufficient to restore the original impressions. Moreover, the line, "Too flattering sweet to be substantial" anticipates the events to come. Even more pointed adumbration of the probable course of events is conveyed through the characteristic imagery of this scene in a speech of Juliet's which shortly precedes Romeo's on "blessed night":

> Although I joy in thee,
> I have no joy of this contract tonight;
> It is too rash, too unadvised, too sudden,
> Too like the lightning, which doth cease to be
> Ere one can say it lightens.   (2.2.116–20)

This too carries the suggestion of intense light against a background of darkness, but with now an ominous implication which anticipates the violent upsetting of their joy and the final catastrophe. The same effect is repeated in Friar Laurence's remark before he marries the lovers:

> These violent delights have violent ends,
> And in their triumph die, like fire and powder,
> Which as they kiss consume.   (2.6.9–11)

The prevailing figurative development is thus given a twist which serves to cast the shadow of the coming catastrophe over the brilliance of the opening.

The mutations of these dominant figures continue, and they are kept in close relation with the movement of the play. Mercutio and Tybalt are slain, Romeo banished. Juliet, unaware of these calamities, waits for the night and Romeo. The long soliloquy which opens the scene is, in effect, an extensive elaboration of those brief suggestions in the balcony scene favorable to the night, which had checked Juliet's blushes and revealed her love:

> Gallop apace, you fiery-footed steeds,
> Towards Phoebus' lodging; such a waggoner
> As Phaethon would whip you to the west,
> And bring in cloudy night immediately.
> Spread thy close curtain, love-performing night,
> That runaway's eyes may wink, and Romeo
> Leap to these arms, untalked of and unseen.
> Lovers can see to do their amorous rites
> And by their own beauties; or, if love be blind,
> It best agrees with night. Come, civil night,
> Thou sober-suited matron, all in black,
> And learn me how to lose a winning match,
> Played for a pair of stainless maidenhoods;
> Hood my unmanned blood, bating my cheeks,
> With thy black mantle; till strange love, grown bold,
> Think true love acted simple modesty.
> Come, night; come, Romeo; come thou day in night;
> Whiter than new snow on a raven's back.
> Come, gentle night; come, loving, black-browed night,
> Give me my Romeo; and when he shall die,
> Take him and cut him out in little stars,
> And he will make the face of heaven so fine
> That all the world will be in love with night,
> And pay no worship to the garish sun.   (3.2.1–25)

The same symbols are here, but the emphasis is distinctly on suggestions of night, which is associated with sensual pleasure and love. Romeo is associated with the characteristic suggestions of light— the stars against the face of heaven, the "day in night"—but unlike the first development of these figurative oppositions, the night is predominant and is associated with their joy. Though the figure of the snow on a raven's back is brilliant, it is not free of ominous impressions; compare it, for example, with two earlier ones on the same model, in which Romeo likens Juliet to a rich jewel in an Ethiop's ear or snowy dove trooping with crows (1.5.47–50). There is a distinct change in the relative force of the images, and this change is carried to its farthest point in the scene in the chamber.

Nothing much "happens" in this episode: the lovers say farewell after many lines about the dawn, lines which have become stock examples of Shakespeare's powers of description and of the beauties into which he was driven by lack of adequate lighting facilities on the Elizabethan stage. But there is more than mere description here, which could have been compressed into fewer lines to serve so simple a function as indicating the time of day, and there is much which a modern stage technician cannot replace. The scene of the parting is little more than a working out in a new form and in a new relation of the imagery of light and darkness:

> *Juliet.* Wilt thou be gone? it is not yet near day.
> It was the nightingale and not the lark,
> That pierced the fearful hollow of thine ear;
> Nightly she sings in yond pomegranate-tree.
> Believe me, love, it was the nightingale.
> *Romeo.* It was the lark, the herald of the morn,
> No nightingale. Look, love, what envious streaks
> Do lace the severing clouds in yonder east.
> Night's candles are burnt out, and jocund day
> Stands tiptoe on the misty mountain tops.
> I must be gone and live, or stay and die.
> *Juliet.* Yond light is not daylight, I know it, I;
> It is some meteor that the sun exhales,
> To be to thee this night a torch-bearer,
> And light thee on thy way to Mantua;
> Therefore stay yet; thou need'st not to be gone.
> *Romeo.* Let me be ta'en; let me be put to death;
> I am content, so thou wilt have it so.
> I'll say yon grey is not the morning's eye,
> 'Tis but the pale reflex of Cynthia's brow;
> Nor that is not the lark, whose notes do beat
> The vaulty heaven so high above our heads.
> I have more care to stay than will to go.
> Come, death, and welcome, Juliet wills it so.
> How is't, my soul? let's talk; it is not day.

> *Juliet.*   It is, it is! Hie hence, be gone, away!
> It is the lark that sings so out of tune,
> Straining sharp discords and unpleasing sharps . . . .
>   (3.5.1–28)

There is no longer any identification of the lovers with symbols of light; in this scene all symbols of light are alien to their joy and tied to their sorrow. For this scene is the turning point of the play. The lovers, having known one moment of peace and union, are separated under harsh and unpropitious circumstances. The reversal is clearly emphasized in Juliet's line,

> O, now be gone; more light and light it grows;   (3.5.35)

and in Romeo's answer,

> More light and light; more dark and dark our woes.   (3.5.36)

One further step remains to point this reversal of the imagery unmistakably to the conclusion, and this takes place in Juliet's speech before Romeo descends:

> Then window, let day in, and let life out.   (3.5.41)

When the lovers meet again it is in the darkness of the tomb, where the final and permanent consummation takes place. Between the scene of farewell and that of their death in the tomb, the images of light and darkness almost completely disappear in the play, and return to prominence only with Romeo's entrance into the tomb with the body of Paris:

> A grave? O no! a lantern, slaughtered youth,
> For here lies Juliet, and her beauty makes
> This vault a feasting presence full of light.   (5.3.84–86)

At the moment of final union in death, the language in Romeo's speech, though tinged with macabre somberness, returns once more to those notions of brilliance in the midst of darkness which announced his first glimpse of Juliet.

In their prominence and in their close relation to the action, the images just discussed tend to dim the others, but not to eclipse them. Some of the more important of these remain to be considered. The star images, for example, sometimes carry a significance deriving from the common notion that the stars govern men's fates, a significance which is established in the Prologue:

> From forth the fatal loins of these two foes
> A pair of star-crossed lovers take their life.

Similarly in Romeo's speech before he enters the revels at Capulet's:

> . . . my mind misgives
> Some consequence yet hanging in the stars
> Shall bitterly begin his fearful date
> With this night's revels . . . . (1.4.106–9)

These images clearly presage the final consequence of events, but they also emphasize the importance of influences lying outside of the individual's control, which play an important part in this plot of cross-purposes and accidents. The other star images are not all freighted with these ominous inferences, but, in at least one instance, appropriately enough in the scene in the chamber before Romeo's departure, two spheres of meaning are deliberately combined:

> Yond light is not daylight, I know it, I;
> It is some meteor that the sun exhales,
> To be to thee this night a torch-bearer
> And light thee on thy way to Mantua . . . . (3.5.12–15)

Juliet seems to be talking of meteors innocently enough here, but they were commonly regarded as portents of danger and frequently thus alluded to in the drama. At the end, when the star images reappear, they combine with the sense of ill fate a sense of triumph over destiny in death. When Romeo is told that Juliet is dead, he speaks in a tone of resolution:

> Is it even so? Then I defy you, stars! (5.1.24)

In his final speech, in which so many of the leading images find a place, the stars once more stand for the fatality which has followed them, but the lines have the same defiance and sense of bitter triumph:

> O, here
> Will I set up my everlasting rest,
> And shake the yoke of inauspicious stars
> From this world-wearied flesh. (5.3.109–12)

Images derived from voyaging constitute a minor sequence, but one which is tied in closely to the action and carried through to the end. The first of such images concludes Romeo's speech of misgiving before they set off for the revels at Capulet's house:

> But he that hath the steerage of my course,
> Direct my sail! (1.4.112–13)

The sense of fatality is replaced in the next instance by the sense of high adventure when the figure appears during the scene at the balcony:

> I am no pilot; yet wert thou as far
> As that vast shore washed with the farthest sea,
> I should adventure for such merchandise.   (2.2.82–85)

Of somewhat different order, but conveying the same impression, is Romeo's reference to the rope ladder,

> Which to the high top-gallant of my joy
> Must be my convoy in the secret night.   (2.4.202–3)

The image is just glanced at with suggestions of turmoil in Romeo's reference to his "betossed soul" on the journey from Mantua (5.3.76). And it comes full circle at the moment Romeo drinks the poison:

> Come, bitter conduct, come, unsavory guide!
> Thou desperate pilot, now at once run on
> The dashing rocks thy sea-sick weary bark!   (5.3.116–18)

The brave adventure has failed; the image now returns to the original implications of fatality and impresses suggestions of welcome ruin.

Since death is the inevitable end for the lovers, the references to death take on a special significance from the start, and it is appropriate to the play that most of the figures of speech involving death are combined with ideas of marriage or love. Juliet says, as she sends the nurse to inquire Romeo's identity,

> Go ask his name. If he be married,
> My grave is like to be my wedding bed.   (1.5.136–37)

The hyperbole prefigures the whole tragic resolution of the play. Romeo's "love-devouring death" (2.6.7) contains a slightly different association of these ideas, for in most such metaphors, death is represented as the rival lover or the ravisher. Such a metaphor is used to express Juliet's despair at the news of Romeo's banishment:

> I'll to my wedding bed,
> And death, not Romeo, take my maidenhead.   (3.2.136–37)

The metaphor is altered to make it applicable to Romeo in Friar Laurence's announcement of the Prince's doom for the killing of Tybalt, and, though death is not explicitly mentioned, the fatal implications are present:

> Romeo, come forth; come forth, thou fearful man.
> Affliction is enamoured of thy parts,
> And thou art wedded to calamity.   (3.3.1–3)

All other uses of this metaphor apply to Juliet. Lady Capulet petulantly exclaims on Juliet's refusal to marry Paris, "I would the fool were married to her grave" (3.5.141). The remark is almost a duplicate of Juliet's first use of the conceit, and the effect is one of unpleasant irony. A few lines further, in Juliet's desperate request to delay the marriage to Paris, the hyperbole is developed still further to the point where it almost literally predicates the concluding episodes:

> Or, if you do not, make the bridal bed
> In the dim monument where Tybalt lies.   (3.5.202–3)

This development establishes the appropriateness of Capulet's announcement to Paris of Juliet's death:

> O son! the night before thy wedding-day
> Hath Death lain with thy wife. There she lies,
> Flower as she was, deflowered by him.
> Death is my son-in-law, Death is my heir;
> My daughter he has wedded.   (4.5.35–39)

In the tomb scene, where the other leading images come to their completion in Romeo's last speeches, the metaphor of death the grim lover reaches its final development, intensified by references to Juliet's beauty and by the infusion of the primary suggestions of light and darkness and night:

> Death, that hath sucked the honey of thy breath,
> Hath had no power yet upon thy beauty.
> Thou art not conquered; beauty's ensign yet
> Is crimson in thy lips and in thy cheeks,
> And death's pale flag is not advanced there . . . .
>   . . . . Ah, dear Juliet,
> Why art thou yet so fair? Shall I believe
> That unsubstantial Death is amorous,
> And that the lean abhorred monster keeps
> Thee here in dark to be his paramour?
> For fear of that, I still will stay with thee,
> And never from this palace of dim night
> Depart again.   (5.3.92–108)

One feature of the diction of this play which demands some comment is the extraordinary amount of wordplay, which has been noted as a sign of early composition, and of which Samuel Johnson said: "His pathetic strains are always polluted with some unexpected depravations. His persons, however distressed, have a conceit left them in their misery, a miserable conceit." Something might still be said, therefore, for the appropriateness of at least some of the wordplay. Psychological probability—apparently the test of propriety implied in Johnson's condemnation—need not rule out all the wordplay; for instance, Romeo's words before the maskers enter Capulet's—

> . . . You have dancing shoes
> With nimble soles; I have a soul of lead
> So stakes me to the ground I cannot move   (1.4.14–16)

—are in a spirit of ironic jesting which is Romeo's usual mood in his talk with the effervescent Mercutio. Similarly, with Mercutio's "Ask for me tomorrow, and you shall find me a grave man," which is beyond dispute "in character." But like the other sorts of manipulations in the language of the play, it is necessary to judge the relevance of the wordplay not wholly in terms of assumptions about human nature, or appropriateness to characters, or in isolation. For instance, Capulet's statement—

> There she lies,
> Flower as she was, deflowered by him [death]   (4.5.36–37)

takes color from other allusions to death and to the grave, and is related to other references to flowers which are associated with love and with Juliet (1.2.29; 1.3.77; 2.2.121–22; 5.3.12). Moreover, there is something in the nature of this play that lends itself to paradox, as Juliet's speech on learning the identity of Romeo indicates:

> My only love sprung from my only hate!
> Too early seen unknown, and known too late!
> Prodigious birth of love it is to me
> That I must love a loathed enemy.   (1.5.140–43)

There are few devices that relate apparent opposites with more evident effect than do various forms of wordplay. Thus the Prologue to the second act:

> But passion lends them power, time means, to meet,
> Temp'ring extremities with extreme sweet.

Similarly, Romeo's remark to the Friar:

> What less than dooms-day is the Prince's doom?[30]   (3.3.9)

But the best example of the functional use of wordplay occurs in one of Juliet's speeches in the chamber scene:

> It is the lark that sings so out of tune,
> Straining harsh discords and unpleasing sharps.
> Some say the lark makes sweet division;
> This doth not so, for she divideth us. (3.5.27–30)

We have already noticed how important the shift in the dark and light images is in this scene. It is the bird of dawning here that sings in discords and sharps; and the pun on division, a word suggesting harmony of parts in its technical musical meaning, and separation in its common meaning, is one other means of pointing up the tragic irony in the situation and of calling attention to the crucial turning point in the action which the scene represents.

When even such reputed trivialities as puns find a significant part in the large scheme of the play, it is not surprising that *Romeo and Juliet* does not suffer from the survivals of the stylistic artifices of the early experiments in tragedy which left their mark on it. They are either reduced to a subordinate role in the style of the play or are made to serve new purposes. The important role is given to images which function dynamically in relation to the action, for the effectiveness of the principal images lies not in their consistency but in their alteration, and the same source of imagery can express, for example, the despair as well as the joy of the lovers. Each crucial symbol or figure of speech is effective in its place for the moment, but it also glances ahead or reflects what has preceded, so that it not only conforms to the exigencies of the action at any given point and helps to sustain the probabilities which govern the play, but it contributes to a cumulative development which gains increased force for later images from those which have preceded them. Thus when the leading images reappear in Romeo's speeches in the tomb at the moment of the catastrophe, they are made to convey the entire reversal of the play; implicit in them is the original disproportion in the situation which initiated the events of the play, and the inevitable change from intense mutual joy to death.

What is true of *Romeo and Juliet* is also true for all the later trage-dies, with only the qualification that the later tragedies possess greater depth and show a more mature artistry, and that no single formula is sufficient to describe the particular way in which the diction is made to function in any given play. Each play must be regarded as a unique problem—*Julius Caesar* represents, for instance, a different solution of the problem of style and imagery from *Hamlet*, let us say. Each play, however, reveals the same closely integrated, dramatic way of handling language, of making, that is, the diction and imagery play an essential role in the scheme of necessity and probability which determines and shapes the action. Nothing could be critically more confusing, therefore, than to regard the big speeches, the familiar soliloquies, and the like, as lyrical interludes, or separable beauties, or to perpetuate as a legitimate critical necessity, as anything more than a temporary expedient, the distinction between Shakespeare the poet and Shakespeare the dramatist. Such a distinction can arise out of either too narrow a conception of the nature and function of drama, or too specialized a conception of the nature of poetry. In any case, it does violence to the remarkable unity of Shakespeare's art. It is out of the question, and for the moment not relevant, to demonstrate this thesis in the case of every one of the great tragedies; but if *Romeo and Juliet* be regarded as too simple a structure, relatively speaking, to support so far-reaching a generalization, *King Lear*, in many ways the most imposing of the great tragedies, is certainly free of this objection and may be regarded as a satisfactory supplement to the earlier play by way of illustration.

It is necessary to realize certain peculiarities of the action of *Lear* before the diction and imagery can be seen in proper relation to it. In one respect, the plot structure is somewhat different from that of the other tragedies in the inclusion of the Gloucester story. For the most part, Shakespeare did not conform in his tragedies to the prevailing popular taste for multiple plot lines within a given play. In many Elizabethan plays, the various plots have little connection with one another, and the subordinate plots could with some trifling manipulation be wholly eliminated. Occasionally, connection is suggested by the treatment of a similar kind of theme or problem—for instance, the two complementary stories each dealing with chastity in *A Woman Killed with Kindness*—but the dramatic connections are negligible, and the two are not related in a single action. The Gloucester plot in *Lear* is not of this sort. The outcome of the play would not be what it is without the participation of Gloucester and especially of Edmund and Edgar. In addition, the relation of father and children is fundamental to both. The subordinate narrative is thus brought within the whole structural scheme of the play, so that it is hardly proper to call it a sub-plot at all. Edmund, Cornwall, Goneril, and Regan are associated together in character and in their effect on the plot; so are Kent, Albany, Edgar, and Cordelia; Gloucester and Lear both undergo suffering at the hands of their unnatural children. There is therefore no disharmony in the diction arising from the multiple threads in the plot; on the contrary, with certain exceptions, the minor plot reinforces the imagery necessary to the primary plot.

Because of this reciprocal relationship, the central position of Lear in the play is never confused, and it is always clear that he is the protagonist. The term, protagonist, however, as applied to Lear must be dissociated from such accidental suggestions of positive and sustained action in the plot as are implicit in popular usage. In the sense that what he does affects the final disposition of the characters in the play, Lear is active only in the opening scenes. He casts Cordelia out of his favor, and he banishes Kent. These acts establish the condition which permits the evil of Goneril, Regan, Cornwall, and indirectly Edmund to flourish. Lear's next decision separates him from his unnatural daughters and sends him out alone. But though from this point on he is relatively passive in the intrigue which resolves the play, he dominates the play in his physical and mental anguish. These intervening scenes represent something more, however, than Lear's passion, his suffering, and his madness. At the outset Lear does violence to his one need for happiness in breaking with Cordelia; toward the end of the play he is reconciled with her, content to live with her even in prison, "like birds i' the cage." Such a sentiment would have been repugnant and unthinkable to him when the play opens. It involves, therefore, the abandonment of most of what Lear had assumed to be valuable and true, for otherwise the meeting with Cordelia could not have taken place on the terms on which it does. It is for this reason that what goes on in Lear's mind between these two extremities in the action takes on such significance. It is an essential part of the action, in fact, since the resolution depends upon it. The long scenes which show us the unsettling of Lear's wit are not pure unreason and are not meant to be.

> O, matter and impertinency mixed!
> Reason in madness, (4.6.78–79)

Edgar exclaims. The "impertinency" is full of vague associations and pointed implications, and the "matter" comprises a sustained and not wholly disordered process of reflection. It is significant that the diction becomes increasingly intense, the imagery increasingly complex, during the central portion of the play which represents Lear's suffering and madness.

In this portion of the play the Fool, Edgar as Mad Tom, and Gloucester function, in a way, as instruments for giving occasion and appropriate focus for the projection of Lear's mind along its tortuous path. Strictly speaking, this development begins with Kent's objection to the king's denunciation of Cordelia. The issue is there clearly and explicitly stated, and Kent is banished. The Fool really continues the function which Kent served of blunt and truthful speaking, but in a new context. As Lear comes to the knowledge of the evil disposition of his two daughters, the Fool serves to draw to the surface the recognition of the error and folly which Lear strives to keep down, since that way madness lies. The comic obliquity and ironic indirectness of the Fool's comments are thus related to his function as the reminder of the folly Lear wishes to forget. The imagery in his witticisms is humiliating; for instance:

I have used it, nuncle, e'er since thou mad'st thy daughters thy mothers; for when thou gav'st them the rod, and put'st down thine own breeches,
> Then they for sudden joy did weep,
> And I for sorrow sung,
> That such a king should play bo-peep,
> And go the fools among.   (1.4.187–94)

And this alternates with outright explicit bluntness: "Thou shouldst not have been old till thou hadst been wise." During this portion of the play the bias of Lear's thought is largely personal. To the Fool's reminders he keeps up a counterpoint of remarks like "I did her wrong," "I will forget my nature," "Let me not be mad." In the first outpouring of his indignation he curses Goneril and begs nature to make her sterile or breed in her ungrateful children (1.4.296–311). In the scene with Regan he pleads for his hundred knights on the score of the dignity proper to him as a man. When he understands the settled purpose of his daughters, he begs for patience and vows terrible revenges which he cannot name. This utmost expression of futility marks the end of the first stage, for neither noble anger nor fierce revenge are the ways to his salvation. From this point on, though the personal impetus to his thoughts is always clear, his reflections take on a more general turn. His first speech in the storm is an extension of his curse on his daughter, but where he had condemned Goneril to sterility he now prays for the destruction of "nature's germens" that "breed ingrateful man" (3.2.1–9). When Kent offers him the shelter of the hovel, he wonders at the art of our necessities which "can make base things precious" (3.2.68–73): he who had once insisted on his hundred knights now finds luxury in straw. He prays before he enters the hovel, and it is not for noble anger or revenge but for the "poor naked wretches" who "bide the pelting of this pitiless storm" (3.4.26–36). At this point Edgar enters the play as Mad Tom, and though the Fool continues as an important accessory until his disappearance at the end of Act III, Edgar becomes the principal occasion and motive of Lear's outpourings. The wildness of Edgar's appearance and the strange medley of his speeches are in closer harmony with the extravagant turmoil of Lear's madness. Moreover, Lear's mind has now been carried beyond the preoccupation with wholly personal issues of which the Fool was the prompter. In his search for essentials, Lear regards Mad Tom, naked and facing the storm, as "unaccommodated man," stripped of all his trimmings. Where once he had urged his hundred knights on Regan with "O, reason not the need," he now sees Edgar and exclaims, "Thou art the thing itself." Edgar, who had known all the wickedness and folly of the world, is now unadorned man, and Lear looks on him in his frenzy as a "noble philosopher." He appoints him as the "learned justice," along with the "sapient sir," the Fool, to conduct the trial of Regan and Goneril.

In the final scene of Lear's madness, Gloucester offers the occasion for Lear's remarks. Many of the earlier themes return, but nowhere else does Lear express so clearly his recognition of the false flattery on which his early opinions rested (4.6.97–107). And in the presence of the wretched Gloucester his humanity comes out most clearly:

If thou wilt weep my fortunes, take my eyes.
I know thee well enough; thy name is Gloucester.
Thou must be patient; we came crying hither.
Thou know'st, the first time that we smell the air,
We wawl and cry. I will preach to thee, mark . . . .
When we are born, we cry that we are come
To this great stage of fools.   (4.6.180–87)

What had been in the storm sympathy for the Fool and then pity for houseless poverty, is now recognition of the pathetic lot of all human life. Though in the very next line he gloats at the remote hope of a violent revenge, nevertheless Lear had come a great way. In the course of his agony he had probed many essential questions— the nature of man, the basis of human evil, the animality and the evil of procreation, the perversions of justice and power, the problem of human suffering—and he had expressed both humility and pity. There could be little more for him to learn.

When he recovers Cordelia and in part his sanity, the loss of the battle and of his liberty weigh little on his mind against the simple knowledge that he has found the real source of his happiness. Then Cordelia dies. In all his wild and earnest questionings during his suffering, the problem of death is singularly absent. The extreme poignancy of this moment of the play arises from the fact that, after what seemed like a resolution of all his woes, he is driven to raise the unanswerable question of the useless injustice of Cordelia's death:

> . . . No, no, no life!
> Why should a dog, a horse, a rat, have life,
> And thou no breath at all? Thou'lt come no more,
> Never, never, never, never, never! (5.3.305–8)

The action thus brings into prominent relief the militant process of unvarnished and unchecked evil in the two daughters and their allies, the torment and agony of Lear, as of Gloucester, and the moral issues which are raised by the violent conflict in the play. That these things can be represented on so stupendous a scale and impress themselves with such great force is partly owing to the manner in which the world of the play is conceived and projected. No play of Shakespeare's is more clearly removed out of the plane in which the minutiae of daily life, the local considerations of time and place, play an important part. There are few localized indications of setting with the exception of references to Dover; on the contrary, all the suggestions are those of a simple and elemental surrounding. The characters are distinguished and opposed with such precise sharpness that Bradley commented on what he felt to be an allegorizing tendency in the play;[31] and indeed, though they are certainly not allegorical, the characters are brought very close to the bare and stripped manifestation of passion and folly. Questions which are occasionally raised concerning the "improbability" of the play—whether Lear could or would have behaved in the presence of the court toward his best-loved Cordelia as he does in the opening scene, or whether Gloucester and Edgar are not more gullible than one has known his neighbors or himself to be under analogous circumstances—are somewhat beside the point, and to raise them with any seriousness is to misjudge the play and reveal confusion concerning its art. Recognition of the tragic difficulties latent in the relations of fathers and children, of the terrible power of unbridled evil, or of the gullibility of trustful virtue, is sufficient to render this play clearly intelligible and the characters sufficiently like us for the purposes of dramatic art.

Only on such primary and fundamental premises would it have been possible to create the brilliant acts of villainy, the repulsive vividness of evil in action, the tragic errors of affection, and the monumental torrents of passion which make up this play. And only on such premises would it have been possible for the language, unhampered by even minor considerations of verisimilitude, to exploit fully and vividly whatever resources of expression the play required. The impression of magnitude in this play is one of the commonplaces of Shakespearean criticism. To a great extent that impression is brought about by the infusion throughout the play of suggestions of an elemental and grandiose nature, which make their appearance in the first scene of the play in Lear's dispossession of Cordelia:

> For, by the sacred radiance of the sun,
> The mysteries of Hecate and the night,
> By all the operation of the orbs
> From whom we do exist and cease to be,
> Here I disclaim all my paternal care,
> Propinquity and property of blood,
> And as a stranger to my heart and me
> Hold thee, from this, for ever. (1.1.111–18)

Allusions to storms, to the procreative forces of nature, to the heavenly bodies diffused throughout the play give to the actions and sentiments not only a grandeur in scale but endow the specific events of the play with the widest possible kind of generality.

To appreciate fully the manifold relationships and the organization of the diction and the imagery, however, it is necessary to realize in addition the ethical context in which the actions and thoughts of the characters have their being. As a poetical work,

King Lear does not offer grounds for a systematic philosophical analysis. Moreover, the play cannot be regarded as existing primarily to recommend a specific ethical philosophy or to raise a moral problem, nor does the thought emerge as a convenient kernel of wisdom which may be sententiously phrased and carried away. But in a serious action like *Lear*, characters are represented as making choices, weighing possibilities, taking a stand on issues, and the like. Particularly in the case of Lear himself, the violent searching into the fundamental questions with which his unexpected troubles have confronted him places these issues in an inescapable prominence. Certain ethical premises emerge, therefore, to which the problems and dilemmas of the characters are referred.

These premises can be brought to light most directly through the most ubiquitous single term in the play—nature, and its derivative forms, natural and unnatural. The words "kind" and "unkind" must also be taken into account (for instance, 4.3.44, 3.2.16), since in Elizabethan usage they had a wider meaning than at present; for instance, the expressions "law of nature" and "law of kind" were practically synonymous. The term "nature" and its variants and analogues invariably carry one or another of the important philosophical implications with which it was freighted in Shakespeare's day.[32] Frequently it is opposed to some contrary notion, like brutish or savage, either directly or by implication. In only a few instances is it possible to assign to a particular use of the term a single specific definition, and for the most part any single use embraces two or more closely related meanings. Such ambiguities, however, do not impair the discernible scheme of meanings which the term carries and which are vital to the understanding of the play.

Certain of the uses are simple and have meanings commonplace today. Nature sometimes denotes individual bias of character, as when Edmund says,

> . . . some good I mean to do,
> Despite of mine own nature,   (5.3.243–44)

or when he remarks concerning Edgar,

> . . . a brother noble
> Whose nature is so far from doing harms
> That he suspects none.   (1.2.195–97)

At times it denotes man's physical capacities: Kent remarks during the storm,

> Man's nature cannot carry
> The affliction nor the fear.   (3.2.48–49)

In this sense it is usually associated with the distress and the infirmities of Lear. Such uses are, however, secondary in importance, for neither matters of individual temperament, nor physical man as distinct from other aspects of his being or from the whole scheme of the universe, are of primary importance in *King Lear*. In its most significant role it carries the meaning of man as man, distinct from a lower order of creation. When Lear says of "Poor Tom,"

> Death traitor! nothing could have subdued nature
> To such a lowness but his unkind daughters,   (3.4.72–73)

he implies that the naked derelict has become degraded to a level which violates the dignity proper to man. In its widest uses it refers directly to conduct proper and becoming to man, or its opposite; thus, Lear's "unkind daughters" above, Gloucester's "Unnatural, destested brutish villain" (1.2.81), and France's appeal to Lear for Cordelia,

> . . . Sure, her offense
> Must be of such unnatural degree,
> That monsters it . . .   (1.1.221–23)

More specifically, the various uses of the term imply the existence of certain personal and social ties, such as those of parents and children, which are conceived of as natural in the sense that man's will to uphold them renders him distinct from brute creation and that their preservation is vital to the integrity of man's human relations. Nature implies, that is, conformity to the proper law of man's being. Such a meaning is present in Lear's plea to Regan:

> . . . Thou better know'st
> The offices of nature, bond of childhood,
> Effects of courtesy, dues of gratitude.   (2.4.180–82)

It is implicit in Gloucester's comment on the brutal treatment of Lear by his daughters, "Alack, alack, Edmund, I like not this unnatural dealing" (3.3.1), and in Edmund's hypocritically pious interest in astrological predictions, "I promise you the effects he writes of succeed unhappily; as of unnaturalness between the child and parent" (1.2.156–58; see also 3.5.3). There are few instances, in fact, in which these crucial terms do not cover this range of meanings.

Among the characters who are ranged on the side of Lear, the term nature when used as an ethical norm takes for granted the existence of an inherent force productive of moral order, violation of which degrades man and produces violent disorder. Of the characters opposed to Lear, Edmund expresses a divergent view. The two attitudes are clearly opposed in two speeches which appear early in the play in close proximity. The second of these is Gloucester's:

These late eclipses in the sun and moon portend no good to us. Though the wisdom of nature can reason it thus and thus, yet nature finds itself scourged by the sequent events. Love cools, friendship falls off, brothers divide: in cities, mutinies; in countries, discord; in palaces, treason; and the bond cracked 'twixt son and father. This villain of mine comes under the prediction; there's son against father: the King falls from the bias of nature; there's father against child. We have seen the best of our time; machinations, hollowness, treachery, and all ruinous disorders, follow us disquietly to our graves.   (1.2.112–27)

The fact that Gloucester takes for granted a relationship between unusual astronomical phenomena and disorders among men has perturbed many a critic, especially as the only clear skepticism concerning astrology as "an admirable evasion of whoremaster man" is expressed by the villain Edmund. The question is not without its interest but it is not significant for the moment: the important philosophical opposition which separates the agents of the play is not the matter of belief in astrology. More to the purpose is the analogy which is implied in Gloucester's comments between the prodigies of the physical world and those of the moral world: just as the former are in a sense a deviation from the normal order of physical nature, so too any violation of the moral laws of nature is assumed to be followed by catastrophes in the social order. Edmund, on the other hand, though he talks the cant of this view in his hypocritical moments, explicitly denies any such ethical assumptions and in his first soliloquy expounds a philosophy of nature quite the antithesis of this:

> Thou, Nature, art my goddess; to thy law
> My services are bound. Wherefore should I
> Stand in the plague of custom, and permit

> The curiosity of nations to deprive me,
> For that I am some twelve or fourteen moonshines
> Lag of a brother?   (1.2.1-6)

The law of nature means to Edmund the dictates of passion, the force of the individual will, the instinct for survival. In opposition to this law he places the laws which men adopt to maintain social order; these he regards as accepted customs and as "the curiosity of nations." In these views he may be regarded as the spokesman of those whose ruthless conduct in the play merits them the odium of "unnaturalness" from those who oppose them.

One further distinction is necessary to avoid any possible confusion between this speech of Edmund's and Lear's curse in which nature is also invoked as a goddess:

> Hear, Nature! hear, dear goddess, hear!
> Suspend thy purpose, if thou didst intend
> To make this creature fruitful!
> Into her womb convey sterility!
> Dry up in her the organs of increase,
> And from her derogate body never spring
> A babe to honor her! If she must teem,
> Create her child of spleen, that it may live
> And be a thwart disnatured torment to her!   (1.4.296-305)

This is not Edmund's goddess. Lear invokes in his curse on Goneril a nature which is the creative and generative force of the universe, the *natura naturans* of medieval and Renaissance thought. This meaning is glanced at in his prayer to the elements in the storm—

> Crack nature's moulds, all germens spill at once
> That makes ingrateful man.   (3.2.8-9)

In consequence of the interplay of these various related meanings, every use of the term nature and its derivatives becomes charged with a high potential of meaning and implication. When Kent, for example, talks of the "unnatural and bemadding sorrow" of Lear, the word "unnatural" implies a sorrow which strikes at the essential core of his being, undermines the foundation of his equilibrium, and is beyond man's capacity to endure. Such usage is the opposite of philosophical clarity, and it is necessary that this should be so. By its protean character, the term ceases to be merely denominative and extends itself to large and general proportions. Its importance is rooted in the particular situation of the play, to which, reciprocally, it lends a cosmic grandeur and generality. Those elemental suggestions which, as we have noticed, help to give the play its magnitude are thus not mere rant but derive their force from the closeness of their relation to this central point of reference. It is therefore somewhat paradoxical for G. Wilson Knight—who is impressed by the largeness of this play—to say, "It is, indeed, curious that so storm-furious a play as *Lear* should have so trivial a domestic basis.[33] Viewed in the light of the ethics of nature to which the actions of the play are referred, the opening situation is no more trivial than the slip in the fault which brings about an earthquake. In fact, in the ethical premises which are implicit in the interrelated uses of the term nature the whole scheme of the play is adumbrated. The tragedy opens with an action on the part of Lear that rives the bonds which keep the moral world of the play together, and chaos ensues. Against the destructive forces of disorder which are thus unloosed, neither virtue nor vice can hope to survive or remain unscathed until the storm has spent its fury. The king falls from the bias of nature, and the world of the play finds itself scathed by the sequent events.

From this intimate relation between the ethical bias of the play and the action, certain of the principal sustained developments in the imagery are, as it were, generated—notably the storm images and the animal images. The storm itself which accompanies Lear during the third act is artistically appropriate and probable in more than one way. It begins immediately after Lear is sent out by his daughter. Its coming is announced at the end of the second act in Gloucester's expression of concern for the old king in the open country, and in Cornwall's comment which closes the act:

> Shut up your doors, my lord; 'tis a wild night:
> My Regan counsels well. Come out o' the storm.   (2.4.311–12)

It coincides therefore with the final cleavage in Lear's family and with the beginning of the violent and tormenting events which are its consequence. It also coincides with the turmoil in Lear's mind which ends in madness. It is certainly no mere piece of theatrical excitement but part of an extended metaphorical proportion implied in Gloucester's speech on the late eclipses: the storm is a great upheaval in nature, a titanic conflict of the elements, and is thus related analogically on the one hand to the rending of the social fabric brought about by the "unnatural" conduct of Lear, his older daughters, and Edmund, and on the other to the "unnatural and bemadding sorrow" of the king.

The storm images enter the language of the play somewhat earlier than this point. Combined with reference to other malignant forces of nature they occur in Lear's curses on his daughter:

> Blasts and fogs upon thee! (1.4.321)

> All the stored vengeance of heaven fall
> On her ingrateful top! (2.4.164–65)

> You nimble lightnings, dart your blinding flames
> Into her scornful eyes! Infect her beauty,
> You fen-sucked fogs, drawn by the powerful sun,
> To fall and blast her pride! (2.4.167–70)

Here the images associate the violence of Lear's feelings and the stress of his unhappiness with the violent and powerful operation of the elements. Other references to storms anticipate the actual storm itself but also have the effect of distinguishing between the physical discomfort of the elements and the more acute suffering induced by "unnatural" man. Thus Edgar resolves that he will

> . . . with presented nakedness outface
> The winds and persecutions of the sky. (2.3.11–12)

In the same way, Lear refuses to accept his daughters' terms:

> No, rather I abjure all roofs and choose
> To wage against the enmity o' the air. (2.4.211–12)

And the analogy between the external storm and that within is explicitly drawn in Lear's speech to Kent during the turmoil of the elements:

> Thou think'st 'tis much that this contentious storm
> Invades us to the skin; so 'tis to thee;
> But where the greater malady is fixed,
> The lesser is scarce felt . . . .
> . . . . When the mind's free,
> The body's delicate; the tempest in my mind
> Doth from my senses take all feeling else
> Save what beats there. (3.4.6–14)

The effectiveness of the storm as part of the play is due in part to the exploitation of this analogy. Lear uses storm images to describe the distraction of his mind; conversely, though the physical violence of the storm is vividly insisted on, the physical turmoil is time and again described in human terms. Sometimes it is in terms of physical human acts:

> Blow, winds, and crack your cheeks!   (3.2.1)
>
> Rumble thy bellyful!   (3.2.14)
>
> Such groans of roaring wind and rain.   (3.2.47)
>
>   . . . this contentious storm
> Invades us to the skin.   (3.4.6–7)

More often the descriptive terms allude to human thoughts and passions:

> Rage, blow.   (3.2.1)
>
> You sulphurous and thought-executing fires.   (3.2.4)
>
>   Then let fall
> Your horrible pleasure.   (3.2.18–19)
>
>   . . . the wrathful skies
> Gallow the very wanderers of the dark.   (3.2.43–44)
>
> The tyranny of the open night's too rough
> For nature to endure.   (3.4.2–3)
>
> Poor naked creatures, wheresoe'er you are,
> That bide the pelting of this pitiless storm.   (3.2.28–29)

In this way the storm becomes the image of the tempest in the mind of Lear.

The animal images grow out somewhat differently from the ethical framework in its relation to the action.[34] Since the word natural signifies in its ethical context behavior that is consonant with the properties of man as man, the word unnatural is identified with non-human properties and is often coupled with them; for instance, Gloucester says of Edgar, "Unnatural, detested, brutish villain!" (1.2.81–82). France asks to know how the best loved Cordelia could

> Commit a thing so monstrous, to dismantle
> So many folds of favour. Sure, her offence
> Must be of such unnatural degree
> That monsters it . . .   (1.1.220–23)

The words monster and monstrous are common in the play. Lear exclaims against "Monster ingratitude" (1.5.42). Cornwall's servant fears that if no harm befalls the two daughters "Women will

all turn monsters" (3.7.102). Albany tells Goneril, "Bemonster not
thy feature" (4.2.63), and he cries out against her proved perfidy,
"Most monstrous!" (5.3.159). Such expressions not only suggest the
absence of qualities like kindness and mercy but the denial of all
those reasonable controls over selfish action on which human society
depends. Thus, Albany tells Goneril,

> If that the heavens do not their visible spirits
> Send quickly down to tame these vile offences,
> It will come,
> Humanity must perforce prey on itself,
> Like monsters of the deep.   (4.2.46–50)

From this distinction between the natural and the monstrous, the
animal images which are associated with the two daughters derive
their special force. From the moment Lear's wrath is aroused against
Goneril the figures drawn from fierce and savage animals come in
quick succession. He denounces ingratitude as more hideous than a
sea monster (1.4.281–83). He calls Goneril a "detested kite"
(1.4.284), and exclaims,

> How sharper than a serpent's tooth it is
> To have a thankless child!   (1.4.310–11)

He warns her that when Regan hears of this "She'll flay thy wolvish
visage" (1.4.330), and when he goes to Regan he complains,

> O Regan, she hath tied
> Sharp-toothed unkindness, like a vulture, here.   (2.4.136–37)
> . . . struck me with her tongue
> Most serpent-like, upon the very heart.   (2.4.162–63)

Most of these are directed at Goneril because she is the first to reveal
her true nature, but they help to establish character for both since
Regan is clearly of the same stamp, and eventually the images are
applied without discrimination between them. Lear calls them she-
foxes (3.6.24), and Gloucester defies them both:

> . . . I would not see thy cruel nails
> Pluck out his poor old eyes; nor thy fierce sister
> In his anointed flesh stick boarish fangs.   (3.7.56–58)

When Albany comes to understand their villainy he employs similar
epithets: "Tigers, not daughters" (4.2.40), and of Goneril "this
gilded serpent" (5.3.84). As a compliant agent of these sisters, Oswald comes in for his share of animal epithets, though all of them
are of a belittling sort, mostly having to do with dogs. "How now!"

says Lear, "where's that mongrel" (1.4.53), and a little later shouts at him, "You whoreson dog! you slave! you cur!" (1.4.88). Kent calls him the "son and heir of a mongrel bitch" (2.2.23), and describes him as one "knowing naught, like dogs, but following" (2.2.86). Because Oswald sometimes cuts a ridiculous figure, Kent calls him a goose which he will send cackling home (2.2.89), and because, though lacking the brilliance of his masters, he nevertheless aids them materially in a loathsome way, Kent says of him:

> Such smiling rogues as these
> Like rats, oft bite the holy cords a-twain
> Which are too intrinse to unloose . . . . (2.2.79–81)

Certain ones of the animal images glance only obliquely at the two daughters. Lear tells Regan that, rather than return to Goneril, he would "be a comrade of the wolf and the owl" (2.4.213), and Gloucester—

> If wolves had at thy gate howled that stern time,
> Thou shouldst have said, "Good porter, turn the key."
>   (3.7.63–64)

Such figures still depend on a comparison of human and animal behavior to the disparagement of the daughters, but they convey the additional impression that when close human ties are once dissolved, man's conduct is something less tolerable than bestial. They are the figurative counterpart of Cordelia's searching remark,

> Had you not been their father, these white flakes
> Did challenge pity of them. (4.7.30–31)

—a sentiment which she reinforces with a similar image in the same speech:

> Mine enemy's dog,
> Though he had bit me, should have stood that night
> Against my fire. (4.7.36–38)

Inhumanity becomes not simply equivalent to monstrous and brutish—or rather, it is implied that when humanity becomes worthy of such epithets it manifests a distinctive quality of evil which it reserves for its own kind.

Distinct from these animal images which are associated with Regan and Goneril is another group which is concentrated in the central portion of the play during Lear's wild excursions into the problems of human life. They are related to his search for the nature of "unaccommodated man" stripped of his protective support of finery and comfort and flattery; and they have the effect of undermining the dignity of man and reducing his actions to triviality or grossness. Lear exclaims when he sees Edgar in his horrid disguise, "Is man no more than this? Consider him well. Thou ow'st the worm no silk, the beast no hide, the sheep no wool, the cat no perfume" (3.4.107–9). Though no analogy is drawn, what this statement does is to make man's dignity and politeness depend on nothing more than accessories borrowed from the leavings of animals. A more direct attack of the same sort is the following:

> The wren goes to't, and the small gilded fly
> Does letcher in my sight.
> Let copulation thrive . . . .
> Behold yond simp'ring dame,
> Whose face between her forks presages snow,
> That minces virtue, and does shake the head
> To hear of pleasure's name,—
> The fitchew, nor the soiled horse, goes to't
> With a more riotous appetite.   (4.6.114–25)

There is nothing in the sexual acts of man beyond what they have in common with the casual couplings of insects and the mating of animals. The dignity of authority and justice suffers similarly: "Thou hast seen a farmer's dog bark at a begger? . . . And the creature run from the cur? There thou mightst behold the great image of authority: a dog's obeyed in office" (4.6.158–63). Such images help project the lowest ebb in Lear's disillusionment and loathing for man. In the case of Gloucester, an animal simile drawn from the same category is used to express the lowest ebb of his pessimism:

> As flies to wanton boys, are we to the gods.
> They kill us for their sport.   (4.1.38–39)

All of the animal images are unflattering, vicious, or belittling in their nature. To this there is one exception, and it is all the more striking for its isolation among all the others. It occurs when Lear and Cordelia, finally reconciled, are being led away to prison:

> . . . Come, let's away to prison:
> We two alone will sing like birds i' the cage.
> When thou dost ask me blessing, I'll kneel down
> And ask of thee forgiveness. So we'll live,

> And pray, and sing, and tell old tales, and laugh
> At gilded butterflies . . . (5.3.8–13)

Taken by itself, this might almost be thought of as a little too decorative and perhaps a little too sentimental. In its context, preceded by so many animal images of an opposite sort, it is startling, and brings to this moment an attractive but pathetic beauty. Its uniqueness among the images emphasizes the singularity of the moment in the play which it signalizes. Not long after, there is a return to the familiar animal references as Lear contemplates the dead Cordelia:

> No, no, no life!
> Why should a dog, a horse, a rat, have life,
> And thou no breath at all? (5.3.305–7)

The associations which by this time have been built up around animal images bring echoes, however vague, from the rest of the play and thus add to the pathos of Lear's regret.

Since *Lear* is to a large extent a play of suffering, many of the images help to convey the sense of physical and mental agony. It is not always possible to make a clear separation of this function of certain images from other functions—for instance, many of the storm images. There are, however, a considerable number of images, which Caroline Spurgeon was the first to point out, expressing notions of strain, torsion, sharp bodily contact, and the like, which emphasize Lear's torments.[35] These are sometimes combined with storm and animal images, and frequently are constructed in such a way as to bear also on the violent wrenching of the normal human ties which is conspicuously developed in many other ways. This last emphasis is clear in one of the earliest of such images of bodily strain:

> O most small fault,
> How ugly didst thou in Cordelia show!
> Which, like an engine, wrenched my frame of nature
> From the fixed place. (1.4.288–91)

Representative examples will show how these images often are combined to sustain more than one vital impression while at the same time bringing to the fore the sense of agony:

> . . . struck me with her tongue,
> Most serpent-like, upon the very heart. (2.4.162–63)
> . . . this heart
> Shall break into a hundred thousand flaws,
> Or ere I'll weep. (2.4.287–89)

> . . . Caitiff, to pieces shake,
> That under covert and convenient seeming
> Has practised on man's life. (3.2.55–57)

> . . . Filial ingratitude!
> Is it not as this mouth should tear this hand
> For lifting food to't? (3.4.14–16)

I here take my oath before this honorable assembly, she kicked the poor king her father. (3.6.48–50)

This vein in the imagery of *Lear* is reflected in a speech of Kent's when Gloucester urges them to flee the shelter: "This rest might yet have balmed thy broken sinews" (3.6.105). Images of this sort are systematically developed chiefly in the central portions of the play where the suffering of Lear is necessarily prominent. They lie back of two very striking figures, however, which appear later in the play. One of these is in Lear's speech when he awakens from the sleep induced by the physician and sees Cordelia:

> You do me wrong to take me out o' the grave.
> Thou art a soul in bliss; but I am bound
> Upon a wheel of fire, that mine own tears
> Do scald like molten lead. (4.7.45–48)

This is a complex speech, but the suggestion of being racked on the wheel is its central feature. It is significant that it is on such suggestions that the play ends, and that the peace of Lear is expressed in Kent's speech as freedom from the kind of physical torture which earlier had been one means of expressing his suffering:

> Vex not his ghost; O, let him pass! He hates him
> That would upon the rack of this tough world
> Stretch him out longer. (5.3.313–15)

To do complete justice to the art of *King Lear* it would be necessary to carry the analysis beyond this demonstration of the intimate relationship between the principal lines of development in the diction and imagery and the organizational scheme of the whole play. For example, the wheel of fire image should be further viewed in the light of scattered references to fire such as—

> Her eyes are fierce; but thine
> Do comfort and not burn. (2.4.175–76)

> You sulphurous and thought-executing fires,
> Vaunt-couriers of oak-cleaving thunderbolts,
> Singe my white hair. (3.2.4–6)

—and of the earlier references to tears—for example,

> Life and death! I am ashamed
> That thou hast power to shake my manhood thus;
> That these hot tears, which break from me perforce,
> Should make thee worth them.   (1.4.318–21)

>   . . . touch me with noble anger,
> And let not women's weapons, water-drops,
> Stain my man's cheeks.   (2.4.279–81)

In addition, there are apparently isolated images that need to be brought into proper relation with the others; the breaking of human ties is expressed, for instance, in figures of speech which suggest the rending of an organic structure. Some of these have been already quoted in another connection, like Lear's figure of ingratitude tearing the hand that feeds it, but with these should be noticed Albany's condemnation of Goneril:

> I fear your disposition.
> That nature which contemns its origin
> Cannot be bordered certain in itself.
> She that herself will sliver and disbranch
> From her material sap, perforce must wither
> And come to deadly use.   (4.2.31–36)

There are some figures which appear not to be extensively developed, but which reflect on one another in a striking way: for instance, Kent's remark to Lear in the opening scene—

> Kill thy physician, and thy fee bestow
> Upon the foul disease   (1.1.165–66)

compared with Lear's condemnation of Goneril—

> But yet thou art my flesh, my blood, my daughter;
> Or rather a disease that's in my flesh,
> Which I must needs call mine: thou art a boil,
> A plague-sore, an embossed carbuncle,
> In my corrupted blood.   (2.4.224–28)

And there is also the problem of the curious scheme of associations which ties together the apparently incoherent and whirling words of the fool, of Edgar as Mad Tom, and of the mad Lear.

All these matters would vastly complicate and extend the analysis, but, though their elucidation would enhance our perceptions about the play, it would not alter what this necessarily simplified discussion reveals concerning the important role which the diction and imagery play among the determinant elements of this great and intensely-conceived dramatic structure. Similarly, a consideration of the other tragedies of Shakespeare from the same point of view is out of the question for practical reasons, but, though it would be a great advantage in enlarging the limited view afforded by the present study, it would not radically alter the general impression provided by this admittedly inadequate treatment of Shakespeare's art. It is not necessary, in any case, to go beyond the two plays dealt with to insist at least on the limited conclusion that certainly in them the possibilities of Elizabethan tragedy have been brought to a remarkable artistic discipline, and in the case of *Lear* have been realized on a scale that dwarfs all but the greatest of tragedies in dramatic literature.

IV

Other than Shakespeare's, there was no genius among his contemporaries or successors which proved a catalyst strong enough to effect an organization of the possibilities of the Elizabethan tragic style on the same scale and with the same wholeness. There were good craftsmen and even men of genius, who employed similar or analogous technical methods and who left their individual mark on the drama of their times. Moreover, nearly all the dramatists from Marlowe to Shirley share a capacity for imaginative use of language, for arresting and revealing metaphors, and for brilliant images; and among no other group of dramatists has this talent revealed itself so generally. Nevertheless, in comparison with the work of Shakespeare, the tragedies of the other dramatists of his time are as the factors of a comprehensive formula. Merely to insist, however, on the unique creative capacity of Shakespeare is to evade a number of interesting and important critical problems which this conclusion raises, and to place at an unnecessary disadvantage plays of genuine interest and distinction. It is necessary to see what were the consequences in the form and in the diction of individual variations in emphasis, in materials, and in focus.

On the basis of what has been observed so far about Elizabethan drama, an important distinction must first be drawn before considering individual dramatists and plays. In the tragedies of Shakespeare, it has been shown, the language of poetry and the demands of drama are brought into a close and essential relationship, and in this respect they bring to completion the developments in verse tragedy which preceded them. The nature of these plays demands verse as the norm for dialogue, and formal unity and magnitude are achieved with the intimate cooperation of poetically manipulated diction. Leaving aside for the moment individual variations, and the limitations of individual dramatists and individual plays, it may further be said that Elizabethan tragedy generally is, at its best, a poetically-conceived dramatic art in the sense that verse and the language of poetry are not merely used as a convenient or ornate instrument of dialogue but as an essential feature of a serious drama. Nevertheless, since verse had become so firmly established as the proper medium for serious plays, its use became also a matter of convention. In consequence, it might well appear where the nature of the materials did not necessarily demand it, or it might be used without regard for its serious function and only by way of a surface brilliance. In the first instance, verse dialogue might be made to serve well enough but would be unnecessary, and in another age would have been replaced by prose; in the second, verse would be merely a theatrically expected feature which might be used for theatrically brilliant effects. To distinguish these developments from those which are more strictly in the main line of tradition, it will be necessary first to consider the cases of Thomas Heywood, and of Beaumont and Fletcher.

Although in his long and prolific career Heywood wrote in a large number of popular styles, the original strain in his work is to be found chiefly in his so-called domestic plays. Among these, *A Woman Killed with Kindness* is the most finished and shows up to best advantage Heywood's special contribution to the drama of his day. Leaving out of consideration the sub-plot, which is almost completely distinct from the main action, the play is quite simple in outline. It begins with the marriage of Frankford, a well-to-do country gentleman, to an attractive and well-endowed young woman of his class. The prospects for happiness seem great, but the wife is seduced by Wendoll, a young man whom Frankford has generously urged to stay with them. Frankford, informed by a faithful servant, discovers their guilt, and banishes his wife from his sight to one of his manors. There she refuses all food and pines penitently away. Just before her death, Frankford consents to see her and forgives her. Except for occasional foreshortening of time which modern critics seem to object to, the play is skillfully and effectively handled. Such fine moments as Nicholas' revelation of his suspicions to his master and the maid's staying of Frankford's hand from murder and earning his thanks are indications of Heywood's keen sense of theatrical effectiveness, gained without forcing and without sacrifice of honesty and directness of means.

It is not only its good qualities as a play which have given this work its importance in the histories of English drama, but the fact that it is unusual for its day in its use of a domestic plot and of an upper middle class setting for tragedy. Heywood himself seems to have been conscious of doing something unexpected in the hint he gives in the Prologue:

> Look for no glorious state; our Muse is bent
> Upon a barren subject, a bare scene.

These deviations from the common practice of Elizabethan tragedy have been regarded as in themselves highly important; the usual argument is that the Elizabethans unnecessarily limited themselves by generally writing tragedies about people in high station and disregarding the fact that the woes of ordinary men are as great and as moving as those of great men. But this criticism is often made without any account being taken of why the Elizabethan writers of tragedy avoided such material as Heywood's and of the radical alteration in the nature of the tragic play which was involved in Heywood's use of them. The effect of the change from this conventional setting can be seen in the character of Frankford, as revealed in the following soliloquy:

> How happy am I amongst other men,
> That in my mean estate embrace content!
> I am a gentleman, and by my birth
> Companion with a king; a king's no more.
> I am possessed of many fair revenues,
> Sufficient to maintain a gentleman;
> Touching my mind, I am studied in all arts,
> The riches of my thoughts; and of my time
> Have been a good proficient; but the chief
> Of all the sweet felicities on earth,
> I have a fair, a chaste, and loving wife—
> Perfection all, all truth, all ornament.
> If man on earth may truly happy be,
> Of these at once possessed, sure I am he. (2.1.1.–14)*

*Line references are to Katherine Bates's edition of *A Woman Killed with Kindness* (Boston, 1917).

Frankford is the flower of his class, an admirable civilized type, but his limitations as the main figure of a great action can be seen in the very definition of his virtues, and particularly in his assertion that he is happy among other men because in his mean estate he embraces content. This may be the goal of all true philosophy, but it is not enough for the tragic hero. In the course of the play, Frankford loses his wife, "the chief/Of all the sweet felicities on earth," and he loses his content, but he does not lose himself—his tolerance (at least by contemporary standards), his capable mind, his ability to act humanely.

Comparison with *Othello* will illustrate the difference, and it will also show how misleading classification by types can be, since *Othello* has been sometimes placed along with *A Woman Killed with Kindness* in the category of domestic drama. Othello loses more than Desdemona and his domestic happiness: he loses his sense of fitness, his magnificent self-possession, his nobility of mind. Such of his virtues as are not utterly destroyed are distorted to perversions of their natural functioning, like his desire for ocular proof and his strong sense of justice. Thus, in the course of the action, whatever is basic to a definition of Othello is involved in such a way as to be undermined or defeated. In this difference between *Othello* and Heywood's play is to be found one of the principal distinctions between tragedy and the kind of serious play to which certain modern critics have applied the term "drame"—plays in which the main characters face a trying situation and confront a difficult problem, any solution to which seems to involve them in possibly unhappy consequences. In tragedy, the course of the action involves the character essentially, so that those qualities without which the character could not be realized at all are directly challenged and brought to a critical test. Not only is the character of Frankford defined in terms which cannot embrace actions and feelings of great power, but his basic qualities remain in large part unthreatened by the action. *Othello* is tragic; *A Woman Killed with Kindness* is sad and pathetic. In consequence, great demands need not be placed on the diction, and the peculiar advantages of verse drama are, of necessity, restricted in their function

A further influence on the diction comes from Heywood's treatment of the setting. In part, his close attention to the details of the milieu arises from the fact that Heywood has placed the source of

Frankford's happiness and dignity in the good things which his station in life can bring him, and hence the social environment becomes important in the characterization of the central figure. The ability to suggest in a few vivid strokes the special features of the life of his times is one of the marks of Heywood's work; even in so extravagant and romantic an adventure story as *The Fair Maid of the West*, the opening tavern scenes give an effective picture of life in a contemporary seaport town. In *A Woman Killed with Kindness*, this characteristic gift is particularly useful, since in the nature of the play the establishment of the environment is something more than a technical flourish. The festivities both of the guests and the servants at the wedding, the hawking contest which initiates the subplot, the quiet comfort of Frankford's home life, all help establish the environment within which Frankford finds his content. Under the circumstances, the diction needs to be restrained within certain limits of verisimilitude which will preserve the effectiveness of the carefully suggested setting.

The norm, therefore, for the dialogue is an easy, conversational treatment of the verse, and clear, simple diction generally free of figurative suggestions:

> Y'are well met sir. Now, in troth, my husband,
> Before he took horse, had a great desire
> To speak with you; we sought about the house,
> Halooed into the fields, sent every way,
> But could not meet you. Therefore he enjoined me
> To do unto you his most kind commends.
> Nay, more; he wills you, as you prize his love,
> Or hold in estimation his kind friendship,
> To make bold in his absence, and command
> Even as himself were present in the house;
> For you must keep his table, use his servants,
> And be a present Frankford in his absence.   (2.3.70–81)

At the same time, however, Heywood preserves certain artifices made possible by the use of verse. There are numerous couplet rhymes, not used for the most part to signalize the ending of a scene as is common in many Elizabethan plays, but to bring to notice an important speech or a crucial turn of events; for instance, immediately following Frankford's urging on Wendoll the freedom of his house:

> *Anne.*   As far as modesty may well extend,

It is my duty to receive your friend.
Frank.   To dinner. Come, sir, from this present day,
Welcome to me forever. Come, away!   (2.1.79–82)

Notable among these is Anne's dying speech:

Pardoned on earth, soul, thou in heaven art free;
Once more thy wife dies, thus embracing thee.   (5.5.82–83)

Verisimilitude is abandoned completely here in the interest of emphasizing the pathos of the restoration of Anne to the status of wife at the moment of her death, and of pointing up the paradox of her dying twice, first through her banishment from her husband and then at the moment of her restoration to him. Similarly with the artifice of the wordplay in the card-playing scene, when every one of the card terms is used with double meanings either by the guilty lovers or Frankford, a device which gives this scene a studied air not common with the rest.

The use of figurative language is reserved usually for the moments of great emotional strain, as, for instance, in Wendoll's soliloquy before declaring his love to Anne and in the scene with her which immediately ensues. Some of these figures have an air of labored artifice about them, like those in Frankford's speech following the servant's insistence on his wife's guilt:

Thou hast killed me with a weapon whose sharp point
Hath pricked quite through and through my shiv'ring heart.
Drops of cold sweat sit dangling on my hairs,
Like morning's dew upon the golden flowers.   (3.2.61–64)

The simile about the dew seems thrust in to satisfy accepted notions of what is appropriate at such moments of a tragedy and not generated by the demands of this particular play. Not all, however, are of this order. Frankford's speech as he enters the house at night to trap the lovers is effective without strain:

A general silence hath surprised the house,
And this is the last door. Astonishment,
Fear, and amazement beat upon my heart,
Even as a madman beats upon a drum.   (4.4.23–26)

An illustration of the extremes in the use of figures is the two speeches on Anne's lute. One of these is Frankford's, when it is discovered that Anne's lute has been left behind:

Her lute! O God! Upon this instrument
Her fingers have run quick division,

> Sweeter than that which now divides our hearts.
> These frets have made me pleasant, that have now
> Frets of my heartstrings made.   (5.2.13–17)

Comparison with the puns on musical terms in the chamber scene in *Romeo and Juliet* will show the vast difference in method: here the extended wordplay is an intrusion since artifices of this sort are not demanded by the nature of the play but are, in effect, alien to it. Anne's speech occurs when the servant returns her lute after overtaking her on the road:

> I know the lute. Oft have I sung to thee;
> We are both out of tune, both out of time.   (5.3.20–21)

The utter simplicity of this renders it far less exceptionable; it takes advantage of the possibilities of verse dialogue without destroying abruptly the effect of conversational speech which is the established norm for the play. On many occasions, therefore, the established conventions of diction of contemporary tragedy enabled Heywood to give point or emphasis to important moments of his play, but it is unlikely that except for the universal adoption of verse as the medium proper to tragedy Heywood could have written this play as he had, and his acceptance of the convention at times is responsible for occasional forcing and strain of expression. He often used the resources of verse drama to momentary advantage, but they were not essential to what he was trying to do in the play.

Superficially, the plays of Beaumont and Fletcher have so many of the features of the characteristic Elizabethan dramatic style that older critics were wont to rank these dramatists next only to Shakespeare. Actually, however, their plays are in many ways a radical departure in essential respects from the best work of their contemporaries; and nowhere is the difference clearer than in their use of verse not so much as an organic feature of a poetic drama but as a superficial means for securing poetic effects. Indication of the change is to be found in the peculiarities of the blank verse in their plays, chiefly in metrical eccentricities most noticeable at the end of the line where additional weak syllables, double and triple endings, and the like, produce a quality of abruptness:

> I do appear the same, the same Evadne,
> Dressed in the shames I lived in, the same monster.
> But these are names of honor to what I am;
> I do present myself the foulest creature,

> Most poisonous, dangerous, and despised of men,
> Lerna e'er bred or Nilus. I am hell . . .
>   (*Maid's Tragedy*, 4.1.229–34)*

Fletcher is usually held responsible for the peculiarities of this metrical idiom, but the question of attribution is for the moment unimportant. What is important is that such treatment of the line destroys the impression of formalized rhythm and appears to aim at the effect of unpremeditated discourse. Seventeenth-century dramatists had mastered the art of manipulating blank verse with freedom and flexibility, but the tricks with meter which are common in the plays of Beaumont and Fletcher represent something more than this. They act in such a way as to make verse appear to be not verse. The effect on the diction is to open a back door to verisimilitude, and at the same time to permit the use of poetical effects whenever these seem desirable.

The roots of the matter, however, go deeper than this. The characteristic product of Beaumont and Fletcher (as well as of Fletcher alone and with other collaborators) is beautifully designed to achieve the maximum in theatrical effects. The tragi-comedies (or dramatic romances) reveal this quality most readily. The plots are designed so as to bring about a variety of extraordinary situations, a medley of high passions, and a number of surprises. The denouement depends on relevant knowledge concealed from the audience, such as the identity of Bellario in *Philaster* or the fact that Arbaces is not the true prince in *A King and No King*, so that dependence on probabilities strongly built up and clearly established is out of the question. In consequence, characters are reduced to the merest outline; they could not otherwise be so easily manipulated to suit the needs of excitement and surprise, nor to be made the mouthpieces for such varying emotional states. Philaster is in turn Romeo, Hamlet, Othello, and Timon. The diction, consequently, cannot be directed toward establishing probabilities of character and the like, and where it does not become a matter of decoration, becomes largely the instrument for expression of passion. The tragi-comedies are, of course, a highly specialized product, and consideration of them would have been out of place here except that they reveal more clearly than other plays of Beaumont and Fletcher

---

*Line references are to P. A. Daniel's edition of *The Maid's Tragedy* in the variorum edition of *The Works of Beaumont and Fletcher* (London, 1904).

characteristics which appear in all. The tragedies are in general constructed with more regard for directness and probability of movement, but they are, *mutatis mutandis*, a product of much the same sort.

The Maid's Tragedy, generally assumed to be their best in this genre, is an excellent illustration of the point. The intrigue is brilliantly manipulated. The play opens on the wedding night of Amintor, who has jilted Aspatia at the request of the king to marry Evadne. Melantius, brother of Evadne, arrives from the wars for the occasion. Amintor discovers to his horror, however, that Evadne has married him only as a means of protecting her position as mistress of the king. In due time Melantius forces Amintor to reveal his secret, and demands of his sister that she restore the good name of their family and expiate for the wrongs done to Amintor by killing the king. In a revulsion of feeling she begs forgiveness of Amintor and then kills the king. Aspatia is unknowingly killed by Amintor, and Evadne and Amintor both commit suicide. Barring the few scenes devoted to showing the pathos of Aspatia's plight, and the overdoing of the buffoonery of Calianax, there is no digressing, and the action moves with economy and force. Yet it is adjusted so as to produce excitements and surprises of much the same sort as *Philaster*. The surprise of Melantius who greets Aspatia as the bride and is amazed to learn that his sister is to be the bride of his friend, and the surprise of Amintor when he is told of his position by the cold and ruthless Evadne are superior to those in the romances only because they are more effectively managed by being used as devices of exposition and because they are not accomplished at the expense of the necessities of the situation. There are also a number of scenes —for instance, Evadne's enlightenment of Amintor on their wedding night, Melantius' wresting of Amintor's secret, Melantius' persuasion of Evadne, Evadne's final discourse with the king before the murder—which are built on the conflict of will between two persons and are worked out almost as set pieces in the ebb and flow of sentiment and passion. What distinguishes this tragedy from the romances is that in the latter many of the situations and incidents can lead in either of two directions, whereas in the tragedy that is not the case, and hence there is more force in these emotional conflicts and tirades because they grow necessarily and inevitably out of what has preceded.

These effects of sharpness and brilliance are, in part, also dependent on the use of characters of limited range, clearly defined but
lacking subtlety, complexity, or depth, and their participation in
the action is therefore direct and forceful. Since one of the principal
functions of the diction in Elizabethan drama is to establish imaginatively and symbolically the probabilities of character, and to extend and enlarge knowledge of them beyond those boundaries
easily defined by other means, it follows that for such characters as
appear in this play the peculiar merits of Elizabethan poetic drama
would not be indispensable. In one other respect, this play involves
a narrowing focus. The play deals with kings and courtiers, but
the royal setting is not made the occasion, as in Shakespeare or
Chapman, for viewing man's actions under circumstances favorable
to their fullest and most intense and most highly-developed manifestation; it is a reflection of a particularized society with codes and
mores having no very large reference beyond themselves. The
principles on the basis of which the characters explain their motives
and reason out their actions are honor and loyalty, understood
largely in terms of the limited conventions of the society within
which they operate. This, too, has the effect of enabling the action
to move clearly and forcefully, and giving to the oppositions and
conflicts of character simplicity and freedom from diffuseness. A
narrow localized code such as that to which the actions of the
characters are referred in this play, however, restricts the range
from which analogies might be drawn and imaginative associations established, though it offers opportunity for rhetorical expressions of feeling; it therefore makes for sharpness and brilliance
but not for depth and magnitude.

In consequence of these conditions, the diction is lucid and energetic, but it is less metaphorical in aspect than is generally the case
with the important tragedies of the age. The rhythms are managed
to give the phrases effective balance and accent, but still to give the
speeches conversational ease:

> *Melantius.*   I fear thou art grown too fickle, for I hear
> A lady mourns for thee, men say, to death,
> Forsaken of thee, on what terms I know not.
> *Amintor.*   She had my promise; but the king forbade it,
> And made me make this worthy change, thy sister,
> Accompanied with graces above her;
> And with whom I long to lose my lusty youth

And grow old in her arms.
Melantius.   Be prosperous!   (1.1.135–43)

The language becomes figurative noticeably in the scenes of conflict between characters; figures of speech become cumulative, that is, at moments when argument and passion are the matter of the speeches, as, for instance, in the scene between Melantius and Evadne:

Melantius.   Quench me this mighty humor, and then tell me
Whose whore you are; for you are one, I know it.
Let all mine honors perish but I'll find him,
Though he lie locked up in thy blood! Be sudden;
There is no facing it; and be not flattered.
The burnt air, when the Dog reigns, is not fouler
Than thy contagious name, till thy repentance
(If the gods grant thee any) purge thy sickness.
Evadne.   Be gone! You are my brother; that's your safety.
Melantius.   I'll be a wolf first. 'Tis, to be thy brother,
An infamy below the sin of coward.
I am as far from being part of thee
As thou art from thy virtue. Seek a kindred
Mongst sensual beasts and make a goat thy brother;
A goat is cooler.   (4.1.55–69)

Hyperbole is a fairly common rhetorical figure, and that is not unusual when the artifices of language become, where they are not merely adornments of phrase, the language of the passions. Such treatment appears not only in the outburst of violent feeling; it is the same in the pathos of the forlorn Aspatia:

Then, my good girls, be more than women, wise;
At least more wise than I was; and be sure
You credit anything the light gives life to,
Before a man. Rather believe the sea
Weeps for the ruined merchant, when he roars;
Rather, the wind courts but the pregnant sails,
When the strong cordage cracks; rather, the sun
Comes but to kiss the fruit in wealthy autumn,
When all falls blasted.   (2.2.14–22)

Only at rare moments is there a suggestion of the usual brilliance of illumination through figurative language which is commonly associated with Elizabethan tragedy. One of these is Evadne's speech to Amintor when she appears with a knife and her hands all bloody:

Noble Amintor, put off thy amaze,

Let thine eyes loose, and speak. Am I not fair?
Looks not Evadne beauteous with these rites now?
Were those hours half so lovely in thine eyes
When our hands met before the holy man?
I was too foul within to look fair then.   (5.4.116–22)

The use of the word "rites" for the murder by which she expiates her crime and the coupling of the idea with the cruel wedding represent precisely the sort of synthesis of opposites through imagery which so often gives illumination in the drama of this age. Nowhere else in the play is the sensuality, beauty, and hardness of Evadne made so vivid as in this speech. But these are not the usual methods of Beaumont and Fletcher.

Of its kind, *The Maid's Tragedy* is a striking performance. It is not, however, in the strictest sense poetically conceived tragedy. Poetry is here an adjunct of the brilliant moment, a final refinement of theatrical emphasis, and not organically related to everything else in the play. In this respect it differs from the work of Shakespeare. It differs fundamentally, too, from the best plays of other important writers of tragedy of the age, now to be discussed; for, whereas in each of these the problem is approached in a different way and the results reveal somewhere a limitation of range and even artistic failure in comparison with Shakespeare, in all of them tragedy is conceived of as a serious form in which verisimilitude is not to be aimed at in the diction, nor merely ornament and theatrical brilliance.

In this respect, the work of Chapman represents in its gravity and earnestness an excellent contrast to that of Beaumont and Fletcher. The characteristic marks of Chapman's tragedy are an almost studied seriousness of tone, an involved style which gives the impression of being deliberately obscure, and a thoroughgoing figurative manner of expression. These qualities are indicative of the intellectual bias of his mind, and they come about almost necessarily from the ends toward which he directed his work in tragedy. He emphasized, as did Jonson, the didactic function of tragedy: in the Dedication to *The Revenge of Bussy d'Ambois* he defined the soul of tragedy as "material instruction, elegant and sententious excitation to virtue, and deflection from her contrary"; and in one of Clermont's speeches in the same play (3.4.14–25), he expressed in more general terms the didactic end of writing. Such comments might be suspected of being mere clichés, but not in the case of Chapman. His art as a writer of tragedy was conditioned in large part by his desire to make use of the form as a vehicle for his convictions and reflections about man.

The earliest of his extant tragedies, *Bussy d'Ambois*, was also the most successful theatrically and is the one by which he is best known. Dryden's vigorous disapproval of the play is generally known. What is significant about Dryden's comments in the Dedication to *The Spanish Friar*, however, is not merely the fact of the denunciation, but the disappointment which Dryden experienced in reading the play after having been impressed by it in the theatre: "I have sometimes wondered in the reading, what has become of those glaring colors which amazed me in *Bussy d'Ambois* in the theatre; but when I had taken up what I supposed a fallen star, I found I had been cozened with a jelly . . . ." Dryden may have had less taste for Chapman's style and what he described as "a dwarfish thought, dressed up in gigantic words" than present day readers may, and today it is unlikely that anyone will ever see a performance of this play and thus be able to compare his own experiences with Dryden's, but there is an implication in the criticism of a lack of balance, a division of force, which is also apparent on careful reading.

The plot of *Bussy* is derived loosely from French history. The historical Bussy died in 1579. Chapman begins his play with Bussy poor and rejected. He is a man with an overwhelming passion for self-fulfillment and a desire to be a "complete man" in the sense of realizing his capacities to the full. He is the embodiment of the ideals of "virtue" and "noblesse" which are discussed frequently during the play. Bussy is taken up by Monsieur (Alençon, brother of the king) and brought to court, where he braves the royal minions, courts the wives of the nobles, and eventually wins the support of the king. Partly because of this support and partly because Bussy is successful in wooing Tamyra, the wife of Montsurry, Monsieur decides to undo him. Tamyra is forced to make an assignation, and Bussy is trapped and murdered. Chapman gives this plot a good deal of theatrically effective development. The contrasts are vivid, and some of the scenes are vigorously and tensely handled; for instance, Bussy's wooing of the Guise's wife, the talk with the nobles which leads to the duel, and the outspoken "anatomizing" which Bussy and Monsieur perform on each other. Moreover, in the ap-

pearance of the ghost of the Friar, the conjuring of Behemoth, the
torturing and stabbing of Tamyra, and the shooting down of Bussy,
the play affords all the conventional stage excitements which were
common features of the popular drama. Yet these things, though
they may have been the basis of its popularity, do not describe its
true nature. If anything, they get in the way of what Chapman
seems to have conceived of as the true importance of his play. At
least, that is the conclusion which one is forced to accept after a
study of the style and the sentiments.

Like all of Chapman's plays, *Bussy d'Ambois* is written in a style
which at first seems primarily distinguished by turgidity and obscurity. These are, however, the defects of his style and not its
characteristics. They result from the occasional looseness of syntax
of his long and involved sentences, and from the ingrained figurative density of his language. Moreover, through this instrument
Chapman essayed to convey serious and sometimes involved ideas.
Chapman could write crisp and vigorous dialogue when he chose.
He also shows a taste for witty word patterns, vaguely suggestive of
the early days of dramatic blank verse; there are dozens of instances
of such tricks as the following:

> And if I truss not, let me not be trusted.
>
> The genius, and th' ingenious soul of d'Ambois.

There are, moreover, numerous instances of metaphors in which
concentration is effected by an implicit suggestion of relations:

> You have beheld some Gorgon; feel, O feel
> How you are turned to stone.   (5.1.136–38)*

But Chapman's preference is for extended speeches couched in
figurative language, and in general for figures which are explicitly
introduced and explained and elaborated quite fully. There are
numerous "as" or "as when" similes, for instance. Sometimes a
figure once introduced is made the basis of a long development, as
in Bussy's speech on how he will pursue corruption and humbug,
which is based on the idea of hawking introduced by the King's,
"Fly at him and his brood! I cast thee off" (3.2.19ff). In a typical
instance, the speech will consist of some reflection expressed almost
wholly through figures of speech:

*Line references are to T. M. Parrott's edition of the tragedies, Volume I of *The Plays
of George Chapman* (London and New York, 1910).

We cannot keep our constant course in virtue.
What is alike at all parts? Every day
Differs from other: every hour and minute;
Ay, every thought in our false clock of life,
Oft-times inverts the whole circumference:
We must be sometimes one, sometimes another:
Our bodies are but thick clouds to our souls,
Through which they cannot shine when they desire:
When all the stars, and even the sun himself,
Must stay the vapors' times that he exhales
Before he can make good his beams to us:
O, how can we, that are but motes to him,
Wandering at random in his ordered rays,
Disperse our passions' fumes, with our weak labours,
That are more thick and black than all earth's vapors?
                                        (3.1.72–86)

The peculiar construction of Chapman's characteristic figurative developments renders less likely the use of schemes of related images such as are characteristic of Shakespeare's tragedies. There are, however, a few in *Bussy*: several are derived from the sea, a few from trees, some from animals, and some from contrasts of light and darkness. Not all of the images in any given category add up to schematic development, however. Images of light and darkness are concentrated in two places chiefly. The first relate to Monsieur's desire to raise Bussy to eminence and are introduced by the lines,

Who, discontent with his neglected worth,
Neglects the light, and loves obscure abodes.   (1.1.47–48)

They are turned to new meanings by Monsieur's line, "Up, man; the sun shines on thee" (1.1.55; see also 1.1.61–63, 75–81). The other group of such images is concentrated in the conjuration scene and is introduced by the Friar's remark,

We soon will take the darkness from his face,
That did that deed of darkness.   (4.2.38–39)

There is no discernible connection between these two developments; each group of images is useful to define a situation, but there is no attempt apparently to use these light-dark figures in any consistent relation. The same might be said for a great number of the animal images, although some of them are quite clearly associated with the character of Bussy himself. In the scene which leads to the duel, Pyrrhot says insolently to Bussy, "We held discourse of a perfumed ass, that being disguised in a lion's case, imagined himself a lion: I hope that touched not you" (1.2.206–8). Since the lion is a common image for a man of valor, often distinguished from the politician as the fox, this speech is a sneer at Bussy's evaluation of himself. The king, speaking of Bussy's detractors, refers to envy as a kite that "feeds on outcast entrails" (2.1.5–16), and later likens flatterers to kites that "check at sparrows," and Bussy to an eagle and a falcon (3.2.1–5). When Monsieur candidly gives his opinion of Bussy, he expresses his low opinion of Bussy's aggressive qualities by describing him as one who "dares as much as a wild horse or tiger," and accuses him of doing any vile act to feed "the ravenous wolf of thy most cannibal valor" (3.2.423–30). The tiger image seems to glance at a speech of Monsieur made shortly before this when, in planning his trap for Bussy, he alludes to his thirst to play "with the fell tiger, up in darkness tied" (3.2.315–17).

The sea and tree images are relatively few, but they are developed in a conspicuous way in their relation to Bussy, and occur among the crucial speeches in the play. In his first speech Monsieur says of Bussy:

> His deeds inimitable, like the sea
> That shuts still as it opes, and leaves no tracts
> Nor prints of precedent for mean men's facts.   (1.1.38–40)

And in the scene in which Bussy braves the nobles in court, Monsieur says in an aside:

> His great heart will not down, 'tis like the sea,
> That partly by his own internal heat,
> Partly the stars' daily and nightly motion,
> The divers frames, but chiefly by the moon,
> Bristled with surges, never will be won,
> (No, not when th' hearts of all those powers are burst)
> To make retreat into his settled home,
> Till he be crowned with his own quiet foam.   (1.2.156–65)

This speech epitomizes the tragedy of Bussy. And it is a characteristic example of Chapman's toughness of style and obscurity of imagery: it would take considerable ingenuity to decide the precise relationship of the scientific references to the idea expressed. In the last of Monsieur's comments on Bussy, the sea is the symbol of Fortune swinging about the "restless state of virtue" (5.2.46–54). The place of Fortune in the lives of such supermen as Bussy is expressed more

completely, however, by means of the most fully developed of the
few tree images:

> Yet as the winds sing through a hollow tree
> And (since it lets them pass through) let it stand;
> But a tree solid (since it gives no way
> To their wild rage) they rend up by the root:
> So this whole man
> (That will not wind with every crooked way,
> Trod by the servile world) shall reel and fall
> Before the frantic puffs of blind-born chance,
> That pipes through empty men, and makes them dance.
>
> (5.2.37–44)

These speeches provide an important clue to the underlying development of this play. They express ideas almost entirely through
imagery, and the images are systematically elaborated. Moreover,
though they relate to Bussy, they possess a high degree of generality,
particularly the two contiguous ones of the sea and of the tree in
relation to the idea of Fortune. The context of these last two is
also illuminating. The speech of Monsieur in which they occur is
part of a long discussion between him and the Guise on the process
of nature which produces such men, their peculiar relation to the
contingencies of Fortune, and the tragic dignity of their fall. The
discussion does not supply anything without which the plot would
be incomplete or less well understood, and the speakers are not
really appropriate for these sentiments. The Guise and Monsieur
are waiting to trap Bussy and destroy him; the Guise has from the
start despised Bussy as an upstart, and Monsieur is tired of his bravado and jealous of his success. It is clear that Chapman is merely
using the occasion immediately before Bussy's downfall to explore
more fully the nature of the problem posed by Bussy, rather than
to establish the role of the plotters to him. It is the ideas abstractly
considered which interest Chapman here, and not the dramatic
situation. Traces of this concern appear throughout. One of these is
a trick Chapman has of generalizing a given situation. For instance,
the Friar is conducting Bussy through the secret passage to Tamyra,
and expresses his pleasure at bringing two such worthy objects of
love together; he continues:

> You know her worths and virtues, for report
> Of all that know is to a man a knowledge:
> You know, besides, that our affections' storm,
> Raised in our blood, no reason can reform.   (2.2.138–41)

This is Chapman succumbing to the fascination of the problem of report and knowledge, of passion and reason, and surely not the Friar instructing Bussy, who has already proved himself a pretty subtle disputer of abstract questions. The most conspicuous features of the style are bound up with this philosophical direction in the development. That so relatively few of the images develop into any schematic relationship may be ascribed to the fact that they are not primarily directed toward developing the probabilities of the action, but are selected for their effectiveness in the figurative expression of the ideas raised by it. The method, too, of explicit and extended elaboration of figures, the recondite nature of some of the images, and the involved phrasing are less suited to the requirements of dramatic dialogue than to the imaginative expression of thought.

The story of Bussy interested Chapman as a particular case of the problem of a great and aspiring character, and of the place of the "whole man," the man of "virtue" and "noblesse," among other men. What is the relation of such a man to positive law and to the sovereign power and authority of the state and the king?—the issue is raised and debated in the scene in which Monsieur asks pardon for Bussy after the duel (2.1). How do such men stand against the contingencies of Fortune?—the question opens the play and is several times given expression. This was a favorite area of speculation for Chapman, and he repeatedly dealt with it in his tragedies. Clermont is another type of such a man who is faced with the necessity of taking private vengeance; Byron is a man of great capacities who believes himself to be above the law and even above loyalty to the king; Chabot is a man of great talents, though less aggressive than Byron, who refuses to act treasonably but who refuses to admit the arbitrary power of the king to force him into compromise with his nobility and demand for truth. The great weakness of *Bussy d'Ambois* is that the plot and the concessions to the demands of a popular stage bring about confusion of these issues, and the style which Chapman found most useful for his philosophical explorations was unsuited to the demands of a stage piece having all the bustle and even some of the claptrap of a popular thriller. The conjuration scenes and the predictions of the spirits, the several appearances of the ghost of the Friar occupy too much room in the play merely to make clear that Bussy would be false to his will if he permitted augury to stand in his way (5.3.70ff), a point which could have been made with much less mummery; and if that is not the function of these episodes it is hard to determine what is. It is also puzzling that the seduction of Tamyra should be the main focus of the intrigue, and that Bussy should be broken through his persistence in meeting her. How his pursuit of her is related to his passion for noblesse is not clear; Bussy appears cynical in his remarks about women, and the discussions of her honor and his worthiness in the matter by the Friar and Bussy and Tamyra have something of the air of sophistry about them—in any case they are too closely bound up with elaborate court conventions to tie in properly with the grand generality of the problems on which the play is focused. For the plot in its aspect as an intrigue, moreover, the style and the almost metaphysical toughness of the imagery seem hardly appropriate. Chapman was doing two things at once. Dryden, having come to the play with a sense of its theatrical excitement uppermost, was disappointed that a serious reading revealed a style hardly consonant with those effects: his reasoning from this experience may have been wrong, but his diagnosis of a divided play was not. The modern reader, who must remain unaware of the excitement which theatre goers of another age found in *Bussy d'Ambois*, will also feel the same lack of integration, though he will more likely conclude that precisely where Dryden found virtues lie the defects of the play, and that Chapman's main concern to which he devoted his richest poetical gifts was at odds with the framework which he employed.

This conclusion seems borne out by the character of his other tragedies. The development of Chapman was not in the direction of a more complete fusion of his talents as a poet to the exigencies of dramatic composition, but of an elimination as far as possible of those features of the drama which interfered with the ends which he wished his poetry to serve—the imaginative presentation of those somber ethical issues which are at the heart of all his acknowledged tragedies. There is a slight hint that Chapman was aware of his difficulties when, after a long discussion by Clermont in *The Revenge of Bussy*, Baligny is made to say,

> Well, sir, I cannot when I meet with you
> But thus digress a little, for my learning,
> From any other business I intend.   (2.1.235–37)

He came closest to an artistic solution of his problem in the double tragedy of *The Conspiracy and Tragedy of Charles Duke of Byron*. The play is based on events in France almost strictly contemporaneous with its composition; but there is little sense of the political intrigues and the pressure of events in Chapman's treatment, rather the events are brought at once to a plane of philosophical generality. How completely immersed Chapman is in the ethical and political problem is suggested by the scene in which Byron succumbs to the King's entreaties and kneels and confesses his treason: no attempt is made to reveal the crisis in Byron's mind or his emotional struggle that leads to his submission; his act is merely a resolution of a combat between spokesmen for two contending ethical and political philosophies.[36] The speeches are long and stately, there are numerous figures of speech of an epic quality, and the style has a massive and often richly textured beauty. One is tempted to express respect for the Blackfriars' audiences who saw this play and apparently with approval, though the closeness of the events and the similarity of Byron's career with that of Essex, to whom he is likened, must have given the whole performance a quality of vividness no longer possible to recapture. The obvious lack of playing qualities does not prevent this play, when judged on its own terms, from being a minor classic, even though it appears to be now generally neglected while duller and less distinguished works of the period survive more prominently if only in the handbooks. Whatever its merits, however, the significant thing for the moment is that when Chapman arrived at the happiest solution for making tragedy a vehicle for thought and an "elegant and sententious excitation to virtue," the resulting product had come dangerously close to losing its nature as drama.

Jonson had in common with Chapman a desire to preserve the old dignity and gravity of tragedy. But Jonson had thought out the problems of drama from a wide perspective, and, as his scattered critical reflections show, he never lost sight of the importance of preserving its fundamental nature as a unified action. He felt, however, that many of the features of the popular drama were a serious handicap in the realization of this end. Jonson therefore protested against many of the practices of the theatre of his day, particularly those which destroyed unity and violated all dramatic decorum, and those which imposed on the imagination and credulity of the audience by crude tricks of staging, frequent shifting of the scene,

presentation of spectacles like battles on a stage which reduced
them to trifling proportions, and the like. He urged a respect for
the best features of ancient drama, though he warned, in the
posthumous *Timber*, that the ancients must be regarded as guides,
not commanders, and he questioned, in the Induction to *Everyman
out of His Humour*, whether the development of ancient drama did
not establish plenty of warrant for innovations on the part of the
moderns. He also disliked extravagance of language; he protested
in *Timber* against flying from nature like "the Tamerlaines and the
Tamerchams of the last age," and ridiculed the rhetoric of *The
Spanish Tragedy* in his *Everyman in His Humour*. Finally, he expressed
frequently his conviction that the dramatist must never forget that
his function is to instruct as well as to delight.

Whatever the merit of these views, as the critical conscience of
his age, Jonson forced the distinction between drama as an entertainment business and as an art, and he helped to call attention to
the high dignity of the dramatist's calling. The precise practical
consequences in his own plays of his theoretical speculations are
perhaps less easy to establish. In general, Jonson saw with justice
that there was a great deal of sloppiness, injudicious mixture, and
extravagance in the drama of his day, and apparently unable to
concede that artistic fusion was possible with devices which resulted
often in disorder, he seems to have held as bad in themselves the
practices which produced such flaws. He apparently concluded that
artistic salvation was to be found in rejecting as many of these
practices as feasible and making use of whatever one could reasonably and sensibly take over from the dramatic literature of the
ancients, which was free of those practices and conventions.

Jonson's two tragedies, *Sejanus* and *Catiline*, were both total failures
on the stage. Of the two, *Sejanus* is generally regarded as the better,
but it is never treated with anything more than qualified respect by
modern critics. Like all the rest of Jonson's work, it shows the marks
of careful planning and rigorous attention to detail, and the restraint of the artist who is also a critic. In his remarks to the reader
of the 1605 edition of *Sejanus*, he confesses freely having violated
the laws of time and having omitted a chorus, and his defense is
that the moderns have not excelled in these practices, and that it
is neither needful nor possible "to such auditors as commonly things
are presented, to observe the old state and splendor of dramatic

poems, with preservation of any popular delight." Having admitted
these defections in detail and these concessions, however, he con-
tends that in essentials he has been faithful: "In the meantime, if in
truth of argument, dignity of persons, gravity and height of elocution, fullness and frequency of sentence, I have discharged the other
offices of a tragic writer, let not the absence of these forms be im-
puted to me, wherein I shall give you the occasion hereafter, and
without my boast, to think I could better prescribe than omit the
due use for want of a convenient knowledge." The phrasing recalls
critical comments from the early days of English tragedy, and, in
fact, the play itself is in some ways a throwback to those early days
of adaptations of Seneca in its long discourses, the eloquent description of the Nuntius, and the sententious remarks set off in the
printed text by quotation marks. Both Jonson's desire to model his
practice to some extent on the ancient drama and his conviction
that drama must instruct would explain some of these similarities
with a style of English tragedy presumably quite extinct in Jonson's
time. Only in a limited respect, however, would these superficial
features describe the nature of *Sejanus* as a poetic tragedy.

The principal point of distinction in style is that which distinguishes all later tragedies from those written before, say, *Tamburlaine* and *The Spanish Tragedy*—the line is not controlled by any
devices of patterning. Jonson's attitude toward such rhetorical
tricks is clear in his ridicule of Kyd's lines "O eyes, no eyes, but
fountains fraught with tears," etc. Jonson's blank verse is designed
with the rhythms of well-phrased, even somewhat formal, discourse
as its basis. It shows up to best advantage in the senate scene—
probably the most effective generally in the play—in which Silius
is accused and, after braving his enemies, takes his own life:

> *Silius.*   Tell thy moil of patience.
> I am a Roman. What are my crimes? Proclaim them.
> I am too rich, too honest for the times?
> Have I or treasure, jewels, land, or houses
> That some informer gapes for? Is my strength
> Too much to be admitted, or my knowledge?
> These now are crimes.
> *Afer.*   Nay, Silius, if the name
> Of crime so touch thee, with what impotence
> Wilt thou endure the matter to be searched?   (3.167–75)*

*Line references are to the Herford and Simpson edition of *Sejanus* in Volume IV of
their *Ben Jonson* (Oxford, 1932).

The smooth sophistries of Afer and the other partisans of Sejanus, and the outspoken frankness and indignation of Silius are finely brought out, and for the give and take of senate house rhetoric, Jonson's verse seems brilliantly adapted. Unfortunately there are few such occasions. There are, on the other hand, many long speeches in which more seems to be said than the purpose demands, such as Macro's long analysis of his position (4.714–43), or the chorus-like comment of Arruntius and other good Romans on the dreadful events, much of which becomes an oft-told tale and does not advance the action at all.

It is not through lack of technical skill in writing that the common and not wholly just accusation of dullness finds support in this play, however, and it is not because of an ascetic plainness in the diction. It may surprise the casual reader of this play that Jonson shows the same zest in the use of figurative language and the same fecundity in the creation of striking images which is characteristic of the Elizabethan dramatists generally. Some of the most effective of these occur in the speeches of Arruntius, who is something of a chorus, in his condemnation of the ruling political régime:

> We that know the evil
> Should hunt the palace rats, or give them bane;
> Fright hence these worse than ravens, that devour
> The quick, where they but prey upon the dead. (1.426–29)

As another instance, Silius' comment on Sejanus' ruthless elimination of the checks to his power might be cited: "No tree that stops his prospect but must fall" (2.500). Once attention is directed toward such figures, they are seen to be quite generously diffused throughout the play. Moreover, to a limited degree, some of these figures develop into a consistent scheme of suggestions such as have been noticed in the plays of Shakespeare. These are the animal images—a favorite source of imagery in Elizabethan tragedy—which are largely used to characterize the faction of Sejanus, and, in lesser number, images of sparks and flames to suggest the virtues of the old Roman character in opposition to the decadent times; for example, Arruntius' speech,

> O, they are fled the light. Those mighty spirits
> Lie raked up with their ashes in their urns,
> And not a spark of their eternal fire
> Glows in a present bosom. (1.97–100)

The jackals of Sejanus do not usually talk in figurative language, but in the scene in which Latiaris traps Sabinus into expressing his views in the presence of hidden witnesses, Jonson ingeniously suggests Latiaris' hypocrisy by having him use these characteristic images of the virtuous Romans (4.142–61). In an analogous way, Jonson suggests hypocrisy and evasion through the use of figurative language in Sejanus' wooing of Livia (2.1ff), and Tiberius' public statements (for instance, 1.439ff, 3.35ff). For the most part the images serve either this rhetorical function, or are employed to express the indignation of the virtuous Romans and to insinuate the dignity of the true ancient Roman ideals against the cheap political and personal decadence of Tiberius and Sejanus. As a secondary function, they glance at the magnitude of the prodigious events which take place, as in the case of the Nuntius' speech at the end (5.866–70), and in some of Sejanus' confident and bragging speeches; for instance, his welcoming of the threat of dangerous opposition:

> Winds lose their strength, when they do empty fly,
> Unmet of woods or building; great fires die,
> That want their matter to withstand them.   (5.17–19)

They are not all in this dignified and temperate vein, however. Jonson hated the rant and extravagance of the old tragedies, but he comes dangerously close to duplicating them in the following lines of Sejanus:

> By you that fools call gods,
> Hang all the sky with your prodigious signs,
> Fill earth with monsters, drop the scorpion down
> Out of the zodiac, or the fiercer lion,
> Shake off the loosened globe from her long hinge,
> Roll all the world in darkness, and let loose
> Th' enraged winds to turn up groves and towns!
> When I do fear again, let me be struck
> With forked fire, and unpitied die;
> Who fears is worthy of calamity.   (5.390–99)

The examples cited do not, of course, give an indication of the extent to which the figurative treatment of the diction functions in the play. The remarkable thing is that in spite of the elaborate and profuse development which it represents, it does not add up to a great deal in the end. And the reason for this is to be found in the nature of the action and the manner in which it is organized. Sejanus is an unscrupulous, politically ambitious climber. The emperor Tiberius, who has raised him to eminence, is indifferent to the welfare of the state, but he covets his power if only because it gives him the security and opportunity for the life of lavish luxury and debauchery which he leads. Sejanus is his tool, and when Sejanus asks to marry Livia, whom he has debauched and whose husband he has poisoned with her aid, Tiberius checks him, realizing that the marriage would bring him too close to the throne. Sejanus, however, regains his hold on Tiberius by the lucky chance of saving the emperor's life, and, blindly underestimating the shrewdness of Tiberius and coming to regard Fortune as his slave, goes on ruthlessly eliminating possible claimants to the emperor's seat and executing dissident patricians. Tiberius sees this game and sets up Macro to undermine Sejanus. Macro is no ally of the Roman virtues, however—merely another Sejanus who sees a chance for his own advancement. It is Tiberius who finally settles the issue between these two exponents of unscrupulous politics, and it is a mark of Jonson's ingenuity that he has effectively created Tiberius to establish the probabilities in a situation which has something in it of a game of cards between two masters of dishonest poker where anything might happen. At the proper moment, after Macro has lulled Sejanus' fears and disarmed his forces, Tiberius calls a meeting of the senate and causes to be read a letter which completely removes Sejanus from power and puts him at the mercy of the senate and the mob. This letter is a masterpiece of its kind: it is, in a sense, the play in miniature, first praising Sejanus, then qualifying the praise, suggesting possibilities for more honor and power, and then threatening to check the power he holds, so that the senate does not know what the ultimate import of the letter is to be until the final sentence. The play ends with a report by the Nuntius of the violent destruction of Sejanus by the mob, and even of his helpless children.

It will be seen that the whole action can be stated in its essence without reference to the characters who uphold the traditional Roman virtues of political freedom and personal decency, even though their speeches constitute a very large part of the play. Arruntius is continually in the foreground, and yet nothing he says or does affects the outcome at all. Silius has his moment before he commits suicide in the senate, but he is merely the most conspicuous and heroic of the victims. The overthrow of Sejanus for which all good men prayed means only the elevation of the equally fiendish Macro. It is little wonder that many speeches are dull going, since they are often merely repetitions of what is obvious in the play and are in no way dramatically effective. The opening scene is an illuminating example of the method which this arrangement forces on Jonson. The first hundred-eighty-odd lines are used to establish the corrupt political situation, but principally they consist of speeches by the anti-Sejanus faction inveighing against the men and the times, recalling the great days of noble Roman men, and, in general, establishing the standard of the Roman ideal against which the political and personal corruption of Sejanus and Tiberius may be measured. This having been done, Sejanus enters and is shown momentarily as the smooth politician in power. The preparation for his entrance is not in the best sense dramatic—that is, he does not enter to a situation which demands a response on his part, but to a rhetorically eloquent description of virtues he does not possess. Moreover, since none of the exponents of these virtues are active in the play, since no single one of these persons opposes Sejanus or influences his rise and fall very directly as part of the action, their long harangues seem largely beside the point. Significantly, the closing speeches are by Lepidus and Arruntius, the two remaining virtuous Romans, and they talk feelingly about the uncertainties of Fortune and the foolishness of striving, like Sejanus, to high station and trusting to slippery chance. If this is all the whole thing amounts to, then it is hard to understand why there was so elaborate and painstaking an antithesis built up between the vicious personal power politics of Sejanus and the selfless probity and honor of the old Roman ideal.

The effect on the diction of this construction is twofold. On the one hand, since the most elaborate development in the diction occurs in the speeches of characters who are largely passive in the main action, the imagery cannot very readily be made integral to the play in the sense that it is closely related to the features which provide necessity and probability. Hence, much of this development becomes merely a kind of appropriate accompaniment, satisfying the demand for "gravity and height of elocution, fullness and frequency of sentence." Moreover, any attempt, under the circumstances, to tie this action to associations of grandeur and magnitude is bound to be largely mechanical. The principal characters are

drawn with the sharpness of analysis and closeness of observation
which is Jonson's distinction in his comedies. Sejanus and Tiberius
are really brilliant studies of wanton desire for power and luxury,
divorced from all human or social feeling. But to talk about shaking
the globe from its hinge or forcing the sun to run backward to the
east is hardly in keeping with the scale on which the play is drawn.
When Sejanus, exulting in his growing power, says,

> The world knows only two, that's Rome and I.
> My roof receives me not; 'tis air I tread;
> And at each step I feel my advanced head
> Knock out a star in heaven! (5.1.6–9)

—the effect is ludicrous. Tamburlaine might have been able to
speak those lines, but Sejanus cannot without appearing ridiculous
in a way which the speech as a whole does not call for.

Jonson achieved in plot and character the logical clarity and
sharpness he admired and for which he sacrificed methods which
led some of his contemporaries to disunity and diffuseness, but
which enabled the best of this drama to gain amplitude and largeness and, in the case of Shakespeare, an organic and poetic unity.
In consequence, his attempts to endow the play with the quality of
magnitude by the customary devices of figurative language led, on
occasion, to the very extravagance he deplored. Moreover, Jonson
desired to preserve the dignity of ancient tragedy, though without
necessarily imitating all its stock devices; but his realization that its
conventional devices could not be grafted on to the popular tragedy
of the contemporary theatre led him to develop at great length a
feature of his play which lay largely out of the main action, with the
result that it served merely as an instrument for the lofty didactic
discourse which Jonson felt to be a part of drama, but which becomes neither in its sentiments nor its imagery an integral part of
the play.

Webster apparently shared with Jonson the feeling that the popular methods of drama were inimical to the highest possibilities of
tragic art; in the prefatory note to the reader in *The White Devil* he
admitted that he had written "no true dramatic poem" and gave
as his reason the impossibility of pleasing the usual audiences with
genuine tragedy. Whether Webster would have written the fine
things for which his admirers have placed him second only to Shakespeare had he repudiated the dramatic art of his times is an un-

answerable question; but his concessions to the dramatic conventions popular in his day have unquestionably been responsible for much of the dispraise which he has earned. In William Archer's denunciation of the illogicality and "ramshackle looseness" of Elizabethan drama, Webster is placed in the bad eminence of the horrible example. He has, in fact, come to occupy a central position in the debate about the merits and peculiar structure of Elizabethan tragedy, and the extremes of enthusiasm and dislike are so great in his case, as to appear an irreconcilable contrast in taste.[37] Into this controversy it would be unprofitable now to enter, though it is important to recognize its existence since it implies that Webster is not the kind of writer who breeds boredom and indifference, and since it puts one on guard against the blindness of either party of enthusiasts. It is important to understand what in the ecstasies of Lamb made Archer indignant; on the other hand, it is equally important to realize that though *The Duchess of Malfi* might have been improved if Webster could have had the advantage of Archer's suggestions, it would have been utterly ruined had he followed all of them.

The defense of Webster, especially since Archer's criticism, has been vigorous and often judicious, notably in the general studies of Ellis-Fermor and Bradbrook already referred to, in Rupert Brooke's earlier small book on Webster, and in the introductory material to F. L. Lucas' edition of Webster. The general direction of these defenses has been to call attention to Webster's splendid poetry (which no only really denies), and to insist on a proper understanding of the methods and ends of Elizabethan tragedy. Lucas' statement is representative: "It was a succession of great moments that they [the audience] wanted on the stage, not a well-made play . . . . If a dramatist gave them great situations, ablaze with passion and poetry, it would have seemed to them a chilly sort of pedantry that peered too closely into the machinery by which these were produced."[38] Without detracting from the excellence of Lucas' discussion, it is important to take precautions against this line of argument. We do not extenuate the political short-sightedness and cynical indifference of the late Roman emperors because the Roman public seemed to approve of bread and circuses. Shakespeare, who wrote for the same audience as Webster, did not fall into gross ineptitude and "ramshackle looseness" in doing so. What the whole controversy seems to point to is that, whereas Webster possessed perhaps more than any other seventeenth-century writer of tragedy except Shakespeare a gift for intense and figurative language and skill in adapting this language to dramatic dialogue, he failed, un-like Shakespeare, to avoid the more obvious theatrical evasions and the violations of logical consequences to which the conventions and current devices of this drama so readily lent themselves, and against which Jonson protested.

Since *The Duchess of Malfi* has been at the center of the critical battle, it calls for careful consideration. The Duchess, young and a widow, is warned by her brothers, the Cardinal and Duke Ferdi-nand, that it is their wish she should never marry again. She never-theless marries her steward, Antonio, in a secret private ceremony. The brothers place a paid creature, Bosola, in her service as their intelligencer. He discovers the birth of the Duchess' first child, in-forms the brothers, and becomes the agent of their persecutions. These do not begin until after the discovery of the birth of the third child and of the fact that Antonio is the father. The brothers then unloose their hatred: the Duchess is tormented and finally strangled to death, and plots are laid against Antonio. In the last act, the Duke goes mad, the Cardinal is distracted by his conscience, Bosola repents and turns against his patrons, Antonio in gloomy despera-tion and ignorance hopes for reconciliation, and all these meet their deaths in a final convergence of conflicting purposes and cross aims. To bring all this to pass, Webster uses many stratagems and de-vices for which he has been criticized. Principally, he has been ac-cused of failing to preserve logical connections between episodes and to follow incidents to their proper consequences, of destroying concentration by spinning out his play after the Duchess' death, of substituting physical horrors for tragic fear, and of failing to make the behavior of his principal characters clear and consistent. On this last point, Lucas has called attention to Italian Renaissance customs and social codes to lend plausibility to the conduct of the characters, but if Webster himself fails to make clear this basis of understanding and consistency, if only by implication, the play may still be regarded as slightly imperfect in the respect that it does not clearly or consistently enough construct its own special world.

In the matter of character, it is unlikely that all the objections can be argued away, particularly in the case of the two brothers. The only explanation of the Cardinal's participation in the oppression of the Duchess is his contempt for a marriage beneath her rank and the consequent insult to the "royal blood of Arragon and Castile" (2.5.30–32)* This does not, however, explain his insistence with Ferdinand that she must not marry again on any account—the initial factor in the opening situation. Ferdinand's only clear statement of his motives comes late in the play: he expresses indifference to the meanness of the match, but admits he hoped to gain her wealth by her death as a widow (4.2.301–5). Even if Archer's objection that Webster has forgotten the Duchess' son by her first marriage is set aside, Ferdinand's statement still fails to explain his savagery toward the Duchess. But whereas in the explicit elucidation of his design Webster must be admitted to be often clumsy and faulty, in the diction and imagery there is a high degree of harmony and consistency, and where the language is so metaphorical in aspect, this feature of the play cannot be neglected in any final understanding of its meaning. It is particularly the case in such a play where the characters are of the sort who are not inspired to action through a clearly perceived purpose or a resolutely held philosophy, or a highly prized aim, but who all, in varying degrees, suggest a lack of certainty of purpose, a darkened vision, or a disordered will. Significantly, almost all of them are at some time or other referred to as melancholy, a term which signified a recognized psychopathology with symptoms varying all the way from quiet or cynical disillusion to madness. For such characters, a symbolic method of insight has certain advantages over an explicit one. Not that explicit guides are lacking: there are precise statements about all of the leading characters by others and by themselves which in their aggregate are sufficient to make a great deal clear, and which give a clue to the scheme of images supporting and in turn developing these lines of characterization.

Ferdinand may be used as an illustration since he is the most perplexing of the characters and since the methods used in his case are more complex. He is early referred to as "a most perverse and turbulent nature" (1.1.169), and in the course of the play he becomes violently insane. The scene with the Cardinal following his discovery of the Duchess' first child shows him in all his violence and

*Line references are to F. L. Lucas' edition of the play, in his edition of *The Complete Works of John Webster* (London, 1927), Volume II.

perversity, and his speeches are a frightening composite of images from natural upheavals, disease, physical violence, animals, and the like. These are not merely blood and thunder extravagances to show anger and indignation, but mirrors of his psychological disorder. There are clear signs of this intent. Ferdinand himself exclaims:

> Methinks I see her laughing!
> Excellent hyena! Talk to me somewhat, quickly,
> Or my imagination will carry me
> To see her in the shameful act of sin.   (2.5.51–54)

Clearly the symbolism is meant to reflect his diseased imagination and disordered violence of spirit. This is further signalized by such remarks from the Cardinal as "You fly beyond your reason," or "Come, put yourself in tune," and, more fully, by the following speech:

> How idly shows this rage, which carries you,
> As men conveyed by witches through the air,
> On violent whirlwinds! This intemperate noise
> Fitly resembles deaf men's shrill discourse,
> Who talk aloud, thinking all other men
> To have their imperfection.   (2.5.65–70)

The first part of this speech turns back on the Duke the kinds of images which he has been hurling at the Duchess and thus shows that they are applicable not to her but to him; the rest of the speech describes the psychology of the Duke and also gives a clue to the method in the imagery in his case. This method is one of the ways in which the disorder of his mind is made apparent, since Ferdinand alone misstates the events of the play in accord with the rankness that lies within him; the others, however foul themselves, perceive their relative position more clearly and there is no such complex reversal of values in the imagery which they employ. The imagery is in the case of the Duke clearly an important—rather an essential—means in the presentation of a complex and difficult psychological case, and to disregard it is to come short of understanding the character.

The simplest way of realizing the use of the figures is to follow through the most frequent categories of images. This method inevitably involves some distortion—for instance, it does not reveal the points of concentration in imagery, nor the association of several categories in sequence—but any scheme of analysis will involve distortion in the case of a writer like Webster who writes consistently in figurative terms. It will help, nevertheless, to illuminate the association of the images with character, situation, and the suffering of the Duchess.

Animal and bird images are among the commonest and most frequent. One of the earliest occurs in a vivid description by Bosola of the rank wealth of the court of the two brothers and their repulsive hangers-on: "He and his brother are like plum trees that grow crooked over standing pools; they are rich and o'erladen with fruit, but none but crows, pies, and caterpillars feed on them" (1.1.50ff). The loathsome and venomous qualities of the Cardinal are enforced by such phrases as, "The spring in his face is nothing but the engendering of toads" (1.1.159), and "The law to him/Is like a foul, black cobweb to a spider" (1.1.180–81); his Machiavellian shrewdness in the more conventional figure of "the old fox" (5.2.156). Animal images are directly applied to Frederick in descriptions of him by others, such as "He lifts up's nose like a foul porpoise before/A storm" (3.3.64–65), or

> A very salamander lives in's eyes
> To mock the eager violence of fire.   (3.3.59–60)

Wolf images appear in his condemnation of the Duchess. In his interview with her he rails,

> The howling of a wolf
> Is music to thee, screech owl.   (3.2.105–6)

And when Bosola tries to rouse his pity for the strangled children he replies,

> The death
> Of young wolves is never to be pitied.   (4.2.274–75)

These have an interesting relation to the Duke: when he goes mad after the murder of the Duchess, his case is diagnosed as lycanthropia:

> In those that are possessed with't there o'erflows
> Such melancholy humor, they imagine
> Themselves to be transformed into wolves.   (5.2.9–11)

The venal character of Bosola's relation to the brothers, as well as its repulsive aspect, is brought out in animal images. When slighted by the Cardinal he says, "I will thrive some way. Blackbirds fatten

best in hard weather" (1.1.39); similarly when he explains his aims
to Antonio: "Could I be one of the flatt'ring panders, I would hang
on their ears like a horseleech, till I were full, and then drop off"
(1.1.53–55; also 5.2.348–50). Antonio, who suspects him, calls
him an "impudent snake" (2.3.52), and expresses his suspicion of
Bosola's role as intelligencer in the phrase, "this mole does undermine me" (2.3.13).

Animal images are also a common means of expressing the opposition to the lovers; for instance, Antonio's reference to blood-
hounds abroad (3.5.60), his anxiety for his children to "save them
from the tiger" (3.5.101), and the Duchess' exclamation to Bosola,
"Puff, let me blow these vipers from me" (4.1.107). This accumulation of animal images also forms the basis of a contrast through
which the position of Antonio and the Duchess is expressed. Against
the opposition of their foes, these two are remarkably passive. The
Duchess shows initiative and forcefulness in the wooing scene,
though withal a great deal of charm, but she proves unequal to the
machinations and persecutions of her brothers and Bosola so that
her strength is seen primarily in the courage of her suffering. Antonio is not of much help in the wooing scene and he is not much
help when their troubles confront them. Accordingly, in their distress they are associated with beautiful but helpless birds. Thus the
Duchess says to Antonio when they are banished:

> The birds that live i' th' field
> On the wild benefit of nature, live
> Happier than we, for they may choose their mates,
> And carol their sweet pleasures to the spring. (3.5.25–28)

Bosola, justifying to her the order of banishment for Antonio, tells
the Duchess:

> I would have you tell me whether
> Is that note worse that frights the silly birds
> Out of the corn, or that which doth allure them
> To the nets? You have hearkened to the last too much.
> (3.5.117–20)

And similarly when the Duchess replies to Bosola's assurance that
her brothers pity her:

> Pity! With such a pity men preserve alive
> Pheasants and quails, when they are not fat enough
> To be eaten. (3.5.129–31)

Finally, when Cariola tries to comfort her about the future, the Duchess interrupts:

> Thou art a fool.
> The robin redbreast and the nightingale
> Never live long in cages.   (4.2.14–16)

The cumulative effect of these animal and bird images is striking. Just how high a potential such a development can generate may be seen in the force of a single word in the Duchess' speech before she is murdered:

> Go tell my brothers, when I am laid out,
> They then may *feed* in quiet.   (4.2.243–44)

The malignancy of the men who torment the Duchess is accentuated by means of allusions to demoniac forces. Many of these are commonplace enough, but their frequency gives the setting for the more striking ones. The divided nature of Bosola—who says of himself "sometimes the devil doth preach" (1.1.318)—is summed up by Antonio,

> You would look up to heaven, but I think
> The devil, that rules i' th' air, stands in your light.   (2.1.97–98)

As they apply to the Cardinal, such allusions also carry suggestion of villainous shrewdness, certainly proper for the best Machiavellian of the lot; for instance, Bosola says of him, "Some fellows, they say, are possessed with the devil, but this great fellow were able to possess the greatest devil, and make him worse" (1.1.45–48; also 1.1.187–90). In the case of the Duke, there is in such images an additional sense of mysterious malevolence, increased by allusions to witchcraft. Such implications are effectively expressed when Antonio says of the apparent indifference of the Duke,

> Those houses that are haunted are most still
> Till the Devil be up,   (3.1.25–26)

and in Delio's remark to the courtiers on the occasion of an ominous appearance of the brothers at court,

> In such a deformed silence, witches whisper
> Their charms.   (3.3.70–71)

As is often the case with images which are identified with the forces against the Duchess, these infernal images also become the symbol of her suffering, expressive in this instance of the torment of her long endurance:

> That's the greatest torture souls feel in hell—
> In hell, that they must live and cannot die.   (4.1.82–83)

After the death of the Duchess, when the villains are troubled and uncertain in their minds, hell becomes the image of their ill conscience. Thus Bosola begs the strangled Duchess to return and lead his soul "out of this sensible hell" (4.2.369); when she seems to open her eyes, "heaven in it seems to ope, that late was shut" (4.2.373); and when she dies, his guilty conscience is "a perspective/That shows us hell" (4.2.385–86). The Cardinal ponders a theological paradox about the fire of hell, and sees strange objects in his fish ponds (5.5.1–7). And Ferdinand, in his one lucid moment of repentance when he sees things in their right perspective, upbraids Bosola for following his orders with

> Where shalt thou find this judgment registered
> Unless in hell?   (4.2.326–27)

Images derived from fire are almost wholly associated with the Duke and refer to his fierce and unreasoning violence and to the effects he visits on others. "'Tis not your whore's milk that shall quench my wildfire," he says in anticipation of his punishments of the Duchess, "but your whore's blood" (2.5.63–64). The torments he imagines for her are ingenious and obscene executions by fire (2.5.87–94), and, with characteristic application to the Duchess of images which reveal his own perversions, he describes her heart as a hollow bullet "filled with unquenchable wildfire" (3.2.136–37), and her guilt as treading on "hot, burning cultures" (3.1.68–69) These and other similar images form the background of the imagery which epitomizes the suffering of the Duchess in a speech shortly before her murder:

> I am not mad yet, to my cause of sorrow.
> Th' heaven o'er my head seems made of molten brass,
> The earth of flaming sulphur, yet I am not mad.   (4.2.26–28)

Storm and tempest imagery functions in much the same way. It is anticipated early in the play when the Duchess, prevailing on Antonio to marry her, attempts to quiet his apprehensions about her brothers:

> All discord without this circumference
> Is only to be pitied, and not feared.
> Yet should they know it, time will easily
> Scatter the tempest.   (1.1.537–40)

With the discovery of the marriage by the brothers, the fire and tempest images enter the play:

> *Cardinal.*   Why do you make yourself
> So wild a tempest?
> *Ferdinand.*   Would I could be one
> That I might toss her palace 'bout her ears,
> Root up her goodly forests, blast her meads,
> And lay her general territory as waste
> As she hath done her honors.   (2.5.23–29)

The Cardinal's later speech directs this figure at the Duke, combining it with the characteristic one of withcraft:

> How idly shows this rage, which carries you,
> As men conveyed by witches through the air,
> On violent whirlwinds.   (2.5.65–67)

Hence the appropriateness of the Duchess' speech to Bosola's pretence that he comes on a conciliatory mission:

> See, see, like to calm weather
> At sea before a tempest, false hearts speak fair
> To those they intend most mischief,   (3.5.34–36)

and, with a modification of the image, of Antonio's statement on the Duke's apparent inaction:

> He is so quiet that he seems to sleep
> The tempest out, as dormice do in winter.   (3.1.24–25)

The suggestions of violence in the storm images, supplemented by references to thunder, earthquakes, and the like, are also sustained by figures derived from battles and implements of warfare. These are explicitly introduced in the Duchess' expression of her determination to follow her intentions against the will of her brothers:

> Even in this hate, as men in some great battles,
> By apprehending danger, have achieved
> Almost impossible actions (I have heard soldiers say so),
> So I through frights and threat'nings will assay
> This dangerous venture.   (1.1.385–89)

They are suggested by implication during the wedding ceremony:

> Bless, Heaven, this sacred Gordian, which let violence
> Never untwine.   (1.1.549–50)

As Lucas points out, the one thing which the Gordian knot inevitably recalls is that it was cut by the sword.[39] This line of imagery is brought in again during the period of persecution. Thus when Bosola knocks at the door of their apartment:

> *Antonio.* . . . Who knocks? More earthquakes?
> *Duchess.*   I stand
> As if a mine beneath my feet were ready
> To be blown up.   (3.2.185–88)

And when the Duchess is hunted and knows herself to be defeated,

> O misery! Like to a rusty o'ercharged cannon,
> Shall I never fly in pieces?   (3.5.121–22)

On the other side, Bosola remarks that the vengeance of the brothers "Like two chained-bullets still goes arm in arm" (4.2.347). And there is the sinister description of Ferdinand laughing, "Like a deadly cannon/That lightens ere it smokes" (3.3.66–67).

But this is not merely an evil and violent world; it is corrupt and gross and unhealthy. This impression grows from the persistent use of such words as foul, dark, rank, rotten, pestilent, and others of a synonymous nature, and from multiplication of images bearing on disease, drugs, and decay. Since images of this sort are very common and in general duplicate in their course the development of the other leading categories, a few of the more important illustrations will suffice. Ferdinand's use of images of disease shows his customary reversal of reference, as for instance his urging the Cardinal to take measures against the Duchess for her conduct:

> Apply desperate physic.
> We must not now use balsamum, but fire,
> The smarting cupping glass, for that's the mean
> To purge infected blood, such blood as hers.   (2.5.33–36)

Similarly, when she takes a pilgrimage to conceal her escape:

> That, that damns her. Methinks her fault and beauty
> Blended together, show like leprosy—
> The whiter the fouler.   (3.3.74–76)

But in his lucid moment of repentance, Ferdinand applies this imagery also to himself:

> Her marriage—
> That drew a stream of gall quite through my heart. (4.2.305–6)

Another revealing instance is Antonio's use of "ague" twice to describe his life: "Come, I'll be out of this ague" (5.3.59), and in his dying words,

> Pleasure of life, what is't? Only the good hours
> Of an ague; merely a preparative to rest,
> To endure vexation.   (5.4.78–80)

Aside from the Duke's application of images of corruption to the Duchess—for instance, his warning to her that she lives in "a rank pasture" (1.1.340)—the most striking occur in Bosola's speeches, chiefly in his descriptions of the brothers; for example:

> Your brother and yourself are worthy men!
> You have a pair of hearts are hollow graves,
> Rotten and rotting others.   (4.2.344–46)

These are the principal categories of imagery and diction, and they play a major part in the development and interrelationship of the various parts of the play. Some minor features need, however, to be considered. It has been noticed frequently of this play that the characters do not seem capable always of clear and conscious volition, and that they have a sense of fatality concerning their actions. These suggestions are conveyed in a series of references to drama and the theatre, the most highly developed of which occur toward the end of the play. Two come from the Duchess in the scenes immediately before her death.

> Who must dispatch me?
> I account this world a tedious theatre,
> For I do play a part in't 'gainst my will.   (4.1.98–100)

> Fortune seems only to have her eyesight
> To behold my tragedy.   (4.2.37–38)

When Ferdinand sees things clearly for a moment following the murder of the Duchess, he says of Bosola's part in it,

> For thee (as we observe in tragedies
> That a good actor many times is cursed
> For playing a villain's part), I hate thee for't.   (4.2.307–9)

Bosola also sees himself in the same light as

> . . . an actor in the main of all
> Much 'gainst mine own good nature.   (5.5.106–7)

And in a similar figure he accounts for the accidental stabbing of Antonio:

> In a mist: I know not how;
> Such a mistake as I have often seen
> In a play.   (5.5.118–20)

These figures have also the effect of lending an air of plausibility to the accumulation of cross-purposes and accidents which converge at the end of the action.

In addition to sustained categories of images in the play, there are individual figures of great power which such an analysis does not bring out, as, for instance, that which precedes the wooing of Antonio, a metaphor not only charged with emotional suggestion, but also prefiguring the whole play:

> Wish me good speed,
> For I am going into a wilderness
> Where I shall find nor path nor friendly clue
> To be my guide. (1.1.403–7)

There is, moreover, a great deal of interpenetration and crossing of lines of suggestion in the diction which it would prolong the discussion too far to bring out in full detail. One instance, however, deserves notice since it involves the most famous line in the play, Ferdinand's utterance on viewing the dead Duchess:

> Cover her face! Mine eyes dazzle; she died young. (4.2.281)

The Duke's eyes acquire a special symbolic significance. It is said of his eyes that a salamander lives in them; to see her husband, he says, he would change them for those of a basilisk; and when he goes mad he complains of "cruel sore eyes."

While this analysis of the diction and imagery in Webster's most famous play can make no claims to completeness, it nevertheless makes clear enough a remarkable ordered design which is more than decorative and which is intimately related in a dynamic way to the primary features of *The Duchess of Malfi*. The weaknesses of the play and the beauty of particular aspects of the writing have been so fully and brilliantly discussed elsewhere that it would be repetitious to cover that ground again in detail after due acknowledgment has been made of these matters and the fruits of the discussion taken sufficiently into account. The important thing for the moment is that whatever unflattering adjectives may be applicable to the technical ineptitudes of Webster, there is nothing silly or ramshackle about the language of the play, and whatever surprising beauties arrest us in the reading, the remarkable feature of Webster as a writer of dramatic verse is his effective use of the instruments of poetry to illuminate and develop his difficult materials. One of the impressive features of the Elizabethan writers of tragedy is the undaunted spirit with which they approached even the most puzzling and forbidding aspects of human experience. They were not unresponsive to the charms of innocence or the dignity of balanced self-possession, yet they did not hesitate to reveal the most sordid depths of perversity, the most puzzling neuroticisms, or the most pathetic loss of sanity which men might become prey to. There is something bold and courageous about their attempt to encompass the wide range between the splendor and degradation of human life. They would have scarcely succeeded to the extent that they did, however, had they not brought to the service of their exploration of these recondite and difficult materials their method of using language symbolically, their felicity in effecting unusual analogies and correspondences in their figures of speech, and their manipulation of the linguistic environment to give individual words unexpected effectiveness and depth. To bring all this under the discipline of a well-ordered and technically unexceptionable dramatic scheme required apparently more comprehensive powers than most of these dramatists possessed. It is Webster's limitation that, like certain others of his fellow dramatists, he fell back at times on the easy shorthand of theatrical effectiveness to carry him over difficulties in the solution of the technical problems which stood in his way. We do not have to make a virtue of his failures; at the same time we have also to bear in mind that tidiness and logic of design is more to be expected in the case of a play like, say, *The Silver Box* than of *The Duchess of Malfi*.

These observations on Webster leave out of consideration one or two matters which, while they do not serve to modify materially what has been said, are useful in affording a more complete view of his art and further illumination on the general question of Elizabethan tragedy. One conspicuous feature of *The Duchess* is the large number of sententious precepts and apothegms, printed usually with quotation marks or in italics to set them off, which are scattered throughout, suggestive of the earlier experiments in the evolution of a tragic style. Some of these have a close enough bearing on the direction of the thought or sentiment of the speech not to jar greatly, like Bosola's lines which finish off the scene in which he has discovered the secret of the first child:

> Though lust do mask in ne'er so strange disguise,
> She's oft found witty, but is never wise.   (2.3.92–93)

But many of them, like Delio's words to Antonio to the effect that
old friends are the best, seem too thin for the purpose, and sometimes inappropriate and out of place. A case in point is Ferdinand's
remark, spoken in soliloquy, on Bosola, who has just told the Duke
what he thinks of him:

> That friend a great man's ruin strongly checks,
> Who rails into his belief all his defects.   (3.1.116–17)

Since Ferdinand has just been railing in his best vein, and has no
intention of keeping Bosola any longer than he can use him without
trouble, this statement has the effect of an intrusion and is clearly
introduced for its own sake. The most striking instance of this is the
lines of Delio which conclude the play:

> "Integrity of life is fame's best friend,
> Which nobly, beyond death, shall crown the end."

There could hardly be a less fitting sentiment on which to end this
dark and gloomy tragedy. If these are attempts on Webster's part
to preserve what he could of the "height of style, and gravity of persons . . . . the sententious chorus, and . . . . the passionate and
weighty Nuntius" which he regretfully sacrificed, in the note to the
reader in *The White Devil*, to the demands of an unappreciative
auditory, we might well be thankful for the ignorance of the spectators which forced him into another vein. In any case, both in
method and content, these sentences are out of key. They are explicit, literal, and possess an air of wit. This last quality is also the
mark of two allegorical narratives, one by Ferdinand to illustrate
the nature of reputation (3.2.142–58) and another on the merit of
wretchedness by the Duchess (3.5.150–69), which belie the speaker
and the situation and bring the commonplace book and the rhetorical exercise into undue prominence. They are survivals of an earlier
style, strengthened and supported in this later date by the conventionally accepted precepts about tragedy. These devices never
become a part of the play but are like beads on a string. Their very
distinctiveness, however, makes it possible to separate them, as it
were, so that they do not materially interfere with the order and
effectiveness of the diction which has already been discussed. They
are even more sharply at odds with the prevailing mood of the play.
Where all the characters seem somewhat lost, where none of them
seems to have any certainty and the best has only endurance and

courage in suffering to sustain her, appeal to such nuggets of wisdom seems inadequate. Or, to put it in another way, the probabilities in this play are not given direction by the implications of a moral system and hence the appearance of these maxims is misleading. However, their effect is not sufficient to obscure the quality of somber melancholy and serious disillusion which pervades this play.

This mood is important in any understanding of Webster. It is incorporated into the prevailing imagery. The oppositions in the action of this play do not create an opposition of values which might serve, as is the case often with Shakespeare, as a basis for contrasting categories of imagery and unexpected correspondences between them. The character who dominates the play is Bosola, the base villain against his will, who begs the Duke to go no further and who discovers the lack of reward for useful villains in the world of courts and princes. The long episode with the courtier and old lady (2.1) has no function whatsoever except to give Bosola's bitter and ironic vein an opportunity:

> What a thing is in this outward form of man
> To be beloved? We account it ominous
> If nature do produce a colt, or lamb,
> A fawn, or goat, in any limb resembling
> A man, and fly from 't as a prodigy.
> Man stands amazed to see his deformity
> In any other creature but himself.
> But in our own flesh, though we bear diseases
> Which have their true names only ta'en from beasts,
> As the most ulcerous wolf and swinish measle;
> Though we are eaten up of lice and worms;
> And though continually we bear about us
> A rotten and dead body, we delight
> To hide it in rich tissue. All our fear,
> Nay, all our terror, is lest our physician
> Should put us in the ground to be made sweet.   (2.1.47–63)

There are other episodes which have little function except to introduce a kind of harsh satire (3.3.12–42; 4.2.49–52) and which play on bitter themes beyond the apparent needs of the moment (4.2.123–31). It is not Delio's apothegms which properly underscore this play, but Antonio's reflection that the pleasures of life are "only the good hours/Of an ague," and particularly Bosola's dying words,

O, this gloomy world!
In what a shadow, or deep pit of darkness,
Doth womanish and fearful mankind live!   (5.5.124–26)

In this respect *The Duchess* may be compared with Webster's slightly earlier play, *The White Devil*, in which the role of Bosola is duplicated by Falmineo. The action is more brilliantly contrived than that of the later play, and a sympathetic critic might have been able, without resort to any sophistry, to persuade even Archer that it compares not unfavorably with some of his miracles of construction. In general, the same categories of sources for the imagery prevail, and the same ironic and melancholy reflections dominate the play, with perhaps a more prevailingly cynical note. The differences arise partly from the circumstance that the two lovers in this case, Vittoria and Brachiano, who are opposed again by a cardinal and a duke, are themselves equally ruthless and expert in intrigue and are admirable chiefly for their strong and genuine love for one another and, especially Vittoria, for an arresting brilliance of character. Even less, therefore, do the dramatic oppositions afford a basis for contrasting values in the imagery. Flamineo, the counterpart of Bosola in this play, may be distinguished for being a more colorful rogue and more aggressively cynical, but he is like Bosola in dominating the play and establishing a pervading mood of disillusion.

This common mood, and the repetition of the device of the melancholy tool-villain as a principal device for projecting it, suggest an interesting artistic consequence of the philosophic bias from which these plays apparently were written. In the tragedies of Shakespeare, and to an extent those of Marlowe and Chapman, wherever the diction and imagery do not immediately serve the ends of necessity and probability, they play a major role in extending the bounds of the play and in giving it generality and magnitude. Where, however, as in the case of Webster, disillusion and uncertainty are the principal sources of inspiration, the imagery and diction, to the extent that they do not help develop necessity and probability, serve chiefly to exploit a quality of melancholy, sardonic irony, and satirical bitterness, which sometimes overflows the frame of the action in finding expression. More extreme effects of this melancholy vein and its satiric expression may be observed in Cyril Tourneur.

The case of Cyril Tourneur is that of a writer of real poetic gifts

who found the most direct release of his talents through an acceptance of a ready-made popular dramatic convention. Both of the
tragedies usually ascribed to him, *The Revenger's Tragedy* (1607) and
The Atheist's Tragedy (1611), are reworkings of the revenge-play
formula, which was introduced by Kyd and which enjoyed considerable popularity during the first decade of the seventeenth
century. Of the two, *The Revenger's Tragedy* is universally acknowledged in all respects the more brilliant, but many of its features appear crude and ludicrous today, and such an honest attempt at
critical evaluation as that of Allardyce Nicoll in his edition of
Tourneur's works, though it calls attention to many excellent dramatic virtues, cannot wholly bridge the gap between the two ages
and eliminate entirely the sense of almost perverse ingenuity which
the play retains. The fact is that *The Revenger's Tragedy* would have
been inconceivable, and even to its own audience incredible, without some two decades of preparation in a dramatic tradition.

The main character is called Vindice—the Revenger—an indication of an understanding between the audience and the dramatist
concerning both the propriety and the nature of such a protagonist.
The probabilities governing such a character are largely taken for
granted, since familiarity with such a dramatic figure would reduce
the need for elaborate statement and analysis of these probabilities
of character. By way of analogy, any audience at a crime or detective moving picture will know at once that the large, stupid police
inspector is not going to solve the crime and that any hypothesis he
proposes is necessarily the wrong one, that he will be astonished at
the private detective's researches, and will finally attempt to convey
the impression that he was pretty well up on the matter himself—
or perhaps it is better to say that any such character can be portrayed without any explanation, and that any deviation from this
scheme will be in the nature of a trick on the audience or will demand fuller analysis of character. Vindice appears with the skull of
his one-time sweetheart, poisoned nine years before by the Duke
whose lascivious proposals she had rejected. Vindice is bent on
revenge. Why he has failed to secure revenge for nine years is never
explained. The lapse of time has made him characteristically bitter,
even antic, in his disposition and that is enough. The skull of his
mistress is the constant reminder of his one purpose (there is no
ghost), and also furnishes occasion for reflections about death and

the vanities of life (3.5.57–110)* Disguise is used not once but several times. The revenge takes place, conventionally enough, in a masque at the end, only in this case the true masquers are also planning to do some killing during their performance, and hence the earlier appearance of the false masquers, who are Vindice and his brother and their assistants, and who take their place to accomplish their own revenge, provides a fine piece of irony, and when the real masquers enter, the slaughter becomes complex indeed.

It is as though Tourneur, relieved of the necessity of giving probability other than that supplied by the recognition of an established scheme, pushed his development in the direction of maximum variation within the scheme. This is clear in the major factor of the revenge itself. Since no explanation of delay is apparently necessary, nor any analysis of conflicts within the character of Vindice, the purpose of the revenger becomes not simply the accomplishment of his revenge but the achievement of revenge with the fullest degree of ingenuity and horror. He declares that the death of his beloved "shall be revenged after no common action" (3.5.74); he regrets the loss of one opportunity to slay the Duke's son, Lussurioso, under peculiarly vivid circumstances—"Oh I'm mad to lose such a sweet opportunity" (5.1.19); and his brother Hippolito says in admiration,

> Brother, I do applaud thy constant vengeance,
> The quaintness of thy malice above thought. (3.5.111–12)

This perverse indulgence in the fine art of revenge as against the necessary accomplishment of an act of justice otherwise unattainable is matched by the lurid evil against which Vindice's energies are directed. It is announced in Vindice's opening speech:

> Duke: Royal lecher; go, gray haired adultery,
> And thou his son, as impious steeped as he,
> And thou his bastard true-begot in evil,
> And thou his Duchess that will do with devil,
> Four excellent characters. (1.1.1–5)

This omits mention of two other sons not a whit behind these four in evil. The court of the Duke is steeped in villainy and lust of all kinds; Tourneur has devised within this group of paragons of vice

---

*Line references are to Allardyce Nicoll's edition of *The Revenger's Tragedy* in his edition of *The Works of Cyril Tourneur* (London, 1929).

almost every possible combination of treachery and lechery. Vindice is therefore continually absorbed with the vicious inclination of man to sin, particularly in sexual matters, and with the evil of the times, and his loathing and nausea are principal features of the play. So obsessed is he that when Lussurioso sends him to tempt his own sister, he goes in disguise and uses his utmost persuasion, and when defeated by his sister, unwilling to let well enough alone, he tempts his mother, this time successfully, to try to corrupt his sister. His success in this affair further feeds his animus against evil.

All of the features of this play can be duplicated in earlier revenge plays—the need for revenge against one beyond the law, the delay of the revenge, the passionate revulsion of the avenger against the concealed or open injustice and evil which he must combat, and his sardonic and melancholy reflections on his problem. But in *The Revenger's Tragedy*, neither the complex ethical conflicts which this raises in the avenger, nor the effects on him psychologically are explored. Tourneur has selected the recognized features of this kind of play and, assuming a general understanding of their dramatic validity, arranged them into a consistent and self-contained pattern. In a sense, the procedure might be likened to a chess problem posed by an expert who assumes that his audience knows the conventions which govern the restricted movements of individual pieces and the possibilities of the game, and then demonstrates the solution in such a way as to encompass the maximum number of variant situations latent in the problem.

It is not at first apparent that the kind of excellence of expression which distinguishes this play is in large part dependent upon the development which has been described. Criticisms of the play generally recognize the remarkable poetic gifts shown in it, but since this is usually accompanied by an air of apology for the matter, the connection between the two tends to be lost. The almost geometrical trimness of the design, the lack of subtlety yet variety in the development, make possible the hard brilliance of diction, the sharp oppositions and antitheses, the ironic contrasts and twists in the imagery. The control of probabilities in large part through the ready reliance on dramatic tradition eliminates the necessity of placing the diction and imagery in the service of reinforcing probabilities (establishing character, exploring subtleties of sentiment and motive, preparing for and anticipating reversal, and the like), and permits concentration on the theme of rampant vice and distorted values, represented by the hideous court, and the central source of feeling for Vindice, who dominates the play. The opening speech of the play launches at once into this vein:

> O that marrowless age
> Would stuff the hollow bones with damned desires,
> And, stead of heat, kindle infernal fires
> Within the spendthrift veins of a dry duke,
> A parched and juiceless luxur. O God! one
> That has scarce blood enough to live upon,
> And he to riot it like a son and heir.   (1.1.8–14)

The sustained concentration on this almost fascinated loathing and indignation and the quality of the expression suggest strongly the satire of the late sixteenth and early seventeenth centuries, particularly of Marston, between whom and Tourneur, Allardyce Nicoll finds some points of connection.[40] The insistence on these matters beyond the needs of the plot is signalized by remarks of Hippolito following Vindice's outbursts, such as, "Nay brother you reach out a'th'/Verge now" (1.3.19), "You flow well, brother" (2.2.162), and "Brother, y'ave spoke that right" (3.5.69), as well as by occasional sudden returns to the plot in such remarks as Vindice's "Now to my tragic business" (3.5.102) after an extended diatribe, and Hippolito's "O, Brother, you forget our business" (4.4.86) on a similar occasion. Since the business moves easily enough in its conventional predetermined grooves, it is quite convenient to pause frequently and allow the bitter current of sentiment to flow.

Isolation of the most prominent devices of Tourneur's writing will help illustrate the characteristic ways through which he gains his brilliant effects. For one thing, he handles his verse with familiarity of phrasing and idiom which goes far toward giving an air of naturalness to the lurid events, without at the same time sacrificing tenseness in the rhythms:

> *Vindice.*   Nay but hear me,
> He desires now that will command hereafter,
> Therefore be wise, I speak as more a friend
> To you than him. Madam, I know y'are poor,
> And lack the day, there are too many poor ladies already—
> Why should you vex the number? 'tis despised.
> Live wealthy, rightly understand the world,
> And chide away that foolish, country girl

Keeps company with your daughter, chastity.
Mother.   O fie, fie, the riches of the world cannot hire a
   mother to such a most unnatural task.
Vindice.   No, but a thousand angels can;
Men have no power, angels must work you to't.   (2.1.86–99)

The concentration on the theme of triumphant lust and evil is
brought out by the frequent occurrence of such words as heat and
blood, and the appearance in several places of images suggestive of
disease and of darkness or artificial light. Disease is the symbol of
sin or the curse of an ill conscience; for example, Vindice says to his
mother when she repents,

Now the disease has left you; how leprously
That office would have clinged unto your forehead.   (4.4.71–72)

And to the Duke, to whose dying moments he wishes to bring increased torment,

             . . . now I'll begin
To stick thy soul with ulcers; I will make
Thy spirit grievous sore, it shall not rest,
But like some pestilent man toss in thy breast.   (3.5.186–89)

Night is the symbol of stealthy sin, and Vindice's diatribes against
night (2.2.149–61; 1.3.109–18) establish these suggestions fully.
Hence, for instance, when Vindice comments on the Duke's desire
to have an assignation in a dark room for better privacy, the idea
acquires an increased viciousness through its association with these
images:

To greet him with a lady,
In some fit place veiled from the eyes ath' court,
Some darkened blushless angle, that is guilty
Of his forefathers' lusts, and great folks' riots,
To which I easily (to maintain my shape)
Consented, and did wish his impudent grace
To meet her here in this unsunned lodge,
Wherein 'tis night at noon . . . .   (3.5.13–20)

In this connection it will be noticed that the brightness of the court
is referred to in terms of artificial light—its revels, for instance,
"when torchlight made an artificial noon." (1.4.31).

Recurrent schemes of imagery are not, however, the main device
on which Tourneur depends. The principal effect of the sustained
assault against the triumphant corruption of the life represented by

the Duke's court comes from setting its keenest desires and its most cherished values either explicitly or, for the most part, by inference, against the contrasting measure of temperance and virtue, and its vanities against the oblivion of death. Its desires are physical, its brilliance artificial, its activity feverish and unnatural. In exploiting these qualities, the diction arrives at its most vivid effects; in insinuating the more sober values against the vicious and perverse ones of lust and villainy, it secures its most effective contrasts and its sharpest ironies. Suggestion of physical effects, of anatomical processes, is one of the commonest features of the diction: "parched and juiceless luxur" (1.1.12); "uttering words sweet and thick" (1.2.-205); "Thy veins are swelled with lust, this [dagger] shall unfill 'em" (2.2.114)—these are samplings. The figures of speech are at times but an extension of this effect; for instance, the Duke's panders "fed the ravenous vulture of his lust" (1.4.50), where the metaphorical word vulture introduces the moral judgment. A similar vividness of detail results from the way in which the accoutrements of court life are described to accentuate its vanity or evil. The simplest method used is represented by an expression like "the costly-perfumed people," which acquires a sharp ironic edge of condemnation in its context:

> Impudence!
> Thou Goddess of the palace, mistress of mistresses
> To whom the costly-perfumed people pray.   (1.3.5–7)

A typical example of Tourneur's more involved figures occurs in Vindice's address to the skeleton of his former love:

> Advance thee, O thou terror to fat folks,
> To have their costly three-piled flesh worn off
> As bare as this.   (1.1.48–50)

Fat folks is a reference to the well-fed luxury of the court, but "costly three-piled flesh" is a brilliant development of the idea: "three-piled" refers to an expensive and rich velvet, the wearing-out of which would be a blow to one's fashionable pride, and the identification of this idea with the wasting of a luxuriously fed body and the terror to indolent and vicious people of contemplating this event produces an extraordinary concentration of suggestions. In such a phrase as "some stirring dish was my first father" (1.2.201), there is a somewhat different method of identifying a concrete detail with a large sphere of activity and implying at the same time a moral revulsion: "stirring dish" suggests both the unnatural animation of a life of luxury and the tempting incitements to evil, and in equating "dish" with "father" there is both a revolting reduction of the procreative act to vicious triviality and an implied condemnation of an attitude which disregards the responsibilities of the act. The contrast between the values of a life of vice and of the life of virtue is sometimes explicitly brought out in antithesis, such as the brilliant one which completes the following speech:

> There had been boiling lead again,
> The duke's son's great concubine:
> A drab of state, a cloth, a silver slut,
> To have her train borne up, and her soul trail i' th' dirt; great.
> (4.4.78–81)

At times it is brought out in an ironic inversion of values:

> Now cuckolds are a-coining, apace, apace, apace, apace.
> And careful sisters spin that thread i' th' night,
> That does maintain them and their bawds i' th' day!
> (2.2.158–60)

The words "careful sisters spin that thread" literally apply to thrifty, honest, industrious women; hence the effect of irony in using it for whores. There is also, finally, a grotesque humor which sometimes arises from the pervading preoccupation with physical things—

> Tell but some woman a secret over night,
> Your doctor may find it in the urinal i' th' morning.   (1.3.93–94)

or from a comic twist to the inversion of values, as, for instance, in Vindice's pretense of horror at discovering the body of the Duke in the garments of Piato—

> O, rascal, was he not ashamed
> To put the Duke into a greasy doublet?   (5.1.75–76)

—as though the awfulness of the act consisted in doing violence to the Duke's fastidiousness and his right to wear fine clothes.

Further analysis would reveal besides these principal devices certain others, or variations on these, but in general most of the effects would be found to arise from great fertility of invention in relating the diction to the perverse and false values of a life of sin and to the various aspects of such a life which bring up a sense of loathing that cannot be put by. The celebrated passages from the play, quoted at some length in T. S. Eliot's essay on Tourneur, consist in large part of combinations of the devices already discussed. It is the case with the following speech, the conclusion of which has been admired, though it is necessary to see it all to get its full effect:

> O Dutch lust! fulsome lust!
> Drunken procreation, which begets so many drunkards;
> Some father dreads not, gone to bed in wine, to slide from the mother
> And cling the daughter-in-law;
> Some uncles are adulterous with their nieces,
> Brothers with brothers' wives—O hour of incest!
> Any kin now next to the rim a'th' sister
> Is man's meat in these days; and in the morning
> When they are up and dressed, and the mask is on,
> Who can perceive this, save that eternal eye
> That sees through flesh and all? Well, if anything be damned,
> It will be twelve o'clock at night. That twelve
> Will never scape; it is the Judas of the hours, wherein
> Honest salvation is betrayed to sin.   (1.3.65–80)

Vindice's reflections on the skull of his dead sweetheart, which is unusual for its striking and eccentric images, is developed around a comparison of values, and its images largely sustain this comparison through an ingenious identification and equivalance between some concrete object connected with the accoutrements or activities of the life of vanity and the attitudes and activities of this life themselves:

> And now methinks I could e'en chide myself
> For doating on her beauty, though her death
> Shall be revenged after no common action.
> Does the silkworm expend her yellow labors
> For thee? for thee does she undo herself?
> Are Lordships sold to maintain ladyships
> For the poor benefit of a bewitching minute?
> Why does yon fellow falsify highways
> And put his life between the judge's lips,
> To refine such a thing? keeps horses and men
> To beat their valours for her?   (3.5.72–82)

Such a method has much in common with that of the satirist, where a standard, explicit or implied, is established, against which the object of satire is revealed as undesirable, whether as revolting, grotesque, or comic, and where invective may be combined with vivid insistence on reprehensible aspects of the object of satire in order further to discredit it.

In this fact may be found both the distinction and the limitations of Tourneur's performance, for, after making all allowance for over-simplification, it is nonetheless the case that the play gives occasion for the fine and brilliant things in it, though it cannot be said that it is a fine and brilliant play. What gave distinction to the finest of the revenge plays was not the accumulation of conventional features which became the common property of the type, but the kinds of probabilities which were introduced into the basic dramatic formula. By themselves, these conventional features appear merely lurid, sensational, and extravagant, and *The Revenger's Tragedy* relies rather too heavily on the conventions themselves. This method allowed for the concentrated development of the mood of melancholy revulsion against evil and of sardonic indignation, which is also a characteristic mark of many plays of this type, and may be recognized, for instance, as one aspect of the character of Hamlet and practically the whole of Malevole in Marston's *Malcontent*. The speeches enlarging on this mood, which occupy so large a place in *The Revenger's Tragedy*, are finely moulded and well suited for effective speaking on the stage, but they are not, in the most complete sense, dramatic since they are to so large an extent distinct from an intimate and continued concern with the action and the probabilities by which it is controlled. It is largely in consequence of this that, whereas the writing is frequently vivid, brilliant, and imaginative, the scheme of the action which gives occasion to it seems alien, overspecialized, academic, and arbitrary.

With John Ford, the line of succession of Elizabethan tragedy may be regarded as virtually at an end. His first important play of which we have knowledge, *The Lover's Melancholy*, was probably acted in 1629. His three tragedies, *'Tis Pity She's a Whore, Love's Sacrifice*, and *The Broken Heart*, were printed in 1633, and *Perkin Warbeck*, a chronicle history, was printed in 1634. Less than ten years remained before the closing of the theatres, and Ford's clearly is the only original excursion in tragedy of any importance before that time. The notoriety of *'Tis Pity She's a Whore*, with its story of incest between brother and sister, has tended to place all of Ford's work in a distorted focus, particularly in discussions of "decadence" in the drama. Whatever this may be taken to mean in any given context, the view that Ford depended on situations which strike horror and unnerve the moral sense in order to compensate for the exhaustion of novelty in the usual subjects can no longer be unqualifiedly accepted.[41] Ford's straightforward facing of the situations with which he deals does not permit evasion and sophistry—compare, for instance, the pruriency and equivocalness of the incest situation in *A King and No King*—and one of the characteristic features of Ford's tragedies is the serious and earnest way in which he calls attention to the moral problems raised by the action. Moreover, the style of Ford, in its most original and characteristic aspects, is hardly fit instrument for lurid excitement.

The Broken Heart is perhaps the most satisfactory of his tragedies for detailed study; it is generally regarded as a better play than *Love's Sacrifice*, and it is not vexed by the question which is inevitably raised in the case of *'Tis Pity* as to why Ford should have handled the subject at all and done so not unsympathetically. Yet it has affinities with the others and in many ways best illustrates the artistic consequences of Ford's subjects and methods. The plot of *The Broken Heart* involves a group of closely interrelated characters most of them distressed by some sort of love furstration. Orgilus, who had been betrothed to Penthea, is tormented by the injustice of her being given in marriage against her will to a nobleman, Bassanes, by her proud brother, Ithocles, and also by seeing her inconsiderately treated by her jealous husband. Penthea submits to her lot and is faithful to her vow of marriage, but she is miserable and loses her mind and then dies. Bassanes is tortured by unreasoning jealousy. Ithocles, returning home a conqueror, falls in love with the princess Callantha, but suffers at first in silence fearful of the differences in rank. When he discovers that Callantha responds to his affection, he is happy, though he is haunted by the specter of his sister and of Orgilus whom he now knows he has wronged. His happiness is short lived, however, for on the death of Penthea, Orgilus traps him and kills him. Callantha, at the moment of becoming the ruler on the death of her father, hears of the death of Ithocles, and after making due preparations for the well-being of the kingdom, dies of a broken heart. Two lovers emerge happy; Euphranea, sister of Orgilus, and Prophilus, friend of Ithocles, discover their love, secure the reluctant consent of Orgilus, and are married just before the several catastrophes overcome the others. They are what Orgilus and Penthea should have been, had not disregard of natural affection by Ithocles and Bassanes twisted a noble love into the slow torture of frustrated passion which watches its own ruin. The others range in between. There is a division of interest and sympathy among these persons; "The plot," writes T. S. Eliot in his essay on Ford, "is somewhat overloaded and distracted by the affairs of unfortunate personages, all of whom have an equal claim on our attention." But it is clear that Ford was primarily concerned in revealing the various forms and degrees of the unhappiness of unfulfilled love and managed his plot so as to provide the maximum number of variations on the problem. The method is analytical in its nature: the plot is a prism which breaks up the situation into its component and related parts, and although, as Eliot points out, normal dramatic concentration is lost, there is skill shown in the emergence of all these possibilities without resort to obvious technical ingenuities.

A hint of the analytical bent of Ford's mind is to be found in the morality or humors type of names, with definitions in the *dramatis personae*: Orgilus, *Angry*: Bassanes, *Vexation*; Ithocles, *Honor of Loveliness*; etc. This device is a sign of a special technique of characterization which in this instance lends itself to Ford's interest in psychological problems. The seriousness of this interest is apparent in an earlier play, *The Lover's Melancholy*, which deals with aspects of melancholy. There is a reference to Burton in a marginal note, and the masque which the physician Corax puts on in the play can be shown to be dependent very closely on the descriptions of symptoms of the various forms of melancholia in *The Anatomy of Melancholy*. Ford's probing of psychological distortions is sympathetic, but is done with a concern for the technical grounds of understanding such phenomena. Bassanes is the most obvious example of what Ford is up to. Orgilus gives a systematic analysis of the causes of Bassanes' jealousy (1.1.57–70)* and during the play Bassanes is given ample opportunity to show what the extremes of jealousy can make a man perform. When Bassanes is called upon at the end to assume serious responsibilities of state, the suggestion seems preposterous, since there is nothing to show him to be anything else but

*Line references are to S. P. Sherman's edition of *The Broken Heart* in the Belles-Lettres series (Boston and London, 1915).

what his name indicates him to be, a vexed and self-tormented man. Where Othello is a magnificent man racked and finally ruined by jealousy, Bassanes is a casebook specimen. None of the others are handled with such cold-blooded attention to the textbooks, but the method is essentially the same. There are guide posts of varying degrees of explicitness to the conduct of the characters. Tecnicus tells Orgilus,

> Ah, Orgilus,
> Neglects in young men of delights and life
> Run often to extremities; they care not
> For harms to others who contemn their own. (1.3.15–18)

Penthea helps to define her own case:

> . . . beauty, pomp,
> With every sensuality our giddiness
> Doth frame an idol, are unconstant friends,
> When any troubled passion makes assault
> On the unguarded castle of the mind. (3.5.19–23)

And Ithocles reflects that, though morality keeps the soul in tune,

> It physics not the sickness of a mind
> Broken with griefs. Strong fevers are not eased
> With counsel, but with best receipts and means:
> Means, speedy means and certain; that's the cure. (2.2.12–15)

The general principle is expressed by Nearchus:

> . . . affections injured
> By tyranny or rigor of compulsion,
> Like tempest-threatened trees unfirmly rooted,
> Ne'er spring to timely growth. Observe, for instance,
> Life-spent Penthea and unhappy Orgilus. (4.2.205–9)

The important characters run their course, each displaying the particular form which love frustration takes in his case.

Ford is, however, equally preoccupied with the moral problems posed by his play, with reference both to the restrictions of social forms and laws which conflict with the claims of love, and to the demands of personal honor which the characters, caught in various dilemmas, must try to satisfy. The word "honor" appears very frequently during the play, and the ideal is represented by Penthea, who satisfies the demands of the laws of marriage by remaining faithful to Bassanes even to being ruthless with Orgilus' feelings, but pines away to death because she is unable to satisfy the higher

demands of purity which the claims of mutual and sincere love between her and Orgilus make on her:

> . . . she that's wife to Orgilus, and lives
> In known adultery with Bassanes,
> Is at the best a whore.   (3.2.73–75)

Death is the only solution of such an irreconcilable conflict of
principles. The grounds of true honor are explicitly reasoned for
Orgilus' benefit by Tecnicus the philosopher, who occupies a position in this play similar to that of the Friar in *'Tis Pity.* In a long
speech (3.1) Tecnicus distinguishes honor based on opinion and the
performance of acts prompted by passion from true honor based on
virtue and reason and made valorous by a desire for justice. Tecnicus' analysis establishes the norm for the ethical basis of the play as
the speech of Nearchus establishes the norm for the psychological
basis. Against this definition of law and honor the actions of the
various characters are measured.

   Such a method is to some degree not too closely dependent on the
kind of contribution which language used poetically can make.
Where the procedure is analytical, explicit modes of expression and
literally-defined words will do. This is, of course, stating the absolute
extremes, though the condition is fully met in Tecnicus' long discourse on honor, if nowhere else. Taken in general, however, this
play reveals the same figurative quality in diction which is the
common property of all the drama of this tradition. Even in those
speeches directed toward establishing the basic premises of Ford's
analysis, such phrases as "the unguarded castle of the mind,"
"tempest-threatened trees unfirmly rooted" add greatly to the expression. Moreover, Orgilus' death speech recalls the intensity
which Elizabethan dramatists regularly infused into those moments:

> A mist hangs o'er mine eyes; the sun's bright splendor
> Is clouded in an everlasting shadow.
> Welcome, thou ice that sitt'st about my heart;
> No heat can ever thaw thee.   (5.2.153–56)

The first two lines seem hardly more than a conventional strain, but
the last two, in view of the association of the word "heat" with passion and the idea of coldness with chastity and virtue throughout
the play, have a genuine and essential brilliance about them. For
the most part, however, the figurative language of this play aids in
giving effectiveness and force to the expression rather than additional depth of meaning. Again to state it in extremes, in Webster,

for example, figurative language is absolutely essential; in Ford, it is auxiliary.

At least two qualifications need to be added. The extreme case of emotional frustration as well as of personal honor is Penthea, who embodies the tragic paradox that adherence to one principle of virtue produces not only misery but, from the viewpoint of another principle, actual sin. Around this theme the diction plays, often with a suggestion of paradox. Orgilus alludes to Ithocles as a poisonous stalk of aconite who has "ravished all health, all comfort of a happy life," he describes Penthea as "wedded to this torture," and contrasts her state as "before contracted mine" with now "yoked to a most barbarous thralldom," and he refers to Bassanes' affection as "a kind of monster-love" (1.1.36–70). The word thralldom is used several times in reference to Penthea's marriage, and Ithocles calls it a "resolved martyrdom" for which she will become a worshipped deity (3.2.80–83). The ethical paradox is alluded to in Orgilus' reference to Ithocles' arrogance which "wrought the rape/On grieved Penthea's purity" (3.4.26–27); but the most elaborate development of this sort occurs in one of Penthea's speeches during her madness:

> O, my wracked honor, ruined by those tyrants,
> A cruel brother and a desperate dotage!
> There is no peace left for a ravished wife
> Widowed by lawless marriage; to all memory
> Penthea's, poor Penthea's, name is strumpeted.   (4.2.144–48)

In addition, the idea of death hangs heavily over the play; Penthea, and even Ithocles, see death ahead of them, though it is again in Penthea that this motif is centered. It is a theme that lends itself to figurative expression, but nowhere does it find more effective and full statement than in the scene of Penthea's madness:

> Sure, if we were all Sirens, we should sing pitifully.
> And 'twere a comely music, when in parts
> One sang another's knell. The turtle sighs
> When he hath lost his mate; and yet some say
> A' must be dead first. 'Tis a fine deceit
> To pass away in a dream; indeed, I've slept
> With mine eyes open a great while. No falsehood
> Equals a broken faith; there's not a hair
> Sticks on my head but, like a leaden plummet,
> It sinks me to the grave. I must creep thither;
> The journey is not long.   (4.2.69–79)

This, like certain other speeches in the mad scene, is more richly imaginative in expression than the rest of the play, but it possesses a general quality in the rhythms and in the quietness of movement which is a mark of Ford's most original qualities as a writer of dramatic verse. There is, however, not the great concentration in imagery of the earlier dramatists in such passages; the figures are deliberately laid out:

> Glories
> Of human greatness are but pleasing dreams
> And shadows soon decaying; on the stage
> Of my mortality my youth hath acted
> Some scenes of vanity, drawn out at length
> By varied pleasures, sweetened in the mixture,
> But tragical in issue; beauty, pomp,
> With every sensuality our giddiness
> Doth frame an idol, are unconstant friends,
> When any troubled passion makes assault
> On the unguarded castle of the mind. (3.5.13–23)

This kind of writing is finely adapted to a quality of Ford's work to which many critics have called attention—the effect of inaction, the masque-like character of his plays. In the scene between Penthea and Ithocles, the movement is for a moment quite arrested and the dialogue takes on the aspect of antiphonal chorus on their mutual unhappiness:

> *Ithocles.*   I consume
> In languishing affections for that trespass,
> Yet cannot die.
> *Penthea.*   The handmaid to the wages
> Of country toil drinks the untroubled streams
> With leaping kids and with the bleating lambs,
> And so allays her thirst secure, whiles I
> Quench my hot sighs with fleetings of my tears.
> *Ithocles.* The laborer doth eat his coarsest bread,
> Earned with his sweat, and lies him down to sleep,
> While every bit I touch turns in digestion
> To gall as bitter as Penthea's curse.
> Put me to any penance for my tyranny,
> And I will call thee merciful.
> *Penthea.*   Pray, kill me;
> Rid me from living with a jealous husband.
> Then we will join in friendship, be again
> Brother and sister. (3.2.52–67)

Such passages bring into sharp relief one of the most puzzling problems in Ford. Against the quiet lyric artifice of such lines, the relentless and objective analysis of Bassanes seems incompatible, crude and comic, though considered by itself there is much brilliance in this portrait with acute observation and vividness of detail. This is different from the kind of artistic confusion which obtains in a play like *The Changeling*, where a comic sub-plot beneath contempt interferes with the uninterrupted movement of the tragic main plot; it is, in fact, a more serious matter. Bassanes is part of the main action, and also a part of the scheme of analytic disclosures in the psychology of thwarted love. To illustrate the problem in another way, the scene in which Callantha continues to dance while three separate messages of calamity are whispered to her has been highly admired as well as condemned. Her death scene is handled in some-what the same striking way; she tidies up her affairs, places a wed-ding ring on the dead Ithocles, calls for the song she had ordered for the occasion, and then, pat, dies of a broken heart. Whether this is good or bad, theatrical or genuinely moving, can hardly be an-swered as matters stand. Regarded in the light of the masque-like features of the play, accentuated, incidentally, by the songs appro-priately interspersed throughout, the artifices of her conduct are hardly out of place, and hence not necessarily too "theatrical," since that is a term wholly relative in its application. But in the light of the exacting psychological and moral excursions in the play, these scenes may seem to trifle somewhat. The point can be illus-trated again by comparing the death of Callantha with that of Orgilus, condemned for the murder of Ithocles. He asks to be his own executioner, announces himself an expert in blood-letting, gives instructions for binding his arms at the right point, and, while some of the witnesses are shaken at the sight, alludes to his symp-toms. These two do not live and breathe in the same way. There seems to be no single point of reference from which the whole play may be approached. And something of the same sort may be said of the language. To what has already been noticed on this score the following illustration may be added from a speech of Bassanes during Penthea's madness:

> Let the sun first
> Be wrapped up in an everlasting darkness,
> Before the light of nature, chiefly formed
> For the whole world's delight, feel an eclipse
> So universal. (4.2.81–85)

Considered by itself, it is a forceful image of the terror in contem-

plating the loss of mind, "the light of nature." Orgilus sneers at the
speech as the ravings of a dotard, and it does seem absurd and forced
both in the general stylistic context of the play and in relation to
previous speeches of Bassanes. It is impossible to know precisely how
to accept it. It sounds like a survival from Ford's dramatic antecedents which has not been adjusted to the needs of the moment or
the play. There are still many echoes of the old thunder in his plays,
but for the most part they are like distant reverberations after the
storm has passed.

In his essay on Ford, T. S. Eliot likens him to Beaumont and
Fletcher in the respect that, compared with Shakespeare, "They
speak another and cruder language. In their poetry there is no
symbolic value; theirs is good poetry and good drama, but it is
poetry and drama of the surface." [42] The severest part of this judgment is in associating Ford with Beaumont and Fletcher. In their
handling of diction, Beaumont and Fletcher represent a radical
break with the other important writers of tragedy. Ford's thinness
and crudity do not arise from the same causes. Ford was neither an
unworthy nor an unwise inheritor of the Elizabethan tradition. His
difficulty was that much which he inherited was unsuitable to the
moods and emotions and materials which he tried to work out
dramatically. To some extent he devised instruments and means of
his own, but the weight of the past was so great that he was unable
to get sufficiently clear of it to arrive at a wholly original organization of his art which would render mutually compatible the means
which he had devised and the ends to which they were appropriate.
In one important respect he was still like the men who preceded
him: he had the same interest in the figurative use of language, and
the same desire to employ verse and the language of poetry not
merely as a convenient or ornate instrument of dialogue but as an
essential part of a serious dramatic art.

Ford's was, in any case, a serious attempt to adapt the traditions of Elizabethan tragedy to original ends. It was, as has been
said, the last such attempt. The fate of this tradition can be seen in
Shirley's best-known tragedy, *The Cardinal* (1641), written just before the closing of the theatres by Parliament placed an abrupt end
to all normal dramatic activity. *The Cardinal* is a technically competent piece of work. Shirley could have taught Webster, whose
plays this tragedy recalls, a number of useful lessons in smooth and

plausible play-building. The dialogue is well handled and there are even vivid and striking figures of speech, effectively, if economically, used. But there is nothing new, nothing memorable. It is what any clever, trained dramatist might have done with small effort and a good knowledge of the standard successes of the immediate past. Above all, the vividness of the language is a clever trick, and establishment of fine and close relations which exist in the other plays between the imagery and the other features of the play is now a lost art. This is clearly the end. There is no telling how much longer such synthetic pieces would have continued to be written had the Puritans not taken a hand in the matter themselves, but nothing but a violent shift in direction could have restored vitality to tragedy.

A glance at Shirley's other plays will show what is taking place. The original work in drama was not any longer in tragedy but in such plays as *The Lady of Pleasure*. This, like some of Massinger's comedies, is a serious work. Comedy appears in satirically conceived types, and in a few grotesque and ludicrous situations and episodes, but the main concern of the play is the almost disastrous absorption of Sir Thomas Bornwell and his wife in the costly and dissolute social whirl of fashionable London from which they are saved, just before financial and personal ruin overtakes them, by their timely return to good judgment and a proper sense of values. In this, as in several other of his plays, Shirley is interested in the personal relations of his characters to an important social problem of his times, and accordingly his depiction of this society is meticulous and detailed so that the problem can be grasped in all its importance and contemporary relevance. The play is in verse, but clearly verse remains as a survival of a tradition, for the diction, the idiom, the rhythms are those of everyday speech; no other treatment would have been suited to the exacting verisimilitude of the rest of the play. Had not the closing of the theatres checked normal development in the drama, it is not unlikely that realistic social drama would have come into full flower some two centuries before it came into being as a new and vitalizing force in the theatre during the closing years of the nineteenth century. As it is, this line of development survived, if at all, in the brilliant comedies of wit and manners of the Restoration. Tragedy found its way back through the new idiom of the heroic play.

CHAPTER III

TRAGEDY AND THE HEROIC PLAY

"There is no bays to be expected in their walks," wrote Dryden of the Elizabethan dramatists. No dramatist of the Restoration had a clearer notion than he of the impossibility of doing again what they had done so completely. Dryden became a leading exponent of the new form of serious drama, known as the heroic play, and was the most able expositor of its aims and defender of its possibilities. Nevertheless, the trace of regret noticeable in the line quoted above from the *Essay of Dramatic Poesy* appears elsewhere. In the preface of *Don Sebastian* Dryden complains that though love and honor, "the mistaken topics of tragedy," are quite worn out, he is "still condemned to work in these exhausted mines." And in the prologue to the last of his rhymed heroic plays, *Aureng-Zebe*, he writes:

> What verse can do, he has performed in this,
> Which he presumes the most correct of his;
> But spite of all his pride, a secret shame
> Invades his breast at Shakespeare's sacred name:
> Awed when he hears his god-like Romans rage,
> He, in a just despair, would quit the stage.

The shift which occurred in 1677 when Dryden and Nathaniel Lee turned from rhymed heroic plays to blank verse tragedy is a sign not so much of a vitalizing corrective to an error in artistic judgment, as of a general feeling that the mines were being exhausted, and with rather disappointing rapidity. The whole phenomenon is indicative of a brave and consistent attempt, which was only partly successful, to continue serious drama in a form that would give the dramatist a new impetus and provide exploration in new ways.[1]

I

At the outset, the new type of heroic drama was adopted with considerable enthusiasm. It was, in one sense, a continuation of an

Elizabethan style represented in the work of Beaumont and Fletcher, whose plays, on the testimony of Dryden, were the most popular among those of the older dramatists when the theatres reopened on the accession of Charles II. It was also—Dryden's protests to the contrary notwithstanding—derived in some measure from the polished and much admired work of French dramatists, notably Corneille. There were those critics and apologists, moreover, who saw in the rhymed heroic play which quickly established itself as the characteristic serious drama of the times, an improvement over previous drama, not only for the currently fashionable reasons that it was more "regular" and in conformity with rule than that of the Elizabethans, but because it had increased the potentialities of serious plays even above those of antiquity. Principally, the additional feature was that the passions proper to tragedy, which had formerly been those of pity and terror, were now increased by the attention given to "admiration." Thus, Saint-Evremond, a writer who enjoyed a reputation in England, wrote in his *De la tragédie ancienne et moderne* (1672):

Avec les bons examples que nous donnons au public, sur le théâtre; avec ces agréables sentiments d'amour et d'admiration, discrètement ajoutés à une crainte et à une pitié rectifiées, on arrivera chez nous à la perfection que désire Horace:—*omne tulit punctum qui miscuit utile dulci*—ce qui ne pouvait jamais être, selon les règles de l'ancienne tragédie.

Setting aside the question of whether many of the writers who used these terms understood properly what Aristotle had meant by pity and fear, there existed a general impression that the serious drama of the later seventeenth century had added a new element to the form, an element which gave it a kinship with the epic. The theoreticians—and the dramatists in general felt apologetic when they did not follow them—may have been arbitrary in their definition of the tragic hero and the kind of plots proper to serious plays, but they all agreed that such plays should be elevated and lofty in character; and, though there was much discussion concerning the particular kind of verse desirable, there was also general agreement that the language must be appropriately "heightened." Dryden remarks in his *Essay of Heroic Plays*, "It is very clear to all who understand poetry, that serious plays ought not to imitate conversation too nearly." If the plays which this age produced have been found by posterity to possess a false grandeur and a tinsel magnificence, it is not for want of much thought and honest effort on the part of its practitioners, nor for their failure to appreciate the nature and the difficulty of their task.

The heroic play written in rhymed couplets became the characteristic form of serious drama for nearly two decades after the reopening of the theatres in 1660. Following its initial vogue, unhappy endings increased in popularity over happy endings, and blank verse generally replaced the heroic couplet. But the essential characteristics of heroic drama had taken deep root, and drama until the middle years of the eighteenth century shows traces of the essential features of the type. The answer, then, to the problem of what happened to serious drama in the years following the Restoration is to be sought in the heroic play itself, a form for which modern taste entertains at best an amused tolerance. The problem of coming to a real understanding of these plays, however, is complicated by more than our lack of taste for them. Criticism has repeatedly called attention to the consistency with which dramatists of the period restricted themselves through a slavish following of such arbitrary critical principles as the unities and decorum, the inference being that, as a result, these writers forsook the opportunity for achieving the amplitude and grandeur of Shakespearean drama. It may very well be that such a writer as Dryden, forcing himself to compose within unwelcome mechanical restrictions, failed to give his natural bent the scope which it demanded. But it is wrong to contend from this that observation of the unities is in itself a mark of narrowness in serious drama. Greek tragedies usually conform to these limits, and, however different they may be from Shakespearean tragedy, they lack neither magnitude nor richness and depth of language. It was a critical error to insist that the unities are an indispensable requirement of all good plays, but in a mechanical way, the unities incorporate the truth that drama demands concentration, and they must not in themselves be held responsible for the failures of Restoration and eighteenth-century dramatists.

The searching out of the essential character of the heroic play is complicated by the comments of the dramatists themselves on their own works. They take it for granted that perfection in the ordering of the "design" is a primary desideratum of dramatic excellence, and one gathers that whatever else they failed to do, they could not be held delinquent with reference to the first principle of Aristotle's *Poetics*, that plot is the soul of a tragedy. They did, as a matter of fact, achieve a certain tidiness in the relation of their scenes and a neat solution of the difficulties in which they placed their main character, but an examination of the plays themselves leads to the conviction that in the last analysis the action was a contrivance of secondary interest with them. The action is always managed in such a way as to produce the maximum number of dilemmas for the hero, so that each episode produces a crisis which the dramatist treats so as to display the expression of intense states of passion, or of sharp clashes in point of view between two opposing characters, or of the weighing of conflicting possibilities of choice, or of the persuasion of one character by another. The rival claims of love and duty were the most popular basis for the construction of plots, though minor conflicts of a different sort appear, and on this scheme it was possible to devise plots which generated scenes illustrative of every conceivable variation of the essential oppositon.[2]

The extraordinary amount of discussion about "the rules" by the critics of the age has effectively obscured how much theoretical support this particular feature of the heroic play and its progeny really received. An illustration occurs in Dryden's *Essay of Dramatic Poesy*. Since this work deliberately aims to display the variety of contemporary opinions on fundamental dramatic questions, a point of agreement among all the speakers is of peculiar interest. When Lisideius, therefore, says in defending the French practice of single plots, that it has "gained more liberty for verse" and given French dramatists leisure "to represent the passions (which we have acknowledged to be the poet's work)," the parenthesis takes on distinct importance for being casually assumed to be incontrovertible and for remaining uncontradicted. Lisideius' speech seems to glance at a distinction made shortly before by Eugenius when, commenting on the kinds of "concernments of lovers" which may be expressed at large, and on the expectation of the audience in this matter "who watch the movements of their [the characters'] minds, as much as the changes of their fortunes," he finally adds: "For the imaging of the first is properly the work of a poet; the latter he borrows from the historian." This antithesis clearly sets the plot in a secondary position and places the painting of the passions and sentiments as the primary function of the poet. Examples could be multiplied. From this point of view, the plot can be regarded as a contrivance—however meticulously controlled and circumscribed by rules—for enabling the poet to exercise his proper function in the delineation of thought and passion as aspects of character. In practice, so far as the heroic play went, the plot was merely a device which produced the condition for emotional and dialectical displays.

The behavior of Almanzor in *The Conquest of Granada* will illustrate the types of situations used in the heroic play and the kinds of probabilities which were determinant in bringing about the characteristic effects which have been described. On his first appearance, he takes the part of the Abencerrages in a factional quarrel, because they appear to be the weaker side. He fights for Boabdelin, king of Granada, against the Spaniards because he is a guest of the city. He turns against Boabdelin because he was forbidden to free a noble Spanish prisoner in order to have the pleasure of capturing him again the next day, and he makes Abdalla king. He then sees Almahide, Boabdelin's mistress, and at once falls in love with her. Because Abdalla refuses to grant him Almahide over the claims of another supporter of the revolt, he goes back to Boabdelin and dethrones the usurper whom he has just set on the throne. He then turns against Boabdelin, who will not give up Almahide. In each case there is a question of superior claims on his elaborate code of conduct which motivate the decision. There are numerous similar questions of conduct which involve other characters, but it is perhaps unfair to consider this play further since it is a particularly extravagant example. *Aureng-Zebe*, the last of Dryden's rhymed heroic plays, is generally recognized as a more temperate and polished performance of this kind and will better serve as a test case.

There is no substitute for reading *Aureng-Zebe* to appreciate the complex interrelation of opposing wills, trying dilemmas and desperate passions. The old emperor has four sons, three of whom are in arms against him; only one, Aureng-Zebe, is faithful. As the play opens, Morat, the son of the emperor's present wife, Nourmahal, is preparing to besiege the city, while Aureng-Zebe is just returning from having successfully defeated the other two brothers. Aureng-Zebe gets but a cool reception for his pains, for it transpires that the old emperor loves Indamora, a captive queen and the love of

Aureng-Zebe. Thus for the hero the essential conflict is one of duty to his father and devotion to his love. He cannot take the easy solution of using force to bring his father's revolting passion to an end since that would be to violate his honor both as a son and as a loyal subject. Yet he can never consent to abandon Indamora, death being the only alternative he will consider to life without her. To this primary conflict are added others. The emperor, to get Aureng-Zebe out of the way, betrays the city to Morat, and Aureng-Zebe would have died quickly but for new developments. Nourmahal falls in love with him, and puts off the moment of his death in order to win his love. His resolute stand against her powers of persuasion nearly proves his undoing, but Morat interferes. He has himself fallen a prey to Indamora's charms, cast off his wife Melesinda and consented to a short reprieve in order to improve his chances with Indamora. The possibilities of combination at this juncture are considerable, though the hero seems at a stalemate. Morat precipitates matters by occupying the citadel he had promised to leave to the emperor, and his treachery at last gives Aureng-Zebe a chance to fight him. Before this, he could have fought Morat only by taking advantage of public grievances and by putting himself at the head of an army, a project which could not fail considering his prowess in arms, but he would thus be fighting his father, and this would have been dishonorable. But Nourmahal has in the meantime also taken steps against Morat, apparently to preserve Aureng-Zebe. When she hears Aureng-Zebe is dead, she decides to find some consolation in vengeance by killing Indamora. But Morat fights his way through, mortally wounded, just in time to save Indamora. Shortly before this, he had been convinced of the wrongness of his acts and the error of his philosophy of action by Indamora's reasoning—force of argument never produced greater marvels than in heroic drama—and so he dies a nobler man than he had lived. Nothing is left now but to have Aureng-Zebe enter triumphant, for the report of his death had been false. But the play cannot end without a scene of passion and reconciliation. Once before he had suspected the integrity of Indamora's love, when she secured a reprieve for him from Morat, and now he has been convinced all over again, for he enters just as Morat dies on Indamora's lap. So delicate is the calculus of love and honor that, even after he is convinced Indamora did not love the dying Morat, he can still object:

> Your gratitude for his defense was shown;
> It proved you valued life when I was gone.   (5.5.15–16)*

It is the emperor who finally brings in the misjudged Indamora for the final reunion, just after Nourmahal expires from poison. There are a number of elements which this brief summary does not take into account; for instance, the unfortunate Arimant who also loves Indamora and is tortured by the choice of acting as her willing servant and thus furthering Aureng-Zebe's cause, or of being deprived the sight of her. There is the unhappy Melesinda who gives demonstration of true love to the last. But this brief analysis should suffice to indicate the episodes charactersitic of the play.

Every complication in the play is attended by its proper emotional display or by a dialectical presentation of the issues involved. And the dilemmas are made always clear and explicit. Thus the emperor says, after dismissing Aureng-Zebe from their first interview:

> Yet to detain him makes my love appear;
> I hate his presence and his absence fear.   (1.342–43)

And Aureng-Zebe sums up his problem at the end of the first act:

> I to a son's and lover's praise aspire,
> And must fulfil the parts which both require.   (1.465–66)

When the emperor realizes that Morat is going to demand more than he wishes to give, the same balancing of issues occurs:

> Morat's design a doubtful meaning bears:
> In Aureng-Zebe true loyalty appears.
> He for my safety, does his own despise;
> Still, with his wrongs, I find his duty rise.
> I feel my virtue struggling in my soul,
> But stronger passion does its power control.   (3.268–73)

These samplings are typical enough so that multiplication of instances is unnecessary. The oppositions which they imply are often made the basis of extended debates, in which the issues are analyzed largely in intellectual terms. These are particularly effective when the disputants represent opposing philosophies of conduct. The following is part of the dialogue between Morat and Indamora, during which she succeeds in "converting" Morat, though not in convincing him to abandon his love for her:

*Line references are to the edition of *Aureng-Zebe* in David Stevens' *Types of English Drama, 1660-1780* (Boston, 1923).

> *Morat.*   Birthright's a vulgar road to kingly sway;
> 'Tis every dull-got elder brother's way.
> Dropped from above, he lights into a throne,
> Grows of a piece with that he sits upon;
> Heav'n's choice—a low, inglorious, rightful drone.
> But who by force a sceptre does obtain,
> Shows he can govern that which he could gain.
> Right comes of course, whate'er he was before;
> Murder and usurpation are no more.
> *Indamora.*   By your own laws you such dominion make,
> As every stronger power has right to take:
> And parricide will so deform your name,
> That dispossessing you will give a claim.
> Who next usurps, will a just prince appear,
> So much your ruin will his reign endear.
> *Morat.*   I without guilt would mount the royal seat,
> But yet 'tis necessary to be great.
> *Indamora.*   All greatness is in virtue understood;
> 'Tis only necessary to be good . . . . (5.66-84)

At times the debate involves a choice in which the character must
decide between rival claims on his particular code of conduct. In
extreme cases, when no one is available to act as an opposite or a
second to the debate, the argument must go on in soliloquy. Thus
Aureng-Zebe, when Indamora leaves after being unable to convince him of her innocence in the last scene of the play:

> Go! Though thou leav'st me tortured on the rack,
> 'Twixt shame and pride, I cannot call thee back.
> —She's guiltless, and I should submit—but oh!
> When she exacts it, can I stoop so low?
> —Yes, for she's guiltless—but she's haughty too.
> Great souls long struggle ere they own a crime.
> She's gone—and leaves me no repenting time.
> I'll call her now—sure, if she loves, she'll stay!
> Linger, at least, or not go far away.
>   (Looks to the door, and returns)
> Forever lost! and I repent too late.
> My foolish pride would set my whole estate,
> Till, at one throw, I lost all back to Fate. (5.564-75)

The possibilities for unexpected turns in the action are realized
in some calculated incidents of surprise. The most strikingly presented of these is the revelation of Morat's love for Indamora. She
and Melesinda have just been pleading for clemency from him,
when he dismisses his wife to speak to Indamora alone:

> *Morat.* . . . Queen, that you may not fruitless tears employ,
> I bring you news to fill your heart with joy.
> Your lover, king of all the east shall reign;
> For Aureng-Zebe tomorrow shall be slain.
> *Indamora.*   The hopes you raised y'ave blasted with a breath:
> With triumphs you began, but end with death.
> Did you not say my lover should be king?
> *Morat.*   I, in Morat, the best of lovers bring.
> For one, forsaken both of earth and heav'n
> Your kinder stars a nobler choice have given . . . .   (3.497–506)

Because, moreover, the plot is so contrived as to place the characters
frequently in situations that require each time the extreme manifestation of their virtues and powers, there is frequent occasion for
passionate outbursts, laments, and other expressions of aroused
feelings.[3] The form they take may be illustrated by Aureng-Zebe's
contrition after he has falsely accused Indamora in his jealousy:

> Behold these dying eyes, see their submissive awe—
> These tears, which fear of death could never draw!
> Hear you that sigh? from my heaved heart it passed,
> And said, "If you forgive not, 'tis my last."
> Love mounts and rolls about my stormy mind
> Like fire that's borne by a tempestuous wind.
> Oh, I could stifle you, with eager haste!
> Devour your kisses with my hungry taste!
> Rush on you—eat you!—wander o'er each part,
> Raving with pleasure, snatch you to my heart!
> Then hold you off, and gaze!—then, with new rage,
> Invade you till my conscious limbs presage
> Torrents of joy, which all their banks o'erflow!
> So lost, so blest, as I but then could know.   (4.529–542)

When these characteristic features of Dryden's play are multiplied
to their full plenitude it is possible to appreciate the new orientation
of dramatic material which was accomplished in the heroic play.
For although individual differences distinguished the works of the
several writers, and although various writers like Lee and Orrery
reveal the stamp of their own peculiar talents in their plays, the essential features of these plays remain alike in all. Invariably they are
marked by the same kinds of conflicts, with love and honor pre-
dominating, and with the same straining after multiplicity of episode, each one revealing the variant possibilities which could arise
from a given situation, so that action is overwhelmed in intricacy

and becomes in the end merely an instrument for generating episodes capable of such treatment. This was, in a sort, an achievement in the interest of variety, a quality often insisted upon by the critics. It may be that the straining after diversity was stimulated by the desire to introduce into the drama something of the copiousness of the epic, with which, as we have seen, the heroic play was thought to have some affinities. [4] But this does not explain the particular sort of diversity which appears in these plays. In the comparison of French and English drama which Neander makes in Dryden's *Essay of Dramatic Poesy* he contrasts the barrenness of the French plots with "the variety and copiousness of the English," but he is here talking principally about the older English dramatists. The kind of variety which the Elizabethans indulged in was, in part, denied Dryden and his contemporaries because of the restraints which they accepted in the unities and the principle of decorum. They did the most, however, with a different kind of variety, which consisted in producing as great a multiplicity of arrangements of the pieces as was compatible with some degree of consistency in their movements and the need for arriving at a particular final arrangement of them.

To bring this about on so elaborate a scale, it became necessary to resort to contrivances of various sorts. Dryden justified the happy ending as opposed to the tragic by insisting, in the Preface to *The Spanish Friar*, that it costs a writer more pains to find a probable means to recover all than to resort to the convenience of a dagger and poison cup that are always available in any dramatic extremity. Dryden may be excused for so gross a caricature of the catastrophe attendant on a fine tragedy on the grounds that he was engaged in a piece of special pleading. He knew as well as anyone that there was also available the last minute entrance of the hero in time to avert calamity, the sudden and inexplicable change of heart, the startling and unexpected coincidence to save all and bring about not only a happy ending but all those dozens of striking oppositions and reversals that are the chief feature of heroic tragedy. And this suggests another property of the action in these plays, since the inclusion of one important accident or coincidence in a serious play is generally sufficient to raise the question of whether artistic necessity and probability have not been weakened thereby. In these plays several of them seemed not to have caused any concern, so useful did they prove in providing the sort of interest which the dramatists sought.

Under the circumstances it would be irrelevant to complain that the characters lack "psychological subtlety" or "depth" or any of the other qualities which critics have found these plays deficient in. To say that these characters are not very good is to neglect the fact that they are very good for their purpose; that, in fact, for the kind of work in which they exist they could not be other than they are. At the same time, the very extravagance of the heroes of these plays encourages conjecture. What bred these fantastic creatures? The Elizabethans had created their heroes in the light of the impressive ideals which their age had thought possible in the warrior, the courtier, and the king. But these ideals had vanished during the intervening years and left no parallels. Neither in the court of Charles II nor in the increaisngly important center of national culture, the "city" (what did the cultivated urbanity insinuated by *The Spectator* have to offer the tragic poet?), was there anything comparable to the possibilities which had encouraged the impressive idealizations of the moralists and the courtesy-book writers of an earlier age. The dramatist in search of the stuff out of which to mould the heroic figure ended up with an extravagant artifice, a fantastic puppet, who, though useless for the purpose of serious tragedy, could at least serve as an ornate pawn in a sequence of surprising moves and as a mouthpiece for elevated sentiments and strong passions.

II

Whatever may be objected against these dramatists, it must be conceded that they apparently understood the artistic conditions within which they were operating, and this applies to the kind of verse they used and their handling of the diction. The couplet rhyme has often impressed English critics since the Restoration as an unfortunate medium for serious drama, and the question was debated with some vigor even during the best days of the heroic play, particularly in the controversy between Dryden and Sir Robert Howard. [5] The verdict must go to Dryden in this, to the extent, at least, that he repeatedly insisted on the inadmissibility of the argument from strict verisimilitude. That argument, he saw, would condemn rhyme as being unreasonable in dialogue, but it would also apply to blank verse, and it would lead to an admission merely of the prose of daily discourse as alone proper to dialogue. This, Dryden reasoned, was absurd; and in his *Defence of an Essay of Dramatic Poesy* he cleared himself from the position of having pursued anything "so ridiculous as to dispute whether prose or verse be nearest to ordinary conversation," and pointed out that the important question was whether verse "be natural or not in plays." The raising of the argument on these grounds, however, indicates that the unquestioned acceptance of verse as a requisite of serious drama had been considerably weakened, since the argument from verisimilitude leads logically where Dryden insisted it would: to the elimination of verse. For the moment, however, this critical conflict seems to have enhanced the claims of rhyme, for if serious drama is regarded as a form traditionally associated with artifice of speech, rhyme makes unmistakable the existence of artifice by exaggerating the distinction between the medium of the play and ordinary discourse. This distinction is clearly implied in Dryden's resolution of the issue. Moreover, the problem for the dramatist was made more acute by the circumstance that during the later years of the seventeenth century, language in all forms of discourse was undergoing a development in the direction of clarity and perspicuity. The two factors taken together may be regarded as an encouragement of rhyme since they forced a sharpening of the distinction between dramatic art and reality.

It is a little artificial, however, to fix merely on the fact of rhyme as the mark of distinction between the verse of Elizabethan drama and heroic drama, although it is the most obvious and one which has important consequences. For the heroic couplet as written during the restoration and the early eighteenth century had certain peculiarities, whether used in dramatic or non-dramatic verse, which it is important to bear in mind in considering the language of these plays. Partly through the force of philosophical influences, which had an indirect effect on style, partly through a desire to avoid the obscurities and technical ingenuities which resulted from the tradition of seventeenth-century metaphysical poetry, the poets of the Restoration aimed toward clarity and perspicuity as one of the merits of diction. In this they sacrificed to some extent figures which secure their effect by diffusing the literal clarity of phrase and increasing the suggestions which it is capable of sustaining. They made the most, however, of such devices as antitheses, in which opposing notions are cleanly and often unexpectedly opposed, and of paradox, in which, by a sudden turn, elements normally anti-thetical are put into close relations. They became expert in various means for producing irony, and mastered the trick of placing a subordinate phrase where it would suddenly reverse the emphasis placed on the preceding part of the statement. And such devices were assisted by the construction of the distich, which became the basic metrical unit, and by the rhyme which in most instances brought a grammatical unit to its completion. Though these devices were exploited most methodically and prodigally by Pope, they are essential features of most Restoration verse, and any of Dryden's poems, for instance, will provide examples.

> No written laws can be so plain, so pure,
> But wit may gloss and malice may obscure.

> Did wisely from expensive sins refrain
> And never broke the Sabbath but for gain.

These are from Dryden. The following neat example of paradox is from Rochester:

> Merely for safety, after fame they thirst;
> For all men would be cowards if they durst.

These devices do not exhaust the stock in trade of the Restoration poets, but they played an important part in rendering a clear and precise diction fit for poetic purposes. At least, for *their* poetic purposes. Much of the verse written during the eighteenth century is of a persuasive order—satire, whose end is to convince that certain things are undesirable and at the same time to insinuate a more acceptable norm of judgment or conduct; or philosophic poetry, like the religious poems of Dryden, in which verse is a final resource to make the material attractive and ingratiating, and to bring out the brilliance of the logic. There is little question that for these particular purposes the heroic couplet proved an admirable instrument.

A little reflection will show why, with a degree of modification necessary for dramatic uses, it was also beautifully adapted to heroic drama.[6] The numerous debates lent themselves perfectly to the brilliant rhetorical possibilities of the couplet.[7] A comparison of the following lines from *The Hind and the Panther* with the passages of debate quoted above from *Aureng-Zebe* will show, moreover, how close the affinity can be between the philosophic poem and the dramatic debate:

> "Friend," said the Hind, "you quit your former ground,
> Where all your faith you did on Scripture found:
> Now, 'tis tradition joined to Holy Writ;
> But thus your memory betrays your wit."
> "No," said the Panther, "for in that I view
> When your tradition's forged, and when 'tis true.
> I set them by the rule, and as they square
> Or deviate from undoubted doctrine there,
> This oral fiction, that old faith declare."
> (*Hind.*) "The Council steered, it seems, a different course;
> They tried the Scripture by tradition's force;
> But you tradition by the Scripture try;
> Pursued by sects, from this to that you fly,
> Nor dare on one foundation to rely.
> The World is then deposed, and in this view
> You rule the Scripture, not the Scripture you."

Since in every heroic play a principal feature is the several scenes in which, under the impetus of a clash of arguments, a character is swayed from one conviction or loyalty to another, or remains inflexible in the face of the forensic assault, verse which lent itself so admirably to the services of philosophic analysis and persuasion would be equally effective in this drama.[8] It might, in fact, be reasonably maintained that the dramatists were tempted to multiply scenes for which they had so admirable an instrument. It became, indeed, difficult to avoid the forensic touch wherever a decision was contemplated. The following excerpt from Sir Charles Sedley's *Antony and Cleopatra*, showing the lovers faced with the need of separation, is not in the strictest sense a characteristic verbal conflict, but the language and style, with the general aphorisms, the neat antitheses, has the effect of cancelling the quality of personal emotion from the speeches and lending them the air of a debate on general issues:

> *Cleopatra.*   But then your love, in absence, will it last?
> Men think of joys to come and slight the past.
> *Antony.*   My heart shall like those trees the east does show
> Where blossoms and ripe fruits hang on one bough,
> With new desires, soft hopes, at once be pressed;

> And all those riper joys, love gives the blest.
> Courage and love shall sway each in their turn,
> I'll fight to conquer, conquer to return.
> Seeming ambitious of the public view,
> I'll make my private end and dearer, you.
> This storm once past, in peace and love we'll reign,
> Like the immortal gods, the giants slain.
> *Cleopatra.*   Moments to absent lovers tedious grow;
> 'Tis not how time, but how the mind does go
> And once Antonius would have thought so too.

Since, also, these plays abound in sharp dilemmas and clear cut oppositions, the capacity of this verse for paradox and antithesis was turned to good use. The quandary of the hero in Orrery's *Mustapha* affords a good example:

> Fortune did never in one day design
> For any heart, four torments great as mine;
> I to my friend and brother rival am;
> She who did kindle, would put out my flame;
> I from my father's anger must remove,
> And that does banish me from her I love.

A similar instance might be cited from Sedley's *Antony and Cleopatra* Macenas, assigned to see that Octavia does not kill herself, falls in love with her, and consents for her sake to do his best to preserve Antony. This puts him in a difficult position with Octavia:

> Whom, whilst he lives I never can enjoy,
> And if he dies she will herself destroy.
> I am undone; obey or disobey!
> I needs must perish, but may choose my way.

And, to return to Dryden once more, Indamora's reflections when she is threatened with death have a similar character:

> I wish to die, yet dare not death endure;
> Detest the medicine, yet desire the cure.   (5.207–08)

Moreover, the same qualities of balance, opposition, antithesis, and the like, which are so sharply revealed in the verse unit of the couplet, are to be found in the structure and development of longer units—in a scene, for example, or in an individual speech. Such passages as are usually cited to illustrate the special merits of the style of these plays have these characteristics, as, for example, the following from *Aureng-Zebe*:

> When I consider life, 'tis all a cheat;

Yet, fooled with hope, men favor the deceit.
Trust on, and think to-morrow will repay.
Tomorrow's falser than the former day—
Lies worse, and, while it says we shall be blest
With some new joys, cuts off what we possessed.
Strange cozenage! None would live past years again,
Yet all hope pleasure in what yet remain!
And, from the dregs of life, think to receive
What the first sprightly running could not give.
I'm tired of waiting for this chemic gold,
Which fools us young and beggars us when old.   (4.33–44)

It is possible to appreciate from these examples that language and a metrical scheme capable of these effects were less well suited to the kind of imagery which gives distinction to Shakespearean tragedy. Yet a careful reading of *Aureng-Zebe*, to return to our type case, reveals a surprising number of striking figures of speech. The concluding lines of the passage just quoted contain two ingenious and attractive metaphors, for example. One might well ask why it is that this feature of the play leaves so little impression on reading, that, in fact, critics should comment on its style and show such little concern for a feature which on examination appears very prominent. The fault does not lie with the critics. However numerous and however powerful the images might be, there were other features of these plays, as we have seen, which overshadowed them. In addition, the peculiar genius of couplet verse as written during the Restoration and eighteenth century was of the sort to conceal the more colorful and diffuse effects of the images which were used; it cancelled them, as it were, by its pointedness, its clarity of balance and antithesis, its attention to paradox, its ringing finality of rhyme. These features draw the attention away, by the superior and continued emphasis which they receive, from the broad associations, the depth, possessed by any figure isolated from its framework and setting. He would be a sharp or learned critic who on reading the isolated line,

Where slumber abbots, purple as their wines,

would declare that it came from *The Dunciad*. What effects their medium was capable of, these poets realized with much brilliance; by their very competence, however, they were restricted from making full use of effects of another sort.

The force of the images is affected not only by the mechanics of the verse but also by the mechanics of the figures of speech. Essentially, a figure of speech is an analogy; a proportion is set up between what is literally intended and a symbol which expresses some aspect of the intention more forcefully or with the possibility of larger inferences than a direct statement will permit. The relationship between the two parts of a figure may be explicit, as in a simile, in which a sign such as "like," or the "as when" of the more elaborate epic type of simile, separates the two parts and calls attention to the device as a formal equivalence of unlike elements. In a metaphor, on the other hand, the identity is implicit. There are degrees of explicitness, however, between these two in the construction of the image. Consider, for example, the following from *Aureng-Zebe*:

> Beauty a monarch is,
> Which kingly power magnificently proves
> By crowds of slaves, and peopled empire loves. (2.73-75)

This is a metaphor, yet the opening line, except for the omission of the word "like," is a statement of the analogy on the basis of which the succeeding lines are constructed. There are other means for giving explicitness to an image; for instance, a general statement might precede or follow the figure as an indication of its precise applicability, as in the following from a speech of Morat:

> Fondness is still th' effect of new delight,
> And marriage but the pleasure of a day;
> The metal's base, the gilding worn away. (4.247-49)

These are indications merely of the devices by means of which the mechanics of a figure may be suggested. In the heroic plays, barring certain figurative words such as flame and fire which are common equivalents for love, the greatest number of the images are, generally speaking, built on an explicit pattern including even occasional "as when" similes of the epic style. Now, although the concentrated metaphor is as artful as any of the devices of poetry, such explicit figures as the simile, by virtue of the fact that they are so constructed as to call attention to their nature as ornaments of discourse, convey more immediately an impression of artifice, particularly when they appear in any considerable number. Especially is this the case in a play, where the dialogue often takes on an air of self-consciousness as a result.

It is necessary, however, to look beyond the mechanics of the verse and the imagery; for the nature of these plays being what it is, the role of the images, their relation to the other parts of the play, is different from that in Elizabethan, particularly Shakespearean, tragedy. An examination of the images in *Aureng-Zebe* will illustrate how this is the case.

The greatest number of the figures of speech is concerned in some manner with love, a condition appropriate enough in the light of the fact that the principal characters are involved in nearly every possible combination of love relations which the plot will allow. Many of these are based on ideas of fire. Aureng-Zebe tells Indamora:

> Love mounts and rolls about my stormy mind
> Like fire that's borne by a tempestuous wind. (4.533–34)

Such images suggest youthful and impetuous love, but they are not distinctive in the sense that they are peculiar to Aureng-Zebe in such a way as to distinguish him from anyone else or to imply any particular course in his role as a lover. The reason is that others use much the same imagery in much the same way. Thus the emperor tells Indamora:

> No, 'tis resistance that inflames desire,
> Sharpens the darts of love, and blows his fire. (2.164–65)

And to the jealous Nourmahal:

> Have patience!—my first flames can ne'er decay. (2.220)

When Nourmahal expresses contempt for the emperor's aged pretensions to love, her scorn shows through the same images:

> You importune it with a false desire,
> Which sparkles out, and makes no solid fire. (2.298–99)

A more ingenious variant is Arimant's reply to Indamora's refusal to consider him except as a friend:

> Think you my aged veins so faintly beat,
> They rise no higher than to friendship's heat?
> So weak your charms that, like a winter's night
> Twinkling with stars, they freeze me while they light? (2.86–89)

These various instances may differ in the particular thought they may wish to express, but they have in common a uniform figurative use of the notion of fire. Flame and fire, that is, have been accepted as appropriate elevating devices for love, and have practically become synonymous with the word. A glance at any of the other Restoration heroic plays will supply confirmation of this view, since in all of them flames and fire are regularly used to denote an overpowering love; and, in fact, when the word love appears unadorned, it almost strikes one as more strange in the context of these speeches than the usual figurative synonyms. The images appear to serve as means for securing the heightening of language which was thought proper for serious plays, and are not in general organized to establish essential discriminations among characters or to function as indices to the unfolding of the action. Occasionally, the conventional image appears in novel form, as in the speech of Melesinda as she leaves to sacrifice herself on the funeral pyre of her husband:

> My love was such, it needed no return,
> But could, though he supplied no fuel, burn;
> Rich in itself, like elemental fire,
> Whose pureness does no aliment require.   (5.627–30)

But in its essential structure, this image does not differ from the rest: fire is equivalent to love, and there are various kinds of love as there are of fire. Only rarely does an image break the conventional mould: Morat's dying speech, though still very much within the standard formula, carries the identity of love and fire a step further:

> I leave you not, for my expanded mind
> Grows up to Heav'n, while it to you is joined.
> Not quitting, but enlarged! A blazing fire,
> Fed from the brand.   (5.433–36)

The image here acquires an ambiguity which extends its meaning beyond that of intense physical passion.

Among the other images pertaining to love, those which concern themselves with the wounds, darts, and other of the current military symbols have a role in the play similar in many respects to those of fire. There are the wounds, for example, of the lover. Thus Arimant:

> O Indamora, hide these fatal eyes!
> Too deep they wound whom they too soon surprise!   (2.31–32)

> So weak I am, I with a frown am slain;
> You need have used but half so much disdain.   (2.69–70)

There are references to the darts of love, and an elaborate military image in Nourmahal's justification of her evil passion:

> I fought it to the last—and love has won
> A bloody conquest, which destruction brought,
> And ruined all the country where he fought.   (3.373–75)

Distinction might be made among these, but they bear too convincingly the stamp of current poetical counters to be very impressive. More elaborate are the love images derived from navigation. In these the lover is a mariner and his condition is likened to some exigency of the mariner's life. The emperor thus describes his failure to interest Indamora:

> Unmoved she stood, and deaf to all my prayers
> As seas and winds to sinking mariners.
> But seas grow calm, and winds are reconciled:
> Her tyrant beauty never grows more mild.   (1.266–69)

In the same imagery, Aureng-Zebe announces the arrival of Indamora:

> But here she comes!
> In the calm harbor of whose gentle breast,
> My tempest-beaten soul may safely rest.   (1.354–56)

The figure is used to express Arimant's disappointment that he is to be no more than a friend to Indamora:

> So mariners mistake the promised coast,
> And with full sails on the blind rocks are lost.   (2.84–85)

By another rearrangement, it is made to express Indamora's desire to be free of Aureng-Zebe's jealous rages:

> Now, with full sails, into the port I move,
> And safely can unlade my breast of love—
> Quiet and calm. Why should I then go back
> To tempt the second hazard of a wrack?   (4.525–28)

The possibilities for variation are greater in this image, and the examples cited show more individual character than those, say, from fire, but the manipulation of the images is the same: the lover is the mariner, his state is likened to some situation in navigation.

These images reveal nothing distinctive about the character, and cannot be clearly related to anything outside of the immediate moment in which they are uttered, when they are often appropriate and decorative. One exceptional use of the voyaging image occurs in a speech of Morat's following his reformation by Indamora:

> Renown and fame in vain I courted long,
> And still pursued them, though directed wrong.
> In hazard and in toils I heard they lay;
> Sailed farther than the coast, but missed my way.
> Now you have given me virtue for my guide,

And with true honor ballasted my pride,
Unjust dominion I no more pursue;
I quit all other claims but those to you.   (5.112–19)

This may be paralleled with the somewhat unusual use made of the
fire image in Morat's case. It illustrates, moreover, another interesting feature of the imagery. It is one of the few instances in which
honor is given symbolical treatment in the play; and this is remarkable when it is realized that the dilemmas caused by the clash of love
and honor are the *primum mobile* of the play. What we should expect
if the imagery were used in some organic relation to the play would
be a figurative treatment of honor along with love in a way which
would bring out the essential opposition and final resolution of these
elements. As it happens, only late in the play, and only in the case of
Morat, is there any such development in the imagery.

There are a number of other recurrent images which suggest general properties, such as the wine images which sometimes stand for
the flush of youthful joy and power, or, as dregs, for the decay of
age. The most striking of such recurrent images are those referring
to the sun, which suggest royalty and manly vigor, and to flowers,
which suggest female delicacy and beauty. The sun image occurs
early in the play as a symbol of the emperor's declining powers:

He promised in his east a glorious race;
Now, sunk from his meridian, sets apace.
But as the sun when he from noon declines,
And, with abated heat, less fiercely shines,
Seems to grow milder as he goes away,
Pleasing himself with the remains of day;
So he who, in his youth, for glory strove,
Would recompense his age with ease and love.   (1.80–87)

Among other casual and conventional uses, such as the emperor's
reference to Arimant as "warmed by my beams," Morat's assertion
of his ambition appears impressive:

Methinks, all pleasure is in greatness found.
Kings, like heav'n's eye, should spread their beams around,
Pleased to be seen while glory's race they run.
Rest is not for the chariot of the sun.   (3.166–69)

The flower images are used by the emperor in an insincere speech of
flattery to Nourmahal, and in her contemptuous reply to him allud-
ing to the beauty which may not "be gathered by such withered
hands." They are alluded to in the occasional use of the word

"bloom." Most strikingly they are used with reference to Mele-sinda. Indamora speaks of Melesinda's sorrow after being rejected by Morat:

> Your head reclined (as hiding grief from view),
> Droops, like a rose, surcharged with morning dew.   (3.74–75)

In her reply, Melesinda combines the sun and flower images:

> Can flowers but droop in absence of the sun,
> Which waked their sweets?—and mine, alas! is gone.   (3.76–77)

This comes close to accomplishing the kind of fusion of determinant images which is a feature of the best Elizabethan writing.

Several other images have a similar kind of distinction. Among the numerous animal images there are a few which stand out not only because of their ingenuity separately considered, but because they are illuminatingly attached to some important feature of the play. One of these occurs during an altercation between Aureng-Zebe and Morat:

> *Aureng-Zebe.*   When thou wert formed, Heav'n did a man begin;
> But the brute soul, by chance, was shuffled in.
> In woods and wilds thy monarchy maintain,
> Where valiant beasts, by force and rapine, reign.
> In life's next scene, if transmigration be,
> Some bear, or lion, is reserved for thee.
> *Morat.*   Take heed thou com'st not in that lion's way!
> I prophesy, thou wilt thy soul convey
> Into a lamb, and be again my prey.   (3.304–12)

As a figurative implication relating to character, this is among the better passages in the play. Two others have a similar distinction. The emperor, conscious of his guilt but unable to resist his passion, says:

> O Aureng-Zebe! thy virtues shine too bright,
> They flash too fierce: I, like a bird of night,
> Shut my dull eyes, and sicken at the sight.   (1.322–24)

In close proximity to this comes Aureng-Zebe's speech to Indamora, the object of the Emperor's affection:

> Care shuns thy walks; as at the cheerful light,
> The groaning ghosts and birds obscene take flight.   (1.359–60)

The number of figures of speech of this order, however, is limited. Of the great number of miscellaneous images which the play contains, the greatest number cannot be brought into any such intimate relation with the parts of the play. Many individual images occur which may be good in the sense that a clear and explicable relation exists between the symbol and the idea implied by it, but which appear less serviceable when judged by the closeness of their relation to the play as a whole. Some of these might be called out of key. Consider the following instance. Morat is killed trying to reach Indamora, and it later transpires that Melesinda has urged him to come. The speech in which she reports this concludes with the following lines:

> I called him hither—'twas my fatal breath,
> And I the screech-owl that proclaimed his death.   (5.364–65)

It is true that a screech owl's call was traditionally considered a por-tent of death, and in this sense it is ingenious to refer to Melesinda as a screech owl—but only if the figure is judged in isolation, for it does violence to all the other suggestions which have been attached to her and is inappropriate to a character who is very nearly an allegorical symbol of eternal and unselfish love. Similarly with the following speech in which Aureng-Zebe, just returned victorious from the wars, replies to Indamora's suggestion that he give her up:

> Bid the laborious hind,
> Whose hardened hands did long in tillage toil,
> Neglect the promised harvest of the soil.   (1.367–69)

The reluctance to give up the fruits of toil, both sides of the simile have in common; but "laborious hind" introduces a totally false note in connection with a character whom we are to consider as impetuous, daring, and created for valor and love.

Other images are misleading in a somewhat different way through the same circumstance of being good for a particular moment. In their first interview, Indamora tells Aureng-Zebe that, though she still loves him, it will be disastrous for both if she responds to his affections. Aureng-Zebe's reply contains the following lines:

> In Death's dark bowers our bridals we will keep
> And his cold hand
> Shall draw the curtain when we go to sleep.   (1.427–29)

This speech may be considered a forceful expression of the hero's state of mind. In order to appreciate its failure to establish any larger relations, we may recall how, frequently, in the tragedies of Shakespeare a figure of speech occurring early in the play and quite appropriate to its immediate context, anticipates in a brilliant way the resolution of the entire action. This one obviously does not do so; in fact, it is a false scent. It is perhaps one of the difficulties of an action which is to end happily after many hairbreadth approaches to disaster that it will require the utmost in the art of figurative language to express the dark moments of the play and yet anticipate the fortunate outcome. Perhaps it would be improper to press the point in the case of the speech just quoted were it not in a sense symptomatic; there is little, for instance, to be said in extenuation of the following speech by Aureng-Zebe near the end of the play when he inadvertently witnesses Indamora's concern over the death of Morat:

> I begin
> To stagger, but I'll prop myself within.
> The specious tower no ruin shall disclose,
> Till down at once the mighty fabric goes. (5.425–28)

It is so clearly obvious at this point that the mighty fabric will do no such thing that the speech merely leaves one with a sense of false and inflated elevation. We come in time, as it were, to have no faith in these figures; we do not trust them. And we lose also the cumulative force acquired in a progressive development of key images, which at times gives to some climaxing figure of speech in Shakespeare a terrifying grandeur.

III

By 1677 the day of the heroic play in rhymed couplets was over. In that year Nathaniel Lee wrote *The Rival Queens* in blank verse, and Dryden also abandoned the couplet in *All for Love* which appeared a few months later. Thomas Otway followed suit in 1679 with *The History and Fall of Caius Marius*. The leading dramatists had thus set the new style and the rest perforce followed. The mere change from rhyme need not of itself imply, however, a radical alteration in the drama. But couplet verse during the Restoration had involved, as we have seen, so characteristic a use of language that abandonment of it might well have entailed considerable alteration or shift of emphasis in the handling of the diction. In addition, these changes might have encouraged elimination or subordination of the kinds of episodes which lent themselves to the effects of couplet verse. The use of blank verse did in fact bring these tragedies more nearly in line with the Elizabethan tradition, and historians of the drama have noted various ways in which the influence of Shakespeare may be discerned in these blank verse plays. In the case of Dryden's first blank verse tragedy, we have not only the choice of subject, but his own statement that he had gone directly to Shakespeare for his model: "I hope I may affirm, and without vanity, that, by imitating him, I have excelled myself throughout the play." That dramatists continued for some time to work under the shadow of the Elizabethans may be seen also in the choice by Nicholas Rowe during the early years of the eighteenth century of such subjects as Tamerlane, Jane Shore, and Lady Jane Grey for his tragedies, and in the several attempts by various dramatists to rewrite certain Shakespearean tragedies, of which the most notable example is Nahum Tate's adaptation of *King Lear*. Moreover, an occasional relaxing appears from the strict application of such rules as that of decorum, as in the supplementary comic plot in Thomas Southerne's *Oroonoko* and the few harsh comic scenes in Otway's *Venice Preserved* dealing with Antonio's love for Aquilina.

An enumeration of these changes, however, gives an exaggerated view of what actually happened. These dramatists did not restore tragedy to the pattern of Shakespeare or even that of his contemporaries and immediate successors; and it involves probably an incorrect estimate of their aim to make a point of the fact that they did not do so. They returned to a great dramatic tradition which they loved and respected, in order to discover new sources of inspiration through which they might modify a contemporary tradition they rightly judged to be limited in its possibilities and exhausted. But the effects of heroic drama never quite left them; in some form its impress can be seen in nearly all serious drama to the end of the eighteenth century. The continuation of the style can be most simply realized in the preservation of certain types of episodes and the use of certain kinds of motives which seem inseparably a part of the heroic play. In *The Rival Queens*, commonly regarded as Lee's best play, there are everywhere indications of the tradition from which it sprang. By way of illustration may be noticed the scene in which Statira and Roxana, the rivals for Alexander's affections, argue things out with elegant violence. More particularly, there is the scene in which Statira, who has sworn never to see

Alexander again, has what she believes is to be a last interview with him. The scene places the two in a series of nice dilemmas as persuasion moves them from one resolution and emotion to another, beginning with Statira in cold disdain and finally ending, after a last debate, with Statira in Alexander's arms. There are also the characteristic exhibits of passion:

> Ha! could you wish me to forget Statira!
> The star, which brightens Alexander's life,
> His guide by day, and goddess of his nights!
> I feel her now, she beats in every pulse,
> Throbs at my heart, and circles with my blood.

These lines, though they are in blank verse, have the quality, which Bonamy Dobrée called attention to in the verse in Addison's *Cato*, of having all the effects of heroic couplet verse except for that of rhyme.

Lee's play might be expected, as the first to make the break from couplets, to possess more clearly the marks of heroic drama. Survivals still remain, however, in so apparently novel an instance as *Oroonoko* (1696), a play dealing with a Noble Savage in a West Indian setting of slave merchants, colonist planters, and hostile Indians, with a supplementary plot done in the spirit of Restoration comedy and quite separate from the story of the princely slave. The story which Oroonoko tells of the violent love of his father for his beautiful Imoinda and the separation which he forced on the two lovers when he discovered that he could not enjoy her is reminiscent of the numerous "unnatural" passions which appear in heroic drama. The meeting of the two through the merest chance as slaves may have more in common with the Jacobean dramatic romances than with the accidents and unexpected turns of heroic drama, but the point is a delicate one. Particularly striking, however, is how much the noble savage has in common with such heroes as Aureng-Zebe—his irresistible prowess as a warrior and his readiness to put himself at the head of a force and triumph single-handed; his undying affection (he lacks jealousy, however); the utter nobility of his sentiments, and the readiness with which he weighs rival claims on his code of conduct. This last appears in several crucial incidents which involve his decision after an argument or a weighing within himself of the attendant possibilities. One is not surprised to hear him say:

> To Honour bound! and yet a slave to Love!
> I am distracted by their rival Powers,
> And both will be obeyed.

Nor to have him state his cruel dilemma, in the face of the need to kill the fair Imoinda, with a neat antithesis characteristic of the heroes of another day:

> I cannot, as I would, dispose of thee:
> And, as I ought, I dare not. Oh Imoinda!

There survives in the revision of *King Lear* made by Nahum Tate a curious example of how far the heroic play had altered the current conception of the tragic pattern and how completely out of the question was any thoroughgoing abandonment of its characteristic features. It would be trivial to raise the question of Tate's version of *Lear* only to strike once more a straw man already much battered by the slings and arrows of outraged criticism. That Tate should have rewritten this great tragedy so as to permit a happy ending, with Lear once more king and Cordelia married to Edgar, has provoked offense and amusement for more than a century, not to mention horror at the taste of an age that applauded such a desecration. Too general a conclusion cannot be deduced from what Tate chose to do to *Lear* since, after all, Tate was at best a second-rate poet, but the fact remains that his version replaced Shakespeare's for many years. Dr. Johnson was inclined to support the preference for Tate's preservation of "the final triumph of persecuted virtue." "In the present case," he wrote, "the public has decided. Cordelia, from the time of Tate, has always retired with victory and felicity." And even A. C. Bradley is not inclined to heap too much scorn on Tate's attempt to mitigate the awful terror of Shakespeare's conclusion. However, to debate the question of the unhappy ending, and raise once more argument about poetic justice to which Johnson appealed in justification of his preference would be largely to mislead the present search for those features of Restoration drama which left a permanent impression on succeeding serious plays.

Tate approached Shakespeare's play in a wholly respectful attitude, and actually preserved much of the original—too much, one is inclined to think, for the good of his own revision. He was particularly impressed by the language. He wrote in the Dedication:

The images and languages are so odd and surprising, and yet so agreeable and proper, that whilst we grant that none but Shakespeare could have formed such conceptions; yet we are satisfied that they were the only things in the world that ought to be said on those occasions.

Yet he could not have fully understood the play, for while he professed to admire the diction, he discovered no coherent design, and it is particularly revealing that the stratagem he hit upon to give the play unity was a love plot:

I found the whole . . . . a heap of jewels, unstrung, and unpolished; yet so dazzling in their disorder, that I soon perceived I had seized a treasure. 'Twas my good fortune to light on one expedient to rectify what was wanting in the regularity and probability of the tale, which was to run through the whole, as love betwixt Edgar and Cordelia, that never changed word with each other in the original. This renders Cordelia's indifference and her father's passion in the first scene, probable. It likewise gives countenance to Edgar's disguise, making that a generous design that was before a poor shift to save his life. The distress of the story is evidently heightened by it; and it particularly gave occasion for a new scene or two, of more success (perhaps) than merit.

That he should have been pleased with himself in having "heightened" the "distress of the story" may at first sight seem inexplicable in the light of the already appalling amount of distress which Shakespeare's play possesses and the fact that Tate's version mitigates it by altering the conclusion. But a glance at what Tate added makes it clear that he was not thinking of the same sort of distress. It was the distress of lovers caught in unhappy crises, of virtue exposed to injuries that asked for pity, of noble heroism restrained from exercise of its strength—in short, the kinds of distress which the plots of Restoration heroic drama had made the familiar stock in trade of the serious dramatist.

The love plot is introduced early in the play. Edgar is already out of favor and in love with Cordelia, and Cordelia is destined by her father for Burgundy, from whose "loathed embraces" she wishes to be free. To these complications there is added Cordelia's mistrust of Edgar:

> This baseness of th'ignoble Burgundy,
> Draws just suspicion on the race of men;
> His love was int'rest, so may Edgar's be,
> And he, but with more compliment, dissemble;
> If so, I shall oblige him by denying:
> But if his love be fixed, such constant flame
> As warms our breasts, if such I find his passion,

> My heart as grateful to his trust shall be,
> And cold Cordelia prove as kind as he.

How, under the circumstances, Edgar's love could conceivably be interest is not explained; it is sufficient that Cordelia's suspicion adds one additional complication, though little enough is made of the possibilities involved. A further twist is introduced when Edmund shows signs of being attracted to Cordelia as he watches her pleading with Gloucester to aid in the restoration of Lear to the throne:

> O charming sorrow! How her tears adorn her
> Like dew on flowers; but she is virtuous,
> And I must quench this hopeless fire i' th' kindling.

And a little further on:

> I'll gaze no more,—and yet my eyes are charmed.

Nothing comes of this, and in fact Edmund sends out ruffians to seize Cordelia when she wanders out to the heath to give aid to her father; but the temptation to introduce the possibility of such an infatuation born of many similar developments in heroic drama was too great to resist, and Tate could not refrain from the minor titillation which this hint might afford. The love intrigue involving Edmund, Goneril, and Regan, essential to the original play, fitted in too well to the accepted schemes of heroic drama not be to improved on and enhanced. It is accented a little more deliberately, and treated more fully. The dialogue which occurs when Cornwall asks Edmund to leave so that he may not witness the punishment to be inflicted on Gloucester illustrates the kind of treatment which this aspect of the plot receives:

> *Regan.*   The grotto, sir, within the lower grove
> Has privacy to suit a mourner's thought.
> *Bastard.*   And there I may expect a comforter,
> Ha, madam?
> *Regan.*   What may happen, sir, I know not,
> But 'twas a friend's advice.

The next scene is announced as "A Grotto. Edmund and Regan amourously seated, listening to musick." The rival loves of Regan and Goneril are pointed up in a characteristic word-battle between them which occurs just after Edmund is mortally wounded. The dying Edmund puts an end to it:

> No more, my Queens, of this untimely strife,
> You both deserved my love, and both possessed it.
> Come, soldiers, bear me in, and let
> Your royal presence grace my last minutes;
> Now, Edgar, thy proud conquest I forgive.
> Who would not choose, like me, to yield his breath
> T' have Rival Queens contend for him in death?

His closing words sum up this intrigue in a way which recalls all the neat splendors of the heroic plot. The balanced equality of the two rival queens is preserved by altering the original so that both die from the effects of poison which each had secretly administered to the other at a banquet.

The changes which Tate made "to rectify what was wanting in the regularity and probability of the tale" have the effect of making Edgar the hero, and in consequence it became necessary to preserve as far as possible the qualities which were required for a noble lover and intrepid man of action. Considering the conditions which the plot of the original imposed on Tate, some ingenuity was called for to save Edgar, horrible as Mad Tom, for these purposes. It becomes, therefore, not sufficient that Edgar choose this disguise merely as "a poor shift to save his life"; it has to be made "a generous design." Edgar disguises himself in order to stay near Cordelia and protect her if necessary. His chance comes when he attacks the rogues sent by Edmund after Cordelia in the heath and disposes of them single-handed. Edgar reveals himself to her, after which the horrible object that had spurred Lear's mind to raise bizarrely some of the most searching questions about man, engages with Cordelia in a mutual declaration of love, at the conclusion of which she takes him in her arms. He decides to build a fire to keep her warm and dry:

> Then fierce and wakeful as th' Hesperian Dragon,
> I'll watch beside thee to protect thy sleep;
> Meanwhile the stars shall dart their kindest beams,
> And angels visit my Cordelia's dreams.

The real crime of Tate was not primarily that he gave *Lear* a happy ending, or that he joined Edgar and Cordelia as lovers, or that he made the changes in plot necessary to bring these things about. It was his failure to appreciate the horrible artistic impropriety of preserving many of Shakespeare's lines, the language and images of which he professed to admire and the propriety of

which he was so astonished by, alongside his own writing, in which
the images and language are ordered by quite different means to
quite different ends from those in the original. Consider, for example, the following dialogue introduced early in the play:

> *Edgar.*   Cordelia, royal fair, turn yet once more,
> And e'er successful Burgundy receive
> The treasure of thy beauties from the King,
> E'er happy Burgundy for ever fold thee,
> Cast back one pitying look on wretched Edgar.
> *Cordelia.*   Alas! what would the wretched Edgar with
> The more unfortunate Cordelia?
> Who in obedience to a father's will
> Flies from her Edgar's arms to Burgundy's?

Simply on the score of diction and imagery these speeches have no
place beside the speeches of these characters which are preserved
from Shakespeare. The outbursts of passion on the part of Lear in
the original have some remote affinity with the taste for exhibitions
of passion which are common in heroic drama, but Tate plays
curiously with them:

> Blow winds, and burst your cheeks, rage louder yet,
> Fantastic lightning singe, singe my white head;
> Spout cataracts, and hurricanoes fall
> Till you have drowned the towns and palaces
> Of proud ingrateful man.

Thus, "you sulphurous and thought-executing fires" of the original
becomes "fantastic lightnings"; the words "palaces" and "proud"
are gratuitous; and the lines,

> And thou, all-shaking thunder,
> Strike flat the thick rotundity o' the world!
> Crack nature's moulds, all germens spill at once,

are omitted. In short, most of the figures which relate this passage
to the large scheme of images which runs through the play, to the
immediate turmoil of Lear's mind, and to the thought which lies at
the heart of it are either weakened or destroyed, and all we have is
the expression of violence of feeling and rage. The same thing occurs
as much in what Tate added as in what he omitted. Gloucester says:

> Fly, Edmund, seek him out, wind me into him,
> That I may bite the traitor's heart, and fold
> His bleeding entrails on my vengeful arm.

At the other extreme is the debilitating effect of certain substitutions which he seems to have made in the interest of intensifying the point, but which mar brilliantly the fierce economy of some of Shakespeare's great moments. Thus, for Edmund's

> Yet Edmund was beloved!

He substituted,

> Who would not chuse, like me, to yield his breath
> T' have Rival Queens contend for him in death.

And, most dismal change of all, he preferred to take out Cordelia's sobbing reply to Lear's submission,

> No cause, no cause,

and put in its place,

> O pity, sir, a bleeding heart, and cease
> This killing language.

With which inspired piece of unintended criticism of his efforts we might leave him.

Tate's version of *Lear* is a useful test case because the disharmony of the two traditions—or it is perhaps better to say the attempt to incorporate the recognized merits of an older tradition with the established conventions of the new one—appears in undisguised clarity. It seems to bear out the general impression created by other more original specimens that these dramatists failed to grasp the essential nature of Shakespearean tragedy and that, however much modification might conceal the fact, the plots and the language which they used had affinities rather with the dramatic style best exemplified in its pure form in the heroic play. The fusion, as far as these examples go, resulted at best in an unsuccessful and inharmonious hybrid. Clearly, however, such fine clinical specimens as Tate's *Lear* do not satisfactorily establish a general case. It is necessary to consider plays which recommend themselves for some artistic merits. Among the numerous blank verse tragedies of this age, Otway's *Venice Preserved* (1682) has been repeatedly judged as a piece of distinct merits. Otway has the distinction of being mentioned in Coleridge's *Dejection* as one who "framed the tender lay." Even more unanimous has been the opinion concerning Dryden's *All for Love* (1677) which Bonamy Dobrée called "a proud and lovely masterpiece." The case for Restoration blank verse tragedy might well rest with these two plays.

IV

The plot of *Venice Preserved* is effectively managed. The play opens with the hero, Jaffeir, begging his father-in-law, Priuli, a senator of Venice, to abandon his violent disapproval of his daughter's marriage and save them from poverty and humiliation. His pleas are in vain. Wrathful and desperate, he is met by his devoted friend Pierre, who informs him that he has been dispossessed and his wife driven out of the house on orders signed by Priuli. Pierre encourages Jaffeir's passion for vengeance, and then confides in him the secret of a conspiracy about to go into action, which will destroy all the feeble and proud senators, seize Venice, and restore liberty, dignity, and justice once more. Jaffeir joins and gives up his wife Belvidera as a pledge; but he cannot resist seeing her, and only with difficulty restrains himself from telling the reason for his strange conduct. When she informs him, however, that Renault, an elderly conspirator assigned to protect her, attempted to force himself upon her during the night, he tells her all, and, shattered by Belvidera's pleas to spare her father and the citizenry, he reveals the plot to the senators after receiving a promise of general amnesty. Pierre scorns and humiliates Jaffeir when he discovers his faithlessness. The conspirators ask for death rather than degrading mercy, and the senate reverses its promise to spare them and dooms them to cruel death. Belvidera, urged on by Jaffeir, succeeds in getting forgiveness and sympathy from her father, but Priuli is too late in offering a plea for the condemned men. Jaffeir, though still in love with his wife, realizes the impossibility of further marital happiness when the affection of his wife was the cause of his own violation of an oath and the death of his only friend. He bids farewell to Belvidera and goes to see Pierre for the last time. At Pierre's request, he stabs his friend to save him from the indignity of death on the rack, and then kills himself. Belvidera becomes insane and dies.

Literary critics have pointed out that this plot focuses once more on the familiar love and honor conflict. And, of course, since such a conflict occurs, there are also the inevitable scenes of contention and persuasion which precede the final choice. There is, however, a difference. There is but one crucial conflict, and the whole play leads to it, and the catastrophe derives from it. There is significant difference, too, in the scenes of persuasion and debate, if indeed this word can now be applied to them. These no longer consist of a debate on the issues, of the balancing of intellectually framed positions; they are here in the nature of a direct appeal to intimate feelings, urged in such a way as to make the choice rest with the sentiment which can be appealed to most tellingly. Jaffeir never ceases to be tortured by his betrayal of Pierre, though he is helpless before the pleading of Belvidera. And there are other differences. Jaffeir is not a creature of impossible loyalties, of clear-cut convictions, of heroic and irresistible valor. In the handling of the action, moreover, there is no resorting to such devices as unexpected intrusions, reverses, overhearings, and the like to further and increase complications. The plot development is not conducive to the kind of variety aimed at in the heroic play through a multiplication of possible rearrangements among the agents in the play. As far as the plot goes, Otway succeeded in effecting not merely a disguise or a reshuffling, but a new orientation of the old materials.

These changes are reflected in the language. The balanced antithesis, the deft paradox, are largely gone. Otway has been criticized, in fact, for being diffuse. At his best, he has ease and freedom of rhythm and phrasing, and a gift for using language figuratively, though figures at times seem too fully or meticulously developed:

> Come, lead me forward now like a tame lamb
> To sacrifice, thus in his fatal garlands,
> Decked fine and pleased, the wanton skips and plays,
>   Trots by the enticing flattering Priestess' side,
>   And much transported with his little pride,
>   Forgets his dear companions of the plain
>   Till by her, bound, he's on the altar lain
>   Yet then too hardly bleats, such pleasure's in the pain.
> (4.91–98)*

Such figures, when they appear, lend the speeches an air of deliberateness which makes them needlessly conspicuous. Many images, however, escape this difficulty, even though, as in the following remarks of Pierre to the priest who wishes to attend him at his execution, they come perilously close:

> You want to lead
> My reason blindfold, like a hampered lion,
> Checked of its nobler vigor then, when baited,

*Line references are to Bonamy Dobrée's edition of *Venice Preserved* in *Five Restoration Tragedies* (World's Classics).

> Down to obedient tameness, make it couch,
> And shew strange tricks which you call signs of Faith.
>
> (5.451–55)

Pierre's language usually has a fine brilliance:

> How lovely the Adriatic whore,
> Drest in her flames, will shine!   (2.330–31)

This image, derived from the annual Venetian ceremony of the marriage with the Adriatic, not only shows his scorn for the state and the ruin which he plans for it, but touches glancingly on his resentment against the aged senator who seduced his mistress with gold.

The speeches of Pierre are, in fact, one of the interesting problems in this play. Nearly every time an arresting figure of speech or expression appears, it turns out to be spoken by Pierre. His language at times has an ironic indirection, suggestive of a hidden sense of wrongs and a determination not to weaken under them. The following scene has something of this flavor:

> *Pierre.*   Sure I have stayed too long:
> The clock has struck, and I may lose my proselyte.
> Speak, who goes there?
> *Jaffeir.*   A dog, that comes to howl
> At yonder moon: What's he that asks that question?
> *Pierre.*   A friend to dogs, for they are honest creatures,
> And ne'er betray their masters: never fawn
> On any they love not: Well met, friend:
> Jaffeir!
> *Jaffeir.*   The same. Oh Pierre! Thou art come in season,
> I was just going to pray.
> *Pierre.*   Ah that's mechanic;
> Priests make a trade on 't, and yet starve by it too:
> No praying, it spoils business, and time's precious.   (2.79–92)

Even where he is explicit, his language is strongly imaginative:

> Die—Damn first—what, be decently interred
> In a church-yard, and mingle thy brave dust
> With stinking rogues that rot in dirty winding sheets,
> Surfeit-slain fools, the common dung o' th' soil.   (1.310–13)

Why it is that the speech of Pierre should possess an imaginative brilliance which is usually lacking in the rest, and why the images seldom fuse into any sort of coordinate relation with the play as a whole, is a question in the answer to which lies the secret of the failure of this play to achieve the kind of distinction which appears in the best Elizabethan examples of verse tragedy.

The critical weakness of this play is that everything else is sub-ordinated to what was known as "painting the passions," a quality for which Otway was much admired in his day. What had been one of the characteristic features of heroic drama, the exhibition of states of emotion, he adopted and developed in this play with an exaggerated consistency and sentimental coloring. Belvidera and Jaffeir dominate the scene. They are faced with distress and ruin; they are devotedly in love with each other. The expression of these feelings puts everything else in the play in a secondary position. Moreover, their sentiments are for the most part expressed not through figurative symbols, but by means of explicit and direct description. The diction is ridden with expressions of pity, misery, and melting love. Sometimes all these appeals are combined:

> Lead me, lead me my virgins!
> To that kind voice. My lord, my love, my refuge!
> Happy my eyes, when they behold thy face:
> My heavy heart will leave its doleful beating
> At sight of thee, and bound with sprightful joys.
> Oh smile, as when our loves were in their spring,
> And clear my fainting soul.   (1.343-49)

It is not necessary, however, to look for these effects in set speeches. They are infused prodigally by means of words and phrases which carry their force into every segment of the play. A meager sampling of representative examples will suffice here:

> Kind, good, and tender, as my arms first found thee.
>
> melting kisses sealed our lips
>
> my eager arms
>
> soft breath of love
>
> these desiring arms
>
> a thousand, thousand dear times
>
> these poor streaming eyes
>
> pity the sad heart that's torn with parting
>
> I play the boy and blubber in thy bosom
>
> Come like a panting turtle to thy breast,
> On thy soft bosom, hovering, bill and play.

It is difficult to illustrate the overwhelming number of such touches, and even more difficult to show how these sentiments are insinuated by the casual adjective and the suggestive verb. It is the case, however, that the diction is largely ordered by such considerations.

This assault on the sensibilities proceeds in other ways. There are paintings of sad vignettes, as in Pierre's description of Belvidera's expulsion from her home:

> Hadst thou but seen, as I did, how at last
> Thy beauteous Belvidera, like a wretch
> That's doomed to banishment, came weeping forth,
> Shining through tears, like April suns in showers
> That labor to o'ercome the cloud that loads 'm,
> Whilst two young virgins, on whose arms she leaned,
> Kindly looked up, and at her grief grew sad,
> As if they catched the sorrows that fell from her:
> Even the lewd rabble that were gathered round
> To see the sight, stood mute when they beheld her;
> Governed their roaring throats and grumbled pity;
> I could have hugged the greazy rogues: they pleased me.
>
> (1.273–84)

Except for the last line, the scene had affected even the diction of Pierre. It is also significant that this is merely an elaborate preparation for the scene in which we actually witness the distressed Belvidera led by two virgins. Similarly, after we see the passionate Jaffeir urging Belvidera to sue for mercy from her father for her friends, we are given an extended and highly colored description of his behavior by Belvidera to her father. The scenes of persuasion, we have already noticed, are not treated in the brilliant forensic style of the heroic play, but are directed at the feelings. In this way, though essential to the action, they contribute further to the emphasis on delineation of emotions. One effect which this has on the style is that the rhetorical question, already a commonplace in Restoration drama, occurs frequently:

> Part! must we part? Oh! am I then forsaken?
> Will my love cast me off? have my misfortunes
> Offended him so highly, that he'll leave me?
> Why drag you from me? whither are you going?
> My dear! my life! my love! (2.429–33)

Occasional outbursts of passion usually sustain the prevailing love sentiments, and with great violence and inflation of feeling:

> O, lead me to some desert wide and wild,

Barren as our misfortunes, where my soul
May have its vent: where I may tell aloud
To the high heavens, and every list'ning planet,
With what a boundless stock my bosom's fraught;
Where I may throw my eager arms about thee,
Give loose to love with kisses, kindling joy,
And let off the fire that's in my heart. (1.376–82)

But there are others of sterner note, such as Jaffeir's speech when he knows his friend is doomed:

Final destruction seize on all the world:
Bend down, ye heavens, and shutting round this earth,
Crush the vile globe into its first confusion;
Scorch it, with elemental flames, to one curst cinder,
And all us little creepers in 't, called men,
Burn, burn to nothing: but let Venice burn
Hotter than all the rest: Here kindle Hell
Ne'er to extinguish, and let souls hereafter
Groan here, in all those pains which mine feels now. (5.251–59)

This suggests in a tumid way the fierce explosions in *Lear*, but here it is less impressive. The elemental imagery in *Lear* is integrally related to the determinant elements which direct the action. Here it is not, and the speech is largely pompous rhetoric. And in addition, the appeal to such grandiose notions suffers because it is surrounded so completely by evidences of the touching and the pathetic.

Concentration on such effects reflects at times on the characters to their disadvantage. For example, Belvidera goes to her father after promising Jaffeir that she will not return until she has succeeded in gaining her father's help to reverse the doom placed on his friends. She has not seen her father since he banished her for marrying Jaffeir. It is obviously a big scene. Belvidera does a masterly job, working on the old man's emotions until he agrees to anything. Early in the interview she succeeds in arousing his sympathy. Then:

Belvidera. Lay me, I beg you, lay me
By the dear ashes of my tender mother.
She would have pitied me, had fate yet spared her.
Priuli. By heaven, my aching heart forbodes much mischief.
Tell me thy story, for I'm still thy father.
Belvidera. No, I'm contented.
Priuli. Speak.
Belvidera. No matter.
Priuli. Tell me. (5.83–91)

This is a very deft business in building up an emotional scene; but since we know that Belvidera came for only one reason, and not to make this sentimental request, we are left with some misgivings about the impressions of sincerity and disingenuousness which we are expected to have of her. In more ways than one, the talent of Belvidera for the pathetic touch helps to spoil the play as it does the conspiracy.[9] Jaffeir does not wholly escape either. Aside from his numerous expressions of tender endearment, such phrases as "these poor arms" and "this poor breast" help to cancel out any heroic stature he might possess. The diction does little to suggest anything about him except indignation and self-pity and abject submission to conjugal joys. And this works to the disadvantage of Pierre since it makes unworthy of him the initial error of considering Jaffeir a fit sort of person for the rigors of a political plot.

Thus the ordering of the language in the interest of passion, instead of producing an impression of strength, rather brings about a weakening all along the play. The plot has all the possibility of swift and progressive movement, but the final effect is one of overloaded feeling, almost of stasis.

Dryden's *All for Love; or, The World Well Lost* is generally acknowledged as his best play, and without much question it is the best tragedy of its age. In the Preface to the play Dryden expresses his dissatisfaction with French tragedy and his enthusiasm for Shakespeare, on whose *Antony and Cleopatra* he modeled this play. The subject was a favorite, as Dryden tells us in his Preface:

The death of Antony and Cleopatra is a subject which has been treated by the greatest wits of our nation, after Shakespeare; and by all so variously, that their example has given me the confidence to try myself in this bow of Ulysses amongst the crowd of suitors; and, withal, to take my own measures, in aiming at the mark. I doubt not but the same motive has prevailed with all of us in this attempt; I mean the excellency of the moral: for the chief persons represented were famous patterns of unlawful love; and their end accordingly was unfortunate.

It may be that Dryden was directed to this play among the rest of Shakespeare's tragedies because of the excellency of the moral, in which case the choice artistically was a lucky one. No other of Shakespeare's plays lent itself so readily to the typical Restoration plot structure or could have submitted to its characteristic schemes and patterns without some fatal distortion. Conflicts of love and

honor, decisions that held empire and joy in the balance, great personages, undying loyalties—all these were present in a story certified
by history and glorified by Shakespeare. Dryden worked out the
plot in such a way as to accentuate those features which lent themselves to the prevailing methods of heroic drama, and it is in this and
not merely in the general tidying up, nor in the imposition of the
unities of time and place onto the expansive scheme of Shakespeare's
play, that the important modifications are to be found.

Dryden's play begins with Antony in utter despair, shut off from
the world in the temple of Isis. Actium is a bitter memory; Caesar
is at the gates of Alexandria. At this juncture Ventidius arrives, interrupts Antony's gloomy meditations, upbraids him for his blind
infatuation, and urges him to go to Syria and take personal charge
of twelve veteran legions which he had marched up from Parthia
and which will give him an advantage with which to defeat Caesar.
Antony's hopes as Emperor and his pride as a soldier triumph, and
he resolves to leave at once without so much as taking the risk of
bidding farewell to Cleopatra. As he is departing with his officers,
Alexas, the queen's eunuch, persuades him by clever stratagem to
see Cleopatra once more. He attempts sternly to justify his departure from her, but she convinces him of her loyalty and love, and
Antony gives up all thoughts of leaving. In the enthusiasm of the
moment, he executes a successful surprise attack with his few local
troops on Caesar's army, and returns triumphant to Cleopatra.
Once more Ventidius intrudes, urging the impossibility of further
military successes and the wisdom of using the momentary advantage to make favorable terms with Caesar. To clinch his argument,
he confronts Antony first with his friend Dollabella from Caesar's
forces, and then with Octavia, Antony's wife and Caesar's sister,
and with their children. The combined appeal of these attacks on
his better nature wins out, and he again abandons Cleopatra. In
desperation, Cleopatra listens to Alexas' advice that she should
arouse Antony's jealousy by working on the susceptibilities of Dollabella, once himself infatuated with her, who has been sent by Antony to give his farewell to the queen. The stratagem proves fatal.
Ventidius had overheard Dollabella talking to himself and weighing
the possibility of stating Antony's case in such a way as to recommend his own love to the queen, and he witnesses Cleopatra's efforts
to arouse Dollabella's interest—efforts which failed because her own

faithfulness would not permit her to go on with a distasteful ruse. Ventidius returns, moreover, with Octavia just in time to misinterpret Dollabella's kissing of Cleopatra's hand. Confronted by Ventidius and Octavia, Antony finally believes after Alexas falsely corroborates their evidence. In his utter despair he offends Octavia, who leaves him for good, and he refuses to believe Cleopatra and Dollabella. He is now completely alone. And the last blow is the news that the Egyptian navy has abandoned him and gone over to Caesar. In his mind Cleopatra is now doubly condemned. To shield her from his anger, the high priest Serapion sends her to her monument, and Alexas is placed to meet Antony and repair the damage done by his stupid machinations. But Alexas can only scheme. To soften Antony he tells him that Cleopatra has taken her own life. The news shatters Antony, and he falls on his sword. Cleopatra, fearing the event when she hears of Alexas' falsehood, comes in time to see Antony dying. Faithful to the end, she too takes her own life.

As the plot is managed, Antony oscillates from one allegiance to another as the two opposing sides win him over by one appeal or another. Granted this basic design, the development is ingenious. Each fluctuation makes more permanent his separation from Cleopatra or more difficult his saving of the empire. Ventidius succeeds by appealing to the emperor and warrior. Cleopatra matches this with a proof of her complete devotion and faithfulness. Ventidius overcomes this with the ties of friendship and family. Devotion being not enough, Cleopatra reluctantly tries jealousy, and this destroys both sides. As a last desperate ruse Alexas uses death, and this succeeds all too well. Each probability inherent in the situation is explored and eliminated. At the end, death is the only scheme left for Alexas to try, but death is also the only way out now for the defeated emperor. Only the treachery of the navy remains an unexplained and unpredictable factor in the scheme of forces which drive Antony first one way and then another. This manipulation of the plot has nevertheless one serious disadvantage in that Antony, presumably the protagonist, becomes the battle ground for contending forces, or rather the prize for which they contend. The strategy on one side is managed by Ventidius, on the other by Alexas. The latter is doubly necessary since, to maintain the equal balance between love and honor, Cleopatra is made unswerving in her devotion, with nothing of the coquette about her, and nothing equivocal about her motives; hence the stratagems by which Antony is enticed cannot originate with her: "'Twas thy design brought all this ruin on us," she tells Alexas shortly before the catastrophe. To permit the conflict to proceed by a series of skirmishes, Antony is made open to the claims of the lover (Cleopatra), of the warrior and emperor (Ventidius), the friend (Dollabella), the husband (Octavia), and the father (his two children). The presentation of the conflicting claims appears with least subtlety in the third act, when Ventidius first shows the folly of further attempts at victory, then produces Dollabella, and finally Octavia and the two children. The high point is reached when Octavia sends the children to the wavering Antony; and as the children obey, all the forces are turned on him:

> *Ventidius.*   Was ever sight so moving! Emperor!
> *Dollabella.*   Friend!
> *Octavia.*   Husband!
> *Both Children.*   Father!
> *Antony.*   I am vanquished . . . . (3.406–10)*

It is as though each one calls out his card as he lays it down, and Antony realizes that he has nothing to beat the combination. No other episode in the play is as coldly deliberate as this, but the method in most of them is the same. And the position of Antony as an almost helpless victim of these operations is intensified by such remarks as Alexas' "He melts; we conquer," or Ventidius' "He moves as I would wish him," or Antony's own "Oh, my distracted soul."

It was perhaps inevitable that Dryden should have introduced jealousy among the possibilities for producing further complications in the play, but it is somewhat unfortunate that he should have used it as the critical issue on which the play turns to its final conclusion; for in order to bring it about he had to resort to a number of dramatic contrivances among which the sudden betrayal of a long friendship by Dollabella is the least questionable. This episode made possible a love-honor conflict of a secondary order, since Dollabella must choose between the rival claims of friendship and love; and the play is thus brought closer to the pattern of heroic drama, though

---

*Line references are to Bonamy Dobrée's edition of *All for Love* in *Five Restoration Tragedies* (World's Classics).

not with too great a loss in concentration since, with this exception, the other important conflicts center entirely in Antony. More important in their effect on the play are the other devices, typical of the heroic play, employed to set the stage for Antony's jealousy. It becomes necessary for Ventidius to overhear Dollabella weighing the claims of friendship and love, thus using the dramatic convention of the soliloquy as a talking out loud. It requires Ventidius to leave off his spying on the interview between Dollabella and Cleopatra one moment too soon, and to return to it with Octavia, also one moment too soon—a double coincidence of misunderstandings. To rest the critical turn of affairs on such trifling dramatic tricks tends to weaken an action that in so many other more probable ways predicates a tragic conclusion. Such things might pass in the general atmosphere of the heroic play, but they seem less acceptable here. For the important thing about *All for Love* is that it involves such radical alterations in the characterization and particularly in the language that the total result is quite different from such works as *Aureng-Zebe* or even such blank verse drama as *The Rival Queens*.

The blank verse of *All for Love* is not the heroic couplet gone flabby for want of rhyme, nor is it an uncontrolled instrument for rant and gaudy rhetoric. It is remarkable, in view of the similarities in plot with the heroic play, that there should be so few traces of those brisk paradoxes and tight antitheses which seemed so inseparable a complement of the situation in the language. Occasionally in such a phrase as Ventidius' "You speak a hero, and you move a god," traces of the couplet style appear, and something of the antithetical pointing up of a dilemma occasionally survives in a speech like that of Dollabella when he considers betraying his friend:

> O friendship! friendship!
> Ill canst thou answer this; and reason, worse:
> Unfaithful in th' attempt; hopeless to win;
> And, if I win, undone: mere madness all.   (4.62–65)

More often such phrasing has the effect of Octavia's departing words—

> . . . for I despair
> To have you whole, and scorn to take you half.   (4.491–92)

which add an accent of finality to a beautifully modulated speech.

It is no problem to illustrate the admirable virtues of this verse, for almost any speech will do. The following is Cleopatra's reply to Octavia's accusation that all of Antony's woes can be traced to Cleopatra:

> Yet she who loves him best is Cleopatra.
> If you have suffered, I have suffered more.
> You bear the specious title of a wife,
> To gild your cause, and draw the pitying world
> To favor it: the world contemns poor me;
> For I have lost my honour, lost my fame,
> And stained the glory of my royal house,
> And all to bear the branded name of mistress.
> There wants but life, and that too I would lose
> For him I love.   (3.522–31)

To appreciate further the transformation in style which this play represents, it should be noted that this speech occurs in the only interview between Octavia and Cleopatra, one of those contentions between rival interests which customarily called forth the fullest display of rhetorical brilliance in the heroic play. This verse has the clarity which training in the couplet might have produced, and the discipline; but it has ease and suppleness as well. It is a fine medium capable of absorbing the strain that any dramatic necessity can place upon it.

This style moves with such ease that its effects frequently come off with an almost deceptive simplicity. Consider, for example, the following speech of Antony:

>   How I loved
> Witness ye days and nights, and all your hours,
> That danced away with down upon your feet,
> As all your business were to count my passion.
> One day passed by, and nothing saw but love;
> Another came, and still 'twas only love:
> The suns were wearied out with looking on,
> And I untired with loving.
> I saw you every day, and all the day;
> And every day was still but as the first:
> So eager was I still to see you more.   (2.327–37)

The opening, rather studied, image conveys an impression of trivial gaiety, but the whole passage gives an effect quite other than triviality. The imagery of the passage is derived from units of time— hours, days, nights, diurnal suns—all symbols of earthly flux and

change reinforced by "one," "another," "wearied"; yet the statement in the passage is of permanence and constancy, so that the
speech has an air of paradox about it. And in addition the phrase
"suns were wearied out," the repetitions of "day" convey also the
notions of majesty and immutability of cosmic cycles. This is by no
means one of the more arresting passages in the play, but it serves to
illustrate how the style combines something of the ease of unstudied
discourse with all the studied complexity of poetry. Some of the
Elizabethan freedom and daring in handling of images has been
sacrificed, but the intimate relationship between the possibilities of
the language and the demands of the form has been preserved.

The development of the action proceeds, as we have seen, by a
series of oscillations on the part of Antony, between his love for
Cleopatra and the claims of empire, family, and friendship represented by his Roman loyalties. This opposition of forces working on
Antony is represented in the diction by a scheme of images which
represent the appeal to Antony of these contrasting attractions. The
two appear mutually antagonistic throughout. Thus Ventidius tells
Alexas:

> Go tell thy queen,
> Ventidius is arrived, to end her charms.
> Let your Egyptian timbrels play alone;
> Nor mix effeminate sounds with Roman trumpets.   (1.209–12)

This simple opposition of timbrels and trumpets with its suggestion
of decadent pleasure on the one hand and vigorous strength on the
other, contains the germ of an elaborate development in the diction.
Traces of it appear widely diffused. When Serapion expresses his
fears concerning the outcome of a Roman Victory—

> . . . our plenteous harvests
> Must then redeem the scarceness of their soil.   (1.71–72)

—he is talking about the political consequences of such a victory,
but the diction also balances suggestions of richness and fecundity
against those of sternness and privation. In a more direct way, the
opposition is implied in the images which are directed toward
Ventidius and Alexas, the two leading machinators in the struggle
for Antony. Alexas, giving the devil his due, says of Ventidius:

> Firm to his prince; but, as a friend, not slave.
> He ne'r was of his pleasures; but presides
> O'er all his cooler hours and morning counsels.   (1.111–13)

Ventidius, on the other hand, to whom Alexas is Cleopatra's "darling mischief, her chief engine," and "Antony's other fate," says to him:

> You are of Cleopatra's private counsel,
> Of her bed-counsel, her lascivious hours;
> Are conscious of each nightly change she makes,
> And watch her, as Chaldeans do the moon,
> Can tell what signs she passes through, what day.   (4.378–82)

Words like cool and morning define Ventidius; Alexas is associated with images of night and passion. The particular bias which a given image in this scheme receives is dependent in large part on the position of Antony at any given point in the play. Ventidius finds him under Cleopatra's spell "unbent, unsinewed, made a woman's toy" (1.193); after his resolve to fight, Antony tells his general,

> Thou shalt behold me once again in iron,   (1.497)

and Charmian reports to Cleopatra that she found him

> Incompassed round, I think, with iron statues.   (2.57)

On the other side, centering in Cleopatra and all she represents in contrast to Rome, the images are more elaborately and frequently developed, sometimes implying wantonness and malevolence when spoken by Ventidius or Octavia, or even by Antony when he determines to break from his toils, and at times implying pleasure, gaiety and allurement, as when spoken, for instance, by Antony in his resolve to lose the world for his love. The speeches of Ventidius contain many impressions of the first sort. He tells Alexas:

> Does the mute sacrifice upbraid the priest?
> He knows him not his executioner:
> O, she has decked his ruin with her love,
> Led him in golden bands to gaudy slaughter,
> And made perdition pleasing.   (1.184–88)

All the allurements of Cleopatra and the East are deadly in his eyes; he warns Antony when Alexas brings gifts from her for his departure:

> Now, my best Lord, in honor's name, I ask you,
> For manhood's sake, and for your own dear safety,
> Touch not these poisoned gifts,
> Infected by the sender, touch 'em not,
> Miriads of bluest plagues lie underneath 'em,
> And more than aconite has dipt the silk.   (2.232–37)

In his description of Cleopatra's flight from Actium, intended to call attention to the cowardice which he repeatedly assigns to the east, he nevertheless touches also on the colorful grandeur:

> What haste she made to hoist her purple sails!
> And to appear magnificent in flight.   (2.363–64)

Most of his speeches glance somehow on the combination of color and evil with which he associates Cleopatra and what Octavia calls her "black endearments." Only in Antony's speeches do the attractions of Cleopatra appear in imagery freed from suggestions of taint. Even during his moment of resolve to leave with Ventidius, he can recall his pleasure in terms cleared of reproach:

> How I loved
> Witness ye days and nights, and all your hours,
> That danced away with down upon your feet.   (2.327–29)

Though a few lines further he can state the consequences of his passion in words that convey impression of ruin and decay:

> While within your arms I lay,
> The world fell mouldring from my hands each hour,
> And left me scarce a grasp (I thank your love for't).   (2.344–46)

During the period when he has returned to Cleopatra and before Ventidius' second triumph over him, Antony's speeches create an unsullied impression of her appeal. He speaks of his love in images that symbolize once more the paradox of her ever-fresh charms:

> There's no satiety of love in thee;
> Enjoyed, thou still art new; perpetual spring
> Is in thy arms; the ripened fruit but falls,
> And blossoms rise to fill its empty place;
> And I grow rich by giving.   (3.25–29)

He gives full expression to the high-colored splendor of her attractions in his speech to Dollabella reminding him of their first view of Cleopatra:

> Her galley down the silver Cydnos rowed,
> The tackling silk, the streamers waved with gold,
> The gentle winds were lodged in purple sails;
> Her nymphs, like Nereids, round her couch, were placed;
> Where she another sea-born Venus lay . . . .
> She lay, and leant her cheek upon her hand,
> And cast a look so languishingly sweet,
> As if secure of all beholders' hearts,

> Neglecting she could take 'em. Boys, like Cupids,
> Stood fanning, with their painted wings, the winds
> That played about her face; but if she smiled,
> A darting glory seemed to blaze abroad,
> That men's desiring eyes were never wearied,
> But hung upon the object. To soft flutes
> The silver oars kept time; and while they played
> The hearing gave new pleasure to the sight,
> And both to thought. 'Twas heav'n or somewhat more;
> For she so charmed all hearts, that gazing crowds
> Stood panting on the shore, and wanted breath
> To give their welcome voice. (3.181–202)

This is the most elaborate presentation of those images which color the impression of Cleopatra's claims in the contending forces which divide the allegiance of Antony. With it must be compared Ventidius' speech to Octavia, in which, though confessing her charms, he dyes his speech with suggestions of her malevolence:

> Her eyes have power beyond Thessalian charms
> To draw the moon from heav'n; for eloquence,
> The sea-green sirens taught her voice their flattery;
> And, while she speaks, night steals upon the day,
> Unmarked of those that hear. Then she's so charming,
> Age buds at sight of her, and swells to youth:
> The holy priests gaze on her when she smiles;
> And with heaved hands forgetting gravity,
> They bless her wanton eyes. Even I who hate her,
> With a malignant joy behold such beauty;
> And, while I curse, desire it. (4.267–77)

The extreme expression of the malignant side of the opposition appears in the speeches of Ventidius and Antony after they have witnessed the treachery of the Egyptian fleet. Ventidius:

> Curse on this treach'rous train!
> Their soil and heav'n infect 'em all with baseness;
> And their young souls come tainted to the world
> With the first breath they draw. (5.170–73)

And in the full tide of his despair, Antony speaks now the language of his general, and Cleopatra is not even mentioned in his condemnation of the deadly infection of the east:

> Th' original villain sure no god created;
> He was a bastard of the sun, by Nile.
> Aped into man, with all his mother's mud
> Crusted about his soul. (5.174–77)

Shortly after these speeches, Alexas brings the false report of Cleopatra's death. The conflict in Antony between love and empire
ceases, and this interplay of images representing Antony's divided
soul comes to an end. To follow the course of the diction through
the close of the play, it is necessary to trace other threads.

This scheme of opposed images reflects indirectly on the conflicting demands of Antony's spirit. Of images that bear directly on
his character, there are on the whole comparatively few and those
usually of a general sort, perhaps because the nature of the action is
such as to require him to be open to a number of separate loyalties.
The problem is largely simplified by introducing a wide variety of
images divided between what might be termed Roman and Egyptian qualities. Two speeches of Ventidius early in the play are designed to set the impression of greatness and weakness in Antony:

> Virtue's his path; but sometimes 'tis too narrow
> For his vast soul, and then he starts out wide,
> And bounds into a vice that bears him far
> From his first course, and plunges him in ills:
> But, when his danger makes him find his fault,
> Quick to observe, and full of sharp remorse,
> He censures eagerly his own misdeeds,
> Judging himself with malice to himself,
> And not forgiving what as man he did,
> Because his other parts are more than man.   (1.137–46)

This is a straightforward analysis for the most part, in which the
language aims at sharp definition. Ventidius' other speech on
Antony leans toward over-elaborateness:

> But you, ere love misled your wand'ring eyes,
> Were sure the chief and best of human race,
> Framed in the very pride and boast of nature,
> So perfect, that the gods who formed you, wondered
> At their own skill, and cried, 'A lucky hit
> Has mended our design.' Their envy hindered,
> Else you had been immortal, and a pattern,
> When heav'n would work for ostentation sake,
> To copy out again.   (1.468–76)

Scattered phrases, such as his own reference to his "eagle's wings,"
Cleopatra's "my greater Mars," and the like, keep up the suggestions of greatness, but not in any consistently developed scheme, and
the numerous signs of the glory of his empire are only indirectly re-

lated to impressions of Antony and play another role. A few images touch on his simplicity and honesty. When he has lost Octavia and suspects Cleopatra, Antony says:

> But I am made a shallow-forded stream,
> Seen to the bottom: all my clearness scorned,
> And all my faults exposed! (4.502-4)

In the same mood he tells the apparently faithless Dollabella:

> How could you betray
> This tender heart, which with an infant-fondness
> Lay lulled betwixt your bosoms, and there slept
> Secure of injured faith? (4.563-66)

If the character of Antony emerges from the play as something less than heroic and impressive, the difficulty is to be found partly in the management of the action and partly in the diction: it is the limitations of the man that appear in the vacillating character speaking and acting, and the diction does not do a great deal to add a compensating aura of magnitude.

In an indirect way, the character of Antony gains from the treatment which Octavius Caesar receives. The latter does not appear in the play at all, and thus the conflict of Antony is kept sharp within the limits defined by the other characters, and his defeat is not made a triumph of some other military hero. At the end of the play Antony is able to say:

> O happy Caesar! Thou hast men to lead:
> Think not 'tis thou hast conquered Antony;
> But Rome has conquered Egypt. (5.167-69)

Throughout the play, moreover, the imagery helps to maintain an impression of Caesar as inferior to Antony. He refers to Caesar as "the boy," and in his speeches the images suggest guile rather than heroism:

> Let Caesar spread his subtle nets, like Vulcan. (3.18)

> Nature meant him for an usurer;
> He's fit indeed to buy, not conquer kingdoms. (3.241-42)

In their rise to fame, Antony's is the grander flight:

> Fool that I was, upon my eagle's wings
> I bore this wren, till I was tired with soaring,
> And now he mounts above me. (2.162-64)

The treatment of Caesar thus places the fall of Antony primarily within himself at the same time that it introduces a source of imagery which directly adds to Antony's stature.

In keeping with a scheme which requires a rather clear-cut opposition of issues, Cleopatra is preserved throughout sincerely loyal. It is true, she has twice to prove her love—once, at the beginning when she reveals that she refused favorable terms from Caesar and preferred to be ruined with Antony, and again when she convinces Antony that she had no interest in Dollabella. But at no time can any action of Cleopatra's in the play be interpreted as a sign of disloyalty except by those who oppose her. Moreover, the images which build up suggestions of evil and malevolence around her reflect rather on Antony, since in almost every case they are pointed toward the consequences of his affection on his sterner and more strictly Roman virtues. Such a phrase as Antony's "Took you into my bosom, stained by Caesar" (2.321) is spoken during one of his moments of self-reproach; and the following figure of perfidy is uttered by him in the depth of spirits brought on by the treachery of the Egyptian navy:

> Ingrateful woman!
> Who followed me but as the swallow summer,
> Hatching her young ones in my kindly beams,
> Singing her flatt'ries to my morning wake;
> But, now my winter comes, she spreads her wings
> And seeks the spring of Caesar.   (5.236–41)

Other images tend to cancel these impressions: the "household dove" in the following passage, for instance:

> Nature meant me
> A wife, a silly harmless household dove,
> Fond without art, and kind without deceit;
> But Fortune, that has made a mistress of me,
> Has thrust me out to the wide world, unfurnished
> Of falsehood to be happy.   (4.99–104)

Other images suggest her simplicity and innocence:

> There I till death will his unkindness weep:
> As harmless infants moan themselves to sleep.   (3.550–51)

And still others her sincerity. Thus Dollabella says after he receives convincing demonstration of her devotion to Antony:

> I find your breast fenced round from human reach,
> Transparent as a rock of solid crystal;

Seen through, but never pierced. My friend, my friend!
What endless treasure hast thou thrown away,
And scattered, like an infant, in the Ocean,
Vast sums of wealth which none can gather thence.   (4.228–33)

Neither in the action nor in the imagery is this Cleopatra a serpent of old Nile. At the same time the imagery of the play, if it does not have the effect of destroying these impressions of loyalty and simplicity, does have the effect of identifying her with all the allurements and pleasures of the civilization of which she appears as the most attractive embodiment. Cleopatra gains in stature and impressiveness thereby, so that when Serapion announces his dire news—

> O horror, horror!
> Egypt has been; our latest hour is come:
> The Queen of Nations from her ancient seat,
> Is sunk forever in the dark abyss:
> Time has unrolled her glories to the last,
> And now closed up the volume.   (5.77–82)

—his words seem to convey not so much predictions of the fall of an empire, but the fall of its queen.

The tragic catastrophe is anticipated and prepared for in the images throughout the play, and there is everywhere a close paralleling of the diction with the development of the situations. The portents and supernatural sights announced by Serapion at the outset may be dismissed as a concession to a tragic convention; the supernatural plays no real part, as it does in *Macbeth*, for instance. The important development is begun by the somber impressions indicative of the situation: Antony is at the low ebb in his fortunes and has isolated himself with his own gloomy reflections. We are told by Alexas,

> All southern, from yon hills, the Roman camp
> Hangs o'er us black and threatening, like a storm
> Just breaking on our heads.   (1.45–47)

Antony "makes his heart a prey to black despair" (1.66); he will keep his birthday "with double pomp of sadness" (1.222). His failures haunt him. He tells Ventidius of the disgraceful defeat at Actium, which becomes a symbol of his great decline,

> Here, here it lies; a lump of lead by day,
> And, in my short distracted nightly slumbers,
> The hag that rides my dreams.   (1.313–15)

There are practically no images which give to his downfall suggestions of brilliance except that of the meteor:

> Why was I raised the meteor of the world,
> Hung in the skies, and blazing as I travelled
> Till all my fires were spent; and then cast downward
> To be trod out by Caesar?   (1.224–27)

For the most part they are dreary. Caesar, Antony says,

> . . . . drives me before him
> To the world's ridge, and sweeps me off like rubbish.   (2.166–67)

Ventidius describes Antony as

> Shrunk from the vast extent of all his honors,
> And cramped within a corner of the world.   (1.194–95)

Antony tells Dollabella,

> Thou find'st me at my lowest water-mark.
> The rivers that ran in and raised my fortunes
> Are all dried up, or take another course.
> What I have left is from my native spring;
> I've still a heart that swells, in scorn of fate,
> And lifts me to my banks.   (3.145–50)

Only the last lines imply some measure of contrast to those impressions of aridity and gloom which crowd the first two acts.

Though the concentration of such images occurs in the earlier portions of the play, figures indicative of the collapse of Antony's might extend through the entire fabric. Cleopatra, says Alexas, "winds herself about his mighty ruins" (1.85). Ventidius, observing Antony in his passion, remarks,

> . . . the tempest tears him up by th' roots,
> And on the ground extends the noble ruin.   (1.235–36)

Antony does indeed cast himself down and give himself over to melancholy thoughts:

> Lie there, thou shadow of an Emperor;
> The place thou pressest on thy mother-earth
> Is all thy empire now: now it contains thee;
> Some few days hence, and then 'twill be too large,
> When thou'rt contracted in thy narrow urn,
> Shrunk to a few cold ashes.   (1.237–42)

He tells Cleopatra, "The world fell mould'ring from my hands each hour" (2.346); and when she tries to dissuade him from departure, he asks,

.   .   would you multiply more ruins on me?
This honest man has gathered up the shipwreck of my fortunes.
(2.367–68)

"Ruin," in fact, is the most persistent single word in the play, a recurrent note running throughout.

Heightening these impressions are the references to the fallen empire, invariably introduced to point the magnitude of Antony's decline, and suggestive of activity and greatness. Antony tells Ventidius:

> Fortune came smiling to my youth, and wooed it,
> And purple greatness met my ripened years.
> When first I came to empire, I was borne
> On tides of people, crowding to my triumphs;
> The wish of nations; and the willing world
> Received me as its pledge of future peace.
> I was so great, so happy, so beloved,
> Fate could not ruin me; till I took pains
> And worked against my fortune, chid her from me,
> And turned her loose; yet still she came again.
> My careless days and my luxurious nights
> At length have wearied her, and now she's gone,
> Gone, gone, divorced forever.   (1.337–49)

In a similar vein he talks to Dollabella:

> Thou hast beheld me other than I am.
> Hast thou not seen my morning chambers filled
> With sceptered slaves, who waited to salute me;
> With eastern monarchs, who forgot the sun
> To worship my uprising? Menial kings
> Ran coursing up and down my palace-yard
> Stood silent in my presence, watched my eyes,
> And, at my least command, all started out
> Like racers to the goal.   (3.156–64)

In both instances mention is made of fortune. When Antony comments at the close of this speech, "Fortune is Caesar's now; and what am I?" Ventidius replies, "What you have made your self." In each case the reference is such as to eliminate the possibility that Antony is the victim of fate. These particular references to empire thus help to center the cause of his decline in Antony, and accentuate the drabness of the present. The contrast which these passages bring out deliberately is often implied, as when Antony asks Ventidius,

> Why dost thou drive me from myself, to search
> For foreign aids? to hunt my memory,
> And range all o'er a waste and barren place
> To find a friend? The wretched have no friends.   (3.88–91)

Against the background of this elaborate scheme of images, there
is a fine appropriateness to Antony's speech when he has heard of
the loss of his navy and the death of Cleopatra:

> My torch is out; and the world stands before me
> Like a black desert at the approach of night:
> I'll lay me down and stray no further on.   (5.324–26)

The images thus anticipate and sustain an action which is concerned with the loss of the world and the fall of its hero. But if the
world is well lost, there should properly be some resolution of these
prevailing images of darkness, decay, and barenness into terms that
will convey the shift which the action involves from uncertainty and
misery to certainty and peace. Early in the play Ventidius is told
that Antony has been heard to say in scorn,

> Take all,
> The world's not worth my care.   (1.134–35)

And Ventidius hears these words from Antony himself:

> No, when I found all lost
> Beyond repair, I hid me from the world,
> And learned to scorn it here; which now I do
> So heartily, I think it is not worth
> The cost of keeping.   (1.370–74)

These, however, are words of defeat. The accent changes when he
tells Ventidius that Cleopatra "deserves/More worlds than I can
lose" (1.424–25); and the sentiment becomes not one of defeat but
of triumph when he resolves to stay with her:

> Give, you gods,
> Give to your boy, your Caesar,
> This rattle of a globe to play withal
> This gu-gau world, and put him cheaply off:
> I'll not be pleased with less than Cleopatra.   (2.508–12)

The bravado of this image represents the height of Antony's opti-
mism, and it is not again repeated. For the world and Cleopatra are
not separable; he cannot so readily choose between them. The conditions of the play impose a hard choice on him. If he loses the
empire to Caesar, he loses Cleopatra; if he tries to save the empire,

he must leave her forever. Yet his empire is meaningless to him
without her. His half of the globe he had given her "in dowry with
my heart" (4.560). And when he expresses for the last time his will-
ingness to give up the world, after he believes Cleopatra to be dead,
it is with all these considerations in mind—and the figure for the
world is a ring:

> My Queen is dead.
> I was but great for her; my power, my empire,
> Were but my merchandise to buy her love;
> And conquered kings my factors. Now she's dead,
> Let Caesar take the world—
> An empty circle, since the jewel's gone
> Which made it worth my strife: my being's nauseous;
> For all the bribes of life are gone away.   (5.306–13)

This speech has the air of resignation, and is almost immediately
followed by the somber image of the extinguished torch. After he
has wounded himself, he sees Cleopatra once more, "The one dear
jewel that his haste forgot," and receives final reassurance of her
love. In the speech which follows, spoken just before his death, the
somber and brilliant suggestions are interwoven:

> But grieve not, while thou stay'st,
> My last disastrous times:
> Think we have had a clear and glorious day;
> And heav'n did kindly to delay the storm
> Just till our close of evening.   (5.447–51)

The image breathes reconciliation. It recalls vaguely the bright
images which are associated with Cleopatra in the play. And the
grimness of the extinguished torch and the dark desert is replaced
by the quiet of evening. This impression is recalled by Cleopatra's
speech over his body before she too takes her own life:

> Hail you dear relics
> Of my immortal love!
> O let no impious hand remove you hence;
> But rest forever here: let Egypt give
> His death that peace, which it denied his life.   (5.536–40)

The resolution of the somber images in the case of Cleopatra is on
the whole more brilliant. There is something of the triumphal
about Cleopatra's death that contrasts vividly with Antony's. It
finds its expression in a series of images that are of the nature of
paradox—in their death the lovers conquer Caesar and win the
world:

> Now seat me by my lord. I claim this place;
> For I must conquer Caesar too, like him,
> And win my share of the world.   (5.534–36)

Where in Antony's case, darkness comes as the quiet end of day, in Cleopatra's, darkness itself becomes desirable.

> 'Tis sweet to die, when they would force life on me,
> To rush into the dark abode of death,
> And seize him first; if he be like my love,
> He is not frightful sure.   (5.509–12)

Antony has described death as a friend (5.388ff); Cleopatra as a lover. And her death is not a separation, but a permanent union at last:

>   Let dull Octavia
> Survive to mourn him dead: my nobler fate
> Shall knit our spousals with a tie too strong
> For Roman laws to break.   (5.477–80)

When Charmian asks the reason for her regal attire, she replies:

> Dull that thou art! why 'tis to meet my love,
> As when I saw him first, on Cydnos bank,
> All sparkling, like a goddess; so adorned,
> I'll find him once again: my second spousals
> Shall match my first in glory. Haste, haste, both,
> And dress the bride of Antony.   (5.527–32)

The words of Serapion at the end are a kind of quiet benediction on this final security of death:

>   Sleep, blest pair,
> Secure from human chance, long ages out,
> While all the storms of fate fly o'er your tomb.   (5.590–92)

But it is in the death of Cleopatra that the action and the diction justify the title in its fullest sense—*All for Love*; or, *The World Well Lost*.

It is apparent at times that the scheme of the action created problems in diction which Dryden was not always able to solve happily. There is an occasional thinness and lack of concentration in the images. The role of Antony in the action was in some ways a handicap, and it is significant that in the fifth act, when there is neither need nor opportunity for further choice or change of mind, the language finally builds up into a sustained and cumulative climax. The need to give Dollabella equal place with the rest in the heart of Antony leads to some obvious heightening of the diction—

the amatory images, for example, which help to disturb the larger
scheme of figures in the play—and in fact one gets the impression
that the language is less well managed where Dollabella is concerned than almost anywhere else. These and other similar criticisms would be trivial, except that they help to show the handicaps
which the conventions of the heroic drama placed in Dryden's way.
The really important fact, however, is that Dryden succeeded in
finding a particular modification of the traditions of heroic drama
which permitted a use of language quite different from that which
prevailed in the parent form. He adopted a rhythmic scheme that,
while imposing a formalizing restraint, was nevertheless flexible
enough to be adaptable to any possible dramatic needs. And he gave
his language imaginative weight without losing the clarity and poise
which he had mastered in the couplet. *All for Love* was his one
moment of liberation from some Octavia among the muses who had
kept him within bounds of artistic respectability and frustration. It
was his great achievement that he accomplished once more, on
somewhat new and limited terms, the union of the poetical resources
of language and the requirements of dramatic form. How fine his
accomplishment was may be realized by comparing *All for Love*
with any representative heroic play, and then with any of the efforts
of his fellow dramatists to escape its pattern.

To carry the story into the eighteenth century would be, on the
whole, profitless. A few interesting examples of verse tragedy exist,
to be sure. In comparison with other representative plays of its
time, Addison's *Cato* cannot be dismissed merely as a play which
succeeded by appealing equally to rival political parties, and Bonamy Dobrée commends it for restoring to tragedy its proper action
of a great and noble individual going necessarily to disaster. The
work of John Home, "the Scottish Shakespeare," particularly
Douglas, has some interest for its attempt to find new materials. It is
possible to discover in these and other pieces certain mild merits.
But the search ends in the discovery that most of these plays have
not strayed radically from the contrivances and tricks established
by heroic drama and its blank verse derivatives. The plots often
turn on probabilities of a trivial and surprising order, and the poetic
energy of the verse tends toward the expression of passion or sentiment as the most significant aspect of character. More important
still, not one of these plays possesses any real distinction, and in not

one of them is there any indication of a serious or fresh attempt to come to grips with their artistic problem. New influences and new experiments appear in the closing decade of the century, but they are properly a part of another story.

The long period between the Restoration and the end of the eighteenth century produced one distinguished dramatic poet, who produced one memorable tragedy. Dryden never quite shook off the feeling that he was working under the shadow of the great accomplishments of the Elizabethans, and he had occasional doubts about the way he had chosen. He felt himself to be

> . . . betwixt two ages cast,
> The first of this, and hindmost of the last.[10]

It is as much an indication of his true poetic instincts that he felt these misgivings as that he finally worked out some measure of success.

CHAPTER IV

NINETEENTH-CENTURY TRAGEDY

THE HISTORY of the drama of the nineteenth century is the paradox of a flourishing desert, of malnutrition amidst plenty. There was widespread and general interest in the drama, there were distinguished and able actors, and there were numerous and prolific writers of plays. Moreover, every one of the poets whose names make the century memorable, from Colcridge and Wordsworth to Tennyson and Browning, tried, in some cases repeatedly, to succeed in this species of writing. And yet it is an observation commonplace among historians and critics of the drama that from all this activity there resulted not one unforgettable comedy, not one great tragedy —not one play worthy of being placed in the same rank with the accepted classics of the theatre.

Great failure is almost as much an incitement to analysis as great success; and there is no lack of ingenious and plausible explanations of this paucity of creditable drama, or even of fruitful serious experiment and novelty until the emergence of the "new drama" during the later decades of the century. Was the failure due to the theatrical conditions of the times, with the artificial separation of the two large "legitimate" theatres from the other "illegitimate" ones; the small financial rewards of authors; the "star system"? Was it the aloofness of literary men from the theatre itself? Was it the lack of objectivity among the romantic writers with their emphasis on their personal sensibilities? Was it the imitation of bad models, or the undue veneration for great ones? Was it the prevailing bad taste for spectacle and melodrama?[1] None of the current explanations seems satisfactory by itself. But though further exploration of the problem posed by the nineteenth century may fail to give the final answer, the state of the drama during these times demands serious consideration in the light of the numerous and valiant efforts which were made to restore verse tragedy to its ancient sovereignty.

I

The serious drama of the Restoration had developed in conformity with a tradition established by the heroic play, and for the most part this tradition, though varied in a number of ways, had a controlling effect during the greater part of the eighteenth century. The writers of serious—and that meant poetic—drama during most of the nineteenth century, however, are characterized by diversity of styles and by an eclecticism in the choice of models. In part this was the result of the incredible decline in the standards of popular theatrical composition, which forced serious writers to look elsewhere for inspiration. In part, also, it was due to the continuing effect of certain novelties introduced during the closing years of the eighteenth century, to which the origin of many features of early nineteenth-century drama is to be traced.

There are signs during the closing years of the eighteenth century of an attempt to introduce fresh themes and materials to the worn-out conventions of the drama. The most spectacular and notorious of these was the use of the machinery of the gothic novel. Such works as Walpole's *Mysterious Mother* and Lewis's *Castle Spectre* employ the gothicism, the mystery, and the horror-mongering introduced by the type of popular novel of this period which these writers helped to make popular. Traces of this influence can be seen not only in the melodrama of the nineteenth century, but in the setting of such a serious work as Byron's *Manfred*, and in details of Coleridge's *Remorse*, to name only familiar samples, and in the work of Joanna Baillie, an influential writer who regarded herself as a reformer in the drama. The effect of this gothicism was on the whole not salutary. It provided chiefly a novelty of setting, and narrative conventions which fostered incidents involving surprise and terror, and characters of fixed and exaggerated capacities. It tended to substitute stage business for action, and assaults on the sensibilities for emotion. The possibilities of gothicism as a conventional framework within which tragic themes might be explored were scarcely even perceived. The gothic milieu neither acquired the symbolical quality with which Yeats endowed the Irish legends, nor did it develop into a convenient framework which freed the dramatists from the limitations of versimilitude and enabled them to extend the meaning of the materials to the full stature of tragedy, in some such manner as Shakespeare treated the ancient stories of *Hamlet* and *Lear*, or the Greeks the old myths. Its principal influence was to foster the theatrical.

The elements of gothicism often fused with those of another important influence, the German drama. At its worst, this influence dominated the seventeen-nineties through the work of Kotzebue, in such an excess that parodies and ridicule appeared before the end of the decade. At its best, the German influence can be seen in the interest in Schiller's plays, especially *Die Raüber*, and to a lesser degree in those of Goethe. The immediate effects of this influence were quite short lived. They can be seen, however, in such plays as Coleridge's *Remorse*, Wordsworth's *Borderers*, and Byron's *Werner*. In general, English drama did not profit too greatly from this source, and the rapid decline of Germanic influence indicates the superficial effect which it had. A kind of romantic dash, a heightened individualism of sentiment, the recurrence of certain set schemes of incident is about all that English drama managed to absorb from Schiller and the other Germans. Like gothicism, the vogue for these materials represents chiefly a search for greener pastures, an excursion into novelties and tricks to add a new flavor and to escape from familiar devices. Whatever they may have contributed to current theatrical pieces, they were not a really vitalizing influence to serious writers, and they ended in barrenness. Yet, in themselves, these influences are neither good nor bad. Had not *Cambises* and the *Misfortunes of Arthur* been followed by the work of men like Marlowe and Shakespeare, they might have appeared now as similar blind alleys and vitiating influences. For some reason, the Elizabethans succeeded in developing a great tragedy out of inauspicious beginnings where the writers of the nineteenth century did not.

In view of the uncertain drift of dramatic developments during the later years of the eighteenth century and the early years of the nineteenth, the studied attempts of Joanna Baillie in her *Plays of the Passions* (first series 1798) to come to grips with the problem of tragedy deserves separate attention, especially as she aroused the admiration of such men as Coleridge and Byron. Scott, after a short enthusiasm for the Germans and some attempts to translate Goethe, wrote in 1801, "The 'Plays of the Passions' have put me entirely out of conceit with my Germanized brat."[2] This was only some three years after Baillie published the first volume of plays under this general title. Two later series followed (1802, 1803), and in addition two other volumes of miscellaneous plays, printed in 1804 and 1836. A number of her plays saw production on the stage, though the acclaim of critics for her work outran the response of audiences.

Joanna Baillie believed that the peculiar province of tragedy was the presentation of powerful manifestations of powerful emotions, and in the fourteen plays written in conformity to this theory she essayed to represent in each the operation of some single emotion. Her justification of this scheme appeared in a long preface to the first volume in the series. The most absorbing of all topics, she notes, is the characters and dispositions of men. Knowledge of human nature is gratifying in any species of literature, but in the drama it is indispensable. In the works of the dramatist, "no richness of invention, harmony of language, nor grandeur of sentiment, will supply the place of faithfully delineated nature."[3] And it is in the manifestations of characteristic passions that the nature of man is best revealed. The drama, and particularly tragedy, had not adequately realized these possibilities:

But the last part of the task which I have mentioned as peculiarly belonging to Tragedy,—unveiling the human mind under the dominion of those strong and fixed passions, which, seemingly unprovoked by outward circumstances, will from small beginnings brood within the breast, till all the better disposition, all the fair gifts of nature, are borne down before them, —her poets in general have entirely neglected, and even her first and greatest have but imperfectly attempted. They have made use of the passions to mark their several characters and animate their scenes, rather than to open to our view the nature and portraitures of those great disturbers of the human breast, with whom we are all, more or less, called upon to contend . . . . in Tragedy it is events, more frequently than opposite affections, which are opposed to them; and those often of such force and magnitude, that the passions themselves are almost obscured by the splendour and importance of the transactions to which they are attached.[4]

In conformity with this revised view of the aims and methods of tragedy, Joanna Baillie recommends a reform in the diction:

Besides being thus confined and mutilated, the passions have been, in the greater part of our tragedies, deprived of the very power of making themselves known. Bold and figurative language belongs peculiarly to them. Poets, admiring those bold expressions which a mind, labouring with ideas too strong to be conveyed in the ordinary forms of speech, wildly throws out, taking earth, sea, and sky, and every thing great and terrible in na-

ture, to image forth the violence of its feelings, borrowed them gladly to
adorn the calm sentiments of their premeditated song. It has, therefore,
been thought that the less animated parts of tragedy might be embellished
and enriched. In doing this, however, the passions have been robbed of
their native prerogative; and in adorning with their strong figures and
lofty expressions the calm speeches of the unruffled, it is found that, when
they are called upon to raise their voice, the power of distinguishing themselves has been taken away. This is an injury by no means compensated,
but very greatly aggravated, by embellishing, in return, the speeches of
passion with the ingenious conceits and complete similes of premeditated
thought.[5]

Action is thus placed in a secondary position; the drama is to be
organized around the delineation of character or, more accurately,
around the presentation of passion through which character is made
known. The roots of this theory go back, of course, to the eighteenth
century. It is probable that the tradition of "star" acting which became so firmly established during the nineteenth century, with the
leading actor working on the sensibilities of the audience, had also
something to do with the general approval of this theory of tragedy.

The defect in the theory is that it endangers the prospect of
achieving a fully coordinated dramatic design; the action becomes
a theatrically effective frame within which the display of passion
may be accomplished. Such theory, whatever its original intentions,
might well have had the effect of encouraging rather than discouraging the tawdry plot devices of the times, and the use of some
of the most banal of these in the work of Joanna Baillie herself and
her imitators illustrates the fact. Her solution of the problem of
diction in a poetic drama of this sort rests on a modified principle of
verisimilitude, since language is to be tied to psychological probabilities. Nothing is to be admitted which reveals the author's pre-
meditation; ornament is to be confined to the vigorous outburst of
passion which naturally inclines men to speak in an elevated
manner. Whether this view of the matter is psychologically accurate
or not may be left unquestioned for the moment; its disastrous
effects on the diction of poetic drama, however, can be inferred. To
tie the "poetry" of verse tragedy simply to the expression of the
moments of passion is to misconstrue the dramatic functioning of
the diction in such works. It is only fortunate that Shakespeare, and
the others who, Baillie laments, failed to arrive soon enough at her
view of tragedy, were free of her principles. That Baillie's plays and

theories impressed important writers and critics of the nineteenth century is perhaps less an indication of her direct influence than of how far astray they were.

An interesting sidelight can be thrown on this point from the soliloquies of nineteenth-century drama. The dramatists seem unable to handle the soliloquy, or even an extended speech, dramatically. *Hamlet* is the most reflective and introspective of Shakespeare's plays, yet a comparison of Hamlet's great soliloquies with any soliloquy in any nineteenth-century verse drama will show the difference. Even the opening lines will serve: "To be or not to be"; "O, what a rogue and peasant slave am I"; "How all occasions do inform against me"—set these against such a beginning as that of Tell's apostrophe in Sheridan Knowles' *William Tell*: "Ye crags and peaks, I'm with you once again"—and the difference is clear. Hamlet's speeches are concerned with his will, his motive to action or inaction; Tell at once launches into a rhapsody. A soliloquy is a signal for the expatiation of the sensibilities in almost any nineteenth-century play.

This subtle shift in the handling of the soliloquy raises another problem. The one general influence throughout the entire period, which no serious dramatist escaped wholly, was that of Elizabethan drama, Shakespeare particularly; but the lessons which were learned from this dramatic literature were neither profound nor fundamental ones. Characters were woodenly imitated, figures of speech were indiscriminately borrowed, and, worst of all, archaisms of Elizabethan idiom were unthinkingly retained.

The effect of this admiration for the great dramatic past was for the most part deadening. It might well be asked why, in spite of prevailing theoretical confusions about drama, the imitation of Shakespeare and the other Elizabethans did not act as a leavening force during the nineteenth century, in a manner comparable to the effect of Seneca on the early Elizabethans. For one thing, Seneca had some of the stirring effect of novelty for the Elizabethans, whereas Shakespeare had become an ancient and venerable demi-god, to whom nineteenth-century criticism had given a new profundity. Moreover, Shakespeare was a great dramatic genius, which Seneca was certainly not; and whereas the imitator could absorb readily what Seneca had to offer and then pass on to new developments, the awe-inspiring performance of Shakespeare acted as a kind of deterrent toward fresh excursions, so that new models and sources of inspiration, as Byron apparently felt, seemed desirable if the dramatist was ever to break his tethers with the past. Moreover, Seneca was in a different language, and even a closer imitation of his devices and speeches than any Elizabethan accorded him would still have left the poet untrammeled in the free and original exercise of his powers of expression. Seneca may have imposed an arbitrary rhetorical notion of appropriate dramatic style, but he did not bring about a hybrid language, a respectable tragic vocabulary, a jargon of lofty discourse. Theoretically there is nothing wrong with a writer's arbitrarily composing poetry in the language of some two hundred years before his time, except that there will be nuances of thought and sentiment peculiar to his day for which there will not be adequate or appropriate symbols in the older speech. The imitators of Elizabethan drama, however, did not write Elizabethan English, but an artificial hybrid of the older language and their own. Under these conditions, the poet would be hampered in the use of turns of speech natural to him in his non-dramatic poetry, while on the other hand he would be encouraged to take over ready-made ornaments from his originals and thus become a dealer in a kind of standardized poetic-drama rhetoric, selecting figures not for their essential bearing on the play as a whole, but for their suggestions of conformity with the proper respectable tradition.

The generally unsatisfactory turn to Elizabethan drama is an indirect but important indication of the position of the serious playwright of this age. He had become curiously separated from the current popular theatrical activity. His separation did not consist in the fact that his plays were never performed, for they often were; and, in a sense of, course, plays such as Knowles' *Virginius*, which had a not inconsiderable stage success, Talfourd's *Ion*, or Coleridge's *Remorse*, constitute in themselves an important development in stage style, and one, moreover, in which features which ruled the popular theatre were not wholly absent. The nature of the separation is to be discerned chiefly in an attitude of mind toward the theatre. The poet-dramatist generally felt that he was engaged in a task different in kind from that of the humble, and frequently despicable, purveyor of entertainment for the public. Dryden and Shakespeare could be at once the leading poets and dramatists of their respective ages; what distinguished them from most of their fellow dramatists was not a difference in kind so much as in degree, in the simple fact that they were men of talent and genius. No such closeness with the stage characterized most of the poet-dramatists of the nineteenth century. They wrote as custodians of a noble art, or as reformers. They sometimes wrote with the express intention of not having their plays performed, and the fact that some of these plays were performed in spite of their author's intentions does not alter his position. Thus came into being the "closet drama," a phenomenon almost unique, at least on such a scale, with the nineteenth century.[6]

An illustration of the effects of this attitude is to be found in the work of Bulwer-Lytton, a writer who fared much better in the theatre than the other poetic dramatists of his time, and who apparently had every intention of succeeding there. In the preface of his most ambitious play, *Richelieu*, he wrote:

The length of the Play necessarily requires curtailments on the Stage,— the principal of which are enclosed within brackets. Many of the passages thus omitted, however immaterial to the audience, must obviously be such as the *reader* would be least inclined to dispense with,—viz. those which, without being absolutely essential to the business of the Stage, contain either the subtler strokes of character, or the more poetical embellishments of description.[7]

Bulwer-Lytton reiterates the principal in a note to the opening speech of Act III:

I need not say that the great length of this soliloquy adapts it only for the closet, and that but few of the lines are retained on the stage. To the reader, however, the passages omitted in representation will not, perhaps, be the most uninteresting in the play, and may be deemed necessary to the completion of the Cardinal's portrait,—action on the stage supplying so subtly the place of words in the closet.[8]

This distinction between the stage and the reader carries some curious implications. It suggests a sharp division between what is poetical and what is dramatic, and thus introduces as a matter of practice one of the most vitiating principles in the criticism and composition of verse drama, a notion which penetrated quite far into nineteenth-century criticism. Rightly considered, the criterion of inclusion or exclusion of any part of a play is not whether it is too subtle or too poetic for the rougher and more exciting province of the stage, but whether it contributes anything essential to the elements of necessity and probability which give the play its peculiar quality and contribute to its formal completeness. It is true that even among the Elizabethans revisions by someone experienced in the ways of the theatre were made in the author's manuscript, apparently even in the case of Shakespeare; but the issue involved was merely that of the judgment of the stage manager against that of the author on the propriety of some part or other, and not that of a principle of distinction between beauties appropriate to the theatre in opposition to beauties appropriate to the reader in the closet.

It is a matter of historical record that almost without exception the greatest plays have been written in direct participation with an active theatre and in competition with plays bidding for the favor of the particular audience which gave the theatre its patronage. Whatever the reasons for this fact, the serious dramatists of the nineteenth century were taking risks in the face of experience as a result of their aloofness. Shelley did not like to go to the theatre; Byron did not want to have his plays performed; Browning wrote his later plays for "a purely imaginative stage"; Coleridge and Wordsworth and Tennyson seemed unaware of any need for apprenticeship in the theatre. Later critics have outspokenly taken these poets to task for their aloofness. Their expressed contempt for much current theatrical fare is not necessarily an ill sign, however; it would have been strangely uncritical of them had the opposite been the case. And in their protests they have something in common with certain of the dramatists of the great period during the sixteenth and early seventeenth centuries when the poet and the theatre were much closer than they have been since. Greene expressed a fierce hatred for the compositions of the hack dramatists of his time; Ben Jonson kept up an unending attack against the uncritical crudeness of the average play; Webster regretted that he found it impossible to write in the loftiest tragic manner "with any preservation of popular delight"; and Beaumont's great comic masterpiece, *The Knight of the Burning Pestle*, is a brilliant criticism of the extravagant features of certain plays in demand and of the audiences whose bad taste brought them into being and preserved them. It would be disastrous for the art of popular drama if the more conscientious writers did not protest in word and deed against vitiating influences in the theatre. The error lies not in an attitude of protest toward what is crude and uncritical but in the expressed or implied conviction, against all precedent, that there is never any chance for the serious and conscientious artist in a commercial theatre and before popular audiences.

It has consequently often been maintained that the men of letters would have come off much better as dramatists had they had less scorn for the work of the journeyman playwright and a greater understanding of the popular thrillers. They would not then have deprived their plays of those features of theatrical art which make drama exciting, for the successful writer for the theatre is in possession of trade secrets which it is profitable for the more serious artist to know. This truism cannot be pushed too far, however, in the case of the nineteenth-century men of letters, in view of the really deplorable condition of the theatre of the times; for the tricks which brought popularity to the current favorites might well have irremediably corrupted the serious dramatists. What were these common means of public attraction? The increasingly lavish use of stage contrivances was one—costly scenery, horses, waterfalls, sea battles, and what not. On the side of plot was the reliance on momentarily arresting episodes rather than on closely integrated action, on the extravagant use of hairbreadth coincidences, on the occurrence of just the contingency which is mathematically least likely, on the manifestation of the most inhuman virtues, and the appeal to the crudest sort of *sensibilité*—all tending to an order of probability destructive to a serious action, and entailing thoughts and sentiments, and consequently diction, too thin, too lacking in subtlety and depth, for serious drama. Under such circumstances it is understandable that the poet-dramatists of this age wished to abandon the tawdry mechanisms of theatrical gratification exploited by their contemporaries and looked to established and more dignified models for guidance. The lessons they would have learned from their popular and prolific contemporaries would not serve them too well in the aim which inspired them of bringing once more a worthy tragic drama to England.

It might be maintained, in fact, that the serious artists learned too much from that school. Bulwer-Lytton's *Richelieu* is a useful illustration, since its author combined poetic aspirations with an eye to theatrical success. Though the Cardinal as a great political genius is the central figure, the plot largely turns on the love affair of Julie and du Mauprat, with Richelieu as a kind of *deus ex machina* who saves them from separation and death. The play moves through many rapid changes of situation, involving abruptly broken friend-ships and loyalties, and the search for a fatal document which is brought in just in time, after many abortive attempts and hair-breadth escapes. In the midst of all this, the Cardinal's long dis-courses on statecraft and on his own spiritual trials seem largely forced and in the way. It is the sly wolf of melodrama parading in the ill-fitting sheep's clothing of tragedy. And if Bulwer-Lytton is to be objected to as an unfair illustration, the same point may be made from works of the acknowledged poets. Coleridge's plays have much in common with popular contemporary drama in plot, character, and sentiment. Byron's *Manfred* is saturated with gothi-cism in the setting, and his *Werner* reflects the Germanic vein in contradiction to his expressed abhorrence of it. Archbishop Becket's last-minute rescue of Rosamund in Tennyson's *Becket* is in the man-ner of the thrillers. Instances could be multiplied to show that the poets cast occasional furtive glances at the meretricious goddesses of the theatre while courting the more stately muses. Yet in spite of their concessions, they have earned the dubious title of closet dramatists.

Except, however, as the epithet reflects the attitude of many of these writers toward the theatre, most of the poetical dramas of the nineteenth century do not merit the name of closet drama, in the sense of purely literary drama. The term, closet drama, has come to be loosely used to designate plays which, while suitable to the tastes of fastidious readers, are unfit for the manly excitements of the playing stage. As thus used, the term is constantly breaking down and helps to generate critical confusion. Some plays once per-formed before appreciative audiences are now so far removed from modern stage practices that performance of them would be out of the question: it is unlikely, for instance, that some of the most frequently anthologized Elizabethan tragedies would ever be con-sidered now even for private revivals, yet they were certainly played in their day. Other plays never intended by their authors for per-formance have in fact been staged—*Manfred* is a case in point. And there is *The Cenci*, written for the stage but forced into the category of closet drama on moral and not theatrical grounds. What has given currency to the popular concept of closet drama is the un-satisfactory development of poetic drama during the nineteenth century and the experimental nature of poetic drama in our times.

There is, however, one species of play to which the term closet drama may be applied without confusion. It is possible for a poet to use the act and scene conventions of drama, and to take advantage of the directness and vividness which the method of presentation through characters in dialogue affords, and yet to write in freedom from the limitations which condition the form of a play that must take into account the restrictions imposed by a stage, by the use of actors who must speak lines, or by audiences who must not be perplexed through the use of unfamiliar methods or recondite themes. Because it is unaffected by such considerations, the literary play, properly speaking, never causes confusion. *Prometheus Unbound*, *Samson Agonistes*, and *The Dynasts*—and perhaps Byron's *Cain*—are literary drama in this sense. Attempts to stage these plays do not invalidate the premises on which they are founded. Many examples of nineteenth-century "closet drama" do not preserve these conditions and hence open themselves to judgment on a different basis.

The serious playwright of this age was forced by circumstances into an anomalous position which divided or vitiated his efforts. By virtue of a tacitly assumed convention, he was expected to write in verse, and hence he regarded his work as following a line of descent which could be traced back to the hallowed dramatic masterpieces of other times: his was a position analogous to that of a king dispossessed of his throne who nevertheless feels the responsibility of living up to the family traditions of royalty. The disparity between what the serious dramatist felt called upon to produce and the deplorable state of much current theatrical fare only intensified his aloofness from the popular stage, which amounted in some cases to deliberate repudiation. In spite, therefore, of considerable productivity and relatively frequent production, the verse drama of the age was not the flowering of a vigorous contemporary style which had its roots in the popular theatrical activity of the time. It was a hybrid, kept alive by tradition and by occasional infusions, usually to its disadvantage, from the current theatrical fare.

In consequence, it is not easy to select typical nineteenth-century verse plays for analysis and illustration. There are plays in abundance, but choice is complicated in part by the eclectic character of much of the work and in part by the almost total lack of plays of great merit. Some of the plays which earned high praise in their day—for example, Knowles' *Virginius*, Talfourd's *Ion*, and Milman's *Fazio*—are not distinguished for plot or characterization and, most important of all, show no real poetical skill and merely acknowledge in their use of verse submission to an accepted mode of tragic composition. It is to the plays of those whose fame rests primarily on their work as poets that we must turn to see in all their complex ramifications the problems of the poetic dramatist in the nineteenth century. Of these, the most interesting and important, without much question, are Shelley, Byron, Tennyson, and Browning.

II

Shelley finds a place in the story of nineteenth-century poetic drama by virtue of only one work, *The Cenci*. On the basis of his one dramatic piece, however, Shelley's place is assured. It is not an uncommon opinion that *The Cenci* is the most distinguished tragedy written during the nineteenth century. Moreover, admiration for this play comes not only from literary critics; it has elicited praise from St. John Ervine, who is skilled in the ways of the theatre and who finds numerous instances of felicitious understanding of the demands of the stage.[9] That Shelley should have secured at one try such a measure of success is at first sight paradoxical. He is one of the most subjective and philosophical of our poets, hardly the usual adjectives for a playwright. Moreover, his acquaintance with the stage seems to have been slight, and his customary attitude not one of sympathy for the ways of the playhouse.[10] He was also uncertain of his own ability to write dramatically; Mrs. Shelley wrote in her note to the play:

Shelley most erroneously conceived himself to be destitute of this talent. He believed that one of the first requisites was the capacity of forming and following-up a story or plot. He fancied himself to be defective in this portion of imagination: it was that which gave him least pleasure in the writings of others, though he laid great store by it as the proper framework to support the sublimest efforts of poetry.

What Shelley lacked in the way of intimate familiarity with the theatrical compositions of the contemporary stage, however, he made up in his knowledge of the great classics of the past, both ancient and modern, and the ability he showed in the management of the episodes came largely from clever adaptation of materials which his sympathetic knowledge of these had suggested. Shelley himself seemed unaware of the extent to which he relied on his reading of earlier plays. It is only fair to accept at its face value the note in his preface concerning Beatrice's description of the ravine (3.1.243–65):* "An idea in this speech was suggested by a most sublime passage in *El Purgatorio de San Patricio* of Calderon; the only plagiarism which I have intentionally committed in the whole piece." Yet *The Cenci* is an amazing combination of devices, motifs, and even speeches drawn from other plays. For example, the scene preceding the murder of Cenci resembles the scene of the murder of Duncan in *Macbeth*; the defiance of her judges by Beatrice is strongly reminiscent of Vittoria's behavior during the trial in *The White Devil*; Cenci's curse of Beatrice is modeled after Lear's curse of Goneril; Beatrice's expression of horror at hearing her sentence confirmed suggests Juliet's speech before she takes the sleeping potion; Giacomo's complaint of the pitiful condition of himself and his family suggests Jaffeir's complaints against his senator father-in-law in *Venice Preserved*.[11] How close the parallelisms are at times may be illustrated by the resemblance of the following speeches of Giacomo in Othello's speech before the murder of Desdemona:

> Thou unreplenished lamp! whose narrow fire
> Is shaken by the wind, and on whose edge
> Devouring darkness hovers! Thou small flame,
> Which, as a dying pulse rises and falls,
> Still flickerest up and down, how very soon,
> Did I not feed thee, wouldst thou fail and be
> As thou hadst never been! So wastes and sinks
> Even now, perhaps, the life that kindled mine:
> But that no power can fill with vital oil
> That broken lamp of flesh.   (3.2.9–18)

> (*Lighting the lamp*) And yet once quenched I cannot thus relume
> My father's life.   (3.2.51–52)

This extraordinary subservience to the work of others was not without its advantages for Shelley. Lacking experience in the drama, he found in these various incidents and speeches of the dramatic classics ready-made patterns of arrangement, relationship, order, and intensification. Since he exercised excellent taste in those he used, and since in most instances his borrowings bear some relevance

*Line references are to the Oxford one-volume edition of *The Complete Poetical Works of Percy Bysshe Shelley*, edited by Thomas Hutchinson (Oxford, 1923).

to his story, they lend the appearance of practiced mastery. He was fortunate, too, in his models; he was the better off for not having followed the current stage favorites, or for not allowing his admiration of Coleridge's *Remorse* to lead him astray, or Milman's *Fazio* to influence him more than it did.

Shelley did not, however, escape the disadvantages of such imitation, and the inviting of comparison is not the most important of these. The principal danger in such a practice is that it may encourage dependence on a purely theatrical order of probability; that is, it may prompt the use of episodes and devices not demanded by the formal requirements of the new piece but inspired by the general effectiveness of some feature in the source without reference to its original function. The scene in which Giacomo waits for news of his father's murder is an example. It is midnight; there is "thunder, and the sound of a storm." Giacomo comments on the connection between the storm and the feelings of man. But there is no reason for the storm at all; its appearance is not strongly demanded, as in the case of *Lear*, which Giacomo's words at this point recall. And before Giacomo has spoken a dozen lines the storm is completely forgotten and is never alluded to again, even in stage directions. Giacomo now develops the analogy, already noted, between the dying lamp and his father. A bell strikes the hour, and the reflections shift once more, until Orsino enters to inform Giacomo that the first murder plan has failed. He then calls attention to the fact that the lamp has gone out, whereupon Giacomo returns to the figure about the dying lamp. A comparison with *Othello* will illustrate the difference; there, the putting out of the lamp is called for by the action, at the same time that it is strongly symbolical and leads to the magnificent lines, "Put out the light, and then put out the light." In *The Cenci*, the light goes out by accident merely to add another touch of gloom to the spectacle, along with the storm and the bell, and to provide an opportunity to repeat the already developed metaphor of the lamp borrowed from Shakespeare. The whole episode is superfluous, and nothing depends on it. It gives a big scene to Giacomo, who does not deserve it at all, and brings in a note of pity for Cenci, which is dangerous in view of the sympathy required for Beatrice's relentless opposition to her father. Moreover, such theatrical superfluity affects the diction as well, for where the scene is not dramatically required, the elaborations in the diction may well turn out to be rhetorical ornament, "mere poetry" as Shelley termed it with just deprecation in his preface. This particular scene sets these defects into relief with greater clarity, perhaps, than any other, but there are other moments in the play which do not escape at least a trace of the disadvantages noted in this case.

It is remarkable that Shelley survived these disabilities as well as he did. What saved Shelley was his passionate interest in the story—oppression by parental and ecclesiastical authority of a brave, intelligent, and beautiful girl—which enabled him to introduce his own original conceptions within the framework of an Elizabethan tale, and his great gifts as a poet which enabled him to fuse these mixed sources of inspiration into a high degree of consistency.

The story as Shelley employed it in his play is essentially simple. Count Cenci, old in crimes unpunished by grace of payments to the Pope, is obsessed with a hatred of his family. Because his daughter Beatrice is less defeated in spirit than the rest, and because she denounces him at a banquet which Cenci holds to celebrate the death of two of his sons, he determines to destroy her spirit by committing the unnatural crime of incest. Unprotected against his bestiality, Beatrice and the rest of the family resolve on murder. Unforeseen developments bring them under suspicion, and the hired assassin and members of the family confess under torture. Beatrice never confesses. All the members of the family involved are executed. To this simple framework Shelley added the intrigue of the priest Orsino, formerly a suitor of Beatrice's and still in love with her, who fails to deliver her appeal to the Pope through a villainous design to keep her from her freedom and thus win her as his mistress, and who aids in the schemes to murder Cenci in the hope that his possession of the secret may aid him in keeping Beatrice in his power. This is not, in the execution, too happy a contrivance. Neither is the enlargement of Giacomo's role too successful an attempt at amplification, since his woes and reflections are developed out of all proportion to his actual participation in the action. These and other faults in the treatment of the plot are obvious, but they do not impair too seriously the essential conflict of the play, the terrible struggle between Cenci and Beatrice. Though Shelley faltered immaturely during the progress of the play, he never lost sight of the grim opposition which forms its center.

Cenci's unnatural evil and overweaning hate are the principal

moving forces in his character. In particular, there is Cenci's desire
to consummate his hatred for Beatrice through an incestuous
union. For the most part, Shelley avoids probing into obscure
psychological forces, except for one or two hints. Early in the play
Cenci, describing himself to Camillo as "what your theologians call
hardened," explains how love of pleasure led to love of violence:

> When I was young I thought of nothing else
> But pleasure; and I fed on honey sweets:
> Men, by St. Thomas! cannot live like bees,
> And I grew tired:—yet, till I killed a foe,
> And heard his groans, and heard his children's groans,
> Knew I not what delight was else on earth,
> Which now delights me little. I the rather
> Look on such pangs as terror ill conceals,
> The dry fixed eyeball, the pale quivering lip,
> Which tell me that the spirit weeps within
> Tears bitterer than the bloody sweat of Christ.
> I rarely kill the body, which preserves,
> Like a strong prison, the soul within my power,
> Wherein I feed it with the breath of fear
> For hourly pain.   (1.1.103–17)

This is the only clear attempt to go behind Cenci's acts to their
psychological causes and origins. There is also a suggestion of the
ambivalence of feeling which lies behind the incest, though very
little is made of this, save in the imagery of a limited number of
speeches: for instance, in Cenci's anger after the banquet,

> Thou painted viper!
> Beast that thou art! Fair and yet terrible!
> I know a charm shall make thee meek and tame,   (1.3.165–67)

and in the oscillation of adjectives and figures during Cenci's curse
of Beatrice—words like "bane," "disease," "infects," and "poisons"
alternating with "bright loveliness," "love-kindled lips," and "those
fine limbs" (4.1.115–35). But however brilliant these suggestions,
they are minor notes in the treatment of Cenci. The incest is not
presented as an act with its own peculiar impulses deeply rooted in
Cenci's being, but rather as the most immoral expression of his
generalized hate and indecency. In fact, the treatment of Cenci
does not escape the taint of Baillie's studies in passion, where the
donné is the passion itself and the play reveals the variety and extent
of its manifestations. But there is a grander quality to Cenci than in

the general run of characters cast in the Baillie model. He becomes
the incarnation of the spirit of evil, cosmic in proportions, bearing a

> . . . darker deadlier gloom
> Than the earth's shade, or interlunar air,
> Or constellations quenched in murkiest cloud.   (2.1.189–91)

He is less a mortal than a satanic spirit:

> I do not feel as if I were a man,
> But like a fiend appointed to chastise
> The offences of some unremembered world.   (4.2.160–62)

The wine he drinks in celebration of his sons' death takes on the
form of some obscene Mass:

> Could I believe thou wert their mingled blood,
> Then would I taste thee like a sacrament,
> And pledge with thee the mighty Devil in Hell.   (1.3.81–84)

The process of development of the character is thus an increasing
abstraction, until Cenci becomes the incarnation of evil, a relative
of Milton's Lucifer. It is not therefore any psychological order of
probability which gives magnitude or convincingness to the figure
of Cenci, but rather the generalization of the qualities of unnatural
evil, and the extravagant power in the expression of sensations and
passions which relate to it.

Shelley's own conception of the problem conforms to this view of
his characters: "The person who would treat such a subject," he
writes in his preface, "must increase the ideal and diminish the
actual horror of the events, so that the pleasure which arises from
the poetry which exists in these tempestuous sufferings and crimes
may mitigate the pain of the contemplation of the moral deformity
from which they spring."

Beatrice's character undergoes similar treatment, though not to
such a marked degree. She is in all respects the antithesis of Cenci:
she embodies beauty, firmness of mind, quiet courage, clarity of intellect, freedom from distorting passion, sweetness, light, and life.
To the end, she is pronounced the epitome of these qualities, and in
particular of purity and innocence. The critical difficulty raised by
Beatrice appears in her insistent denial of guilt before her accusers
and judges in a manner that suggests abdication of the qualities of
intellectual integrity and courageous honesty which are ascribed to
her. The answer to this critical problem lies in part in the philosophical conception of innocence and beauty and courage which

she represents. Cenci has lost the claim of being her father; therefore she cannot be guilty of parricide (3.1.37,40). It is not by any human order of relations that she can be innocent; but, in the sense that the forces of evil and authority are at enmity with light and freedom and truth, and that these can survive only by the elimination of the powers of darkness, the murder is merely a justifiable assertion of innocence, a triumph of light and freedom over darkness and oppression. The conduct of Beatrice after the murder, however, tends to obscure this relationship of the character to the act. She insists that the murderer, Marzio, has falsely confessed under torture, and she forces him to accept sole guilt and declare her innocent of parricide. She upbraids her family for confessing, since they have brought dishonor to an ancient name. There seems to be an uncertainty in Shelley's treatment of her, a failure to realize as fully as in the case of Cenci the process of abstraction which might have given full consistency to her actions. The sophistries of Vittoria Corombona, whom Beatrice resembles in the trial scene reminiscent of *The White Devil*, are the defenses of a sinful woman fighting for her freedom against evil and cunning men; Beatrice's, however, must spring from a higher source—they must appear to be other than sophistries or desperate dodges of a clever and strong mind. The difficulty is produced by the fact that Beatrice is seen more frequently than Cenci in purely human relations—in her sympathy with her family and her loyalty to them, in the near-madness of her violated honor, in her relations with Orsino, in her defiance of the processes of law and authority—so that the directing forces which determine her conduct appear divided and not of the same consistency as in the case of Cenci.

Shelley's treatment of his two principal characters, even though he was unable to sustain it with consistency in all respects, saved him in the main from one of the dangers of his reliance on older models, that of making them weak imitations of villains long past their prime and faded replicas of heroines of another day. Shelley wrote of this play, "It is written without any peculiar feelings and opinions which characterize my other compositions; I have attended simply to the impartial development of such characters as it is probable the persons represented really were, together with the greatest degree of popular effect to be produced by such a development."[12] Shelley's contention is not, however, fully borne out by a

comparison of *The Cenci* with some of his other works.[13] The theme
of beauty, innocence, and virtue oppressed by evil and authority
aroused him too deeply to permit purely objective handling of the
leading characters. This was a fortunate circumstance: that Shelley's
language in this play reaches such a high degree of intensity and
feeling is in part the result of his having infused into the main
characters conceptions which had inspired much of his best poetry.

The principal development in the diction centers in Cenci and
Beatrice and in the relations which exist between them. The opposition in the images is introduced in its elementary form in a speech
of Camillo's early in the first scene of the play:

> Where is your gentle daughter?
> Methinks her sweet looks, which make all things else
> Beauteous and glad, might kill the fiend within you.   (1.1.43-45)

Camillo continues,

> I stood beside your dark and fiery youth
> Watching its bold and bad career, as men
> Watch meteors . . . .   (1.1.49-51)

After hearing Cenci's statement of his evil nature and purposes,
Camillo replies:

> Hell's most abandoned fiend
> Did never, in the drunkenness of guilt,
> Speak to his heart as now you speak to me.   (1.1.18-20)

This antithesis of suggestions marks the scheme within which the
principal elaborations occur: on the one hand the dark, violent,
corrupt, satanic; on the other, beauty, light, quiet strength. But
since Beatrice is constantly under the shadow of Cenci, the latter
impressions are overwhelmed, particularly during the early portions of the play, by the somber and the horrible, as appropriate to
the life-in-death which is Beatrice's lot. Her first speech, though
not connected with Cenci, and spoken to her former suitor and apparent friend, introduces in a quiet way suggestions of gloom and
decay that play a dominant part in the associations surrounding her
during most of the play:

> You remember where we held
> That conversation;—nay, we see the spot
> Even from this cypress;—two long years are past
> Since, on an April midnight, underneath

> The moonlight ruins of mount Palatine,
> I did confess to you my secret mind.   (1.2.2–7)

More forcefully these appear in Beatrice's remarks to the guests at the banquet, when she refers to her family as "we the desolate dead" (1.3.104), and later in the same scene:

> [O] that the flowers of this departed spring
> Were fading on my grave!   (1.3.138–39)

Yet implications such as these are cut across from the beginning with others which reflect on Beatrice's essential virtues. Orsino's remarks emphasize her beauty and strength of mind:

>   I fear
> Her subtle mind, her awe-inspiring gaze,
> Whose beams anatomize me nerve by nerve
> And lay me bare . . .   (1.2.83–86)

> Her bright form kneels beside me at the altar . . .   (2.2.133)

Even Cenci's perverted tirades help these suggestions of brightness in such phrases as "fair and yet terrible." Her strength and determination are also brought out, as in the following speech of Lucretia's:

>   . . . you alone stood up, and with strong words
> Checked his unnatural pride; and I could see
> The devil was rebuked that lives in him.
> Until this hour thus have you ever stood
> Like a protecting presence: your firm mind
> Has been our only refuge and defence.   (2.1.44–49)

If these are a minor note during most of the play, it is because the figure of Cenci towers above everyone, and the dark and satanic suggestions are developed not only as they relate to him, but also as they reflect on the horrible influence which he exercises on Beatrice and the rest. The insistence on such phrases as "dark spirit" (1.2.61), "dark and bloody" (2.1.55), on the ironic contrast between Cenci's white hair and his evil soul, as in Beatrice's

>   . . . tyranny and impious hate
> Stand sheltered by a father's hoary hair.   (1.3.100–101)

> Seek out some dark and silent corner, there,
> Bow thy white head before offended God.   (1.3.156–57)

—such reiterations are the repeated fundamental which defines the key. Similar in function is the diffusion through the play of such adjectives as *impious* hate, *deep* wrongs, wrongs *strange* and *monstrous*.

strange ruin, and the like, and the frequent appearance of the word "unnatural." The most elaborate developments in the diction arise from these simple lines and their relation to the opposite terms connected with Beatrice.

In a play so rich in figurative language, it is practicable to illustrate only the most important development of the relations indicated above. The diction receives its first full elaboration in Cenci's toast to the death of his sons:

> Oh, thou bright wine whose purple splendor leaps
> And bubbles gaily in this golden bowl
> Under the lamplight as my spirits do,
> To hear the death of my accursed sons!
> Could I believe thou wert their mingled blood,
> Then would I taste thee like a sacrament,
> And pledge with thee the mighty Devil in Hell,
> Who, if a father's curses, as men say,
> Climb with swift wings after their children's souls,
> And drag them from the very throne of Heaven,
> Now triumphs in my triumph!—But thou art
> Superfluous; I have drunken deep of joy,
> And I will taste no other wine tonight.   (1.3.77–88)

The satanic suggestions predominate in this speech, and with them those of power and energy; for Cenci is a brilliant and dynamic figure, though the peculiar sources of his power convey, in this and other speeches, febrile, nervous, unhealthy implications. These are carried further in the appearance of notions of disease, unwholesomeness, and corruption, usually in speeches of Beatrice. They are introduced prominently in the opening of Act II, when Beatrice enters wild and pale from fear of Cenci's newest and most horrible design:

> . . . . He has trampled me
> Under his feet, and made the blood stream down
> My pallid cheeks. And he has given us all
> Ditch-water, and the fever-stricken flesh
> Of buffaloes, and bade us eat or starve,
> And we have eaten.—He has made me look
> On my beloved Bernardo, when the rust
> Of heavy chains has gangrened his sweet limbs,
> And I have never yet despaired—but now!   (2.1.64–72)

The end of this act introduces the most striking elaboration of the dark-light images, in a speech of Cenci's after he has announced his resolution to take his family to his remote castle, "That savage rock, the Castle of Petrella":

> The all-beholding sun yet shines; I hear
> A busy stir of men about the streets;
> I see the bright sky through the window panes:
> It is a garish, broad, and peering day;
> Loud, light, suspicious, full of eyes and ears,
> And every little corner, nook, and hole
> Is penetrated with the insolent light.
> Come darkness! Yet, what is the day to me?
> And wherefore should I wish for night, who do
> A deed which shall confound both night and day?
> 'Tis she shall grope through a bewildering mist
> Of horror: if there be a sun in heaven
> She shall not dare to look upon its beams;
> Nor feel its warmth. Let her then wish for night;
> The act I think shall soon extinguish all
> For me: I bear a darker deadlier gloom
> Than the earth's shade, or interlunar air,
> Or constellations quenched in murkiest cloud,
> In which I walk secure and unbeheld
> Towards my purpose.   (2.1.174–93)

The speech begins with suggestions of light, but they are all alien to Cenci's taste and to his purpose; it is the dark which he commands. But the suggestions shift to those of mist and foggy obscurity, for the act he contemplates is of a sinister kind more obscure and mysterious than the simple acts of violence and evil he has been guilty of thus far, and it will effectually bar Beatrice from normal humanity. As far as the diction is concerned, it separates her from clear association with light and life—"Let her then wish for night"—and demands fuller development of the gloom and horror which obscure her beauty and clear virtue. As far as the character of Cenci is concerned, in the contrast between the cosmic suggestions of the closing lines and the mundane activities alluded to in the opening ones, the speech continues his abstraction into the incarnation of the spirit of pure evil and oppression in man.

This scene is therefore a preparation for the third act, the first scene of which is little more than a profuse development of the principal imaginative suggestions established thus far. Indeed, if space permitted, proper method of illustration would be to reproduce practically the entire scene with running comment. Beatrice's language at the outset is whirling and wild, since she is represented as unhinged by the terrible injury which has befallen her; yet though what she says may lack form, poetically it is carefully sustained. Her opening words set the tone:

> Reach me that handkerchief!—My brain is hurt;
> My eyes are full of blood; just wipe them for me . . .
> I see but indistinctly . . . .   (3.1.1–3)

The immediate horror in her mind is expressed in terms of whirling and giddy motion:

> The pavement sinks under my feet! The walls
> Spin round! I see a woman weeping there,
> And standing calm and motionless, whilst I
> Slide giddily as the world reels.   (3.1.8–12)

But at once the essential imagery is introduced, in the play of dark and light images, of suggestions of corruption and purity:

> The beautiful blue heaven is flecked with blood!
> The sunshine on the floor is black! The air
> Is changed to vapours such as the dead breathe
> In charnel pits! Pah! I am choked! There creeps
> A clinging, black, contaminating mist
> About me . . . . 'tis substantial, heavy, thick,
> I cannot pluck it from me, for it glues
> My fingers and my limbs to one another,
> And eats into my sinews, and dissolves
> My flesh to a pollution, poisoning
> The subtle, pure, and inmost spirit of life!
> My God! I never knew what the mad felt
> Before; for I am mad beyond all doubt!
> No, I am dead! These putrefying limbs
> Shut round and sepulchre the panting soul
> Which would burst forth into the wandering air!   (3.1.13–27)

The light images are contaminated with blood and with darkness; they are then replaced by those of mist and vapor, which finally change into images of death and corruption stifling the air of life.

Throughout the rest of the scene derivative images and words are woven through the speeches, principally, though not exclusively, in those of Beatrice:

> O blood, which art my father's blood,
> Circling through these contaminated veins,
> If thou, poured forth on the polluted earth,
> Could wash away the crime, and punishment
> By which I suffer . . . . no, that cannot be!   (3.1.95–99)

What are the words which you would have me speak?
I, who can feign no image in my mind
Of that which has transformed me: I, whose thought
Is like a ghost shrouded and folded up
In its own formless horror: of all words,
That minister to mortal intercourse,
Which wouldst thou hear?   (3.1.107–12)

The resolution to murder Cenci introduces the description of the ravine, the place decided upon as the scene of the murder, an elaborate passage which Shelly conceded might possibly be the only detached figure in the play, the only instance of "mere poetry." It was much admired in contemporary criticisms.

Two miles on this side of the fort, the road
Crosses a deep ravine; 'tis rough and narrow,
And winds with short turns down the precipice;
And in its depth there is a mighty rock,
Which has, from unimaginable years,
Sustained itself with terror and with toil
Over a gulf, and with the agony
With which it clings seems slowly coming down;
Even as a wretched soul hour after hour,
Clings to the mass of life; yet clinging, leans;
And leaning, makes more dark the dread abyss
In which it fears to fall: beneath this crag
Huge as despair, as if in weariness,
The melancholy mountain yawns . . . below,
You hear but see not an impetuous torrent
Raging among the caverns, and a bridge
Crosses the chasm; and high above there grow,
With intersecting trunks, from crag to crag,
Cedars, and yews, and pines; whose tangled hair
Is matted in one solid roof of shade
By the dark ivy's twine. At noonday here
'Tis twilight and at sunset blackest night.   (3.1.244–65)

This is actually not as much mere poetry as the scene which follows, Giacomo's soliloquies, with the storm, the bell, and the dying lamp; but Shelley sensed its role as a kind of set piece, with the strain in the deliberate attribution of terror and toil and agony to a rock overhanging a gorge. Yet except for the obvious artifice of the lines, they have a poetic bearing as a kind of symbolic picture of Beatrice's position, courage giving way to desperation, firmness slowly being replaced by despair and resignation. The mingling of ideas of gloom and terror, the suggestions of darkness eclipsing light, scarcely need further comment.

The fourth act contains the murder of Cenci; the Count dominates the first scene, Beatrice the last. The first scene is climaxed by Cenci's curse of Beatrice, which is preceded by the introduction of the familiar images. Of his young son, Bernardo, Cenci says:

> . . . make his youth
> The sepulchre of hope, where evil thoughts
> Shall grow like weeds on a neglected tomb.   (4.1.52–54)

On Beatrice he showers disease-ridden epithets:

> Her spirit shall approach the throne of God
> Plague-spotted with my curses. I will make
> Body and soul a monstrous lump of ruin.   (4.1.93–95)

To his first demand to see her, Beatrice returns the message:

> Go tell my father that I see the gulf
> Of Hell between us two, which he may pass,
> I will not.   (4.1.98–100)

And to his second demand,

> Go tell my father that I see a torrent
> Of his own blood raging between us.   (4.1.113–14)

This reply launches him into his extended curse:

> . . . . God!
> Hear me! If this most specious mass of flesh,
> Which Thou hast made my daughter; this my blood,
> This particle of my divided being;
> Or rather, this my bane and my disease,
> Whose sight infects and poisons me; this devil
> Which sprung from me as from a hell, as meant
> To aught good use; if her bright loveliness
> Was kindled to illumine this dark world;
> If nursed by thy selectest dew of love
> Such virtues blossom in her as should make
> The peace of life, I pray Thee for my sake,
> As Thou the common God and Father art
> Of her, and me, and all; reverse that doom!
> Earth, in the name of God, let her food be
> Poison, until she be encrusted round
> With leprous stains! Heaven, rain upon her head
> The blistering drops of the Maremma's dew,
> Till she be speckled like a toad; parch up
> Those love-enkindled lips, warp those fine limbs

> To loathed lameness! All-beholding sun,
> Strike in thine envy those life-darting eyes
> With thine own blinding beams. (4.1.114–36)

This inverse treatment of Beatrice's virtues, this oscillation and fusion of the bright and lovely with the corrupt and loathsome, is the most effective expression through the imagery of the distorted mirror of Cenci's mind, but the imagery is shortly translated to another plane, for after Cenci curses Beatrice's possible offspring, he dissociates himself from mankind:

> I do not feel as if I were a man,
> But like a fiend appointed to chastise
> The offences of some unremembered world. (4.1.160–62)

And the scene ends on the purely satanic note:

> O, multitudinous Hell, the fiends will shake
> Thine arches with the laughter of their joy!
> There shall be lamentation heard in Heaven
> As o'er an angel fallen; and upon Earth
> All good shall droop and sicken, and ill things
> Shall with a spirit of unnatural life
> Stir and be quickened . . . even as I am now. (4.1.183–89)

This conclusion provides adequate preparation for Beatrice's comments during the scene in which the murder is consummated, which establish the grounds of her declarations of innocence:

> . . . our act
> Will but dislodge a spirit of deep hell
> Out of a human form. (4.2.6–8)

> . . . his death will be
> But as a change of sin-chastising dreams,
> A dark continuance of the Hell within him,
> Which God extinguish! (4.2.32–34)

With the murder of Cenci accomplished, the established suggestions appear in a new relation:

> . . . the world
> Is conscious of a change. Darkness and Hell
> Have swallowed up the vapour they sent forth
> To blacken the sweet light of life. My breath
> Comes, methinks, lighter, and the jellied blood
> Runs freely through my veins. (4.3.39–44)

The images of darkness, decay and hell are banished in this speech of Beatrice, which prepares for her direct, unqualified affirmation

of the themes of light and life, even at the moment when suspicion
falls on her:

> The deed is done,
> And what may follow now regards not me.
> I am as universal as the light;
> Free as the earth-surrounding air; as firm
> As the world's center. Consequence, to me,
> Is as the wind which strikes the solid rock
> But shakes it not.   (4.4.46–52)

In this speech the characterization of Beatrice is carried to an
extreme of generalization, suggestive of a disembodied spirit of free
life, strength, and beauty. The speech is further important for its
bearing on a development which begins in the third act (3.1.119–21;
3.1.365–69) but is accomplished principally in the fifth, which deals
with the trial and condemnation; in increasing numbers, direct
assertions and figurative suggestions appear stressing Beatrice's
sweetness and innocence. There is, for instance, Giacomo's speech:

> She, who alone in this unnatural work,
> Stands like God's angel ministered upon
> By fiends; avenging such a nameless wrong
> As turns black parricide to piety.   (5.1.42–45)

Even Camillo, one of the judges, pronounces her "as pure as speech-
less infancy" (5.2.69); and Beatrice comments on the confessions of
her family:

> O white innocence,
> That thou shouldst wear the mask of guilt to hide
> Thine awful and serenest countenance
> From those who know thee not!   (5.3.24–27)

The insistence on this idea continues to the very end, in Bernardo's
sorrow at seeing "that perfect mirror of pure innocence . . .
shivered to dust" (5.4.129–34), and in Beatrice's admonition to
Bernardo to be constant

> . . . to the faith that I
> Though wrapped in a strange cloud of crime and shame,
> Lived ever holy and unstained.   (5.4.147–49)

The dark and sinister elements in the diction do not completely
disappear. Their appearance is necessitated in part by the charges
and defense at the trial. They enter with unexpected frenzy, however, in Beatrice's response to Camillo's report that the Pope has
refused mercy:

My God! Can it be possible I have
To die so suddenly? So young to go
Under the obscure, cold, rotting, wormy ground!
To be nailed down into a narrow place;
To see no more sweet sunshine; hear no more
Blithe voice of living thing; muse not again
Upon familiar thoughts, sad, yet thus lost—
How fearful! to be nothing! Or to be . . .
What? Oh, where am I? Let me not go mad!
Sweet Heaven, forgive weak thoughts! If there should be
No God, no Heaven, no Earth in the void world;
The wide, gray, lampless, deep, unpeopled world!
If all things then should be . . . my father's spirit,
His eye, his voice, his touch surrounding me;
The atmosphere and breath of my dead life!
If sometimes, as a shape more like himself,
Even the form which tortured me on earth,
Masked in gray hairs and wrinkles, he should come
And wind me in his hellish arms, and fix
His eyes on mine, and drag me down, down, down!
For was he not alone omnipotent
On Earth, and ever present? Even though dead,
Does not his spirit live in all that breathe,
And work for me and mine still the same ruin,
Scorn, pain, despair?   (5.4.48–75)

The curiously surprising effect of this speech is not easy to explain.
Beatrice's magnificent strength, her determination even under
torture, her sustaining of her family's courage, all seem to be violated
and contradicted suddenly by this outburst. Nothing in her purely
human relations during the scenes of the arrest and trial seems to
imply this fear of death, particularly her remarks to the remorseful
Giacomo:

> What 'twas weak to do,
> 'Tis weaker to lament, once being done.   (5.3.11–12)

The lines which immediately follow these offer a clue:

> Take cheer! The God who knew my wrong, and made
> Our speedy act the angel of His wrath,
> Seems, and but seems, to have abandoned us.
> Let us not think that we shall die for this.   (5.3.113–16)

Her strength arises from her conviction that God will never permit
pure evil to triumph; yet though this faith, once destroyed, might
well lead to despair, it need not lead to a cowardly horror of physi-

cal death. It is only when Beatrice is considered in relation to the incarnation of evil in Cenci as the image of light and life that the appropriateness of the speech is more effectively established. The death sentence is the triumph of Cenci, who alone was "omnipotent on earth," and in her judges lives his spirit. The Beatrice who properly speaks in these lines is not the Beatrice who questioned the court and comforted her family, but the Beatrice who said, "I am as universal as the light." The speech illustrates the interesting mixture of the lyric and the dramatic in this work.

Immediately after these lines a note of calm enters in the fine simplicity of Beatrice's words,

> 'Tis past!
> Whatever comes my heart shall sink no more.   (5.4.77–78)

The closing note is one of resignation, but the insistent suggestion in the language is that of cold:

> How tedious, false and cold seem all things. I
> Have met with much injustice in this world;
> No difference has been made by God or man,
> Or any power moulding my wretched lot,
> 'Twixt good or evil, as regarded me.
> I am cut off from the only world I know,
> From light, and life, and love, in youth's sweet prime.
> You do well telling me to trust in God,
> I hope I do trust in Him. In whom else
> Can any trust? And yet my heart is cold.   (5.4.80–89)

> Yet both will soon be cold.
> Oh, trample out that thought! Worse than despair,
> Worse than the bitterness of death, is hope:
> It is the only ill which can find place
> Upon the giddy, sharp and narrow hour
> Tottering beneath us.   (5.4.96–101)

These speeches suggest resignation, if not defeat. And with a final denunciation of "cruel, cold, formal man," Beatrice accepts death:

> Come, obscure Death!
> And wind me in thine all-embracing arms!
> Like a fond mother hide me in thy bosom,
> And rock me to the sleep from which none wake.   (5.4.115–18)

The concluding lines end the play on a domestic touch, full however of dignity and pathos:

> Here, Mother, tie

My girdle for me, and bind up this hair
In any simple knot; ay, that does well.
And yours I see is coming down. How often
Have we done this for one another; now
We shall not do it any more. My Lord,
We are quite ready. Well, 'tis very well.   (5.4.159–65)

Here the human virtues of Beatrice are displayed, the simple pathos of her situation emphasized. There appears to be no resolution in the diction of the principal oppositions which the play develops at such length and with so much insistence. Only, in these last lines, there is an echo of some of Beatrice's words during her distraction:

How comes this hair undone?
Its wandering strings must be what blind me so,
And yet I tied it fast.   (3.1.6–8)

But this echo is remote; from the moment Beatrice says, "Whatever comes my heart shall sink no more," there is little left of the elaborate orchestration of emotions and figurative symbols that is so principal a feature of the diction in this play. Only in the few simple suggestions of cold, in the more even and measured rhythms and simple dignity of the verse, is the sense of Beatrice's resignation in the face of tragedy conveyed.

If, as many have insisted, *The Cenci* is the best single serious play that the nineteenth century produced, the reason does not apparently lie in Shelley's mastery or understanding of the dramatic form, though many scenes are excellent and have impressed men who know the stage. The numerous echoes of other plays show indirectly Shelley's lack of practical skill in the drama, which forced him to rely for many features of his play on some masterpiece suggested by the dramatic exigencies of the moment, even to the language. A lesser writer would have ended up with a ludicrous hybrid or an undigested hodgepodge, lacking not only dramatic coherence, but consistency in the diction. Shelley's poetic powers triumphed over limitations that might well have proved disastrous to others.

Shelley's great talent, however, was in lyric poetry, and a close study of the play reveals that the diction is ordered less by those requirements which are singular with drama than those which obtain in the lyric. The principal consistent development in the diction of the play arises from the opposition of Cenci and Beatrice, an interplay of contrasting suggestions which at times raises these figures to a high degree of abstraction. In this respect the handling of the diction may be compared with such a poem as the "Ode to the West Wind," in which suggestions of death, decay, and corruption alternate with those of animation, life, and regeneration. When Shelley strays from the primary opposition of the play, as in his treatment of Giacomo or Orsino, he is often betrayed into "mere poetry"; when he is inspired by the essential theme of his play, he often writes magnificently, but as if in the lyrical isolation of the moment. Moreover, the diction is characterized also by an expansive quality, a tendency to repeat the same thought in a number of ways, until every conceivable facet of the sentiment is displayed, until every ingredient has been added to form the peculiar flavor of the feelings which are being expressed. It is thus that Shelley works in his other poems; consider, for instance, the series of figures in the opening stanza of "Hymn to Intellectual Beauty," and the train of similes in "To a Skylark."

This is, in fact, a characteristic mark of much Romantic poetry, where the desire to describe exactly the "powerful feelings" which the poets' themes induced often produced sustained series of related analogies, similes, metaphors, which by an accumulation of complementary suggestions limit and define some precise range of feeling. The diction is largely ordered by the definition of feeling, and this is precisely the way, moreover, that Shelley saw his problem in *The Cenci*: "In a dramatic composition," he wrote in his preface, "the imagery and the passion should interpenetrate one another, the former being reserved simply for the full development and illustration of the latter." Such methods, admirably suited to poems of a lyrical nature, are less well adapted to the drama, where properly the diction demands to be ordered finally by the action, and not by emotion. The reiteration is static, seldom progressive and in delicate adjustment to the demands of the narrative. To all the real merits that may be attributed to this play, the ordering of its rich and powerful diction to the full needs of drama is not one. *The Cenci* is an impressive work, but it is not great drama, not merely because Shelley lacked the requisite training in the mechanics of the form, but because he wrote primarily as a lyric poet.

Byron's plays are among the most interesting and creditable of the nineteenth-century efforts to bring high seriousness and artistic dignity once more to English drama.[14] He showed an early interest in the theatre, and during 1815 was one of the committee of amateurs who took over the management of Drury Lane. But he developed a distaste for the popular stage, and professed to have no interest in it for his own plays. He wrote to Thomas Moore with reference to an attempt to produce *Marino Faliero*: "I have written to Murray, to the Lord Chamberlain, and to others, to interfere and preserve me from such an exhibition. I want neither the impertinence of their hisses, nor the insolence of their applause. I write only for the *reader*, and care for nothing but the *silent* approbation of those who close one's book with good humour and quiet contentment . . . . The play is quite unfit for the stage, as a single glance will show them, and, I hope, *has* shown them; and if it were ever so fit, I will never have any thing to do willingly with the theatres."[15] In the preface to the volume containing *Sardanapalus*, *The Two Foscari*, and *Cain*, he wrote: "In publishing the following Tragedies I have only to repeat, that they were not composed with the most remote view to the stage." Such condenscension to the theatre is not normally a healthy sign in one who would write plays; but if we take into consideration the conditions of the theatre of Byron's day, we might find more than snobbish pride in his attitude. To have sought the approval of theatrical producers and actors and the pleasing of the public would have placed almost insuperable obstacles in the way of what he desired for a new drama, in view of the conspicuously degenerate standards which prevailed.

The variety in Byron's dramatic writings and the occasional discrepancies in his expressed views might leave some doubt as to precisely what his aim was; but in general it is not difficult to make out the direction he preferred. Though his *Werner* shows marks of the German school, he decried the popularity of plays composed under this influence. He also disapproved of the tendency to exalt the Elizabethans and to imitate Shakespeare. In his comments to Shelley on *The Cenci* he wrote: "I am not a great admirer of our old dramatists *as models*. I deny that the English have hitherto had a drama at all."[16] He referred to the minor Elizabethans as "your mad old dramatists" and "those turbid mountebanks—always excepting B. Jonson, who was a Scholar and a Classic."[17] He admired Joanna Baillie, however, and referred to her as "our only dramatist since Otway and Southerne,"[18] but his comments on her are so meager that it is not clear what the basis of his admiration was. What is clear is that when Byron expressed himself—as he did often—on the subject of the drama, he showed the greatest enthusiasm for the "classical" tradition, as represented in the ancients, in the French tragedians, or in Alfieri, for whom he had a genuine if qualified admiration.[19] In *English Bards and Scotch Reviewers* he urged Sheridan,

> Give, as thy last memorial to the age,
> One classic drama, and reform the stage.   (ll.584–85)

And in *Hints from Horace* he revealed further his approval of the restricted drama. In his three "historical" plays, he attempted to conform strictly to these traditions, and the letters written during the period of their composition afford ample illustrations of his views. The writing of great tragedy, he maintained "is not to be done by following the old dramatists, who are full of gross faults, pardoned only for the beauty of their language; but by writing naturally and *regularly*, and producing *regular* tragedies."[20] In the same vein he wrote on another occasion: "My dramatic simplicity is *studiously* Greek, and must continue so: *no* reform ever succeeded at first. I admire the old English dramatists; but this is quite another field, and has nothing to do with theirs. I want to make a *regular* English drama, no matter whether for the stage or not, which is not my object,—but a mental theatre."[21]

Actually only three of Byron's plays were executed in conformity to these ideals: *Marino Faliero*, *Sardanapalus*, and *The Two Foscari*, the first written in 1820 and published early in 1821, and the others written in 1821 and published, together with *Cain*, late in the same year. The earlier *Manfred* (1817) and *Cain* (1821) are distinct from these historical dramas in style, and have many qualities in common. There are two unfinished pieces: *Heaven and Earth*, on "a scriptural subject," was written immediately after *Cain*, and, in spite of Byron's protestations of its piety, remained unpublished until 1823; *The Deformed Transformed*, written apparently in 1822 and published in 1824, is a Faustian kind of fragment. The remaining play, *Werner*, appears, in the light of Byron's professed aims, something of a puzzle. Twice he made a start at dramatizing the story which forms the plot, once as a boy of thirteen, and again in 1815 when he was on the Drury Lane committee. On the basis of his mature views on the drama he should have dropped it. And yet once more, in 1821/22, he reconsidered the old idea and published the resulting play in 1822. It would be easy to argue from this that his protestations lacked sincerity, or that at best his impulse to reform sprang from intellectually generated assumptions not entirely in harmony with his own tastes. *Werner* is, in any event, universally regarded as the least impressive of his plays.

The understanding, therefore, of Byron's best effort in the drama involves a consideration of two separate kinds of styles—that represented by *Manfred* and *Cain*, and that by the three "historical" plays. In the latter group *Sardanapalus* is the most elaborate of Byron's attempts at a new drama. *Marino Faliero* is perhaps more striking in the materials of the story and offered better opportunities for dramatic concentration; but it suggests too patently the *Venice Preserved* of Otway, for which Byron had great admiration, and while the restrictions of simplicity which he placed on himself restrained him from employing his gift for grandiose utterance, its frequent passages of lengthy reflection betray Byron at times into monotonous rhetorical eloquence. *Sardanapalus*, on the other hand, has a more complex plot which involves a greater variety of episodes, so that it offered a formidable test of Byron's belief in the conventions of the classical play. It is characterized, moreover, by a greater variety in the style and more subtlety in the language. *Sardanapalus* appears to offer a critical test of the excellence at which Byron aimed, and therefore provides a clearer illustration of the difficulties he encountered in adapting his peculiar poetical gifts to the demands of the classical drama.

Sardanapalus deals with the end of the reign of the mythical last Assyrian king, whose historicity Byron apparently took for granted on the authority of Diodorus Siculus. Effeminate and hedonistic in character, Sardanapalus loathes the arts of war as inhuman and unproductive, and has during his reign provided for his people the opportunity to cultivate the arts of peace, and himself the arts of pleasure. For this he earns the contempt of most men, and while he pursues his pleasures, a conspiracy, headed by a priest whose religion he scorns and a soldier whose occupation he despises, aims at his throne. His minister, Salamenes, brother of the wife whom he has put aside for a Greek slave girl, Myrrha, is still faithful, and uncovers the plot, only to have Sardanapalus set the leaders free because he despises the harsh measures of the realist politician. The freed conspirators make their assault that night in the midst of the king's revelry. Sardanapalus, in the emergency, takes up the un-accustomed sword and performs prodigies of military valor, but the opposing forces are too strong, and, expecting defeat, Sardanapalus sends his wife and his remaining followers to safety, and then dies with his mistress Myrrha on a funeral pyre erected in his palace.

It is not difficult to see the appeal which the figure of the king had for Byron. His deliberate indulgence in pleasure, his defiance of the world's standards for political and moral excellence, his anti-clericalism, his elegant disillusion with the ways of mortals, are com-ponents of a type familiar to any reader of Byron. Unfortunately the hero does not escape the taint of a school-boyish conception in his unfailing readiness of reply, his posturing, his ornate love-making, his easy success as a warrior, and the final magnificence of the last gesture; and these all weaken the hero for tragic purposes and ob-scure his stature and the weight of his sentiments. In this respect *Marino Faliero* is superior, for Marino himself is an imposing and arresting figure with more possibilities for serious tragic develop-ment, and, except for his passionate devotion to the ideas of liberty and justice, has fewer of the characteristics of the standard Byronic figure. This is an important advantage, for the temptations which such a character as Sardanapalus offered Byron for self-justifica-tion and the exploitation of his favorite themes were sufficient to weight the work rather heavily on the side of thought and sentiment and to inspire his moody rhetoric. Nevertheless—and this is one of the principal advantages which Byron derived from adhering to the classic models—the traditions of the form were sufficient in this case to place action in a prominent position in the development of his material, and the forcing of the variety of episodes within the framework of the conventional unities allowed for a minimum dis-sipation of dramatic power. Yet he was pulled two ways—in the direction of expatiation and rhetorical inflation or easy smartness by the proximity of oft-repeated favorite themes, and toward "dramatic simplicity" and economy, by his determination to write "naturally and regularly." In a subtle but nevertheless perceptible way, the strain left its traces in the language.

The opening of the play gives every indication of a sure and practised grasp of the problem in question. Salamenes soliloquizes on the paradox of the king's character and position, and on his own curious loyalty; and the accents of his speech recall like echoes the

cadences of Dryden in the clarity of the diction, in the epigram-
matic turn of phrase, in the crispness of the antitheses:

> He hath wronged his queen, but still he is her lord;
> He hath wronged my sister—still he is my brother;
> He hath wronged his people—still he is their sovereign—
> And I must be his friend as well as subject:
> He must not perish thus. I will not see
> The blood of Nimrod and Semiramis
> Sink in the earth, and thirteen hundred years
> Of Empire ending like a shepherd's tale . . . .
> If born a peasant, he had been a man
> To have reached an empire: to an empire born,
> He will bequeath none; nothing but a name,
> Which his sons will not prize in heritage.   (1.1.1–17)*

It is as if Byron, realizing the qualities of language demanded by
the dramatic tradition he hoped to re-establish, had turned to those
writers who had once tried the same experiment. To practice a
"Greek simplcity," to write naturally and regularly and still to
write poetry—Byron faced the same problem which had confronted Dryden, and apparently sought to solve it the same way.
And the matter of the speech lends itself well to such expression.

The start, however, is deceptive, for such echoes of the style of
Restoration tragedy, and of French tragedy, do not carry very far
into the play. For the most part the desire to write naturally and
regularly led to occasional passages characterized by clarity and
directness of expression:

> I hate all pain,
> Given or received; we have enough within us,
> The meanest vassal as the loftiest monarch,
> Not to add to each other's natural burthen
> Of mortal misery, but rather lessen,
> By mild reciprocal alleviation,
> The fatal penalties imposed on life.   (1.2.348–54)

With this, however, may be contrasted Sardanapalus' description
of Myrrha at the battle:

> I paused
> To look upon her, and her kindled cheek;
> Her large black eyes, that flashed through her long hair
> As it streamed o'er her; her blue veins that rose
> Along her most transparent brow; her nostril

*References are to line numberings given in Ernest Hartley Coleridge's edition of *The
Works of Lord Byron* (London, 1899–1903).

Dilated from its symmetry; her lips
Apart; her voice that clove through all the din,
As a lute pierceth through the cymbal's clash,
Jarred but not drowned by the loud brattling; her
Waved arms, more dazzling with their own born whiteness
Than the steel her hand held, which she caught up
From a dead soldier's grasp; all these things made
Her seem unto the troops a prophetess
Of victory, or Victory herself,
Come down to hail us hers. (3.1.386–99)

Salamenes' immediate reply—"This is too much"—seems all too appropriate. The passage is overloaded, confused in its imagery, and as ostentatiously studied as the central figure in some nineteenth-century historical canvas. It is not a matter merely of good or bad dramatic writing. The style that opened the play has collapsed, its clarity, epigram, and balance giving place—and with greater frequency as the play progresses—to a tortuous accumulation of adjectives and figures. The contrast brings out vividly the fact that the play is cut through and vitiated by an unfortunate confusion of idioms, and a difficulty to settle upon an appropriate and consistent style.

It is possible, by a judicious piecing of certain of the more impressive passages in the play, to arrive at some significant qualifications to the extreme position stated above. A comparison of two important speeches will make this clear. The second act opens at sunset with a soliloquy of the priest Belesus on the eve of the attack:

The Sun goes down: methinks he sets more slowly,
Taking his last look of Assyria's Empire.
How red he glares amongst those deepening clouds,
Like the blood he predicts. If not in vain,
Thou sun that sinkest, and ye stars which rise,
I have outwatched ye, reading ray by ray
The edicts of your orbs, which make Time tremble
For what he brings the nations, 'tis the furthest
Hour of Assyria's years. And yet how calm!
An earthquake should announce so great a fall—
A summer's sun discloses it. Yon disk,
To the star-read Chaldean, bears upon
Its everlasting page the end of what
Seemed everlasting; but oh! thou true Sun!
The burning oracle of all that live,
As fountain of all life, and symbol of

> Him who bestows it, wherefore dost thou limit
> Thy lore unto calamity? Why not
> Unfold the rise of days more worthy thine
> All-glorious burst from ocean? why not dart
> A beam of hope athwart the future years,
> As of wrath to its days?   (2.1.1–22)

The question raised by Belesus finds its answer in Myrrha's speech at the opening of the fifth act following the night of the fatal battle, and the leading image now is the rising sun:

> The day at last has broken. What a night
> Hath ushered it! How beautiful in heaven!
> Though varied with a transitory storm,
> More beautiful in that variety!
> How hideous upon earth! where Peace and Hope,
> And Love and Revel, in an hour were trampled
> By human passions to a human chaos,
> Not yet resolved to separate elements—
> 'Tis warring still! And can the sun so rise,
> So bright, so rolling back the clouds into
> Vapours more lovely than the unclouded sky,
> With golden pinnacles, and snowy mountains,
> And billows purpler than the ocean's making
> In heaven a glorious mockery of the earth,
> So like we almost deem it permanent;
> So fleeting, we can scarcely call it aught
> Beyond a vision, 'tis so transiently
> Scattered along the eternal vault: and yet
> It dwells upon the soul, and soothes the soul,
> And blends itself into the soul, until
> Sunrise and sunset form the haunted epoch
> Of sorrow and of Love; which they who mark not,
> Know not the realms where those twin genii
> (Who chasten and who purify our hearts,
> So that we would not change their sweet rebukes
> For all the boisterous joys that ever shook
> The air with clamour) build the palaces
> Where their fond votaries repose and breathe
> Briefly;—but in that brief cool calm inhale
> Enough of heaven to enable them to bear
> The rest of common, heavy, human hours,
> And dream them through in placid sufferance.
> Though seemingly employed like all the rest
> Of toiling breathers in allotted tasks
> Of pain or pleasure, *two* names for *one* feeling,
> Which our internal, restless agony

Would vary in the sound, although the sense
Escapes our highest efforts to be happy.   (5.1.1–38)

The sun image, representing for the star-reading Belesus the awful
cycle of human calamity, becomes for Myrrha the symbol which
equates love and sorrow, pleasure and pain, and in the transient
beauty of its rising and setting, marks the boundaries of a calm
understanding that is vouchsafed to the true votaries of life and
renders endurable and perhaps comprehensible the "restless agony"
of human experience.

The close similarity between these two passages is clearly not
fortuitous, and the position which they occupy in the play, at the
opening of the second and fifth acts respectively, indicates their importance. Sardanapalus' desire is for pleasure and peace: death, he
says, should come unexpectedly "Midst joy and gentleness, and
mirth and love" (1.2.604). Those who oppose him, the soldier and
the priest and the restless populace, demand action, conquest, traditions appropriate to "the blood of Nimrod and Semiramis," which
are hateful to Sardanapalus: "If they hate me," he insists,

> . . . 'tis because I hate not:
> If they rebel, 'tis because I oppress not.
> Oh, men, ye may be ruled with scythes, not sceptres,
> And mowed down like the grass, else all we reap
> Is rank abundance, and a rotten harvest
> Of discontents infecting the fair soil,
> Making a desert of fertility.   (1.2.412–18)

There are thus opposed throughout the play images suggestive of
life and pleasure, and of death, violence, and unhappiness. The
latter occur with fullest concentration in Sardanapalus' recital of
his dream in Act IV, in which the vision of his warrior ancestors
appears accompanied by grisly images of violence, goblets of blood,
and the like. In a less lurid and more effective manner, they are
suggested in Myrrha's

> The dust we tread upon was once alive
> And wretched . . .   (4.1.65–66)

or in Sardanapalus' reply to Salamenes' exhortations:

> *Salamenes.*   Thy sires have been revered as Gods—
> *Sardanapalus.*   In dust
> And death, where they are neither Gods nor men.
> Talk not of such to me! the worms are Gods;

> At least they banqueted upon your Gods,
> And died for lack of nutriment.
> Those Gods were merely men; look to their issue—
> I feel a thousand mortal things about me,
> But nothing godlike.   (1.2.267–74)

On the other hand are images of love and pleasure, at times even suggesting effeminacy, such as "silken dalliance," but more often brilliance as in the use of the star images in Sardanapalus' description of his proposed banquet (1.2.551ff), or in his reply to Belesus' respect for the astrological significance of the stars:

> I love to watch them in the deep blue vault,
> And to compare them with my Myrrha's eyes;
> I love to see their rays redoubled in
> The tremulous silver of Euphrates' wave,
> As the light breeze of midnight crisps the broad
> And rolling water, sighing through the sedges
> Which fringe his banks . . .
> I see their brilliancy and feel their beauty—
> When they shine on my grave I shall know neither.
>   (2.1.252–68)

These oppositions find a figurative and even philosophical resolution in Myrrha's speech on the rising sun; and they help also to lend some artistic appropriateness to the death by fire, and to Myrrha's speech as she sets the torch to the pyre:

>   Lo!
> I've lit the lamp that lights us to the stars.   (5.1.449–50)

That such an order can be discerned in the imagery, and that the play on quick reading leaves an impression of animation, should not, however, obscure the important fact of its inner confusion. The oppositions which cut through the play, and the conflicts within Sardanapalus himself, are never fully resolved either in the action or in the diction. And this failure produces in the language at times a nervous sort of stylistic hysteria, illustrated in the king's speech to his wife Zarina:

> . . . If e'er we meet again, perhaps
> I may be worthy of you—and, if not
> Remember that my faults, though not atoned for,
> Are *ended*. Yet, I dread thy nature will
> Grieve more above the blighted name and ashes
> Which once were mightiest in Assyria—than—
> But I grow womanish again, and must not;

I must learn sternness now. My sins have all
Been of the softer order—*hide* thy tears—
I do not bid thee *not* to shed them—'twere
Easier to stop Euphrates at its source
Than one tear of a true and tender heart—
But let me not behold them; they unman me
Here when I had remanned myself. My brother,
Lead her away.   (4.1.390–404)

Moreover, the essential disharmony of styles remains a handicap throughout the play. In selected moments there is one sort of power or another, but when the context produces no demand for either Byron falls too often into banality. Sometimes it is the merest rhetorical fakery, the pomp of dead artifice:

. . . . Slave, tell
The Ionian Myrrha we would crave her presence.   (1.2.419–20)

His *Consort's* brother, minion of Ionia!
How darest *thou* name *me* and not blush?   (1.2.40–41)

Sometimes it is plain stilted dullness:

Pania.   With your sanction
I will proceed to the spot, and take such measures
For the assurance of the vacant space
As time and means permit.
Sardanapalus.   About it straight,
And bring me back, as speedily as full
And fair investigation may permit,
Report of the true state of this irruption
Of waters.   (5.1.209–16)

This is not Grecian simplicity.

Mechanically, *Sardanapalus* conforms to Byron's notion of classical principles—a serious and also a "historical" subject in which the fate of empires is involved, adherence to the unities, and even, at times, clarity and restraint of expression. But more was required. Clarity is lacking in the central character: since Byron is not sure of the answer to Sardanapalus' problem, his hero ends in posturing and glib evasions, and what the effect of this is on the language of his speeches has already been suggested. But the difficulty lies even deeper than this. Whatever style might have been devised to meet the requirements of such a play, Byron could not easily have confined himself to it. It lay outside of the current developments in the idioms of poetry and outside even of Byron's own customary idiom in the expression of such sentiments and thoughts as were suggested to him by his material. He was tempted again and again into the grandiose, expansive, and loose imagery of such characteristic pieces as *Childe Harold* and *Manfred*. This style, however considerable its merits, was not suitable for his purposes here, and the play shows every sign of the strain of trying to overcome this tendency and to force the writing into a less diffuse idiom.

Byron's classical plays come in order of composition between *Manfred* and *Cain*. There is something significant in this order, for *Cain* and *Manfred* have more in common with each other than with any of the plays in the middle group. The impression grows as one studies Byron's plays that either Byron had no conviction of real success about the "classical" plays, or that he found in the other plays a happier adaptation of the dramatic form to what he wanted to say. That these two plays are less suited to stage performance than even the classical dramas is not sufficient reason for disregarding them here, since an understanding of the efforts of the century to create a new serious drama is made more difficult by insisting on a distinction which, especially in Byron's case, frequently broke down in practice. *Manfred* and *Cain* are written in dramatic form and they are still among the works that people want to read. There are so few poetical dramas of the nineteenth century which can claim the distinction of being read at all that this gives further warrant for their consideration.

Manfred shows many marks of the gothic and German styles of drama. The opening scene is "a Gothic Gallery. Time, Midnight"; other scenes are laid on the summit of the Jungfrau, and in hall or room of Manfred's castle, and there is a general atmosphere of gothic horror and mystery-mongering in the appearance of spirits, in the awful secret of Manfred's sin. The elements of setting are largely decorative, however, overlaid on the surface of what has been frequently referred to as a Faustian conception. Actually, however, the play is no more strictly a Faustian play than it is a gothic play. Whether Byron's insistence that he did not know Marlowe's play and was not very familiar with Goethe's is the truth or not is not very important; it is simply not very fruitful or accurate to approach the play in Faustian terms. Manfred's power over spirits is an instrument—hopeless it turns out—in his search for the unknowable, in his desire to find the secret of his restlessness and to still the agony of mortal longings and sin. The fact of his power, the ethical significance of his possession of it, are not issues in the play. In the end he learns and accomplishes nothing, dying with his accustomed stoical pride and gloomy defiance. The significant feature of the form of *Manfred* is that there is no action, no resolution. In the strict sense, the form is not dramatic at all, for the parts are not ordered by an action. What the play performs is an exploration of the emotions and the thoughts of Manfred, either through soliloquies, or conversations between Manfred and selected persons who leave the scene not to enter again—the spirits, the chamois hunter, the witch, Arimanes and the spirits, Astarte, the Abbot. His death is thus not the termination of an action, but of this philosophical and emotional study; from the beginning, Manfred can know or experience or suffer nothing more as a mortal. There is no motion, no change. *Manfred* is closet drama in this sense; and the appurtenances of the gothic and Germanic dramas are merely misleading ornaments. It has more in common, essentially, with such works as *Job* and *The Crito* than with *Oedipus* or *Hamlet*.

Byron described *Cain* as "on a metaphysical subject, something in the style of Manfred."[22] *Cain* is a more spectacular and daring performance—in its day it became a *cause célèbre*—and, being free of the surrounding claptrap of current stage traditions, it reveals its essential nature with greater clarity. But the important differences are not great: both plays are inspired by the same theme—the cruel disparity between man's grand and noble aspirations and desires and the agonizing limitations and humiliations of mortality. Manfred is tormented throughout by the sense of sin, as Cain is not until the end, and the terror of death broods over *Cain*, whereas it is a release in *Manfred*; but both heroes are filled with an unquenchable desire to know the ultimate mysteries, both have a fine sense of the beauties of the universe and the splendor of their own noble thoughts, and both are hurt by the injustice of man's position. In both plays the central figure is the instrument through which Byron develops these leading ideas. Though *Cain* is less like a conventional play in its outward lineaments, it is more nearly dramatic than *Manfred*. The problems in Cain's mind are intensified by the contrast of his views with those of his family, who accept the judgment of God on their sin and continue to worship him as good. Cain is comforted by his love for Adah and for their offspring while at the same time he loathes himself for producing miserable victims in his own image. His killing of Abel is not an act of jealousy, but anger at the ready acceptance by an apparently unjust God of a sacrifice performed in a spirit of unquestioning submission by Abel, who stands in the way to prevent the desecration of his altar. Cain's striking of his brother is thus simply the most violent manifestation of his high defiance. At the end, neither his smouldering resentment nor his sense of injustice at man's ignorance and suffering leave Cain, nor his sense of great wrong in the very fabric of human existence, but he is less defiant. His branding and his exile with his family merely accentuate his isolation: he has always been alone, like Manfred. It was of such tortured souls that the Spirit spoke in *Manfred*:

> This is to be a mortal,
> And seek the things beyond mortality. (2.1.157–58)

The selection of the universally known biblical myth gives to this characteristic theme of Byron's both boldness and dignity. Byron made excellent use of the possibility for striking episodes which the story afforded, particularly in the third act, in the heated discourse which leads to the murder, in the renunciation of Cain by his family, and his remorseful and gloomy departure. Nevertheless, the principal appeal which the legend had for him lay in the character of Cain as a mouthpiece for what he himself called a metaphysical subject. That Byron did not succeed in making the myth wholly consistent with his purposes, noticeably in such matters as the Fall and the first appearance of death which stems from it, does not interfere too much with the distinct advantages which Cain offered as the central speculator of the principal themes; and in fact these features of the original story are at times incorporated as spurs to Cain's gloomy and bitter reflections. The play is strong where the myth touches man's universal problems—his apprehension concerning death, his regrets over bearing offspring which must face again the age-old evils of life, his sense of universal injustice. For such contemplations, Byron's Cain is a splendid creation.

The principal innovation which Byron introduced is the appearance of Lucifer and the journey on which he conducts Cain through inter-stellar space and the realm of the dead pre-Adamites. Lucifer is conceived of as a sort of Manichean opposite to God, who finds in Cain a congenial mortal readily encouraged in his doubts about a deity whose goodness he considers specious. The tour, which occupies all of the second act, is intended to confirm Cain's opinions, and to answer his questions about the unknown. This portion seals the philosophical nature of this play, for if the play is regarded as an action, little more can be said for this long episode than that Cain's experiences so fix him in his opinion that he is led to greater anger than usual at Abel's piety and strikes the blow that brings death into the world and his own expulsion from his family. To any reader of the play, this explanation will appear unconvincing. Lucifer is brought in as a means of carrying the thought of the play into deeper and abstruser avenues. Cain's family offer partial opportunity for inciting Cain's mind; Lucifer's appearance offers sharper impetus; and the journey affords a means for introducing speculations about the unknowable. The method suggests *Manfred*, where each of the interlocutors provides further opportunity for emotional and philosophical exploration; and in some respects, Lucifer serves less well than the chamois hunter, the spirits, the abbot in *Manfred*, each representing a distinct view against which Manfred's position can be made clear. For Lucifer is only a more ironic and sophisticated Cain, viewing things the same way, only more confirmed through superior knowledge and practised familiarity with the problems. Thus, he does not offer a dialectical opposite, as it were, so that, once the bright shock of novelty is over, the effect is one of reiteration and repetition. A further weakness arises from Lucifer's supernatural powers and superior penetration into the mysteries, exemplified in his shrewd observations about the future and his entrée into the spirit world of dead creatures; for, since Byron did not know the answers to the questions which Cain raises, neither can his Lucifer, who meets them all with coy sophistry, arch counter-question, knowing hints, and the like. What philosophical or theological inferences Byron intended by these tricks of his Manichean devil is certainly not clear, but the effect is to bring about a large amount of repetition, and, where the answer is clearly out of our grasp, the frequent use of such phrases as "it may be" or "perhaps."

The Lucifer episodes, and particularly the trans-stellar journey, are very useful, however, looked at in another light, in affording sources for enforcing and elevating imaginatively the themes of the play. The tragedy of man's aspiring mind tied to mortality is as-

serted frequently in the play, particularly during the first two acts.
It is the substance of Cain's first talk with Lucifer:

> *Lucifer.*   Mortal!
> *Cain.*   Spirit, who art thou?
> *Lucifer.*   Master of spirits.
> *Cain.*   And being so, canst thou
> Leave them, and walk with dust?
> *Lucifer.*   I know the thoughts
> Of dust, and feel for it, and with you.
> *Cain.*   How!
> You know my thoughts?
> *Lucifer.*   They are the thoughts of all
> Worthy of thought;—'tis your immortal part
> Which speaks within you.   (1.1.98–105)

Cain expresses a loathing for the mortal in him:

>   I live,
> But live to die; and, living, see no thing
> To make death hateful, save an innate clinging,
> A loathsome, and yet all invincible
> Instinct of life, which I abhor, as I
> Despise myself, yet cannot overcome—
> And so I live. Would I had never lived!   (1.1.109–15)

Yet the reflections of his mind give him a sense of greatness:

>   I feel the weight
> Of daily toil, and constant thought: I look
> Around a world where I seem nothing, with
> Thoughts which arise within me, as if they
> Could master all things . . . .   (1.1.174–78)

In the tour with Lucifer what he sees fills him with exaltation:

> Oh Gods! Oh Gods! or whatsoe'er ye are!
> How beautiful ye are! how beautiful
> Your works, or accidents, or whatsoe'er
> They may be! Let me die as atoms die,
> (If that they die), or know ye in your might
> And knowledge! My thoughts are not in this hour
> Unworthy what I see, though my dust is;
> Spirit, let me expire, or see them nearer.   (2.1.110–17)

Yet when he becomes aware of his limitations, he is plunged into
gloom:

> It is not with the earth, though I must till it,
> I feel at war—but that I may not profit

> By what it bears of beautiful, untoiling,
> Nor gratify my thousand swelling thoughts
> With knowledge, nor allay my thousand fears
> Of Death and Life.   (2.2.125–30)

Around this essential opposition of man's mortality and aspiration the whole poem turns, and from this the brooding on death and pain and God's injustice springs. To this the legend is directed, with its trees of knowledge and life, the acceptability of Abel's sacrifice of blood to God, the irony that the one most sensitive of pain should have first brought death. And it is this opposition which makes the details of the journey imaginatively appropriate. For the imagery is derived from opposing categories with suggestions of earth, darkness, loathing, against those of clearness, beauty, infinite extent. The frequency of the words "dust" and "clay" is a direct index to the direction which the diction takes on one side, and they are in most instances opposed to suggestions of mind and infinity, as in the passages quoted above. It is for this reason that the journey through space acquires significance, for it brings into more striking relief the basic images already suggested in the preceding act:

> *Lucifer.*   The maker—Call him
> Which name thou wilt: he makes but to destroy.
> *Cain.*   I knew not that, yet thought it, since I heard
> Of Death: although I know not what it is—
> Yet it seems horrible. I have looked out
> In the vast desolate night in search of him;
> And when I saw gigantic shadows in
> The umbrage of the walls of Eden, chequered
> By the far-flashing of the Cherubs' swords,
> I watched for what I thought was coming; for
> With fear rose longing in my heart to know
> What 'twas which shook us all—but nothing came.
> And then I turned my weary eyes from off
> Our native and forbidden Paradise,
> Up to the lights above us, in the azure,
> Which are so beautiful: shall they, too, die?   (1.1.266–81)

This opposition of the suggestions of "gigantic shadows," the "umbrage of the walls of Eden," and the clear beauty of the starlit heavens reflects the conflict in Cain's spirit. The journey with Lucifer brings these suggestions into closer contact and applies them on a more grandiose scale. As the earth recedes into space, it becomes a symbol of the littleness of man:

> Yon small blue circle, swinging in far ether,
> With an inferior circlet purpler it still,
> Which looks like that which lit our earthly night?
> Is this our Paradise?   (2.1.28–32)

And the trip through space suggests the illimitable scope of man's imprisoned spirit:

> As we move
> Like sunbeams onward, it grows small and smaller,
> And as it waxes little, and then less,
> Gathers a halo round it, like the light
> Which shone the roundest of the stars, when I
> Beheld them from the skirts of Paradise:
> Methinks they both, as we recede from them,
> Appear to join the innumerable stars
> Which are around us; and, as we move on,
> Increase their myriads.   (2.1.34–43)

The implied symbolism of these speeches is brought into close relation with the explicit theme of the play:

> Oh thou beautiful
> And unimaginable ether! and
> Ye multiplying masses of increased
> And still-increasing lights! what are ye? what
> Is this blue wilderness of interminable
> Air, where ye roll along, as I have seen
> The leaves along the limpid streams of Eden?
> Is your course measured for ye? Or do ye
> Sweep on in your unbounded revelry
> Through an aërial universe of endless
> Expansion—at which my soul aches to think—
> Intoxicated with eternity?   (2.1.98–109)

When Cain returns to earth, these impressions continue in the same role. Cain tells Adah:

> I have beheld the immemorial works
> Of endless beings; skirred extinguished worlds;
> And, gazing on eternity, methought
> I had borrowed more by a few drops of ages
> From its immensity: but now I feel
> My littleness again. Well said the Spirit,
> That I was nothing.   (3.1.63–69)

They return again when he speaks with Abel:

> The dead—
> The Immortal—the Unbounded—the Omnipotent—

The overpowering mysteries of space—
The innumerable worlds that were and are—
A whirlwind of such overwhelming things,
Suns, moons, and earths, upon their loud-voiced spheres
Singing in thunder round me, as have made me
Unfit for mortal converse.   (3.1.177–84)

These are the principal and most striking sources of the imagery of the play. Other minor strains appear, some of them arising from the materials of the fable. The rational pre-Adamites visited by Cain, impressive but aimless shadows, are a type of the destiny of lesser man. The two trees of Paradise suggest the paradoxical position of man, whose possession of life and thought ends in nothing but frustration and death:

Cain.   . . . the Tree of Life
Was withheld from us by my father's folly,
While that of Knowledge, by my mother's hate,
Was plucked too soon; and all the fruit is Death.   (1.1.105–8)

The sacrifice introduces images of blood which suggest in the prayer of Cain the harshness of God:

If thou lov'st blood, the shepherd's shrine, which smokes
On my right hand, hath shed it for thy service
In the first of his flock, whose limbs now reek
In sanguinary incense to thy skies.   (3.1.255–58)

Against these he offers the more benign gifts of

. . . the sweet and blooming fruits of earth,
And milder seasons, which the unstained turf
I spread them on now offers in the face
Of the broad sun which ripened them . . . .   (3.1.259–62)

Thus is enhanced the irony that Cain should stain his own hand with blood; and in the end the idea of blood expresses the bitter tragic conflict of his soul:

oh! thou dead
And everlasting witness! whose unsinking
Blood darkens earth and heaven! what thou *now* art
I know not! but if *thou* seest what *I* am,
I think thou wilt forgive him, whom his God
Can ne'er forgive, nor his own soul.   (3.1.528–33)

The striking feature of all the imagery in the play is the consistency with which it opposes one set of images against their contraries. Nowhere in the play do the figures progress or the oppositions fuse. The contrasts are maintained throughout. And this too reveals the essential nature of the play, for at no time are the issues resolved. Cain is even deprived of Manfred's capacity to suffer with theatrical hauteur. In the last lines of the play we leave Cain as we found him:

> *Adah.* Peace with him [Abel]!
> *Cain.* But with me!— (3.1.561)

The play is one impassioned questioning of the ways of God to man. The answers, direct or implied, are but evasions, and they not only fail to satisfy the philosophical demands of the interplay of ideas, but weaken at the same time the language. The fact is seen most apparently in Lucifer's trick of answering by questions:

> *Lucifer.* But as thou saidst
> Of all beloved things thou lovest her
> Who shared thy mother's milk, and giveth hers
> Unto thy children—
> *Cain.* Most assuredly:
> What should I be without her?
> *Lucifer.* What am I?
> *Cain.* Dost thou love nothing?
> *Lucifer.* What does thy God love?
> *Cain.* All things, my father says; but I confess
> I see it not in their allotment here.
> *Lucifer.* And, therefore, thou canst not see if *I* love
> Or no—except some vast and general purpose,
> To which particular things must melt like snows. (2.1.305–15)

Examples might be multiplied. For it is one weakness of Byron as a dramatist that his disposition led him to philosophical drama, and that, having not the mind of a philosopher, he was ill equipped for the special task of being a philosophical poet. Yet in all his plays he verged toward the deeply reflective, and in the plays in which he most seemed to extend and reveal his powers, in *Manfred* and *Cain*, he left the drama ordered by action for drama ordered by a dialectical pattern. What lends power to these is the stirring voice which he gave to the torturing questions of man and to the conflicting emotions which these questions arouse: what weakens them is his illusion that he is writing philosophically. There is thus a suggestion of *profondeur* in these plays—particularly in *Manfred*, though *Cain* does not entirely escape it—which does not bear close scrutiny either philosophically or poetically. At times Byron seems at the end of his resources. The reader of his plays becomes conscious of a recurrent habit of using italics. None of the plays is without this feature, and *Cain* offers numerous illustrations:

> *Cain.*   Alas! the hopeless wretches!
> They too must share my sire's fate, like his sons;
> Like them, too, without having shared the apple;
> Like them, too, without the so dear-bought *knowledge*!
> It was a lying tree—for we *know* nothing.
> At least it *promised knowledge* at the *price*
> Of death—but *knowledge* still: but what *knows* man?
> *Lucifer.*   It may be death leads to the *highest* knowledge!
> At least leads to the *surest* science: therefore
> The Tree was true, though deadly.   (2.2.156–67)

The poet who is reduced to writing thus—and the passage is by no means isolated—is less enviable than the orator who resorts to shouting. The true philosopher-poet meets such a crisis by an illuminating analogy, by a striking marriage of figures, by a dazzling accent on a word that achieves new brilliance through the alchemical effect of its context. It is not too harsh a judgment on Byron to point out that the uncertainty and philosophical immaturity of his mind rendered his diction flabby, at critical points, that the largeness of the conceptions which he strove to express strained the capacity of his language.

While all this is true, Byron appears large in stature alongside other nineteenth-century writers of verse drama. More than most of the others, he faced the problem with a clear recognition of its difficulties. He also sought to break the tyranny of the currently respectable models. And he reached a measure of success. It is not too difficult to urge one to read *Cain*, or even *Sardanapalus* and *Marino Faliero*. It is less easy to do as much for most of the others. The failure of Byron—for in the end no one of the plays shows a full coordination of the component elements nor any compelling formal excellence—is at least an impressive failure.

Tennyson demands attention both because of the number of plays which he composed, and the preëminent position which he occupied as a poet during his lifetime. Of his plays, *Becket* is most worthy of attention. It has many of the same general qualities as his other historical dramas, *Queen Mary* and *Harold*, and is dramatically superior to them. Adapted for the stage by Irving, it became an accepted vehicle for that actor's talents. Other dramatic efforts include two short pieces, *The Cup* and *The Falcon*; a Robin Hood play, *The Foresters*, in which Forest-of-Arden pastoralism and *Midsummer Night's Dream* fairy elements are restored in a heavy-handed way with strong infusion of Victorian morality; and a negligible three act piece, *The Promise of May*. The stature of Tennyson as a dramatist may be measured by *Becket*.

More expertly contrived than the other historical plays, *Becket* nevertheless suffers from lack of concentration and from a confusion in the action. The play opens with a "Prologue," a short scene in which, after some preparation, Henry II offers Becket the Archbishopric of Canterbury to fill the vacancy in the office caused by death. Becket is uncertain. The principal "business" during this scene is a chess game between Henry and Becket, which acquires an obvious symbolical significance. Becket checkmates Henry with his bishop, and the king in annoyance kicks over the board:

> Why, there then—down go bishop and king together.
> I loathe being beaten . . . .

When the action proper begins, Becket has been inducted into the office and has resolved to do his utmost in the interest of the church, though he knows that in so doing he will incur the enmity of Henry, who has committed himself to a policy of enforcing a recognition of the superiority of the civil authority in the realm. The inevitable rift occurs, several attempts at reconciliation fall short of their purpose because of Becket's refusal to accept qualifications even when he has been shown the practical dangers of such persistence, Henry's patience is exhausted, and the barons, no friends of Becket's in any case, find the occasion to kill Becket. The last scene shows us the four barons braving the Archbishop in the church and finally killing him, just as a thunderstorm breaks over the church.

If this statement of the plot gives the impression of a decisive and straightforward action, it is because at least two complicating elements have been eliminated. The decline of Becket, for one thing, is puzzling. It is not easy to determine whether Becket dies a martyr to his ideals, opposed by politicians, villains, and time-servers, or whether for all his great virtue and personal integrity, he paid harshly for his pride, his stubbornness, and his inability to see the practical necessity of compromise. The treatment of Henry is equivocal in somewhat the same way. Part of the difficulty arises from Tennyson's apparent unwillingness to permit the issue of the church versus the state, which he states clearly enough, to be involved directly in the resolution. For, as a second intrusion into the movement of the main action, Tennyson has incorporated another thread in the plot—Henry's love for Rosamund, whom he has hidden in a secret bower known only to Becket, which incurs the hatred of his suspicious queen, Eleanor of Aquitaine, and the ill will of Fitzurse, one of the barons, who hates Becket as a commoner and defender of the people, and who wishes revenge on Rosamund for having once jilted him. Eleanor turns against Becket, not because she does not admire him, but because he will not give her the secret of the bower, and she incites Fitzurse, who becomes a willing tool largely for personal reasons. Moreover, the king speaks the fatal words which the barons take as an excuse to murder Becket, not from political but personal motives: Eleanor, frustrated by Becket in an attempt to kill Rosamund, hastens to tell the king that Becket has sent Rosamund to a nunnery, though failing to tell him why and leaving him to draw the inference that this is a final interference of the Archbishop in his life. Thus, though Henry is spared the opprobrium of being incited for political reasons, the main opposition is made feeble and uncertain, not only because the love plot is so prominent during the course of the play, but because it becomes the instrument by which the main action is resolved.

Tennyson used blank verse for this play with a wide latitude of rhythmic variations. The effect is for the most part quite the opposite of ease and fluidity of motion; it is as if the formal characteristics of the lines as verse were being disguised as far as possible to give the effect of plain discourse, and the speeches are frequently characterized by parentheses, abrupt breaks in thought, ellipses, and at times syntactical looseness. The following speech of Henry's is not unusual:

> Nay, then, I take thee at thy word—believe thee
> The veriest Galahad of old Arthur's hall.
> And so this Rosamund, my true heart wife,
> Not Eleanor—she whom I love indeed
> As a woman should be loved—Why dost thou smile
> So dolorously? (Prologue)

The language is marked by numerous archaisms of form and vocabulary designed, no doubt, to suggest a past era; but such phrases as "he holp the king to break our castles" and "I warrant ye" are certainly inappropriate for Becket's century and succeed merely in generating a bastard Elizabethanism which sets up a barrier to original and vital use of language. At its occasional best, the verse has dignity of movement and the language a studied color and force, as in the following speech of Becket:

> I served King Henry well as Chancellor;
> I am his no more, and I must serve the Church.
> This Canterbury is only less than Rome,
> And all my doubts I fling from me like dust,
> Winnow and scatter all scruples to the wind,
> And all the puissance of the warrior,
> And all the wisdom of the Chancellor,
> And all the heaped experiences of life,
> I cast upon the side of Canterbury—
> Our holy mother Canterbury, who sits
> With tattered robes.   (1.1)

Yet much of the play is written in a manner which could not be distinguished from prose—a little stilted by attempts at dignity and archaism—save for the typographical distribution of the lines on the page. Nevertheless, though the writing does not often become as forceful or figurative as the lines just quoted, there is plenty of elaborateness of diction, particularly in certain portions of the play.

A consideration of the figures of speech and the striking and prominent words in the play is, however, disappointing. It is not only that in so many cases they turn out to be essentially commonplace. In many instances they serve quite clearly only a decorative purpose, the mark of a writer to whom poetical ornamentation of a deft and graceful sort came rather easily. One feature of the play encourages such treatment of language: Eleanor, the queen, is pictured as a troubador and maker of songs and verses, and she herself takes pride in this distinction and indeed takes advantage of her art to give indirectness of statement to some of her sharp observations and taunts. She is given to playing with words, expressing her thoughts with variety of turns and facets:

Louis of France loved me, and I dreamed that I loved Louis of France: and I loved Henry of England, and Henry of England dreamed that he loved me; but the marriage-garland withers even with the putting on, the bright link rusts with the breath of the first after-marriage kiss, the harvest moon is the ripening of the harvest, and the honey-moon is the gall of love; he dies of his honey-moon. I could pity this poor world myself that it is no better ordered.   (Prologue)

This is on the whole a clever device for introducing brilliance and novelty of diction, but there are not many passages even as good as the one just cited, and in general Eleanor palls. Primarily the failure of the character lies in just the fact that with a slight technical excuse for doing it there is so much of a consciously artful nature without much dramatic justification.

There is not, in fact, too much indication that Tennyson understood the necessity of adapting the artifices of language to dramatic ends. A poet who understands the need of some principle of consistency, harmony, or pattern in the language of a graceful lyric may lose sight of the similar necessity on the wider canvas and within the peculiar formal requirements of drama. Herein lies, in fact, the great weakness of Tennyson as a dramatist in verse. For this reason, the play leaves a scattered and diffuse effect; though an occasional striking image reinforces a speech here and there, it seldom shows any close relationship to the determinant elements which give probability to the work. Hence there is loss in magnitude, in concentration, in the intensification of movement which are among the special advantages of language used in a poetical way in drama.

Though this statement of the case is in general just, there are certain qualifications which can be made, indications that Tennyson was not wholly lacking in some elementary grasp of the problem. The fact may best be realized with reference to Rosamund, whose name is a clue to the figures and special words which are characteristically applied to her:

> Thou rose of the world!
> Thou rose of all the roses,   (2.1)

Henry calls her. Her son he calls "the rosebud of my rose." Eleanor herself alludes to her in the retreat built for her by Henry as "one rose in a bower"; and when the queen threatens Rosamund with a dagger, she says,

> What! have I scared the red rose from your face
> Into your heart?   (4.2)

Speeches of Fitzurse, the sullen, crude baron, also carry out this scheme; he refers to her as a blossom, a "rosefaced minion of the King." In addition, there are references to her as a bird restrained in a cage, a moth that must be saved from the flame, etc. Though lacking in vividness or force, these impressions centered in

Rosamund relate to her symbolical, almost allegorical, significance in the play. She is a representative of true feminine beauty, love, utter devotion, and faithfulness. The passionate queen and the vile Fitzurse hate her. The austere Becket is moved by her presence to reflect on the joys of feminine companionship, and takes her protection as a principal duty. The king regards her as the inspirer of his finer and nobler sensibilities; he is represented as muttering:

> I am not worthy of her—this beast-body
> That God has plunged my soul in—I, that taking
> The Fiend's advantage of a throne, so long
> Have wandered among women,—a foul stream
> Thro' fever-breeding levels,—at her side,
> Among these happy dales, run clearer, drop
> The mud I carried, like yon brook, and glass
> The faithful face of heaven—. (2.1)

She scarcely belongs to the same order of characters as the others, and only occasionally seems as one of them.

With reference to Rosamund, the metaphor associated with Henry is that of the sun:

> Oh my life's life, not to smile
> Is all but death to me. My sun, no cloud. (2.1)

This speech of Rosamund's might be taken as typical of a number of others in which this figure is used; they bear a clearly perceptible relation to the figure applied to her. But the sun images are associated with Henry in another connection, in his role as king. Herbert warns Becket of Henry's smile:

> Winter sunshine!
> Beware of opening out thy bosom to it,
> Lest thou, myself, and all thy flock should catch
> An after ague-fit of trembling. (3.3)

In the same scene, Walter Map tells Herbert, "Do you see that great black cloud that hath come over the sun and cast us all into the shadow?" And he continues working out the figure on an elaborate scale. These speeches occur in Act III, but their use is anticipated by an early speech of the king's in Act I, in which he describes how he brought order, peace, and justice out of the chaos of Stephen's reign:

> I made the twilight day,
> And struck a shape from out the vague, and law
> From madness. (1.3)

These uses of the image are more effective than those in connection with the Rosamund episodes and they constitute one of the very few consistent developments in the diction outside of the love plot. But the two are not related.

The defects in the diction of this play may be reduced to two. Where it appears to achieve a kind of consistency in connection with some scheme of relations supported by the action (in this case simply character), the development is concentrated largely in the love plot, a secondary and, as we have observed, a confusing element in the play. In the second place, these images are largely static; developed as they are chiefly around Rosamund, almost an abstract symbol, they undergo practically no dramatic change. Moreover, there is little in the diction to suggest the relations of the two threads in the plot. The point may be further illustrated in the case of Fitzurse, the noble who hates Becket and leads the finally successful efforts to kill him. There are a number of animal images applied to him—he is called a beast, a bear, a hog, a cur—and in almost every case the image is primarily suggestive of his reprehensible conduct toward Rosamund. Only in one instance are these animal figures tied in with the major action, in a speech of Becket's at the end of Act III:

> . . . the wolves of England
> Must murder her one shepherd, that the sheep
> May feed in peace.

But the suggestions involved in the animal images relating to Fitzurse are so prominently of another sort as to isolate this one from the general development in the diction. There is little help from the diction in resolving the initial dramatic ineptitude involved in the relationship of the two threads of the plot.

The effort to give grandeur to Becket through the diction is apparent throughout, but is only partly successful. His speeches often have dignity and strength, and at times they are intensified by effective figures. Thus, he expresses himself on his allegiance to the cause of the church:

> I gash myself asunder from the King,
> Tho' leaving each, a wound; mine own, a grief
> To show the scar forever—his, a hate
> Not ever to be healed.   (1.1)

There is not, however, any consistent accumulation of figures which adds weight to the character at the same time that it intensifies the probabilities which it introduces. Moreover, the preponderance of figures relating to Becket appears in the speeches of the king, or of Becket's opponents, which tend to give picturesque strength to their private annoyance and aversion. Henry says of his mistrust of Becket:

> The bird that moults sings the same song again,
> The snake that sloughs comes out a snake again.   (1.3)

When Becket flees to France, Henry refers to him as a wounded deer fled from his presence and feeding-grounds (2.2.); he is the crow that "hath all but climbed the Roman perch again" (2.2); he has fled the church by night, thief-like, no man pursuing (2.2.). Henry dwells on his favors to Becket:

> I raised him from the puddle of the gutter,
> I made him porcelain from the clay of the city.   (1.3)

> The slave that eat my bread has kicked his king!
> The dog I crammed with dainties worried me!   (5.1)

Other expressions of a similar sort come from his enemies. Says Roger of York, for instance,

> Yes, since he flouts the will of either realm,
> Let either cast him away like a dead dog!   (2.2)

To be sure, these are chiefly expressive of the venom and violence of his opponents; but against these there is no very considerable compensating set of images. A few there are; Foliot calls him a "mitred Herclules" for his strength, for instance. Yet there is little in the diction which enables the cardinal to rise above the expression of opposition by his enemies or the confusions of the action. It is only through the simplicity and dignity of his speeches toward the end of the play that the impression of the cardinal's strength is made evident by means of the diction.

It might at first glance seem surprising that Tennyson's recognized technical virtuosity should have proved unequal to forging a medium proper to drama which, by providing the impetus of intense situations, might be supposed to have encouraged some of his best efforts. The fallacy lies in assuming, first, that a dramatic poet, working with a faulty or uncertain dramatic design, will be likely to coordinate his resources of language to anything like their full concentration; the chances are that he will be led to obvious deco-

ration and ornamentation. It further lies in assuming that because
Tennyson showed real gifts in writing good verse, he could, by
applying the same talents, compose effective dramatic speeches.
Tennyson's chief originality as a technician lay in his ability to use
language for its melody, sound, movement, and the like, with an
overhanging texture of sensuous suggestion. The diction of a play
cannot rise above the level of a writer's essential qualities as an arti-
ficer of language, and Tennyson's peculiar virtues and limitations
as a poet were those least likely to lead to success in the drama.
When he struck on material which lent itself to his characteristic
gifts, as in *The Lotus Eaters* and *Tithonus*, he did his finest work.
These gifts are less useful in drama—at least in such drama as
Tennyson chose to write; and Tennyson found an outlet for them
chiefly in the lyrics, which he scattered through his plays. The
following is one of Rosamund's songs:

> Rainbow, stay,
> Gleam upon gloom
> Bright as my dream,
> Rainbow, stay!
> But it passes away,
> Gloom upon gleam,
> Dark as my doom—
> O rainbow stay.   (3.2)

It is heavy and languid with mechanical virtuosity. And it is thin,
except for a faint symbolism. It illustrates one of the serious weaknesses of this play— a persistent trace of thinness and obviousness
in the imagery. But an even more damaging defect is the failure to
use the devices available to the poet in a dramatic way. Tennyson
was too good a craftsman not to produce some effective lines in his
best play, but his dramas show no real grasp of the necessity for
making the language in a verse play other than momentarily striking or ornamental and decorative.

In the melancholy history of nineteenth-century drama, Browning occupies a unique position. Like Byron, he brought sincere and
intelligent interest, originality, and genuine poetic talents to the
task of writing plays; moreover, his best non-dramatic works, unlike those of Byron, seem to imply the greatest promise of success in
the writing of plays. And he did not lack encouragement. Macready
himself recognized enought talent in *Paracelsus* (1835), Browning's

earliest acknowledged poem, to urge the young poet to write him a play and "save me from going to America." The result was *Strafford*, performed by Macready in 1837, which, though not a success, was at least not too discreditable a first effort. For some years thereafter, Browning tried, though in vain, to write a play which would succeed on the stage. Even *Pippa Passes* (1841), which was not intended for the stage and is frankly an original experiment in dramatic form, gives evidence of this effort: the Jules-Phene episode is influenced by a prominent theatrical success, Bulwer-Lytton's *Lady of Lyons*, and the evidence shows that Browning paid close attention to the work of the one contemporary who seemed to have mastered the trick of writing poetic drama and at the same time drawing the audiences.[23] Browning, however, never succumbed to the facile devices of his more popular contemporary, nor abandoned his search for a fresh and original treatment of dramatic form; he was never, however, to find a wholly satisfactory solution to his problem. Of the six plays following *Pippa Passes*, four were designed for performance: *King Victor and King Charles* (printed 1842) was rejected by Macready, and *The Return of the Druses* (printed 1843) was likewise not performed; *A Blot in the 'Scutcheon* had but slight success—and precipitated Browning's quarrel with Macready; and *Colombe's Birthday* (printed 1844), the last play which Browning wrote expressly for the stage, did not see performance until 1853, when it had a modest success with Helen Faucit at the Haymarket. During the composition of his next play, *Luria* (printed 1846), Browning wrote to Elizabeth Barrett that "it is for a purely imaginative stage," and of his final dramatic effort, *A Soul's Tragedy* (printed 1846), he wrote with such diffidence that Miss Barrett was surprised to find it so good a work. Browning had apparently come to realize that the best fruition of his genius was not to be in the drama.[24]

Though there is general unanimity among critics of Browning that he did not live up to his promise as a dramatist, yet there is clearly reflected in their comments on the plays an interest which goes beyond the attention accorded to the secondary or unsuccessful efforts of an important writer, a recognition of some vitality, or close aim to greatness, which inspires a serious desire to see into their essential nature. And almost invariably, each critic finds some one play which he believes escaped the defects of the rest, and merits esteem and praise, if not as a piece for the theatre, at least as a work for the "closet." Most curious of all is the general lack of agreement among the critics on this point, for each one of the plays has been at one time or another singled out for special distinction. This diversity of opinion is a mark both of Browning's puzzling failure ever to subdue happily the resources of the dramatic form to his purposes, and, at the same time, of the originality and vigor with which he pursued his task. It is true that Browning's work shows traces of other dramatists, and scholars have tracked his footsteps in their snows: Shakespeare's influence has been noted, and even that of Shelley, Bulwer-Lytton, Alfieri.[25] But there is not in Browning's drama anything to arouse immediate memories of earlier models, as, for example, is the case with the Elizabethan parallels in *The Cenci*, or the Germanic features of *Remorse*. None of the common influences left a fatal stigma on his work or exercised a pall on his imagination. His style itself is indication of his independence; almost alone of those who tried to write poetic drama during this period, he largely purged it of pseudo-Elizabethanisms and saved it from becoming a hybrid. He may have profited by the Elizabethans, but he was not ruined by them. The materials he used, the ends he sought, the style he employed, were in the proper sense his own. His failure was not that of subservience to tradition or lack of ideas.

What disturbs most sympathetic readers of Browning is that the author of the dramatic monologues, with their searching into human nature, should have come so short of the mark in drama. Only those, however, schooled in "character analysis" as the principal feature of serious dramatic study could have persevered for long in this bafflement, and there has been no lack of critical answers to their dilemma.[26] For, once the nature of the dramatic monologues is understood, it becomes apparent that there is a fundamental difference between the ends and means employed therein and those required by drama, and hence excellence in the one form does not necessarily imply distinction in the other. In fact, if the dramatic monologue be regarded as the form most suited to Browning's genius, it would be safer to hypothecate on this assumption that Browning would be little more than an ingenious experimenter in the drama. The dramatic monologue seeks to establish the obscure springs of conduct, the hidden motives to action, in a complex individual, or to reveal a human being in a moment of self-understanding. Its end is, in short, the exploration of the human soul. To this end, the individual is viewed in a critical situation which brings into play his hidden motives and impulses and thus reveals the character in its true light. What renders it "dramatic" is but the instrument of discovery, the situation which calls into being the true indices to the character. Now, formally considered, the end of drama cannot be, primarily, the exploration of motive, the discovery of character. Character is demanded as one of the elements, perhaps the most important, which give probability or necessity to the action, but is is precisely this use of character as one of the determinants in a sustained and complete action which Browning seems never to have fully grasped, or perhaps wished to concern himself with.

The plays themselves give evidence enough of Browning's difficulties in coping with this problem, and none perhaps so strikingly as *The Return of the Druses*. Each of the three principal characters is placed by the developing situations of the play into perplexing dilemmas of highly unusual sort. Djabal wishes to save his people, and decides to pose as the god Hakeem in order to arouse them to unity and action; but this stratagem torments him because it promises success through fraud, and because it makes impossible his love for Anael. She, on the other hand, has sworn to marry none but the saviour of her people, but since he is apparently to be the god Hakeem, marriage is out of the question, even though she loves Djabal as a mortal. The situation is further complicated by Loys, the knight-novice who, because of his love for Anael, secures for himself the election as prefect over the Druses in order to replace the corrupt government of his predecessors and thus bring good rule to an oppressed people; yet to secure this office, he must take a vow of knighthood which will make marriage with Anael impossible. Other complications arise which it is needless to mention; the basic ones illustrate clearly enough how rich the possibilities are for soul struggle and analysis. The play is one extended series of monologues in the form of soliloquies, or even lengthy asides, in which the character probes his dilemma; the action is a frame to hang them on. Dialogue becomes a weird talking at cross-purposes, since none of the characters can reveal their true thoughts and intentions, and conversation ends in obscure searching or revelation of soul. Yet there is at least an air of consistency within this elaborate scheme, achieved perhaps because the problems which face these characters are such as inspire only the most academic interest and hence can be displayed in the form of elaborate exercises, as it were, in the presentation of special phases of thought and passion.

Elsewhere, Browning is not very successful in preserving a character clear and intact through the course of a long and involved action. In *King Victor and King Charles*, on the essential matters of Charles' ability to rule, his motives for retaining or giving up the crown, or the particular source of power which his wife has over him, the play is not very illuminating; something profound may lurk there but it is always to seek. In an entirely different way *A Soul's Tragedy* illustrates the same difficulty, though here the solution is neat and effective. The play is in two parts, one in verse, the other in prose: "Act first, being what was called the poetry of Chiappino's life; and act second, its prose," is Browning's note under the title. The first part shows Chiappino arising in a crucial moment to an act of self-sacrifice and heroism; the second shows his corruption with the acquisition of power. Each episode brings out Chiappino's character through a situation capable of forcing one aspect into prominence, and each is clearly and effectively conceived. Yet the dramatist upon instinct would have been concerned primarily with the portion which intervenes, with what Browning left as a hiatus. He would have shown the course of the change and the related steps by which Chiappino is brought to his final humiliation. Browning, on the other hand, selects, as he does in his dramatic monologues, two vital episodes, each implying antecedent developments, and reveals the character through these. Each of these episodes develops, as the monologues often do not, a brief action analogous to a clearly conceived scene in a long play. Within these sharp limits, Browning seems to have done his most successful work in the drama: when he tried to construct a continuum of related scenes in a large-scale dramatic form, either the plots became absurd, or the characters confused and paradoxical. The closer the plays approximate, in purpose and scale, the dramatic monologues, the more effective they seem to become.

It is perhaps for these reasons that *Pippa Passes* remains—for all that it is still the battleground for critical controversey—the only perennial among Browning's excursions into drama.[27] To be sure, it does not conform to the conventional pattern of stage plays, and it was clearly an experimental adaptation of these conventions, a distinct novelty in form. But it possesses exactly those qualities which make *A Soul's Tragedy* effective, and evades the difficulties which bring artistic and logical diffusion to *The Return of the Druses* and *King Victor and King Charles*. Each of the four episodes is distinct from the others, even more so than in *A Soul's Tragedy*, since the separate characters and events have no functional relation with one another. In each case, an individual is placed in a crisis, and the action of the scene, brief and sharp, brings about the self-revelation, the decision, the probing of motives, which lights up the character, shows it in heightened relief, and forces its hidden conflicts to a moment of resolution. Except for the common note of irony contributed by Pippa's conviction that each of these leading figures is worthy of admiration or envy, and the not wholly necessary factor that unwittingly Pippa is herself a principal in certain of these actions, notably the fourth, these episodes are separate and self-contained. In each instance, Pippa's song, breaking in at a crucial moment in the action of the scene, precipitates the final decision, but Pippa is in no sense a principle of unity among the discrete episodes. She appears as an accidental catalyst which hastens the resolution in each case, and her song is a device for crystallizing the crucial moment. Thus *Pippa Passes* is perhaps Browning's best adaptation of the dramatic form, largely because it subdues it most successfully for purposes which find their best fruition in the dramatic monologues. At least two of these episodes—the Ottima-Sebald and the Monsignor-Intendant—may be considered as effective excursions in the one-act play form; but apparently Browning's gifts, or his artistic aims, could carry him no further than these incisive vignettes in playwriting.

The problem of Browning's dramatic style may be viewed in the light of these conclusions, though other considerations need to be raised in addition. One of the commonest charges against it is that of obscurity; but if the distinction between a good and a bad dramatic style depended wholly upon the ease with which an average audience can follow the lines, some notable speeches in Shakespeare would fail the test. One important defect is that Browning is at times difficult to no purpose. Consider the following lines from *The Return of the Druses*:

Does the day break, is the hour imminent

When one deed, when my whole life's deed, my deed
Must be accomplished? Hakeem? Why the God?
Shout, rather, "Djabal, Youssof's child, thought slain
With his whole race, the Druses' Sheiks, this Prefect
Endeavoured to extirpate—saved, a child,
Returns from traversing the world, a man,
Able to take revenge, lead back the march
To Lebanon"—so shout, and who gainsays?   (1.2)

Since the end here is simply exposition, it hardly justifies so cumbersome a method. Prospecting is worth the pains for gold and diamonds, but hardly for a common brick or two, and it must be admitted that Browning exacts labor of his reader without regard to the results. Yet if this were the most damaging objection that could be brought against the style, it would not be unduly important, for in spite of this difficulty, the style of Browning had, under the circumstances, some very obvious advantages.

One of the marks of nineteenth-century poetic drama is the self-conscious dignity which writing in verse seems to have thrust on the writer, with the attendant temptation to indulge in fruitless ornament and commonplace loftiness and to copy the manner of models which possessed the merit of established greatness. By the revolutionary eccentricity of his style, Browning largely escaped the worst of these faults. The very "unnaturalness" of his phrasing, in contrast to the formalities of most dramatic verse, suggested unpremeditated discourse and removed much of the danger of gratuitous elegance and decoration indulged in by many of his contemporaries. In addition, it rendered nearly impossible the hybrid Elizabethanism which lent a touch of staleness to the work of others and which set hindrances in the way of a diction consistent within itself and directed toward the dramatic purpose at hand. There was also the gain of zest and freshness which always accompany a bold turn to fresh paths. Browning's contemporary, Tennyson, took up where the Romantics left off, and the way led him toward greater technical mastery over the style, but also toward a thinning out and dilution of the imagery and diction with a consequent loss of concentration and power. Browning left that path, acquiring qualities often the exact opposite of Tennyson's—roughness where Tennyson had melody and ease, obscurity where Tennyson had transparency, and barenness where Tennyson had ornament.

Both for the qualities of his style and his break with the prevailing idioms in verse, he has been likened to Donne; but beyond a certain point the analogy is misleading. Browning lacked Donne's capacity for brilliant, informing imagery. It is true that, particularly by such devices as ellipses, the style produces an effect of concentration and suggestion which secures at times something of the advantage of figurative language. Nevertheless, he was often betrayed into sheer mannerisms; the overzealous and consistent indulgence of his verbal tricks where they serve no useful purpose is, in fact, one of the disturbing features of his style. He also lacked Donne's impressive intellectual virtuosity and complexity. Browning's thought is essentially too simple for so tortuous a style, and in the purely philosophical or dialectical portions of his work it shows to poor advantage. Where, however, some character is represented as tussling with his thought as in *Paracelsus*, or where the end is some complex exploration in psychology, as in the dramatic monologues, the vagaries of his tortured idiom often fit in admirably.

In the plays, therefore, the style shows to best advantage in soliloquies, or in dialogue which represents the characters as attempting to explain difficult situations or to find their way out of a trying dilemma. It might be said of the style, as of the dramatic design usually followed by Browning, that it is at its functional best when the immediate concern is one of character. Herein lies its failure to be consistently effective in the plays, since only rarely did Browning write with any degree of freedom from the peculiar devices which mark his style. His failure to execute any successful large-scale dramatic design and his failure to adapt his style to dramatic purposes go hand in hand.

Illustration of these points from the bulk of the plays would be cumbersome, yet the constant experimentation of Browning makes the selection of a typical case very difficult. Each play is a special illustration of the general problem. *A Blot in the 'Scutcheon* has at least the advantage of familiarity which few of the other plays of Browning enjoy. Barring *Strafford*, which is admittedly his least original attempt, it comes closer than the rest to the conventional scheme of a play, with a precise and quickly developing action and characters clearly and consistently presented. There is also considerable art in the language and in the use of such emotional and symbolical devices as Tresham's recollections from childhood. It is also relatively free from obscurity and over-subtlety, qualities which lend a dead weight of false profundity to some of the other plays. At the same time, it is not convincing and in many ways it is absurd. Yet it comes toward the end of Browning's attempts to write for the stage, and its failure is in its own way illustrative of Browning's difficulties with the drama.

The action is represented as taking place in the eighteenth century, apparently to provide an appropriate setting for Lord Tresham's fastidious zeal for personal and family honor which determines the course of the play. The play opens with the visit of a youthful neighbor, Lord Mertoun, who comes to ask for Tresham's sister Mildred in marriage. Tresham is favorably impressed and sends word to his sister of his desire to have her meet the young earl in the near future. It appears in a subsequent scene, however, that Mildred has been receiving a young man into her room, who enters her window at midnight after a prearranged signal, and the young man is Mertoun. About the time that Mildred and Mertoun are hopefully discussing the end of their precarious position through the happy acceptance of Mertoun by Tresham as her future husband, an old servant is telling Tresham of having observed an interloper stealing into Mildred's window at various times after receiving a signal. Confronted by Tresham's knowledge of her secret, Mildred admits her sin but refuses to name the young man, and then infuriates her brother by declaring herself willing to receive the attentions of the earl. That night Tresham awaits the arrival of Mildred's visitor, and on his arrival insists on a duel, even when he discovers him to be Mertoun. Mertoun scarcely defends himself and receives his death wound, but before he dies he insists that Tresham alone shall bear the news to Mildred. This the now remorseful Tresham does. Mildred forgives him, and dies, and then Tresham dies also from the effects of poison which he had taken just before the interview.

It is clear from this brief summary that Browning had his eye on theatrical effectiveness, and that he had put aside the piled up complexities of soul-struggle and intricacies of situation which had reached their limits in his preceding play, *The Return of the Druses*. It appears on closer reading that he has also given great thought to the style. Often the peculiar eccentricities of his manner are softened. The language is richer in figurative touches. It is also true that there are slight traces of Elizabethanisms in the style in a way not common with Browning. Since the play also shows traces of the Shakespearean drama in the plot—Benedick and Beatrice have been traced in Guendolen and Austin, and Romeo and Juliet in the young lovers—it may well be that Browning's failures in the drama had made him a little more responsive to guidance from the acknowledged master. The general effect of the Elizabethan style on this play was to modify, at times, the more obvious features of Browning's writing, and at times to spoil it by the unfamiliar and inconsistent traits of another idiom. Neither of these points must, however, be exaggerated; the reader of Browning's verse will have no difficulty recognizing Browning in *A Blot in the 'Scutcheon.*

The simplicity and directness of this play brings to the fore certain interesting details in the diction. At least one clear, if somewhat obvious, development occurs in relation to Mertoun and the idea of the blotted 'scutcheon. In her interview with Guendolen, Mildred says:

> Dear Guendolen, 'tis late!
> When yonder purple pane the climbing moon
> Pierces, I know 'tis midnight. (1.3)

And a few lines later,

> . . . look,
> The moon-beam purpling the dark chamber! (1.3)

When Guendolen leaves, Mildred places her lamp before the purple pane, and at the signal, Mertoun enters through the window. These suggestions of moonlight and color are brought into relation with the action of the play through the fact that Mertoun is regularly viewed in these trysts in a moonlight. As he leaves the chamber from the interview, Mildred watches him:

> His foot is on the yew-tree bough; the turf
> Receives him: now the moonlight as he runs
> Embraces him. (1.3)

In the next scene Gerard's account to Tresham of these visits introduces the same objects—the long avenue of trees leading to the "last great yew tree," the lamp moved from the red to the "small dark-blue pane," and Mertoun's emergence from the window "in a great moonlight" (2). Similarly Tresham says to Mildred after the death of Mertoun:

> Why, as he lay there,
> The moon on his flushed cheek, I gathered all
> The story ere he told it. (3.2)

Tresham's reference to the moon bathing the form of the dead youth comes somewhat unexpectedly, since the whole effect of the scene of the duel is gloomy and darkened. The principal suggestions are produced by the great avenue of trees on the Tresham estate:

> *Tresham.*   Again here! But I cannot lose myself.
> The heath—the orchard—I have traversed glades
> And dells and bosky paths which used to lead
> Into green wild-wood depths, bewildering
> My boy's adventurous step. And now they tend
> Hither or soon or late; the blackest shade
> Breaks up, the thronged trunks of the trees ope wide,
> And the dim turret I have fled from, fronts
> Again my step; the very river put
> Its arm about me and conducted me
> To this detested spot.   (3.1)

In the concluding scenes, these darkened grounds not only establish an appropriate atmospheric gloom for the scene of the death, but they take on an added significance in their almost symbolic character as the physical counterpart of the great ancestral heredity that is vital to Tresham's whole order of life. Thus at the close of the scene in which the young earl dies, Tresham muses on his youth—one of several of his recollections of childhood during critical moments which usually have more than a sentimental irony about them:

> . . . Dear ancient trees
> My fathers planted, and I loved so well!
> What have I done that, like some fabled crime
> Of yore, lets loose a Fury leading thus
> Her miserable dance among you all?
> Oh, never more for me shall winds intone
> With all your tops a vast antiphony,
> Demanding and responding in God's praise!
> Hers ye are now, not mine! Farewell—Farewell!   (3.1)

The yew-tree avenue, moreover, has a regular if subordinate part in the references to Mertoun's trysts with Mildred. As the tragedy progresses to its close, it is appropriate that those elements producing somber impressions should be raised to importance. The effectiveness of this turn will be seen in Tresham's speech to Guendolen:

> When you and Austin wander arm-in-arm
> Through our ancestral grounds, will not a shade

> Be ever on the meadow and the waste—
> Another kind of shade than when the night
> Shuts the woodside with all its whispers up?
> But will you ever so forget his breast
> As carelessly to cross this bloody turf
> Under the black yew avenue?   (3.1)

This speech recalls Mildred's lines in a way which shows the reversal which has been made:

> His foot is on the yew-tree bough; the turf
> Receives him: now the moonlight as he runs
> Embraces him.   (1.3)

This line of interrelations in the diction has at least the merit of maintaining a close association with the main movement in the action; it is functional in the sense that in addition to any purely atmospheric and decorative purpose which the images and suggestions have at the moment, they are tied in a progressive way to the changing course of the plot and to the agents involved in it. Other lines of development in the figures seem to bear a tenuous connection with the main one. There is, for instance, the elaborate use of sunrise images in the scene in Mildred's chamber during her secret meeting with Mertoun, which symbolize their hopes for the future now that Tresham has approved of their marriage, in contrast to the moonlight and secrecy of the past. Mertoun speaks:

> Does a new life, like a young sunrise, break
> On the strange unrest of our night, confused
> With rain and stormy flaw—and will you see
> No dripping blossoms, no fire-tinted drops
> On each live spray, no vapour steaming up,
> And no expressionless glory in the East?   (1.3)

Mildred, brooding on her guilt, seizes on the storm images:

> The night
> You likened our past life to—was it storm
> Throughout to you then, Henry?   (1.3)

Mertoun replies gallantly,

> Of your life
> I spoke—what am I, what my life, to waste
> A thought about when you are by me?—you
> It was, I said my folly called the storm
> And pulled the night upon me. 'Twas day with me—
> Perpetual dawn with me.   (1.3)

Once more these images emerge during the later portion of the scene.

> *Mildred.*   One night more.
> *Mertoun.*   And then—think, then!
> *Mildred.*   Then no sweet courtship-days,
> No dawning consciousness of love for us,
> No strange and palpitating births of sense
> From words and looks, no innocent fears and hopes,
> Reserves and confidences: morning's over!
> *Mertoun.*   How else should love's perfected noontide follow?
> All the dawn promised shall the day perform.   (1.3)

Isolated from the rest of the scene, this sequence reveals more clearly the confusion in its development. Its initial connection with the moonlight images is apparent, but it is less clear what governs its unfolding. The future which was to usher the dawn ultimately is noontide, and what stood for night and storm appears to have been morning. Such a paradoxical play on images might have been capable of brilliant results, except that little more than mutual complimenting plus an all too obvious ingenuity of playing with figures seems to determine the transformation here. The whole episode suggests that consciously or unconsciously Browning had the scene in Juliet's chamber in mind. In any case, a comparison of the two scenes in the matter of diction, though unfair as all comparisons with Shakespeare usually are, makes clear the failure in Browning's case. It will be recalled how brilliantly the night and dawn images in *Romeo and Juliet* are managed, and how precisely and richly they conform, or rather contribute, to the formal scheme of the play. In comparison, the diction in Browning's scene appears haphazard; in the end, no further purpose seems to have been served except an exhaustion of the possibilities in the initial figure, with only slight contributions of a formal sort. Much later in the play the simple dawn image comes into its own, when Mertoun observes Mildred's signal just before Tresham interferes:

> And see my signal rises, Mildred's star!
> I never saw it lovelier than now
> It rises for the last time. If it sets,
> 'Tis that the reassuring sun may dawn.   (3.1)

This speech further illustrates that the elaborate turning about of the initial figure serves no very real purpose.

Several other types of suggestions stand out at various points in the play—those of blood, for example, fire, and death and the grave, the last of which is responsible for one of the most impressive speeches in the play, when Tresham contemplates Mildred's guilt and apparent brazenness:

> What were it silently to waste away
> And see her waste away from this day forth,
> Two scathed things with leisure to repent,
> And grow acquainted with the grave, and die
> Tired out if not at peace, and be forgotten?   (2)

But in most cases the attachment of these to the important determinant elements in the play is very tenuous, and they function principally to intensify sentiment or feeling in a given speech, rather than to weld the speech with all that is important in the play. Nevertheless, there is enough art in the diction of the play to justify, other things being equal, considerable expectation. Unfortunately, other things are not equal.

For one thing, the isolation of the illustrations used above does not bring out numerous other portions of the play in which Browning writes at length in his customary idiom, with its involved tumbling syntax, its elaborate parentheses, its indications of interruption where often no one is interrupting and no one apparently wants to interrupt, and with frequently a curious crude emphasis in the diction.[28] The following speech of Guendolen's will illustrate; it is spoken to Austin just after Tresham denounces Mildred:

> If you spoke on reflection, and if I
> Approved your speech—if you (to put the thing
> At lowest) you the soldier, bound to make
> The king's cause yours and fight for it, and throw
> Regard to others of its right or wrong,
> —If with a death-white woman you can help,
> Let alone sister, let alone a Mildred,
> You left her—or if I, her cousin, friend
> This morning, playfellow but yesterday,
> Who've said, or thought at least a thousand times,
> "I'd serve you if I could," should now face round
> And say, "Ah, that's to only signify . . .   (2)

And so on for twenty-five more lines, while Mildred lies on the floor in a faint. What uses does this style serve in the play? It will be noticed in the first place that the language in this speech is of a distinctly different order from that in the speeches so far dealt with;

language is ordered to a different purpose and apparently serves slightly different ends. The irregularity of the cadences is designed to represent the rhythms of spontaneous discourse in a crisis, just as it does in other cases, such as Tresham's interview with Mildred, or Mertoun's impassioned speeches in Mildred's chamber. Its end is thus a kind of verisimilitude, and it is achieved in part by concealing as far as possible the character of the lines as verse. Thus there is an essential disharmony between such a style and one in which the resources of poetry are frankly employed for whatever purpose they may be found useful; and both find a place, though not without friction, in this play.

Since the best use to which Browning put his peculiar poetical characteristics was in the exploration of character, it might be supposed that, as in the other plays, it would be similarly used here. But there must be genuine depth or complexity of character before the style can be thus employed without sacrificing dignity, and none of the characters in this play justify such an analysis. None of them are introspective in nature, and except for Mildred's simple worry over her past guilt and her casuistry on its moral implications, none of them indulge in much self-analysis; moreover, they are not essentially complex. Consequently the stylistic eccentricities are not a function of difficult ratiocinative processes or of intricate psychological probing, but—except where they are employed in the interest of verisimilitude—of decorum faced with embarrassment, or limited vision straining to realize more than it expected to be called upon to cope with. At least, this is the effect they produce. Moreover, the style reflects often in a curious way on these characters, casting suggestions of frenzy or unbalance; and, it might be added, not only in this play but in all others of Browning's dramatic compositions, it lends to the characters a quality of strangeness and abnormality over and above what the facts in the case would of themselves produce, or of remoteness as of belonging to a cult, the secrets of which the reader can never hope to share fully.

Finally, though Browning came closer in this play to satisfying both in the general design and in the language the conditions of poetic tragedy, he failed also because the materials with which he was dealing were essentially weak, conceived too much with an idea of conventional theatrical brilliance rather than dramatic strength. Some, therefore, have condemned the type of plot for this reason.

But this conclusion does not go far enough. Many plots, it might be argued, even in good tragedies, are tawdry, impossible, full of extravagance. The Elizabethan revenge play affords enough examples. It is largely a matter of what these plots are made to yield. Some revenge tragedies yield little more than fantastic villainy, perverse and lewd evil, and bloodshed and violence. But others, focusing on the dilemma posed to a sensitive and honorable individual of either performing a violent act or permitting evil and injustice to flourish, infused into the play profound psychological and ethical issues, and thus made a plot device essentially theatrical serve the ends of the deepest tragedy of the human spirit. It is not therefore so much the fault of plot outline, as what, finally, are the elements on which its probability and necessity depend. Some of the weakness of the play may be traced to the conception of honor which dominates it, and in particular determines the conduct of Tresham. His approach to honor is that of the fussy connoisseur of a social code, a code which implies a specialized social environment for its existence and therefore narrows the issue of human motives to a sphere where serious and dignified tragedy is impossible. It is a notion better suited to social drama or comedy, and Tresham suffers, as do the rest, from the resulting indignity of absurdity.

Of the irreconcilable contradictions in matter and method in the play, the numerous absurdities of detail are a conspicuous symptom. To bring about the big scenes, to force the action to its violent conclusion, the main characters are deprived of even a trace of common sense. Only Guendolen has a trace of this virtue, and she seems quite helpless, like an attending physician in a madhouse. Situations arise which are grotesque on visualization—Tresham dying slowly from poison, supported by Guendolen and Austin, with the lifeless form of Mildred still clinging to his neck. There is Austin's comment as he looks at Tresham:

> A froth is oozing through his clenched teeth;
> Both lips, where they're not bitten through, are black:
> Speak, dearest Thorold!   (3.2)

And after Tresham's words "Remember me!" what besides concession to conventional pathos inspired the meaningless closing line:

> *Guendolen.*   Ah, Thorold, we can but—remember you!

It seems apparent that Browning was seduced by the established rhetoric of theatrically effective devices to take refuge in such tricks. Only a determination to satisfy, not the poetical requirements of the work, but the desire of an audience for the pathetic could have produced Mildred's sorrowful cry,

> I was so young, I loved him so, I had
> No mother, God forgot me, and I fell.   (1.2)

Dickens, it is said, admired these lines, but at this distance it is almost embarrassing to think that Browning so far forgot his artistic conscience as to use this bright gallery gem, not once, but three times during the course of the play.

In this work, more nearly in conformity with the conventional notions of a play than most of the others, Browning's characteristic gifts could not find their proper soil. There appears, accordingly, some modification of his usual practices, apparently under the inspiration of Shakespearean models, in the peculiarities of his phrasing and in the ordering of the diction, though in these respects the changes are neither very radical nor thoroughgoing. But the modification took also another turn: the more conventional play also led to a reliance on the stock in trade of the theatre, with the result that the characters are narrow and, often, the sentiments forced and the episodes absurd. The materials of the play thus appear inappropriate and unworthy of its best art. Yet when Browning lavished on the drama his strongest and most original talents, he produced, as in *The Return of the Druses*, something less than a play. In the end, he found the happiest solution of his artistic aims, not in the drama, but in the dramatic monologue, and his search for a framework which would enable his favorite device to acquire amplitude and narrative scope ended in *The Ring and the Book*.

Verse drama continued to be written in the nineteenth century after Browning, but not sufficient further insight would be gained by consideration of other examples. The failure of the four writers discussed in detail is the failure of the nineteenth century in serious drama. Since the age tacitly accepted the traditional identification of tragedy with verse drama, distinction could come only from writers who had a poet's gift of language, for the mere use of verse in the hands of a playwright who has only the knack of constructing a plausible or actable play can never rise above banality or at best mediocrity. Moreover, these four, in addition to their great abilities as poets, brought sincerity and seriousness of purpose to their task.

But they were one and all led astray by a failure to grasp the fundamentals of dramatic art and by a misconception of the means at their disposal, and in consequence they never accomplished the subtle fusion of the language of poetry and the needs of drama without which the verse used in plays so often becomes, in Granville-Barker's phrase, effect without cause. Their failure to establish any tradition of poetic drama, their eclecticism in the matter of models, the variety of solutions which they hit upon, are all indications of their uncertainty or confusion. Since they were either unsure or misguided in their notions about drama, they could not always profit in the right way from their models, and were more often hampered by them. Since they were alive to the banalities and vulgar excitements of contemporary popular styles, they could learn little from them except to their own cost. The salvation of nineteenth-century drama could not come from the poet-dramatists.

It came, as might be expected, from men who found in the current popular drama the materials for the reform. It was not through gothic drama, or Joanna Baillie, or Schiller, or Byron, or Browning that the line of descent came, but through such plays as Kotzebue's *False Shame* (as it was entitled in its English adaptation), Bulwer-Lytton's *Money*, Boucicault's *London Assurance*, and Tom Taylor's *The Ticket-of-Leave Man*, inconsequential in themselves but containing the seeds of unrealized possibilities. It was through the efforts of Thomas Robertson that this development reached serious artistic treatment and established the direction which dramatic development was to take. During the sixties, Robertson not only wrote the best of his plays dealing with the issues of contemporary society, but helped materially to alter stage tradition in the matter of scenery and acting so as to harmonize with the naturalistic quality of his plays. Thus was ushered in the prose play dealing realistically with the problems of people in the contemporary world. Bolstered and inspired by the work of Ibsen, this kind of play established itself as the characteristic form of modern drama. Verisimilitude, reportorial exactness, came to be the criterion for plot and characterization. As recently as 1923, in *The Old Drama and the New*, William Archer argued from the success of the new drama the absolute incorrectness of writing in verse at all, and the utter ineptness of older styles.

It is not in point to argue here the merit of the two styles. From the point of view of the future development of drama, even of verse drama, the reform was providential. It cleaned the slate of the unhappy if well-meaning efforts of a succession of writers from the late eighteenth century on who tried to save the drama from itself, and who persevered unprofitably. It left the way open for a fresh attempt. The nineteenth century points the moral, even though it does not greatly adorn the tale. It remains to see whether in modern times the moral has been heeded.

CHAPTER V

THE PRESENT AGE

THE PRESENT century has been hailed as a dramatic renaissance. The roll of prominent names among playwrights is impressive, critical interest in good drama is widespread, and various countries have distinguished themselves, the United States making at last a belated but creditable appearance as a contributor to the world's drama. The founding in Germany, France, England, Ireland, and America of independent organizations for the production of plays which the prevailing commercial theatre did not care (or dare) to consider helped to accelerate new developments, and is evidence of the intelligence and energy of the men who helped to establish the modern theatre.

I

The history of this whole phenomenon is difficult and complex, not because of its large scale or the difficulty of getting a perspective, but because one of the most striking features of the dramatic activity of this age has been the great variety of innovations and experiments both in form and manner of presentation. Yet amid all this great opening up and encouragement of all possibilities, drama in verse has been generally looked upon with suspicion, and the principal style which has stood out from the variety of modern innovation has been the antithesis of verse drama. Since the days of Ibsen and Robertson, the dominant tradition has been what is variously called realism or naturalism. The medium is prose dialogue designed to create the illusion of unpremeditated discourse. The scene is usually contemporary with the author, and the minutiae of the setting are given an important part in the establishment of the world of the play. (If the setting is historical, either a fairly high degree of historical accuracy is maintained, or a breezy modernizing of mores and sentiments is affected.) The kinds of probabilities which operate in the play are made to appear consonant with daily experience within the social milieu established by the play. "Truth to life" has come to be regarded as a primary mark of excellence. These characteristics mark most plays written between such early examples as *Caste* or *A Doll's House* and such more recent successes as *The Little Foxes* and *Golden Boy*.

The issue of verse drama in the present age must accordingly be seen in the light of the central position which realistic prose drama has occupied. The pioneers in this drama, men like Pinero and Jones, wrote in awareness of the importance of their work, and sympathetic critics extolled both the significance of the materials with which their plays dealt and the new conventions of form which they employed. The enthusiasm, as well as the bitter opposition, which the plays of Ibsen aroused in England and somewhat later in America is in another way indicative of the challenging strength inherent in the new form of drama, and of the degree of intensity and excitement with which it once more endowed the stage. Contrasted with the banality, frivolity, and theatrical pomp of the popular drama of the nineteenth century, and the remoteness, the failure to produce one memorable and artistically sound work, of the verse dramatists, the new school of realism might well have generated great enthusiasm. A critic like William Archer, who saw the rise and helped along the success of this drama, may be pardoned the suggestion that it was the happy completion of a necessary process of evolution:

The stage has room, of course, for many forms of drama to which they [the devices of realism] do not apply; and fashion may, from time to time, set strongly in favor of such forms. But I do not believe that Robertsonian realism, as it has been perfected by his successors, will ever be entirely ousted from the position it now holds; for it is only the last term in an inevitable process of evolution.[1]

Historians of the contemporary theater have reflected this enthusiasm for a drama vigorous in its probing of life and meticulous in its observation of it:

The theater today is engaged in the breaking of norms both in the arts of life and in the arts of the presentments of life. If it is to do this the first requirement is that it shall know this life well and present it faithfully. A large part of the activity of the American theater has been given to this elementary research. The playwright has sought to make himself master of the life around him, its habits, customs, characteristic manifestations, surfaces, clichés of thought and action and speech. Observation has been elevated to first place.[2]

The new drama possessed all the advantages which accompany a determined, fresh effort to solve an artistic problem, unhampered by the tameness and confusion of a stale or imitative art. And it succeeded in restoring seriousness and dignity to drama by arousing interest in its attempt to deal with conditions, people, and problems immediately important, and by demonstrating that drama could be a serious artistic vehicle without having to bear the marks of an arid tradition of impossible situations and poetic clichés. This alone was a sufficient accomplishment. It might ultimately prove to be of the highest benefit to poetic drama by virtue of having wiped the slate clean and prepared for a new effort. It is a confirmation of this view that those who in recent years have not abandoned the effort to write serious verse drama approach the task with the tentative air of attacking something new, as though there was nothing in the dramatic tradition which they have inherited from their immediate predecessors which can be of much use to them. But for the time being, the new drama left the poets in some confusion and on the defensive.

The assertion, however, that the dominant tradition in the drama has been realistic is, though a truth, a misleading simplification of the situation. It obscures the importance of the wide range of experimentation which has been indulged in since the nineties of the last century. The career of but one dramatist, Eugene O'Neill, is indicative of how strong has been the impetus to discover new forms and new methods. And this whole phenomenon may be regarded as an attempt, not always conscious to be sure, to enlarge the possibilities or to escape the limitations of realism.

It is no general condemnation of realistic drama to insist that the conventions which govern it operate to eliminate certain features which the serious drama of other times possesses. Though the genius of Ibsen was sufficient to overcome many of these limitations or to render them less obvious, they are quite apparent in the work of most of the English writers of this school, such as Jones, Pinero, Granville-Barker, and Galsworthy, and in many of the successful plays of the English and American theatre since.

In the characteristic play of this school, the particularities of the social environment are among the most important of the given things in the situation governing the action of the play. Hence the peculiar forms of the social milieu are raised to a high place among the determinants of the play and the probabilities which govern the action. One result is that the play is given too precise a local habitation and name. It is a popular criticism of many of these plays today that they are "dated," yet this criticism is not made about much older plays, such as those of the Greeks, which often involve mores and beliefs remote from present day sympathies, or those of Shakespeare, which take for granted political and ethical principles somewhat alien, on occasion, to our times. The narrowing of the world of the play to embrace the minutiae of a particular social milieu tends to weaken in direct proportion its generality and eventually its capacity to arouse a willing response to the scheme of things which governs it. The accidents of the scene may replace its essence. As a further consequence, such a play raises technical difficulties in the way of permitting the exploration of any large and general potentialities, emotional or intellectual, either in the agents of the action or the issues raised by it; or, to state the case in another way, as the accidents of the milieu become important, character necessarily becomes less important among the probabilities of the action. Where the issue is seen largely as a matter of social adjustment, the relationship between the character and the situation becomes less general, and there results the simplified one-dimensional lack of complexity or interest of character which is so often a marked feature of these plays.

The partisan enthusiasts of this drama are inclined to view these limitations as exalted virtues. Thus the author of one of the standard surveys of modern drama remarks:

Rather than agree that no great play can be written about a little man, I should hold that the little man is peculiarly the subject for a great play. In so far as a play magnifies a man it places him above the values that are common to the experience of all men, those values that acquire force from the pressures of social life. Nothing is so puerile, so futile, as man's poor magnitudes. Take a play in which man is shown to be master of his fate and you have a little play. The stage has so long lived under the myth-making convention that even when it presents little men it tends to show them magnified beyond their station by a greater dignity or under a greater ridicule. It has not yet learned to treat the little man—that is, the average member of society—in his relative magnitudes as compared with other men. Until it does learn to do so the stage will not be true to life.[3]

Without disputing the possibility of writing great plays on little men, or raising the question of man's control over his own fate, one might ask the question, What sort of truth and what kind of life? Much may be lost if, in the interest of being "true to life," the dramatist is urged to find his material in the least common denominator of human life. The greatest of the modern dramatists have, in fact, not done so. It is not necessarily incumbent on the dramatist to rival the sociologist, and in any case, he must realize the sacrifices he will have to make when he undertakes the task.

A further limitation of the realistic play arises from the conventions which govern the dialogue. The vigorous repudiation of the soliloquy and the aside by the realists is not so important in itself except as a sign of the way in which they regard the dialogue. Nothing presumably may be uttered by the characters which could not be thought of as having been said under similar circumstances in an actual drawing-room, street, or park. Dialogue is viewed with as strict a regard for verisimilitude as the conditions of an art will permit. This restriction has led to some ingenuity and novelty in methods of exposition, though often it has encouraged shifts and contrivances which make the confidants and asides of another drama look sophisticated in comparison. But the important point is that it has raised almost insuperable barriers in the way of dramatic revelation of complex motives, involved and intense emotions, or subtle cross-currents of thought, which can give richness and depth to a play. Perhaps this difficulty is made even greater in the typical play of the modern realistic school by virtue of the fact that the characters are usually those of an urban and hence reserved sort, so that the dictates of verisimilitude in their case impose an additional restraint on them inimical to the revelation of hidden thoughts or strong feelings. There is little such a character can do in a tense moment except, as Yeats remarked, look into the fireplace.[4] At times the dramatist may take a strong hand, and the result is usually an inappropriate and often embarrassing piece of oratorical display, or a violent translation of some character onto an alien and unprepared-for plane of sensibility and expression.

This, however, does not do justice to the possibilities within the conventions of the realistic style itself to give extension and generality to the materials of the play. The most characteristic form of modern drama would not have provided an outlet for the talents of so many intelligent and serious writers if it had not offered opportunity for considerable scope and at least some reasonable avenues of escape from its more obvious limitations.

Chief, perhaps, of these avenues has been the use of drama as a vehicle for thought, as an instrument for the analysis of general social and other issues and not uncommonly a recommendation of a particular attitude toward the issues raised by the play. To the extent that these issues are of a sort that depend upon a local peculiarity of the mores, this solution does not escape the criticisms already noted above, but it is possible to use the brilliant exactness of observation and intimate association with the current scene to bring into sharp focus a problem of human conduct that has relevance beyond a decade. The drama of ideas within the realistic framework has afforded possibilities for many serious dramatists and has helped to give weight as well as variety to their work. Indeed, this feature of modern drama has led to a decided shift of emphasis in dramatic theory, so that action has come to occupy an inferior position among the requirements of a satisfactory play, being regarded as a triviality of plot and often confused with stage business and bustle. "Plot," says G. B. Shaw, "has always been the curse of serious drama, and indeed of serious literature of any kind."[5] In theory and practice Shaw has brilliantly espoused the cause of "serious" drama in the sense of drama which has some significant social or intellectual purpose. This feature of modern drama has come to be regarded as differentiating it in kind from older drama:

As we watch the progress of tragedy from Aeschylus to Shakespeare, from Shakespeare to the writers of the present day, we can witness an attempt on the part of the playwrights to shake off action in order to depict thought. Ibsen, representative of his own age in this movement, showed to his contemporaries many methods of securing this inwardness. Already Browning had subordinated action to the development of character, but somehow he failed to make the latter sufficiently interesting. Ibsen, by a series of delicate theatrical touches, keeps our attention awake for the appreciation of a drama which is fundamentally static. Nothing really happens in *Ghosts*; the action is more psychological than physical in *A Doll's House* (1879) and in *The Wild Duck*. No effort is made to charm an audience by a set of exciting incidents; rather we are invited into a quiet room and asked to watch the characters there, watch the expressions of their sorrows and joys, and through these sorrows and joys reach to some understanding of their inner selves.[6]

Whether this view of dramatic history is correct is not at the moment the question; the text is important as the expression by a recognized authority in the drama, Allardyce Nicoll, that thought has replaced action as the point of importance in the drama of today. It is a view that has come to be taken for granted in many quarters. Older drama is, of course, not devoid of "thought" or intellectual content, but the position of thought in the scheme of the play is somewhat different. It consists of certain general principles of ethical or political action, certain ways of regarding life itself, which constitute a part of the world of the play and may be tacitly accepted by the author and his audience as proper to the kind of action being developed. It is also an aspect of character, establishing a basis for choice and action. On the other hand, the furor caused in their day by the plays of Ibsen and by certain plays of Shaw, and the disposition of audiences and reviewers to give prominence even in recent years to the social message or philosophical intention of some current play, illustrates the disposition to expect the dramatists to instruct explicitly, to arouse, to debate with, his audience. In recent years the identification of thought and drama has been given new direction by the "leftist" or "Marxist" critics who regard the arts in the light of their capacity as instruments of social action.[7]

The artistic consequences of this change in emphasis are considerable. When the expression of a thesis, the posing of a question, the expression of a particular idea, become the principal end of the play, then the dramatic features—action, character, etc.—become means of recommending it. The play becomes a form of blandishment, a superior method of intellectual seduction, a species of rhetoric. When Mr. Nicoll says that "Ibsen, by a series of delicate theatrical touches, keeps our attention awake for the appreciation of a drama which is fundamentally static," he is saying approximately the same thing. Only, the touches are not always delicate. "Good theatre" and "good show" have in fact become so common a standard in the stock in trade of the modern dramatic critic that the application of other criteria runs the risk of appearing unmanly. From this point of view, as long as the dramatist has the knack for "good theatre," he can keep the audience alive and receptive to his ideas, or can arouse them sufficiently to espouse his cause. Robert Sherwood's *Idiot's Delight*, illustrates the point; it was theatrically brilliant (Mr. Krutch used such phrases as "the slickest contemporary stagecraft" and "accomplished showmanship" in describing it), and it was aimed at an exploration of the conflicting political ideologies of our time. Its structure may be suggested by the fact that whereas a great variety of characters is introduced, scarcely more than three are essential to the action; the rest are employed to provide exposition of German and Italian fascism, communism, pacifism, and the English gentlemanly tradition, in some instances in long speeches done with all the eloquence of a public address. Time is hard on such plays. A dramatist of ideas like Shaw may survive erosion through the inexhaustible effervescence, vitality, and wit of his dialogue, but even Ibsen has not been wholly spared. In his case the effects of time are often exaggerated by the narrowing of critical perspective which the insistence on thought as a primary excellence of drama tends to encourage. It is altogether too common nowadays to object of certain plays of Ibsen that the problems they deal with are no longer of great interest since they raise dead issues long since settled through the adoption of more liberal social views, reforms in the divorce laws, and what not. Such objections are often supercilious. Either these plays were never essentially good and made their mark in their day by presenting currently dangerous or exciting matter, or else we have become so fixed in the habit of identifying dramatic excellence with clever presentation of ideas that we fail to penetrate beyond the intellectual prejudices of the moment to discern the enduring art of the plays. In any case, it is difficult to reconcile the popular view of Ibsen as the greatest figure in the modern theatre with the popular criticism of him as a bore for not keeping up to date. It is noteworthy, however, that such plays as *Hedda Gabler*, in which the "problem" keeps in the background, do not suffer greatly from the common reproach of being old fashioned and "dated."

It is to the credit of modern dramatists that they have striven in various ways to make the drama a vital instrument of public stimulation, and their participation in the issues of their times is a condition of health in them and a spur to creative activity; but it is nevertheless the case that where instruction or stimulation or thought become the primary ends of drama, the dramatist, though he assumes a useful and worthy role, runs the risk of unbalancing the artistic coordination of his means and may end up a rhetorician.

Modern drama has made good use of other means which have

had the effect of circumventing the more obvious limitations of realistic drama through some modification of established conventions. If the typical realistic play gave too little scope for the expression of fundamental emotions or gave too social a direction to the materials of the play, it was still possible to avoid these difficulties by a change in the milieu while remaining faithful to the convention of reportorial exactness and "truth to life" in the dialogue and setting. Rustic life offered, for instance, an environment in which the decorum of urban life had no place, and hence depth of feeling coupled with simplicity and directness of utterance could be employed to uncover uninhibited and primitive emotions. The work of Lascelles Abercrombie and of a number of Irish dramatists is typical of this development, and such a play as Masefield's *Tragedy of Nan* is particularly illuminating because the material seems deliberately chosen with the intention of coming as close as may be to the intensity as well as the poetic quality of older tragedies, especially those employing traditional stories or myths. O'Neill's *Desire under the Elms* makes excellent use of the rural setting in this way, with the additional device of a return to a slightly older era; but the usual tendency in American drama has been to exploit the primitive and often comic possibilities of communities very remote from civilizing influences and having special local peculiarities (MacKaye's *This Fine Pretty World*, for instance). Frequently, in fact, plays with rustic setting bound by the demands of verisimilitude show all too clearly a search for quaint novelties in setting or a display of proficiency in peculiarities of dialect for their own sake. And even at their best, such plays are still hampered by their limitations, for between the exactness of setting which eliminates the sense of remoteness, and the limited capacities of most of the characters, the actions and sentiments may appear crude or brutal rather than stirring or profound as they do in the classic examples of tragedy based on legend or myth.

One special aspect of this concern for settings with local peculiarities has made a contribution sufficiently striking to demand separate notice—a contribution moreover in the matter of diction where modern drama has been perhaps weakest except in the matter of clarity and at times of wit. This development has been particularly noticeable among the dramatists of the Irish school, which on the whole has developed, with one or two exceptions, in the

direction of realism. These plays deal almost exclusively with the
Irish scene. The environment is therefore special and, from the
viewpoint of any urban theatre, relatively unfamiliar—always an
advantage to a writer who wants a little freedom for his imagination—and the characters are highly imaginative and volatile.[8]
Whether the Irish have these qualities is beside the point; they have
been assumed to have them, and the Irish dramatists have made a
distinct convention of the assumption. In addition, the language
employed is a dialect different from the normal conversational
idiom of the theatre, and is loaded with "strange words" and expressions richly metaphorical in character. And, because the language
is popular and idiomatic, there is less danger from the evils of conventional rhetoric. This combination of elements liberates the
dramatist from the restrictions that other writers are hampered by,
yet it does not necessitate his overcoming the current prejudice of
audiences and readers against drama that is remote from what
appears to be the reality of the present. Though restricted to a
language of rather special texture, the Irish dramatist has been un-
confined with respect to just those devices of language which
characterize successful verse drama—highly colored words, words
of a specialized nature, complex metaphorical expressions, and the
like. More than anything else, it is this feature of the best Irish
drama of recent years which gives it its beauty, its richness of effect,
and its complex unity. What would that remarkable play, *The Play-
boy of the Western World*, have been without it?

Certain American plays have found an analogous sort of pictur-
esqueness of flavor in the flourishing slang and popular idiom of this
country. Good popular idiom and slang is always symbolical and
metaphorical in aspect, and the American popular idiom can be
very good. Given an appropriate specialized setting, like that of
What Price Glory, it can supply great vividness to the play. One of
the most skillful users of these possibilities is Clifford Odets. There
is always a sprinkling of New York types, Brooklyn toughs, cab
drivers, gamblers, and what not in his plays to provide occasion for
the sharp accents of popular speech. When Prince (*Rocket to the
Moon*) says of his son-in-law, "He's as mixed up as the twentieth
century," or to the romantic young Cleo, "You'll go down the
road alone like Charlie Chaplin?" the stunt has been carried beyond
the point of striking invective and picturesque characterization to a

moving symbolism. Modern poets, in fact, are becoming aware of the possibilities latent in these racy idioms of language. The limitation of the idiom in these plays, however, arises from the circumstance that it is a secondary thread, though of brilliant color, usually contributed by some relatively minor character; compare, for instance, the speeches of Stark and Cleo in *Rocket to the Moon* during their tenser moments, groping for words or rushing into a heady but vague rhetoric. Such lapses are in general less common in the Irish plays, where the imaginative treatment of the diction permeates more thoroughly the texture of the work; but in both instances the idiom is necessarily restricted by the specialized—and in the whole picture of the possibilities of serious drama, the limited —character of the materials.

Even when the most has been said for such plays, it still remains largely true that modern drama has not availed itself greatly of the capacity of language imaginatively used to suggest analogies, establish consistent and complementary schemes of imagery, and bring to bear on the specific action of the play a complex and extended body of associations to give magnitude and generality to the immediate circumstances of the action. The device which in modern prose drama may be thought of as something of a substitute for this function of diction in the older drama is symbolism. Some feature of the play receives an elaboration over and above its actual bearing on the action, so that it becomes identified with many of the strongest sentiments of the principal characters and becomes a token of the issues which are implicit in the dilemmas and oppositions. The tower in *The Master Builder*, the rat woman in *Little Eyolf*, the bird in *The Sea Gull* are familiar examples. Much speculation and over-refinement of exegesis about such matters have led in some quarters to a repudiation of the importance of symbolism; it is argued that the tower is a real tower, the bird a real bird, etc., and that to think of them otherwise is to carry criticism beyond the legitimate bounds of the simple theatrical force of these features. It is difficult to agree with this view, which might best be interpreted as the desperate effort of critics who would like to save the great modern dramatists any damage from the ineptitudes of some of their less subtle imitators. In any event, symbolism in the form in which it appears in Ibsen and Tchekov has run a rather rapid course to dramatic cliché, and is used sparingly and gingerly by recent dramatists.

For certain other qualities of the poetic drama, modern drama has found a further substitute in the resources of the stage technician, which, it must be admitted, are greater today than they have ever been before in the history of the theatre. Experimentation not only in matters of scenery, lighting, and other devices of illusion, but even in the architecture of the stage to accommodate these mechanical novelties or to conform to some new theory of dramatic presentation has gone very far in our century, and the names of original and important figures in the art are as well known as those of famous playwrights. And it is commonly maintained that these new developments have added a new "poetry" to the modern theatre.[9] We are told that Shakespeare perforce wrote passages of great beauty because he wished to compensate by description for the absence of scenic design and to establish the atmosphere of a scene or to define the mood of a moment. No more need now to write "It was the nightingale and not the lark," or "Night's candles are burnt out," when the trick can be more persuasively turned by means of electricity and paint. And certainly the scenic artist in the modern theatre can do a good deal to produce those elements of heightening and intensification once supplied by language. This is particularly true of lighting, vastly improved in recent years, which has even produced its own type of cliché in the use of shadows and in the insistence on such vivid colors as green and magenta.

There is no denying the great beauty of many modern productions and the addition to emotional strength which modern stage artists have brought to the theatre, but the devices of the stage technician have serious limitations. However extended the scope of all these devices may be, they are on the whole more static and more limited than language and can therefore not be thought of as an adequate substitute for it. In the conventional play the element of spectacle is auxiliary and not essential to the play as play. The devices of spectacle are after all out of the author's hands, and may lead to exaggeration of a meretricious sort, to pointing up unduly, or to supplying something which the play simply lacks. The judicious use of the devices of stage illusion may help to compensate for the absence of suggestion and intensity in the lines of the play, but the exaggeration of their importance and the easy reliance on them may also work to discourage the dramatist's efforts and may result in levelling of the diction. The principal danger lies in the fact that, with the great advance in the theatrical arts, one simple truism seems in danger of being forgotten: the greatness of a production depends on the imagination and technical skill of the director and his associates, but the greatness of the play depends ultimately on the dramatist and on no one else.

The limitations placed on dialogue by verisimilitude have been overcome in various ways. O'Neill took the drastic step in *Strange Interlude* of using the soliloquy to express thoughts not normally revealed in conversations; but there has been relatively little disposition on the part of other dramatists to follow suit. More popular has been the use of the materials of modern psychology for revealing what lies behind the spoken word and the apparent behavior of the characters. Reports of dreams (the mountains of Nebraska in *Rain*), repeated obsessions, conformity on the part of characters to some readily recognized type of "abnormal" behavior (the mother, for instance, in *The Silver Cord*), reference to the more obvious symbols of psychoanalysis, have all been used to overcome the barrier between the spoken word which often conceals and the deeper motives which impel to action. Another method consists of establishing a special environment which acts as a catalyst in breaking down normal inhibitions to self-revelation. Shaw's *Heartbreak House* is a classic example: in the curious atmosphere of Captain Shotover's house the characters expose their innermost secrets under the strange compulsion of the place. Denis Johnston's *Moon in the Yellow River* proceeds in much the same way. For the most part, however, the theatre has exploited this idea in a flashy and pseudo-profound manner—a special environment, the coincidence of compelling circumstances, and the result is *Grand Hotel*, or *The Petrified Forest*, or any of their half-dozen lesser imitations. It is only a step from plays of this sort to the fantastic setting of such a play as *Hotel Universe*, in which all pretense at reality in the setting is abandoned. It is a considerable step, however, and involves a more radical departure from the simple conventions of naturalism than any so far considered.

It need not be inferred on the basis of this analysis of the problems raised by the conventions of realistic drama that at its best it has been a small or shabby thing. To men of genius like Ibsen and Tchekov, its very restrictions were a stimulus to the invention of artistic devices of great originality, which at times introduce unexpected subtlety and depth into their plays. Some of the means which they used are not so obvious in their nature as the devices already discussed. For example, Granville-Barker, in his lectures *On Dramatic Method*, has shown how Ibsen, while preserving the concentration and explicitness essential to his conventions, secured a quality of richness and depth and gained heightening and emotional coloring by a retrospective method which sets the events of the play ironically or tragically against echoes from the past out of which the immediate situations have grown. In Tchekov, apparent irrelevancies which break into the main business of the moment produce by a reflection from the principal dialogue an unlooked-for poignancy. The existence of such subtleties in certain plays, however, does not invalidate the general observation that in its main development and for the generality of its practitioners the realistic play of modern life has tended to confine the imaginative capacities of the dramatist, though it may have stimulated others, and that the various devices which help to mitigate its restrictions have, by themselves, within the limits of the conventions of the tradition, operated largely as palliatives.

The limitations of such plays are responsible, in fact, for certain important developments in modern drama. For one thing, recognition of these characteristic weaknesses has been the chief encouragement of the poets who have tried to make their contribution to the theatre, and the prominence of realistic drama in this century must be kept in mind in any attempt to understand their persistence and the direction which their work has taken. But verse drama has not been the most conspicuous challenge to the prevailing style of modern drama. From the time of Ibsen, dramatists have, in individual instances, abandoned the conventions of realism completely and have used the resources developed in the modern theatre in entirely new ways and for quite new ends. The hell portions of *Man and Superman*, the last scene in *Saint Joan*, and the latter portions of *Back to Methusalah* contain hints of new possibilities realized in limited ways. But the plays which foreshadow most clearly the radical departures from the naturalistic mode are Ibsen's *Peer Gynt* and the later dramas of Strindberg, forerunners of the development in modern drama known as expressionism, which flourished particularly during the first World War and for some two decades thereafter.

Like all such terms, expressionism has been attached to a wide diversity of experiments which have in common a departure from the conventions of realism, and like all experiments of a radical order in the arts, the stimulus which this development in drama afforded has produced results ranging all the way from mannerism and formal confusion to brilliant excursions of an imaginative order. In the full-blown expressionistic play, two conditions may be distinguished. Where symbolism, interest in psychological conditions, and use of advanced arts of stage illusion and design are normally but auxilliary features of realistic drama, they become primary instruments of expression in the expressionistic play. In addition, the point of view is altered, so that the probabilities which govern the observed world of daily experience are no longer presumed to govern the play. Normal impressions are seen as though refracted through some modifying medium, such as the overwrought mind of one of the characters, so that the whole gives the impression of a dream state, or the allegorical bias of the cartoon, or the extravagance and exaggeration of the music hall or vaudeville. It is common to suggest the particular direction of the distortion by such a device as the dream in *Beggar on Horseback*, which comprises most of the play and is sandwiched in between episodes done in a conventional realistic technique, or the blow on the actor's head in *The Old Lady Says "No!"* or the visions of the dying child in *Hannele*. But such a legitimizing device is not always present; in *From Morn to Midnight* or *The Spook Sonata* or the early portions of *The Adding Machine*, for instance, there is no direct "instruction" to the audience of the particular principle of distortion used, but in time all is made clear enough through the character of the speeches, the development of the episodes, and the peculiarities of setting and acting called for by the play. It is for this reason that the stage arrangement of these plays is so important. The design of the setting helps to establish at once the particular kind of world in which the action is taking place, and sets the proper distance between the adopted scale of values and literal representation. Changes of one sort or another in the arrangement and setting usually possess, therefore, some symbolical significance.

Symbolism, in fact, creeps in at all points. In the opening scene of *The Spook Sonata*, for instance, the dialogue is chiefly between the Student and Hummel. Throughout the scene, however, the Janitress and the Dark Lady are present, saying nothing and doing little, but prefiguring by their presence the sinister accumulation of secret evil within their household which is at variance with the impression of elegance and beauty which the Student has received from the attractive outward appearance of the house before he comes to know the truth about its inmates. This simple device of stage arrangement thus assists in the exposition of the contrast—is in fact a part of the exposition itself. This technique is extended to character; individual characters are translated into a realm of allegorical symbols almost at once, not the direct allegory of the morality play, but a kind of fluid identification of characters with a type of behavior, an ethical or psychological concept, and the like, which enables the same character to assume at need more than one role; for instance, Mr. Cady in *Beggar on Horseback* appears as the judge in the trial scene during the dream.

The principle of order cannot be stated categorically for this kind of drama. In *From Morn to Midnight* the development is chronological, beginning with the temptation of the bank clerk which leads to theft, and continuing in sequence with his failure to seduce the beautiful woman, his realization of his miserable error, his hopeless attempts to escape from his crime and from his own thoughts, and his final suicide. In *The Old Lady Says "No!"*, however, time sequences are abandoned: the shifting phantasms in the slugged actor's mind make up the main portion of the play, and the order of the scenes is dependent on a scheme of psychological association, the whole device forming a framework for criticism and satire of modern Dublin life and the political follies and weaknesses of the Irish.[10]

Expressionism has been accused on the one hand of relieving the dramatist from any serious concern for form, and has been praised on the other as an admirable scheme for the projection of moods of confusion and disorder which are a recognized feature of contemporary thought and feeling. Whatever its inherent limitations, however, the method of expressionism has given the dramatist new resources outside the conventional limits of realistic drama for imaginative treatment of his materials. Its future is for the moment uncertain. It has left its mark on the technique of modern popular drama, as witness *Lady in the Dark*. At the same time, there is some feeling that its importance as a serious vehicle is probably over:

according to Joseph Wood Krutch, "As the aims of the didactic playwright were clarified and he came to separate himself more and more clearly from the merely skeptical protestant of the type familiar during the twenties, he turned, sensibly enought, to more direct and less ambiguous forms of expression."[11] However, as recently as 1938 the poet Louis MacNeice wrote, "the man who wants to write tragedy is most likely to succeed in a verse-form or possibly in some form more like Expressionism."[12]

The choice which MacNeice offers is significant, because if expressionism is the most positive step which modern drama has taken in its flight from the confines of the realistic method and represents an alternative to verse drama for the writer of tragedy, what function is left for the poet in the modern theatre, and what direction is he to take if he wishes to write plays? In the light of the actual directions which the poets have taken, the answer appears neither simple nor very clear. To begin with, at no time have they had to circumvent so many impediments or had so much cause for uncertainty. The nineteenth century had apparently placed such a deep curse on verse drama that writing of verse plays had come to be regarded as a retrogression to a bad era from which salvation had but recently come, or at best as a private sport for eccentrics. Until very recently the critics and historians of modern drama were almost unanimous in their opinion that verse drama was a thing of the past.

The experience of three centuries has shown us that the spirit of modern man can no longer produce masterpieces in the impure form in which Shakespeare worked. A thousand attempts to do so have all proved more or less abortive. The two elements of the old drama, imitation and lyrical passion, have at last consummated their divorce. For lyrical passion we go to opera and music drama, for interpretation through imitation we go to the modern realistic play. And surely we ought to recognize that this divorce, so obviously inevitable, is a good and not a bad thing—a sign of health and not of degeneracy.[13]

These are the vigorous accents of William Archer. If there is a suggestion of blundering in the juxtaposition of the words "masterpieces" and "impure form," if the whole analysis seems a little naive today, it must be recalled that Archer was writing as an apologist for an important movement in the drama, and also that the enthusiasts for Shakespeare and the other Elizabethans and the apologists for verse drama had themselves laid the groundwork for his position. An excellent illustration of this is the passage which

Archer himself quotes from an article in the London *Times Literary Supplement*:

In the greatest plays there are moments when the play ceases and something else happens; they arise out of the action of the play, but when they come, it is forgotten—

> Thou remember'st
> Since once I sat upon a promontory
> And heard a mermaid, on a dolphin's back,
> Uttering such a dulcet and harmonious breath
> That the rude sea grew civil at her song.

The actor saying that, should cease to be an actor, should cease to be Oberon even; he, Oberon, and the play, should lose themselves in that music as the singer and Cherubino and the opera are lost when "Voi che sapete" begins. Mozart and Shakespeare are subject to fits of divine absence of mind in which they are called into another state of being, and carry us with them. They too are listening to a music which supersedes even their delightful business; with a wave of the hand they stop it so that the whole world may listen too.[14]

Dismissed by the realists, misled by his friends, the poet-dramatist also found the foundations of his art being mined, either by those who maintained that, as science advances, poetry must necessarily recede, or by those who felt that language itself had become a stale and flaccid medium, or simply by those who believed that the new developments in dramaturgy had far outstripped language as a medium:

We are long past the time when a play can be embodied alone in words. Frequently in this book we have had occasion to refer to the limitations of words as expressive mediums. Not only do words supply a very thin channel through which to pour the water of life. The channel is crowded and clogged with memories of past meanings. And if words are becoming increasingly impotent, then verse is even more nearly valueless. When Arthur Symons says he does not see why people should break silence upon the stage except to speak poetry, he is revealing how little he knows of the stage, or he is employing the term 'poetry' in a more inclusive sense than is common. The stage must, indeed, employ poetry but it is a poetry that is far more extra-literate than literate. It must be a poetry that is composed upon many dimensions and of a multitude of factors. In short, it must be a poetry unlike any that was ever written in a book. Language of speech and written verse has failed to be an instrument of those wide realms of experience and sensation that lie deeper than language. The playwright must create such instrumentalities and employ them with the command with which the versifier of yesterday spun his iambics.[15]

There is an unmistakable note of condescension in the concluding phrase which would be quite chilling were it not for the recollection of that spinner of iambics, William Shakespeare, who touched on experiences "that lie deeper than language" in a way not yet rivalled by the dramatic experimenters of our era alluded to by the author. Yet the persistence of such views, plus the obvious facts of dramatic history, have had a discouraging effect on the poets. Masefield wrote in a prefatory note to *The Tragedy of Nan:*

The poetic impulse of the Renaissance is now spent. The poetic drama, the fruit of that impulse, is now dead. Until a new poetic impulse gathers, playwrights trying for beauty must try to create new forms in which beauty and the high things of the soul may pass from the stage to the mind. Our playwrights have all the powers except that power of exultation which comes from a delighted brooding on excessive, terrible things. That power is seldom granted to man; twice or thrice to a race, perhaps, not oftener. But it seems to me certain that every effort, however humble, towards the achieving of that power helps the genius of a race to obtain it, though the obtaining may be fifty years after the strivers are dead.

The interest in "poetic prose" during the early decades of this century is a product of this discouragement over the state of dramatic poetry. The term refers to the style of such plays as Maeterlinck's *Pelléas et Mélisande*, Wilde's *Salome*, and the characteristic plays of Dunsany. It is a prose style made deliberately mannered and artful, and was therefore regarded as a release from the conversational realism of current drama and at the same time as a substitute for unfashionable and unpopular verse. Synge's *Riders to the Sea* has with some justice helped to foster the conviction that in poetic prose the modern dramatist has found the proper solution to the difficulties which stand in the way of making verse appear plausible on the modern stage. The solution is a compromise, however, and it is now clear that it did not possess as many possibilities as the early enthusiasts hoped for. The dramatist is after all limited by what this type of mannered prose can properly perform. In a play like *Pelléas et Mélisande* is it not simply the poetic prose by itself which distinguishes it from realistic drama. The repetitions, the murmurings, the loose cadences are a conditioning medium, analogous to the rhythm of blank verse or the form of the heroic couplet. What gives the play its special qualities and demands the style is the interpenetrations of symbols (the ring, the sea, the sun, the refrains), the myth element in the story, the deliberate vagueness, the lack of complications. The failure of poetic prose to appeal to more recent writers of poetic drama arises from the fact that the style does not lend itself to the most original and vivid features of the modern poetic idiom, that it does not foster strength and concentration of expression, and that is is not appropriate to the expression of the moods of the present day. The later plays of Sean O'Casey illustrate these difficulties. On occasion, O'Casey introduces speeches in a prose more elaborate and mannered than that which serves for most of the dialogue in the play, and the effect is almost invariably one of sentimental effusiveness which seems to encourage the poetic cliché. Most of the poets who in recent years have been experimenting with the drama have been clearly working for the rehabilitation of verse.

Recently the poets have been advised that the solution to their problem lies in abandoning the stage for the microphone, because, as Archibald MacLeish explains, the lack of a physical stage renders verse less incongruous:

On the stage, verse is often an obstacle because the artifice of verse and the physical reality of the scene do not harmonize: it is for this reason that verse is easily accepted on the stage only where the scene is made remote in time and therefore artificial to begin with, or where the verse is blurred out and made to sound like prose. But over the radio verse is not an obstacle. Over the radio verse has no visual presence to compete with.[16]

The radio may eventually offer the poet a new outlet, but MacLeish has not only misstated the problem—for example, in the uncritical implications of his contention that in the conditions demanded by verse the scene is "artificial to begin with"—but seems actually to have evaded it. No one denies that it is extraordinarily difficult to adjust verse to acted drama, but it has been done, and greatly done. The real question is, how did Shakespeare do it? Sophocles? Racine? Can it be done again?

There has been no lack of attempts, in spite of the wholesale discouragement which the poets have had in the theatre and from the critics. In the present century, verse drama has at least demonstrated its capacity to survive. If it is indeed as dead as many insist, it has nevertheless continued to stir uneasily in its grave, and the exorcisms of critics have not been enough to lay its ghost. Of the considerable number of verse plays which have been written during the present century, it would not be very profitable for present purposes to consider more than a few.[17] For the most part the authors of these plays have been English. Percy MacKaye abandoned his early attempts to write verse plays for experiments in folk plays and pageants on national themes; and, but for the striking exception of Maxwell Anderson, only in very recent years and only in a few isolated instances have American writers displayed any serious interest in the verse play. Not many modern verse plays have enjoyed theatrical popularity, though there have been exceptions. Flecker's *Hassan* had the advantage of elaborate settings and music by Delius and gave the effect of extravaganza in performance, so that its success cannot be regarded as typical. Stephen Phillips was acclaimed early in the century, and more recently Maxwell Anderson has enjoyed an exceptional popularity; and T. S. Eliot's *Murder in the Cathedral* enjoyed a long run in England and had something more than a *succès d'estime* in America. Theatrical success aside, it must be confessed that many of the verse plays of this century possess little besides dignity of manner, meticulous craftsmanship, and isolated good lines; but it must be immediately added that there are instances, even though they are relatively few, which possess originality and distinction. Indeed, though the overall view seems at first glance unimpressive, on closer view the verse plays of the modern age do not in general appear negligible, and some of them acquire stature and significance. A selected few of them repay detailed study, either because they achieved unexpected theatrical success, or because they cast illumination of a special sort on the critical problem, or because, most important of all, they prove to be intrinsically interesting.

II

The century began with what at first appeared as a striking affirmation of the power of verse drama not only to survive but to succeed, in the work of Stephen Phillips, now remembered, if at all, for *Paola and Francesca* (1900), but actually the author of some fourteen plays. Supported in many instances by a popular actor of the old school, Sir Henry Tree, the plays made a brave showing and gained a good deal of popularity. But it was all a deceptive splendor. The fine showing which these plays once made was not owing to great dramatic skill or to any satisfactory organization of dramatic and poetic powers, but to a brilliant sense of theatrical effectiveness, and a romantic and sentimental exploitation of the theme of the supremacy of love and passion. Most of the plays make full use of elaborate stage and scenic effects which must have gone a long way to give the actual performances a brilliance strangely missing now on the printed page. The ending of *Herod* illustrates how far theatrical power substituted for dramatic strength: "Slowly and silently the whole Court melt away, one or two coming and looking on the King, then departing. Herod is left alone by the litter, standing motionless. The Curtain descends: then rises, and it is night, with a few stars. It descends and again rises, and now it is the glimmer of dawn which falls upon Herod and Mariamne, he still standing rigid and with fixed stare in the cataleptic trance." This is spectacular, but it does not resolve the play at all. And it may be said without exaggeration that in the last analysis poetry was for Phillips a kind of theatricality. Ulysses is speaking to Calypso:

> Here would I be at ease upon this isle
> Set in the glassy ocean's azure swoon
> With swards of parsley and of violet
> And poplars shivering in a silvery dream.

It would be as damaging, and as improper, to subject these lines to serious attention as it would to mount the stage during a performance amid the scenery and lighting fixtures, weights and properties, and to inspect the fabrics of the costumes and look close at the painted canvas trees and artificial parsley and violets. *Paola and Francesca* has still a faded and pallid beauty, but Phillips merely continued the conventions of the nineteenth-century verse drama in its least experimental form, with the sole advantage of having a greater knowledge and firmer grasp of the resources of the theatre than his predecessors.

Much more original is the slightly earlier work of John Davidson. He failed just where Phillips succeeded—in the theatre; yet he is an interesting phenomenon, not only because of the variety of ways in which he tried to find a practical solution to his dramatic problems, but because he seemed more aware than most of his contemporaries of what these problems were for the verse dramatist. Davidson's dramas begin with fanciful comedy, *An Unhistorical Pastoral* (written 1877), clearly under Shakespearean influence, and end with two parts of an uncompleted trilogy, *God and Mammon* (1907, 1908), a philosophical work. In between there are historical plays like *Bruce* and *Godfrida*, plays in the contemporary setting like *Smith: a Tragic Farce* and *The Theatrocrat*, and fanciful works, of which the best is perhaps *Scaramouche in Naxos*. The philosophical bent of Davidson's mind led him to value slightly those writings which deal with the surfaces of experience or which use literature as an escape from the realities of man's life, and he regarded poetry as the proper instrument, when rightly used, for the spontaneity, freedom, and liberation from limited common sense which he believed to be the marks of great writing. He favored the drama as a vehicle because, in contrast to the lyric which introduced an element of self-consciousness through exhibitionism, it fostered possibilities for freedom and energy of expression. But Davidson was less sure in what particular form of drama these powers could be best realized in his own day. By the time he wrote *The Theatrocrat* (1905), he had become quite sure that success would be difficult because he had fallen on evil days. Sir Tristram, the actor, says:

> . . . Only once it seems
> The people has a theatre. Drama leaps
> To instant being, power, supremacy:
> From "Gorboduc" to "The Tempest" fifty years;
> And nothing since. Nor can it come again,
> Imagination being an outcast now,
> Unsceptred, unrefreshed, unclad, unknown
> In palace, hut, or hermitage: no home;
> A wandering beldam.

In the Prologue to *Godfrida* (1898) he denied that he was trying to revive Elizabethan or Jacobean verse drama, but only "to write Victorian eclogues"; at the same time he explained why he would not go the way of the world after Ibsen:

Interviewer. But is not verse on the stage a lapse from modernity—a backsliding?

Poet. I think not.

Interviewer. You have expressed somewhat in your writings an intense admiration of Ibsen. Will his influence be found in your play?

Poet. I think not.

Interviewer. Have you ceased to admire Ibsen?

Poet. Oh, no! I share the opinion of those who regard him as the most impressive writer of his time, as the most expert playwright, and most original dramatist the world has seen.

Interviewer. But you are not a disciple?

Poet. No; nothing comes of discipleship except misinterpretation. That seems to me the history of all schools.

Interviewer. But if Ibsen is as great as you say, would it not be wise to follow in his steps?

Poet. No; it would be foolish, as it is unnecessary, to attempt to do over again what Ibsen has done.

Interviewer. Can you not extend the path he has laid down, then?

Poet. No; any step forward from Ibsen would land me in some mystical abyss, or some slough of Naturalism. For me Ibsen is the end, not the beginning.

Davidson at least saw clearly where he stood, though he seemed uncertain of the direction he should take. In *Godfrida* he thought he had found the solution to his problem in romance, which he insisted was "the essence of reality"; earlier in *Scaramouche* he thought "Pantomime . . . to be of best hope," "the childhood of a new poetical comedy," the "likeliest to shoot up in the fabulous manner of the beanstalk, bearing on its branches things of earth and heaven undreamt of in philosophy." In the end, he turned away from such devices to philosophical drama, weakly and melodramatically in *The Theatrocrat* (suggestive of the earlier *Smith*), and with a crude originality in the *Mammon* plays, which are in the direction of dialectical allegory rather than drama. For Davidson had much of the Victorian seriousness of purpose in his view of the arts, which in his case took on the form of a prophetic mission in life to preach an energetic materialism and anti-intellectualism. *The Theatrocrat* shows how far he had come from his notion expressed in *Godfrida* that in the theatre "to give delight is to impart strength most directly, most permanently":

> *Sir Tristram.* We must knead
> The public mind into the shape of this
> To make it possible. The play's the thing!
> *St. James.* Yes; not the pulpit, not the press: the play,
> Loftier and broader than religious rites,
> The mirror of an empire's pride, of man's
> Imagination, from the past released,
> Dowered with the freedom of the universe.

In spite of the clearness with which Davidson recognized his position as a dramatist he could not overcome the difficulties with which he was surrounded—the lack of any established traditions within which he could work, the growing importance of prose social drama, the limitation of his own talents as a poet, and the pressure of his own determination, influenced probably by the new spirit in the drama, to use his art as an instrument for debate and conversion. His writing reflects the confusion of the conflicting elements which shaped his work: there are occasional passages of charming or vigorous statement, but more often the expression is crude and muscular, descending even to strident and ill-mannered rhetoric. But though he remains an isolated phenomenon who started no precedents that others were willing to follow, he illustrates effectively the lot of the poet-dramatist at the turn of the century. In his conviction that the imitation of Ibsen must lead eventually to artistic sterility, that literature at its best should not concern itself with the surfaces of life, and that poetry offers the greatest resources of expression to the serious dramatist, he anticipated at an early date the general direction which the thinking of the poet-dramatists of our century was to take.

The contrast between the success of Phillips and the failure of the more critical Davidson sets the stage in broad terms for the problem of verse drama in the present century. In the first instance, a thorough practical understanding of the theatre coupled with skill in the use of a poetical style which suggested a familiar tradition of verse tragedy gave the effect of mastery; but the work of Phillips seems to indicate that such methods can lead only to momentary and specious triumph. On the other hand, a determined and honest effort to find the proper grounds for the establishment of a modern verse drama forced a search for new forms and conventions and brought about in consequence the loss of security within some established tradition. No matter how one estimates Davidson as a poet, his career seems to raise a difficult question for the modern poet who turns to the drama: if the characteristic dramatic traditions of our times are unsuitable for the poet, and if persistence in his aims separates him from association with the current theatre, can he find a way out of his dilemma and create plays which will be rewarded with acceptance by the stage and will find a useful life outside the covers of a book?

The answer which Thomas Hardy gave to this question in the early years of the century was strongly negative, and *The Dynasts* therefore takes on importance as an illustration of what poetic drama might become if conceived on the basis of his premises. *The Dynasts* is admittedly not a play in the conventional sense at all, but the application of the machinery of drama to a work which has the scale of an epic and the looseness of a panoramic history. Hardy himself clearly saw that his adoption of the dialogue and structural terminology of drama did not consititute a play, and that he was really working in a new kind of form. He wrote in his Preface:

To say, then in the present case, that a writing in play-shape is not to be played, is merely another way of stating that such writing has been done in a form for which there chances to be no brief definition save one already in use for works that it superficially but not entirely resembles.

Though the dramatic form recalled the grandeur of the older drama, Hardy despaired of endowing the modern theatre with similar qualities and hence abandoned the theatre altogether:

Whether mental performance alone may not eventually be the fate of all drama other than that of contemporary or frivolous life, is a kindred question not without interest. The mind naturally flies to the triumphs of the Hellenic and Elizabethan theatre in exhibiting scenes laid "far in the Unapparent," and asks why they should not be repeated. But the meditative world is older, more invidious, more nervous, more quizzical, than it once was, and being unhappily perplexed by—

> Riddles of Death Thebes never knew,

may be less ready and less able than Hellas and old England were to look through the insistent, and often grotesque, substance at the thing signified.

Confined only by a "mental performance," Hardy extended the scope of the drama until he created a new form. What, for instance, would in a normal play be a statement about the setting becomes a principal feature of the imaginative machinery of Hardy's work, at times creating vast panoramic views which cover large areas of a continent, the focus converging until some human action is sharply limned against this huge projection. Other features of the drama receive similar transformations. It might be maintained that Hardy brought to a dignified and large fulfilment the uncertain efforts of the nineteenth century to produce a true closet drama. He abandoned the stage altogether—and in a way never envisioned by many nineteenth-century writers of poetic drama who, if they did write in professed disdain of performance, usually wrote as if still tied to a stage and its limitations. Freed of these limits, Hardy was also freed from the prevailing prepossessions of realism, the identification of the stage with real existence, and at liberty to deal imaginatively with the great forces which are the materials of his play, and poetically with his dialogue. The result, however, was a form which, as he realized, could be called drama only by an almost unwarranted extension of the term. That *The Dynasts* was actually produced does not alter the fact of its basic conception.

The unique position of Hardy's work among the verse plays of the century indicates the determination of the poets to find their solutions within a more conventional understanding of the restrictions of dramatic form—that is, within the limits of some sort of playing area and the capacities of performers. And those who seek for evidence that perhaps Hardy's pessimism about our theatre was perhaps premature might find it in the career of Maxwell Anderson, whose unequivocal success and popularity in recent years is believed by many to presage new promise for the modern theatre. Unquestionably, there is something arresting in the unusual phenomenon of a promising Broadway playwright who turned to verse drama and demonstrated that it could be made acceptable to the public. Moreover, he has not failed to give consideration to the critical issues which his choice had raised. If, as many have contended, the poets fail chiefly because they do not understand the theatre, the case of Maxwell Anderson, whose success demonstrates that he does understand the theatre, might prove to be very illuminating indeed.

Anderson started his career as a poet, publishing verses in magazines and in a little volume, *You Who Have Dreams* (1925), and his first attempt to write drama, *White Desert* (1923), was in verse. It was not, however, by virtue of these relatively slight performances that he came to be known, but through *What Price Glory* (1923), written in collaboration with Laurence Stallings; *Saturday's Children* (1927), and a few other less successful prose plays. With a promising conventional career ahead of him, Anderson turned, in 1930, to the writing of verse plays. He had, in fact, written his first play in verse because, as he tells us, "I was weary of plays in prose that never lifted from the ground."[18] The failure of this play led him to abandon further efforts until he came to the conclusion that "poetic tragedy had never been successfully written about its own place and time." The result was *Elizabeth the Queen* (1930). For Anderson had retained the conviction, from the example of the great acknowledged masterpieces of the world's drama, that all great plays must be verse plays:

To me it is inescapable that prose is the language of information and poetry the language of emotion. Prose can be stretched to carry emotion, and in some exceptional cases, as in Synge's and O'Casey's plays, can occasionally rise to poetic heights by substituting the unfamiliar speech rhythms of an untutored people for the rhythm of verse. But under the strain of an emotion the ordinary prose of our stage breaks down into inarticulateness just as it does in life. Hence the cult of understatement, hence the realistic drama in which the climax is reached in an eloquent gesture or a moment of meaningful silence.

Anderson's perseverance arose from a deep sense of the dramatist's importance: "It is incumbent on the dramatist to be a poet, and incumbent on the poet to be a prophet, dreamer and interpreter of the racial dream." The theatre is a living art and it can play a vital part in transforming the dreams of men into future realities, and Anderson hopes for the appearance of some poet of genius who will direct the course of American drama into fruitful channels, as Aeschylus and Marlowe did at the beginning of Greek and English tragedy respectively. He regards his own efforts modestly as an attempt to encourage some present-day genius in the right direction.

Anderson's sincerity and modesty are enough by themselves to discourage any desire to be damaging or indifferent on the part of a critic; and besides there is his undeniable accomplishment of having scored several successes, notably in *Elizabeth the Queen*, *Mary of Scotland* (1933), and *Winterset* (1935). One is predisposed to deal favorably, or at least cautiously, with a dramatist who has repeatedly forced verse on Broadway and apparently made the audiences like it. Yet it would be wrong to be indulgent through respect or disarmed by practical accomplishment. The popularly successful verse dramatist today needs to be anatomized even more closely than the unsuccessful one.

The choice of Elizabethan times in Anderson's best historical plays contains more than a hint of the dramatic inspiration which lies behind them; in these, and in fact in most of his verse plays, Anderson shows his enthusiasm for the Elizabethan, and particularly the Shakespearean, drama. The lives of the two queens have an understandable attraction for the dramatist, but what is more important in this case is that literary and historical associations prepare us for the acceptance of verse—which might appear inappropriate now in many another historical context—when the setting represents something out of a past with which Shakespeare's and Marlowe's works are vaguely associated. The Elizabethan dramatists did not often base their plots on political events of their own times, but the costumes, the attitudes, the kinds of characters introduced in Anderson's historical pieces are enough like our recollections of Shakespeare and of modern Shakespearean production to assist in rendering a modified blank verse acceptable. For, in spite of the intrusion of modern psychological conceptions in the characterizations, many of the old figures are here—the sinister Machiavellian man of policy, the hard-bitten ambitious woman, the brave young woman attractive for all her indiscretions, the frank-spoken malcontent—they are new and archaic at the same time. The verse—a loose sort of blank verse—is similarly affected with rhythms not quite like the old yet clearly suggesting it, and the diction marked by sprinklings of archaic idioms and words.

What has happened is that, in spite of incidental modernizations, these plays are more nearly an imitation of Shakespeare's history plays than of Shakespeare's methods of treating history dramatically. Shakespeare saw the past in the light of the stern questions and the political crises of his own day, whereas Anderson dresses up the Elizabethan past in terms of Shakespeare. With his understanding of the theatre, Anderson manages also to construct a tense plot, to create plausible figures for the action, and to introduce scenes with sharp opposition and vigorous movement which sustain the interest during performance and even during a casual reading. But this is accomplished at a great loss, and exactly the kind of loss which is destructive to the high purpose which Anderson has set for himself.

Anderson laid the weakness of these plays to the "lively historical sense of our day—a knowledge of period, costume and manners which almost shuts off the writer on historical themes from contemporary comment." There is an element of truth in this view, but it is not impossible under proper conditions for the modern dramatist to use historical material for the purpose of contemporary comment. Shaw, to select but one instance, did so in a number of his plays. It is debateable whether it is the highly developed modern sense of history or the limitation placed on Anderson by the use which he makes of his models which is responsible for the thinness which Anderson himself realized was there. The Elizabethans could make high tragedy out of the materials they selected from history because

of the majesty which they believed to reside in kingship, because of
the high regard in which they held the conduct of the gentleman and
the interest which they had in the question of nobility, and because
they had a keen sense of the passionate self-expression which such
men sought in political action. Anderson could not infuse any of
this into his historical plays today; in fact, he could preserve his
closeness to the models which fascinated him only by diluting those
very features which in a former day gave them magnitude. The
leading characters are conceived merely as intelligent or high-
spirited people not very different in kind from those in many a
current play, but placed in a costume setting with sufficient distance
in time and with the right literary associations to render blank
verse acceptable. They are seen more from the point of view of the
human-interest story rather than from the point of view of tragedy.
The possibilities for poetic treatment are similarly affected. Without
the profound and multiple implications which impressed the Elizabethans in such situations, it becomes impossible to express through
the diction the multiple suggestions, the imaginative synthesis of
related and opposed elements, which the kind of poetic drama that
Anderson set out to write demands, and he is forced back on
shadowy archaisms and on rhetoric.

Distressed at finding himself "labelled a historical and romantic
playwright," Anderson turned to a new solution in *Winterset*, in
which the action takes place in the present and the setting is a
tenement district abutting a river bridgehead, obviously in New
York. The play has come to be regarded as Anderson's best, and
has been highly praised by competent critics and has found its way
into anthologies. It is equally important, however, to mention that
Winterset has also been vigorously assailed, perhaps with even
greater acrimony because it has remained popular.[19] Anderson
himself wrote of this experiment: "*Winterset* is largely in verse, and
treats a contemporary tragic theme, which makes it more of an
experiment than I could wish, for the great masters themselves
never tried to make tragic poetry out of the stuff of their own
times. To do so is to attempt to establish a new convention, one that
may prove impossible of acceptance, but to which I was driven by
the lively historical sense of our day. . . ." In spite of the disap-
proving critics, the generous approval of the play in the theatre
demonstrates that the convention did not prove impossible of ac-

ceptance, and it becomes therefore important to find out why.

For all its modernity of setting and theme, *Winterset* is an elaborate and original combination of Shakespearean situations. The central motive is the Elizabethan favorite of revenge, but a very modern sort of revenge. The youthful hero, Mio Romagna, is driven by the desire to prove the innocence of his father, who was executed some years before for a crime which he did not commit, victimized because he actively promoted a social philosophy at odds with the ruling social powers. Mio is embittered by his experience, and his embitterment has often so strong a flavor of the Elizabethan malcontent that it is impossible not to think of Hamlet. The Romagna case had been reviewed by a professor of law who had noticed the failure of the prosecution to call a material witness, Garth Esdras, and Mio's search for the witness has brought him to this dismal tenement district. There he sees Miriamne, and the two instantly fall beautifully in love with one another. This would be enough to suggest *Romeo and Juliet*, but the parallel is made even stronger when Mio discovers that Miriamne is Garth's sister—his only love sprung from his only hate. A favorite Elizabethan device, madness, is introduced in the form of Judge Gaunt, who has been driven to insanity by the uncertainties which have been preying on his mind since his conduct of the Romagna trial. The review of the case which brings Mio to the tenement area also brings Gaunt. (It also brings Trock, the gangster who really did the murder, who arrives to see if Garth is "safe," and who is the agent of the death of Mio and Miriamne.) It might at first seem far-fetched to identify the old derelict hobo, who asks to be permitted to sleep under the steam pipes in the Esdras hovel, with Mad Tom in *Lear* ("Poor Tom's acold"), were it not for a striking parallel to the mad scene in *Lear*, with the wild wisdom uttered by Gaunt punctuated by the Hobo's silly laughter and comment, to the accompaniment of a storm outside. There is no ghost, but there is a fairly good substitute for one. At the end of Act I, Shadow (the name is suggestive) is shot by Trock's men and thrown in the river. Toward the middle of Act II he too appears at the Esdras house and accuses Trock before he dies, giving Mio just the hint he needs to solve the case. It is hard to believe Shadow is not a ghost, so miraculous seems his improbable if temporary survival from three gunshot wounds, the currents in the river, and the painful trip back, and Trock's remark—"By

God, he's out of his grave!"—helps to lend a suggestion of the supernatural to his appearance. In addition to these parallels there are
echoes in individual speeches which reinforce the more conspicuous
likenesses. Though the situation and characters of *Winterset* are
modern, the dramatic "motifs" are largely those of another day,
and it does not take a learned student of Shakespeare to sense at
least a vague similarity.

This indicates that, in a manner analogous to the historical plays,
a condition which establishes the feasibility of verse as the medium
is the literary associations, and it may be argued that if Anderson
has succeeded in making verse appear appropriate to so modern an
action, it is in part because he has brought into it, as the essential
elements of his pattern, motifs from the golden age of English
tragedy which we associate with rhythmical and elevated language.
An important hint is supplied by the language itself, shot through
with Elizabethan archaisms—pismires, worms (for snakes), sire;
idioms from the past, such as "I would fain look back," "caught so
ripe red-handed," "I fear me," and the like. And the association
with the past is further established by the division between the
speeches done in prose, often in a crisp and popular vein, and those
in verse: generally speaking, the verse passages relate with but few
unimportant exceptions to those features of the play which suggest
analogies with Shakespearean tragedy—the desire for revenge and
the malcontent vein in Mio, the love-at-first-sight sequences, and
the madness of the judge. The only important exceptions are the
chorus-like speeches of Esdras.

The effect of such manipulation of the language is not one of
ordered harmony or of close and progressive relationship to the
action as a whole but one of disunity and contradiction. Mio's
first speech in the play is "Yeah—but I heard something changed
my mind"; but a few lines further on he launches out:

Fell in with a fisherman's family on the coast and went after the beautiful
mackerel fish that swim in the beautiful sea. Family of Greeks—Aristides
Marinos was his lovely name. He sang while he fished. Made the pea-green
Pacific ring with his bastard Greek chanties.

An even more striking contrast occurs when Mio makes his great
discovery:

> This is the thing I've hunted
> over the earth to find out, and I'd be blind

> indeed if I missed it now!
> You heard what he said:
> It was Shadow killed him!

There is nothing remarkable about this portion of the speech, except perhaps the typographical distribution. There are touches in the idiom—"I'd be blind indeed," for instance—which, by lending a trace of formality to these lines distinguishes them slightly from what has preceded; but in the lines which immediately follow a really extraordinary change occurs:

> Now let the night conspire
> with the sperm of hell! It's plain beyond denial
> even to this fox of justice . . . .

The language has suddenly moved on to another plane, and has fallen under the shadow of Shakespeare.

Though these changes are particularly noticeable in the important speeches, the mixture of idioms is so consistent a feature of the method that it sometimes gives an unexpected accent even to incidental lines in the dialogue:

> *Shadow.*   Come on, Trock, you know me.
> Anything you say goes, but give me leave
> to kid a little.

How is the intrusion of "give me leave" to be explained? Presumably it acts as a casual reminder of the poetical norm which functions in other parts of the play, but the principal effect is to inject a literary flavor which is jarring and unsuited to its immediate setting. Admirers of the play have justified the speeches of such characters as Shadow by pointing out that Shakespeare did not hesitate to make murderers, soldiers, adolescents, and what not speak poetically. Unfortunately, it is often difficult to assign any other reason why the characters in *Winterset* do, even though the propriety of the analogy may be granted as a reply to any naive insistence on strict verisimilitude. More important, however, is the fact that whatever else Shakespeare did with his dialogue, he did not make his characters talk a hybrid language compounded, let us say, of his sonnets and *The Canterbury Tales*.

One effect of the shifts in the language is to endow certain of the longer speeches or parts of speeches with a distinctive eloquence, and thus to give emphasis by means of rhetorical isolation to statements having special significance or expressive of intense feeling. It is possible that, consciously or not, this practice represents the practical consequence of a view expressed by Anderson in his essay, "Poetry in the Theatre": "It is inescapable that prose is the language of information and poetry the language of emotion." Since the eighteenth century, there has been a growing insistence that the function of poetry in a play is the expression of emotion, a notion which engenders a limited view, if not a serious misconception, of the nature of verse drama. There are undoubtedly moments in the great verse plays during which the expression of deep feeling or intense passion acquires an obvious eloquence and elevation. But any notion of verse drama which regards the language of these moments as in a separate category from the rest gives to the whole problem a false simplicity and makes for an erratic scheme of development. The speeches in a play may vary all the way from simple statement of fact, or even ribald jesting, to the most profound or impassioned flights, but the question of what language is appropriate is governed not only by the character of the individual speech, but also by the essential nature of the work as a whole, by the artistic idea which informs it, by some general principle which determines the selection and ordering of each part. The accomplishment of complete integration becomes difficult if the moments of greatest feeling are regarded as the proper occasions for moving into a special plane for the expression of emotion through poetry. And it becomes well-nigh impossible if at these critical moments the language passes into a vaguely Shakespearean idiom.

Perhaps the greatest limitation inherent in the method of *Winterset* is that it has interfered with the full realization of the tragic potentialities of the materials of the play. *Winterset* is a tragedy of modern life, and the echoes of the Sacco-Vanzetti case indicate that the play received its inspiration from an episode which touched on some of the most serious issues of the life of our times. Anderson had already concerned himself with the trial in *Gods of the Lightning* (1928), but in *Winterset* the story is sufficiently removed from the immediate circumstances of the original events and sufficiently free of partisan appeal to render it amenable to tragic treatment, and presumably to verse. But the literary associations raised by Anderson's method cut across this modern theme in many ways. They affect, for instance, the tragic hero. The motive of revenge recalls Hamlet, and it recalls him too clearly for the good of the play, al-

though the nature of the revenge and the resolution of Mio's conflict are not the same as in Shakespeare. Even in the speeches which
are in the popular idiom, what Mio says appears at times to be determined by the originals which he suggests. Hamlet puns, and so
Mio must pun. Hamlet unpacks his heart to Horatio with ironic
and learned allusiveness, and so must Mio:

> *Mio.* . . . a hobo has the stench of ten because his shoes are poor.
> *Carr.* Tennyson.
> *Mio.* Right. Jeez, I'm glad we met up again!
> Never knew anybody else that could track me through
> the driven snow of Victorian literature.
> *Carr.* Now you're cribbing from some half-forgotten
> criticism of Ben Jonson's Roman plagiarisms.

And sometimes Mio's reflections seem to take a form which would
have been unlikely had it not been for the melancholy vein in
Hamlet:

> Oh, my friends,
> this fine athletic figure of a man
> that stands so grim before us, what will they find
> when they saw his skull for the last inspection?
> I fear me a little puffball dust will blow away
> rejoining earth our mother—and this same dust,
> this smoke, this ash on the wind, will represent
> all he had left to think with.

Mio in consequence acquires an arch pedantry which is as damaging as it is unintentional. And this is symptomatic of the gravest
flaw, that the method, which often generates a confusion in idiom,
also produces a corresponding confusion in the sentiments and
attitudes of the play. The literary associations produce the curious
hybrid language, and the language emphasizes the literary associations. The use of styles which contain strong echoes from the past
is in itself a sign of the great difficulties encountered by the modern
writer of verse drama, and is to some extent an indirect admission
of weakness, but it is not without possibilities for certain specialized
artistic effects. For instance, it could call attention to the timeless-
ness of the theme, or create ironic comparisons. Certain modern
writers of verse drama, to be considered later, have in fact made use
of literary echoes in this way. In *Winterset,* however, the conjunction
of the Shakespearean and modern idioms has the effect of blurring
the sentiments and thus of detracting from the urgency and significance of what is being said.

All this raises the question of whether Anderson would not have come closer to his goal if he had abandoned verse altogether. As it is, he appears to have fallen into somewhat the same error as the verse dramatists of the nineteenth century, and the comparison which some have suggested with Stephen Phillips is unfair only to this extent, that whereas both men seem to have succeeded because of their knowledge of the theatre rather than because of their understanding of the nature of poetic drama, Anderson is not only the more versatile craftsman, but appears more sincere and serious— as well as more original—in his attempts to bring a greater dignity and magnitude to the drama than the modern theatre seems to have fostered. The sincerity of Anderson and the popular success of many of his plays have had the effect of raising general interest in the question of the possibility of a poetic drama in our times, but his plays cannot be regarded as having contributed greatly to its answer. They are significant as a symptom, but they have not marked out a path that others may fruitfully follow.

III

The work of Anderson places in relief the esoteric nature of the more radical experiments in verse drama during recent years. The novelties resulting from these efforts were the product of a desire to avoid the characteristic features of the conventional drama of the current theatre, and of a determination to escape the banality of continued imitation of older models and practices staled and brought to sterility by much use. In addition, a general inclination to adapt to dramatic uses the idioms and devices original with contemporary poetry added not only to the difficulty of the task but to the strangeness of the product. Among these more rigorous and original excursions into verse drama, two important developments can be distinguished: the first is the work of William Butler Yeats; the second, that of a younger generation of poets whose dramatic writings fall largely within the decade of the thirties.

As a critic, Yeats sought to reveal the failings of the current drama and to trace the foundations on which a new attempt might be raised; as a poet, he experimented over a long period of time in the hopes of discovering new means which would enable the poet to find once more his proper place in the theatre. And he brought to his task one of the unquestionably great poetic gifts of our time.

He came to the theatre chiefly through his interest in the revival of Irish literature; and in the initial efforts to establish a national Irish theatre, Yeats was one of the most energetic leaders, and in a way its spokesman. He believed that the sources of this new theatre should be in genuinely Irish materials: "Ireland in our day has rediscovered the old heroic literature of Ireland, and she has rediscovered the imagination of the folk." For his own part, he preferred to deal "with the heroic legend than with the folk." [20] But it was not merely a nationalistic fervor that inspired this choice of material: in the traditional imaginativeness of the folk, in the still unexploited legends of Ireland, he saw an untapped source for the creation of an imaginative literature grounded in an almost unbroken tradition. He wrote in "Thoughts on Lady Gregory's Translation":

Gaelic-speaking Ireland, because its art has been made, not by the artist choosing his material from whatever he has a mind to, but by adding a little to something which it has taken generations to invent, has always had a popular literature. We cannot say how much that literature has done for the vigour of the race, for who can count the hands its praise of kings and high-hearted queens made hot upon the swordhilt, or the amorous eyes it made lustful for strength and beauty? We remember indeed that when the farming people and the labourers of the towns made their last attempt to cast out England by force of arms they named themselves after the companions of Finn. [21]

Behind this enthusiasm lay a settled and unchanging conviction of the inferiority of realistic drama of contemporary life, in part because it dealt with the surface of commonplace experiences, with changing particulars and not with permanent and essential insights and passions, and in part because it reduced speech to an impersonal and emotionless language. These limitations he regarded as not separate but essentially related aspects of one and the same fatal defect in purpose:

Have we not been in error in demanding from our playwrights personages who do not transcend our common actions any more than our common speech? . . . . Art delights in the exception, for it delights in the soul expressing its own laws and arranging the world about it in its own pattern, as sand strewn upon a drum will change itself into different patterns, according to the notes of music that are sung or played to it. [22]

. . . . . .

The more carefully the play reflected the surface of life the more would the elements be limited to those that naturally display themselves during so many minutes of our ordinary affairs. It is only by extravagance, by an emphasis far greater than that of life as we observe it, that we can crowd into a few minutes the knowledge of years. Shakespeare or Sophocles can so quicken, as it were, the circles of the clock, so heighten the expression of life, that many years can unfold themselves in a few minutes, and it is always Shakespeare or Sophocles, and not Ibsen, that makes us say, 'How true, how often I have felt as that man feels'; or 'How intimately I have come to know those people on the stage.'[23]

The realistic play with its attention on the surface of life, on common actions, concentrates on the accidents of human experience and thus leaves untouched the permanent and the essential:

I have been reading through a bundle of German plays, and have found everywhere a desire not to express hopes and alarms common to every man that ever came into the world, but politics or social passion, a veiled or open propaganda. Now it is duelling that has need of reproof; now it is the ideas of an actress, returning from the free life of the stage, that must be contrasted with the prejudice of an old-fashioned town; now it is the hostility of Christianity and Paganism in our own day that is to find an obscure symbol in a bell thrown from its tower by spirits of the wood. I compare the work of these dramatists with the greater plays of their Scandinavian master, and remember that even he, who has made so many clear-drawn characters, has made us no abundant character, no man of genius in whom we could believe, and that in him also, even when it is Emperor and Galilean that are face to face, even the most momentous figures are subordinate to some tendency, to some movement, to some in-animate energy, or to some process of thought whose very logic has changed it into mechanism—always to something other than human life.[24]

The realists have consequently lost their right to the one indis-pensable quality of all literature—beautiful, vivid, even extrava-gant language. Yeats insisted on the need for learning structure, and it is perhaps suggestive of an awareness of his own failings in that direction that he warned his compatriots that they had little need of "Shakespeare's luxuriance," and urged them to study from the French and Ibsen; but it becomes clear by his constant iteration of the point that he felt the greater need to be magnificence of language:

If one has not fine construction, one has not drama, but if one has not beautiful or powerful and individual speech, one has not literature, or, at any rate, one has not great literature. Rabelais, Villon, Shakespeare, William Blake, would have known one another by their speech. Some of them knew how to construct a story, but all of them had abundant, resonant, beautiful, laughing, living speech.[25]

Lacking this, "the great realists seem to the lovers of beautiful art to be wise in this generation, and for the next generation, perhaps, but not for all generations that are to come."[26] Both from the commonplace materials of the realists, and from their "impersonal language that has come, not out of individual life, nor out of life at all, but out of the necessities of commerce, of parliament, of board schools, of hurried journeys by rail,"[27] Yeats fled for good and all.

The escape from the mediocrity and flatness of modern drama Yeats found through the nationalistic bias which he urged the national theatre to adopt, not, he frequently insisted, for deliberate propaganda but for the purposes of the highest and most enduring art. "Let us learn construction from the masters, and dialogue from ourselves," he wrote in 1901.[28] "From ourselves" because in the speech of the simple countryman, of the imaginative Irishman of the towns, there was a vivid and unspoiled language and elsewhere there was not. In that respect the Irish writer enjoyed the advantages of a Shakespeare drawing from the abundant linguistic resources of his time. "Language was still alive then, alive as it is in Gaelic today, as it is in English-speaking Ireland where the schoolmaster or the newspaper has not corrupted it."[29] "We have looked for the centre of our art where the players of the time of Shakespeare and of Corneille found theirs—in speech, whether it be the perfect mimicry of the conversation of two countrymen of the roads, or that idealised speech poets have imagined for what we think but do not say."[30] For Yeats the perfect vehicle for such speech, as well as for the permanent generality of great art, was myth, or something analogous to it:

I come always back to this thought. There is something of an old wives' tale in fine literature. The makers of it are like an old peasant telling stories of the great famine or the hangings of '98 or his own memories. He has felt something in the depth of his mind and he wants to make it as visible and powerful to our senses as possible. He will use the most extravagant words or illustrations if they suit his purpose. Or he will invent a wild parable, and the more his mind is on fire or the more creative it is, the less he will look at the outer world or value it for its own sake. It gives him metaphors and examples, and that is all.[31]

· · · · ·

Poets have chosen their themes more often from stories that are all, or half, mythological, than from history or stories that give one the sensation of history, understanding, as I think, that the imagination which remembers the proportions of life is but a long wooing, and that it has to forget them before it becomes the torch and the marriage-bed.[32]

Myth is not only the source of passionate utterance, but in its nature approaches to the highest truth, not in the form of sentences and derivative moral significations, but as a sign of transcendent beliefs:

Myth is not . . . a rudimentary form superseded by reflection. Belief is the spring of all action; we assent to the conclusions of reflection but believe what myth presents; belief is love, and the concrete alone is loved; nor is it true that myth has no purpose but to bring round some discovery of a principle or a fact. The saint may touch through myth the utmost reach of human faculty and pass not to reflection but to unity with the source of his being.[33]

There is enough evidence in the great drama of the past to justify these convictions at least as a working principle. How came it then that Yeats, while acting as a prime mover of a movement that has been widely acclaimed, failed to create any plays himself that have been accepted as vital contributions to the drama of our day? One answer suggested is that for all his gifts as a poet he lacked the requisite talents for writing plays, or even for writing verse suitable for dramatic speech. But this answer is too facile, and it is really an evasion, particularly in the case of a man like Yeats who had great talents and who gave every aspect of the problem much painstaking thought, even to experimenting with the proper method of speaking verse on the stage and training actors to do it effectively.

It is significant that the very drama of the Irish school which the world has come to admire filled Yeats with misgivings. He had encouraged the use of native Irish materials, but what he did not realize at first was that the political temper of Ireland and the interest in local details stimulated by his own advice would produce inevitably a special variant of just the kind of drama he had found wanting. Irish drama had the temporary advantage of a picturesque and still unspoiled dialect, but he early realized that the "objectivity" of the people's theatre of Ireland augured ill for his hopes. Surveying the work of the first few years of the movement he wrote, "Yet we did not set out to create this sort of theatre, and its success has been to me a discouragement and a defeat."[34] Only in the plays of Synge did he find any approximation to what he had wanted from the use of the materials of Irish life. And so, though Yeats remained in close contact with the work of the Abbey Theatre and continued to write plays to the end of his career, artistically he found himself in isolation.

If anything, this only confirmed him in the basic principles on which he sought to found his dramatic art, though on the question of what form the plays must take to conform to these principles and to accomplish the ends he sought, and how far these ends could be accomplished, his thinking wavered and underwent modification as he tried first one and then another expedient in practice. Thus, though he still adhered to his conviction that myth is the proper vehicle for deep feelings and for rooted beliefs that lie beyond the conclusions of reflection, he saw that the capacity to treat legends in this way was a function of the strength of one's own awareness of the possession of such beliefs, and that lacking this the artist must be at some disadvantage:

All symbolic art should arise out of a real belief, and that it cannot do so in this age proves that this age is a road and not a resting-place for the imaginative arts. I can only understand others by myself, and I am certain that there are many who are not moved as they desire to be by that solitary light burning in the tower of Prince Athanais, because it has not entered into men's prayers nor lighted any through the sacred dark of religious contemplation.[35]

All his life Yeats tried to find some ground for a scheme of belief, searching in Hindu thought, reading Swedenborg, studying the philosophers, exploring the spirit world through seances, and composing that strange compendium, *A Vision*. Yet though he made of all these things a recondite symbolism for his poetry, he never abandoned his critical faculties about such matters, and seemed to adopt elements from them largely for poetic reasons. It was still true to Yeats that "the end of art is the ecstasy awakened by the presence before an ever-changing mind of what is permanent in the world, or by the arousing of that mind itself into the very delicate and fastidious mood habitual with it when it is seeking those permanent and recurring things," but the fulfillment of these conditions may have to await, he thought, the time "when a new race or a new civilization has made us look upon all with new eyesight."[36]

But in the meantime? Yeats regarded with envy times such as those of Hesiod and Homer when "a man of that unbroken day could have all the subtlety of Shelley, and yet use no image unknown among the common people, and speak no thought that was not a deduction from the common thought."[37] The artistic consequence of the "broken," divided character of modern man was that it encouraged of necessity a subtle and rarefied lyricism:

In literature, partly from the lack of that spoken word which knits us to normal man, we have lost in personality, in our delight in the whole man—blood, imagination, intellect, running together—but have found a new delight, in essences, in states of mind, in pure imagination, in all that comes to us most easily in elaborate music. There are two ways before literature—upward into ever-growing subtlety, with Verhaeren, Mallarmé, with Maeterlinck, until at last, it may be, a new agreement among refined and studious men gives birth to a new passion, and what seems literature becomes religion; or downward, taking the soul with us until all is simplified and solidified again . . . . If the carts have hit our fancy we must have the soul tight within our bodies, for it has grown so fond of a beauty accumulated by subtle generations that it will for a long time be impatient with our thirst for mere force, mere personality, for tumult of the blood. If it begin to slip away we must go after it, for Shelley's Chapel of the Morning Star is better than Burn's beer-house . . . . except at the day's weary end; and it is always better than that uncomfortable place where there is no beer, the machine shop of the realists.[38]

This was the dilemma which Yeats posed for himself, and the choice was inevitable. The modern world no longer felt the interpenetration of force and intellect, imagination and passion, belief and wisdom; it had destroyed the acceptance of the whole man, which other happier ages enjoyed, and which supplied the artist with materials for a vigorous and vivid treatment of his themes. The writer in the modern world, in which observation and reflection had been raised to so high a level of importance and separated from those other functions and needs of man which they could not serve alone, was in a different position from the great writers of the past:

The two great energies of the world that in Shakespeare's day penetrated each other have fallen apart as speech and music fell apart at the Renaissance, and that has brought each to greater freedom, and we have to prepare a stage for the whole wealth of modern lyricism, for an art that is close to pure music for those energies that would free the arts from imitation, that would ally acting to decoration and to the dance.[39]

What was to become of Yeats's early dream of a people's theatre in which the poet was to bring joy to the artisan of the town and the man of the fields? It had pretty much gone by 1919 when he wrote, "I want to create for myself an unpopular theatre and an audience like a secret society where admission is by favour and never to many." All he wanted was "an audience of fifty, a room worthy of it (some great dining-room or drawing-room), half-a-dozen young men and women who can dance and speak verse or play drum, flute and zither." He aimed now at a "mysterious art" working by symbol and suggestion and making use of color, gesture, and rhythm, and, significantly, the writers whom he regards as spiritual affinities in this enterprise are not dramatists; it is to be "a mode of drama Shelley and Keats could have used without ceasing to be themselves, and for which even Blake in the mood of *The Book of Thel* might not have been too obscure." [40] He came to emphasize more and more those features of his plays which enhanced their decorative qualities and their suggestion of symbolism and ritual. He proposed, for instance, writing a series of plays on a limited number of masks. [41] How far Yeats went in the direction of altering the basis of dramatic art can be seen in his comments on *Fighting the Waves*, the revised form in 1935 of *The Only Jealousy of Emer*:

I have retold the story in prose which I have tried to make very simple and left imaginative suggestion to dancers, singers, musicians. I have left the words of the opening and closing lyrics unchanged, for sung to modern music in the modern way they suggest strange patterns to the ear without obtruding upon it their difficult, irrelevant words . . . .

I do not say that it is always necessary when one writes for a general audience to make the words of the dialogue so simple and so matter-of-fact; but it is necessary where the appeal is mainly to the eye and to the ear through songs and music. *Fighting the Waves* is in itself nothing, a mere occasion for sculptor and dancer, for the exciting dramatic music of George Anthiel. [42]

The arduous and passionate efforts of Yeats to restore words to their ancient sovereignty in drama had, in the end, resulted in forms in which words played a secondary role, and the poet became the auxiliary to the costumer, choreographer, and musician.

It is indicative of the direction of Yeats's dramatic experiments that he almost never wrote in the longer forms. In his early advice to prospective contributors to the new Irish theatre he suggested the doubtful expedient of writing at first in short forms as a preliminary exercise toward the mastery of dramatic method. There were nevertheless certain incidental advantages in this practice. The short play represented a sharp break from the formulae of the commercial play and hence from its conventions and clichés. It also discouraged aping of the classics of poetic drama in the manner of the nineteenth century. Yeats searched the accepted classics of tragedy not for models but for an understanding of the essential requisites of serious drama and of the conditions which encouraged its composition. In his effort to get at essentials, however, he reduced the elements of drama to include little more than passion expressed in beautiful language, steadily eliminating as secondary and irrelevant such representational features as all European drama has had in common with realism and harking back to the ritualistic origins of drama for his clues. His persistence in the short form coincided with the general predisposition revealed in his reflections on the drama toward an essentially undramatic direction of development, toward an increasingly lyrical and formalistic treatment of his materials.

His discovery of the Japanese Noh plays provided both a stimulus in this direction and new models to guide him. These plays, the product of the fourteenth and fifteenth centuries, and in subsequent times the concern chiefly of aristocratic Japanese audiences, are a highly formalized combination of dance, song, and speech. The Noh plays provided a framework which eliminated all suggestions of literal imitation and all associations with reality, a condition which Yeats preferred for a free exercise of his talents as a poet, and which at the same time severed all connections with the European stage and the dramatic classics of Western literature. Yeats introduced a ceremony in which three musicians unfold and fold a large cloth while singing or reciting verses, which signalizes the opening or the end of the play and permits the initial characters to enter the playing area and leave it unseen by the audience. This arrangement effected another break with European theatrical traditions by eliminating the proscenium and front curtain. The musicians retire after this ceremony to the rear of the stage and, on occasion, play and sing during the course of the play. They do not function in a way analogous to the chorus of a Greek tragedy, however; they serve to intensify the formal character of the play and translate it almost to the point of ritual, and at the same time their lines provide for the most complete lyrical treatment. Yeats admired the aloof, puppet-like quality of the characters of the Noh plays, and by the use of masks and other devices tried to incorporate some of this quality into his own, so that the characters are little more than tokens or emblems. The characters become parts of a pattern of symbols, and suggest an analogy with the method of the French symbolists whom Yeats admired and who influenced him greatly. Myth and legend came to be for Yeats not the basis of an action, but the scheme for a symbolism.[43]

The general development of Yeats's dramatic work is in the direction of increasing clarity and sharpness of diction, more precise and yet subtle handling of rhythm, and increasing formalization of character and structure. The earlier plays—*The Countess Cathleen* (1892), *The Land of Heart's Desire* (1894), *The Shadowy Waters* (1900), *The King's Threshold* (1903)—show no very radical departures in the treatment of form except for their slightness and the absence of any clearly defined line of action. The indecisive rhythms, the luxuriance and even inflation of language are adapted to suggestions of a dreamy and evanescent sort, better suited to expression of sentiment and mood than to any of the purposes for which verse might be employed in drama as conventionally conceived. Yeats's own remarks to A. E. in 1904 about *The Land of Heart's Desire*—that it had "an exaggeration of sentiment and sentimental beauty which I have come to think unmanly"—indicates his own dissatisfaction with this earlier manner. "The popularity of *The Land of Heart's Desire*," he continued, "seems to me to come not from its merits but because of this weakness."[44] The escape from such weaknesses came not only through the change which becomes generally apparent in Yeats's language and prosody, but through the adaptation of new models, the Japanese Noh plays. The plays in which these methods were first employed in a thoroughgoing manner—grouped in *Plays and Controversies* (1923) as "Four Plays for Dancers"—are *At the Hawk's Well* (1916), *The Dreaming of the Bones* (1919), *The Only Jealousy of Emer* (1919), and *Calvary* (1921).

Calvary is in a slightly separate class in not using Irish myth, and in being freighted with a more apparently philosophical symbolism; moreover, it lacks some of the more spectacular decorative features of dance and costume of the others. It is perhaps a more obvious illustration, however, of how the diction functions in these plays. The play opens with the folding and unfolding of the cloth by the musicians, who sing a neatly constructed lyric. As the musicians take their place at the back of the scene, one musician recites a number of lines announcing the passion of Christ, largely in the meter of the play proper, thus effecting a transition from the idiom of the lyric to the main body of the work. The play proper consists of a dialogue between Lazarus and Christ, a description by the musician of the appearance of the Marys, a dialogue between Judas and Christ, and finally a scene with three Roman soldiers and Christ, a progression vaguely suggestive of a "mystery" drama sequence. This ends in a dance by the soldiers, followed by Christ's, "My Father, why hast thou forsaken Me." The musicians fold and unfold the cloth to conclude the play, singing a lyric like the first in form which recalls the initial imagery and refrains.

The diction is characterized by a persistent use of bird symbols, particularly the heron. The opening song begins:

First Musician
Motionless under the moon-beam,
Up to his feathers in the stream;
Although fish leap, the white heron
Shivers in a dumfounded dream

Second Musician
God has not died for the white heron.

This theme is developed throughout the whole of the opening lyric with the refrain thrice repeated. The same imagery is used on several occasions throughout the play. After the appearance of Christ, the musician sings,

Oh, but the mockers' cry
Makes my heart afraid,
As though a flute of bone
Taken from a heron's thigh,
A heron crazed by the moon,
Were cleverly, softly played.

The moon image occurs quite regularly in some connection with the bird image. Lazarus' final remark, after protesting that Christ has torn him from the peace of the grave, recalls again the bird figure:

Make way for Lazarus that must go search
Among the desert places where there is nothing
But howling wind and solitary birds.

When Judas speaks of the betrayal as a triumph of his will he also makes use of these symbols:

When I planned it
There was no live thing near me but a heron
So full of itself that it seemed terrified.

In the final lyric, the bird references are not restricted to the heron but are obviously suggestive of the same things. It begins:

> Lonely the sea-bird lies at her rest
> Blown like a dawn-blenched parcel of spray
> Upon the wind, or follows her prey
> Under a great wave's hollowing crest.

And the new refrain is,

> God has not appeared to the birds.

One curious image is distantly related to the one about the flute made of a heron's thigh bone. It occurs in the speech of one of the soldiers who speak of casting for Christ's clothes:

> Our dice were carved
> Out of an old sheep's thigh at Ephesus.

There is clearly something beautifully articulated about all this, and the images have a strange and haunting effect—and they can have no more than that to the uninitiated. One who has an acquaintance with Yeats's poems and has had some initiation into his private pattern of symbolism may be clear about much of this at a performance. Or one might first read Yeats's note to the play. Yeats himself admits the deliberate obscurity of the lyrics:

I have written the little songs of the chorus to please myself, confident that singer and composer, when the time came for performance, would certainly make it impossible for the audience to know what the words were.

But this seems perverse, especially as the words of the lyric are alluded to in the play and are highly important there, and it is also curious that Yeats should want it to be clear to a reader who, he says, "can always solve the mystery and learn the secret by turning to a note." The secret is revealed in the note in words ascribed to the mythical Michael Robartes:

Certain birds, especially as I see things, such lonely birds as the heron, hawk, eagle, and swan, are the natural symbols of subjectivity, especially when floating upon the wind alone or alighting upon some pool or river, while the beasts that run upon the ground, especially those that run in packs, are the natural symbols of objective man.

Subjective men are lonely, unique, and hence the association of Lazarus and Judas with the leading images marks them out as subjective men. Yeats continues:

I have used my bird-symbolism in these songs to increase the objective loneliness of Christ by contrasting it with a loneliness, opposite in kind, that unlike His can be, whether joyous or sorrowful, sufficient to itself. I have surrounded him with the images of those He cannot save, not only with the birds, who have served neither God nor Caesar, and await for none or for a different saviour, but with Lazarus and Judas and the Roman soldiers for whom he has died in vain . . . . I have therefore represented in Lazarus and Judas types of the intellectual despair that lay beyond His sympathy, while in the Roman soldiers I suggest a form of objectivity that lay beyond His help.

Now much becomes clear, even to the opposition between the flute of the heron's thigh bone and the soldier's dice made of the bone of an old sheep (an animal that walks the ground and hence a symbol of objectivity). The emphasis on the lots which the soldiers will cast for Christ's garments, their constant reference to gambling, also takes on a new meaning. They are men who have happily acquiesced in a world of contingency:

> . . . you had not found
> More comfortable companions for a deathbed
> Than three old gamblers that have asked for nothing.

What is still not clear is the references to the moon, but these also give up their mystery to one who is familiar with the rest of Yeats's work or who has read in the elaborate scheme of *A Vision* that the moon is the symbol of subjectivity. When all this recondite pattern is straightened out, the work emerges as something beautifully conceived and impressively managed. But it is the antithesis of drama as ordinarily conceived, where the images, properly used, are not static and where they derive their meaning either by association with common human experience and an erudition which may be supposed to be reasonably familiar, or through some scheme of relations established by the play and requiring no knowledge beyond it.

Though *Calvary* is in some respects a special case it serves to illustrate the type of scheme which many of the later plays followed. Though in these the conventions Yeats adapted from the Noh plays are not invariably present, in many ways the plays for dancers represent his favorite solution of the problem, and most of the subsequent plays show the effects of these experiments. The materials, where they are not directly from Irish myth, have the air of child's folk tales or parables. They are treated in a simplified, formalistic way.

Occasionally the play proper will be in prose, as in *Fighting the Waves,* or extremely lucid verse, simple almost to the point of affectation, as in *The Death of Cuhulain,* but in nearly every instance there are the lyrics with their abstruse or recondite symbolism.

Two of the late plays are a departure from these methods, *The Words upon the Window Pane* (1934), and *Purgatory* (published 1940). The former lies quite outside the principal development of Yeats's dramatic work, but *Purgatory* is a striking variant among his excursions in verse drama. There is no survival of the ceremonials of the Noh adaptations—no musicians, no curtain folders, no dancers. There is more than a suggestion of the technique of expressionistic drama in the multiple order of probabilities—the direct speech of the Boy, the brilliant, hard eloquence of the Old Man, the appearance of the figures of their dead progenitors reliving again the critical episodes of their lives in the old burnt-out house; but there is also a suggestion of the contiguity of the natural and supernatural which is common in the Noh plays. Neither of these forms, however, is responsible for the dominant quality of this play. There is a brilliant intensity about it. The verse is hard and lithe. The overhanging luxuriance of the early plays is gone completely. There is also missing the quaint oversimplicity of some of the later plays, or their sly, recondite ironies, or their difficult and obscure symbolism. And the imagery is comprehensible within the scheme established by the play and demands no private initiation into its mysteries.

> Study that house.
> I think about its jokes and stories;
> I try to remember what the butler
> Said to a drunken gamekeeper
> In mid-October, but I cannot.
> If I cannot, none living can.
> Where are the jokes and stories of a house,
> Its threshold gone to patch a pig-sty?
>
>   .   .   .   . .   .
>
> Great people lived and died in this house;
> Magistrates, colonels, members of Parliament,
> Captains and Governors, and long ago
> Men that had fought at Aughrim and the Boyne.
> Some that had gone on Government work
> To London or to India came home to die,
> Or came from London every spring
> To look at the may-blossom in the park.

They had loved the trees that he cut down
To pay what he had lost at cards
Or spent on horses, drink and women;
Had loved the house, had loved all
The intricate passages of the house,
But he killed the house; to kill a house
Where great men grew up, married, died,
I here declare a capital offence.

There is hardly a finer example of the adaptation of the idioms of modern poetry to the requirements of spoken dialogue. The form of the play, however, is scarcely more than an extended dramatic monologue with supporting devices, the Old Man's reflections and outpourings of feeling in the presence of the old house haunted by its former residents being the heart of the whole play.

Starting with an ambition to restore once more dignity and vitality to drama through beauty of speech and to establish a theatre that would become an important institution in the life of a nation, Yeats ended up with a species of writing that was admittedly wholly unsuited to such an audience and that had only a remote and superficial resemblance to the work of Sophocles, Shakespeare, Corneille, Racine—those dramatists of the past whose names are scattered throughout his reflections on the drama. It would be trivial to complain that these verse plays of Yeats (as well as of his principal imitators, Sturge Moore and Gordon Bottomley[45]) are what they are and not something else. If, as is certainly the case, some of these compositions attain artistic fulfillment in their own way, they have fully justified their existence and the experiments which produced them. Confusion arises, however, from identifying them either directly or by implication with older tragic forms, considering them similar in kind, or hoping that by an extension of their scope such plays will fill a role analogous to that of the established classics of tragedy. What they have accomplished has been achieved at the expense of something else. They are a new thing, and we can be grateful for a new kind of beauty; but these experiments will not show the way to a restoration of poetic tragedy to the modern world, and Yeats's own critical writings suggest that they are the result of a compromise born of frustration of his hopes and the realization that the conditions which surrounded him were inimical to the desired end.

IV

The most original and energetic of the recent poets who have turned to the drama—T. S. Eliot, W. H. Auden, Stephen Spender, Louis MacNeice—have not taken the path followed by Yeats. They have, on the contrary, worked with more familiar conventions through various adaptations of devices and methods already in use in modern drama and in analogous forms of popular entertainment. Hardly less than Yeats, however, they have felt constrained to search critically the problems of a modern poetic drama; and to understand the direction which they have taken in their dramatic experiments it is necessary to consider what difficulties they have believed confronted them. Though the basic questions are not essentially different from those considered by Yeats, they are at the same time viewed in a somewhat different way. For the most part, the discussions center in two related problems which have been frequently considered by critics of contemporary poetry generally but which have a peculiar bearing on the role of the modern poet as dramatist: one arises from the problems which confront the modern world, the other from the nature of the modern poetic idiom.

The absorption of contemporary writers in the intellectual and social chaos of modern life has become one of the commonplaces of criticism. If it could be said of the Romantic poets, as Arnold suggested, that they did not know enough, it might be said of these modern poets that they know too much. They seem bowed down by the accumulation of knowledge in the various branches of learning, by the none-too-comforting panorama of history, by the "destructive element" in contemporary thinking, and by the necessity to struggle against their disillusionment in the face of the present disorder. Expressions of concern and uneasiness are everywhere. "What do you think about England, this country of ours where nobody is well," asks Auden in the opening paragraphs of *The Orators*. And C. Day Lewis writes in *A Hope for Poetry*, "The Great War [1914-1918] tore away our youth from its roots." What is particularly important, however, is the realization of these writers that the modern temper affects the poet not only as an intellectual and social being but as an artist. This is a principal theme of *The Destructive Element* by Stephen Spender, who gives Henry James a central place in his study because of what he regards as James's "conviction that European society—and particularly English society—was decadent, combined with his own despair of fulfilling any creative or critical function in civilization as a whole." [46]

Preoccupation with a state of chronic philosophical uncertainty is in many ways a difficult condition for the artist, but it is particularly so for the dramatist. Thought is not the artistic end of tragedy—it is not, that is, the object of imitation in a work ordered by an action. In any serious play, however, the characters are represented in situations which raise ethical issues, they make decisions which involve a consideration of the moral problems which confront them, and their actions are referred to certain premises about conduct which are relevant to the circumstances which surround them. The ideas in a poetic tragedy cannot be precisely reduced to a system, certainly they cannot be summed up in a nugget of wisdom like the moral of a fable, not only because the persons of the play are always speaking "in character," but because, being an imaginative work of art, poetic tragedy is not amenable to a literal and systematic analysis as an intellectual work. The world of a play is defined, however, to some extent by the concepts which govern the actions of the characters and to which judgment of them is referred, and in this sense the "thought" may be seen as constituting an element of probability. For this reason the serious dramatist needs some convictions; he must feel under the compulsion to say something which he believes to be important about human experience, and he must apprehend certain qualities or values about human life, around which he can order his observations and impressions. Complete uncertainty would therefore undo him: he would not know what to do about his characters, unless he escaped into the mathematical tidiness of a pure detective plot or the excitement of a hare-and-hounds story. In that case, he would hardly need such elaborate and searching means as those offered by poetic drama. To this extent, the dramatist's philosophical equipment affects his capacity to write poetically at all.

The kinds of ideas with which he is concerned affects him in a somewhat different way. In classical and Shakespearean tragedy, though the ideas which appear to be implicit in the play are rooted in the thought of the times, the issues which are raised are referred to large and general premises. The very conditions of poetic tragedy make this necessary. If a play hinges, let us say, on whether a character can accept a challenge to a duel from one slightly inferior to himself, or on whether one dare divorce his wife and marry a dancer and thus risk offending his employer who is a deacon in the church, it would be impossible to avoid establishing the social circumstances within which such choices are momentous and decisive, and hence radically affecting the conditions which make the use of verse possible. And if the dramatist wishes to deal with the kinds of issues which require him to instruct, reform, or convert his audience, his methods will have to be primarily rhetorical. Poetic tragedy appears to require that the principles to which the actions of the characters are referred be the most general, and call for no forensic justification. In his essay, "The Possibility of a Poetic Drama," Eliot reflects on the advantage which the Elizabethan dramatist enjoyed in being able, thanks to the " 'temper of the age,' " to take for granted certain habits of mind and ways of regarding recurrent situations in the plays, so that it was necessary for the poet to do "only so much as would make a play his, only what was really essential to make it different from anyone else's." "When there is this economy of effort," he continues, "it is possible to have several, even many, good poets at once. The great ages did not perhaps *produce* much more talent than ours; but less talent was wasted." Under the proper conditions, moreover, the intellectual bias from which a dramatist writes can become the basis for a schematism with reference to which analogies can be drawn, individual words intensified, and oppositions in the imagery referred to and resolved.

A condition of uncertainty and confusion concerning fundamental issues can, accordingly, have the effect of imposing limitations on the direction which a writer's efforts may take. Spender sees the modern writer facing precisely this difficulty:

I have chosen the writers in this book, because they are political-moral artists who are in the dilemma of Hamlet: they find their lives fixed in a world in which there are no external symbols for their inner sense of values. There is no power, and no glory. They are, therefore, forced either to satirize the world by showing it up as it really is . . . . or they are obliged to try and reconcile the world with themselves, by adopting a hopeful evangelizing tone, or they are obliged to invent a set of symbols of their own, and in the eyes of the world, like Hamlet, to feign madness; or they may retreat into the realms of pure art.[47]

In the face of what seems to him chaos, the poet can presumably unpack his heart with words or put an antic disposition on. But whereas in such works as *Ulysses* or *The Waste Land* there is justification and reason for the complexities of expression required by the attitudes described by Spender, there is much less in dramatic composition, which by its nature generally presupposes a stage and an audience, and which is objective in the sense that it represents particular characters feeling, thinking, making choices, and meeting defeat or triumph or both. A dramatist who accepts the view of the world as disorderly and lacking in values can work out the dramatic treatment of his materials in a number of ways: he can probe the social, economic, and ethical problems of the disorganized world which he sees, or satirize its follies, or explore its neuroses, or, having decided on a cure for its ills, become a preacher or propagandist. In none of these modes can the poet's way with langauge be put to its fullest use, if it is indeed required at all, and, more specifically for the modern poets in question, in none of them will the devices of expression which they have worked out for the statement of their private doubts and moods be suitable except in a very limited way.

It would be difficult, if not impossible, however, for the poets to reject utterly the way they have learned to write. There is a close relationship between their peculiar response to the world in which they live and the most original and vigorous characteristics of their style, which they quite properly regard as the outcome of their effort to express imaginatively and honestly the moods and sentiments which affect them most deeply. Abandonment of these hard-won poetic idioms might result in sterility; it could lead to poetic archaisms or mannered artifices of expression, and it might falsify the attitude and temper of the poet in relation to his experiences. Yet for the writing of drama, the style of modern poetry as represented by the poets being considered constitutes something of a handicap; for, one effect—and a notorious effect—of the principal characteristic innovations in modern English poetry is that it has rendered this poetry "difficult" and obscure.

The difficulties of modern poetry are not quite the same as those which confront the sentimental, indifferent, or untrained reader in any concentrated, learned, or complex poem, such as, for instance, *Lycidas* or *Air and Angels*. The obscurity of modern poetry results from its treatment of language and its methods of structure and development. The modern poet is often highly elliptical in his phrasing, he indulges in grammatical license, and he often abandons logical transitions for a system of symbolical development or psychological association not always readily perceptible. The difficulty becomes most acute when the system of relations which obtains is not announced or implicitly revealed in the poem but depends on the possession of a body of knowledge or of private experiences and associations peculiar to the poet, the knowledge of which is nevertheless necessary to explain the meaning of the symbols and images and provides the basis for a multiple scale of significances for them. *The Waste Land* is the most famous single example of this kind of obscurity, but it may be encountered almost anywhere. Eliot's *East Coker*, a more mature and more simply developed poem, illustrates difficulties of the same order. The title is a clue to the poem, yet there is nothing to indicate that it derives its significance from the fact that East Coker is the birthplace of Thomas Elyot, author of *The Governour*, and that from East Coker, Andrew Eliot, to whom the Eliot family traces its origin in America, emigrated to the new continent in the seventeenth century. Other things need to be known; for instance, that the sixteenth-century lines quoted in the early portions of the poem are from *The Governour*. It also helps to know that the opening line, "In my beginning is my end," was a motto woven in an arras which hung in the English residence of Mary Queen of Scots, for this not only gives added poignancy to the line "And to shake the tattered arras woven with a silent motto," but also brings the line immediately into the context of shifting references between the Renaissance and modern times which is one of the principal devices of the poem. [48] Such a poem as Donne's "Good Friday" also has its problems, but they are not of this order precisely: one must know the Ptolemaic system of astronomy and the story of the crucifixion and its significance in Christian theology, but the title would puzzle no one, and the first line, "Let man's soul be a sphere," establishes explicitly the primary scheme of the figurative development. The poem thus asserts and keeps clearly defined the schemes of reference and their transmutations. Any reasonably well read person is thoroughly equipped to find his way through "Good Friday," and this generalization would hold even more true for Donne's own day, but even specialists in Renaissance literature might miss the associations which carry the imaginative exploration of Eliot's theme in *East Coker*. The younger poets—who make a point of their differences from Eliot—nevertheless have many of the same qualities. MacNeice's explanation of the difficulties in his "Perseus" and "Hidden Ice" illustrates the kinds of mysteries which the reader is called upon to fathom in the characteristic poems of this group. If they do not, as MacNeice says, "write obscurely for the Symbolist reason that obscurity is delightful in itself," yet their desire for concentration, their use of dream-state materials, the multiple relations in which they see any given image, all, nevertheless, frequently render their work difficult.

It appears, then, that certain of the characteristic moods and the methods of expression which have been responsible for some of the magnificent effects of modern poetry will either have to be abandoned or modified before modern verse drama can become an established and vital form. The kind of drama which the modern poets apparently would like to create, a drama comparable in character and magnitude, though not precisely in kind, with the great tragedies of the past, would demand these concessions. There are indications, however, that in some essential respects present conditions are not wholly inimical to serious drama in verse on the part of the moderns.

On the intellectual side there has been evidence of an inclination to find a way out of uncertainty and despair, even though the effort to do so sometimes gives the impression of being too deliberate. Eliot's adoption of Anglo-Catholicism is a case in point. His dramatic compositions nearly all spring from his religious interests. *The Rock* was written to promote a church building-fund; *Murder in the Cathedral* represents the struggle of a man to preserve the integrity of his religious convictions and involves the problem of martyrdom; *The Family Reunion* deals with the expiation for crime. Whatever one's opinion of the effect of Eliot's religion on his art may be, it is questionable whether he could have written plays at all without his religious convictions about man's earthly struggle. The younger poets seem also determined to leave the waste land. For the most part they showed an early inclination toward communism. What apparently inspired them in the new social experiment is the possibility which they perceived in it of making an art of political life, of controlling social forces toward a beneficent and just end. This has given them as human beings a sense of direction and of active participation in the modern scene. As artists, however, they have realized the danger which they run in their enthusiasm for what is still a revolutionary program for political action, and they have been careful to explain that they have no inclination to subordinate their poetry to outright propaganda. On this point they have their answer both to the bourgeois reader who mistrusts their sympathies and the communist who resents their concern with themselves as artists. C. Day Lewis' reply to the former is characteristic:

Yet the bourgeois critic must remember that there is no reason why poetry should not also be propaganda; the effect of invocation, of poetry, and of propaganda is to create a state of mind; and it is not enough to say that poetry must do unconsciously what propaganda does consciously, for that would be to dismiss all didactic poetry from that of the Bible downwards. All one can say is that propaganda verse is to be condemned when the didactic is achieved at the expense of the poetic: poetry in fact, whatever else it may or may not be, must be poetry—a sound, if obvious, conclusion.[50]

To the communist they point out that, as Spender puts it, "The writer is primarily interested in man, and not in systems, not even in a good economic system."[51] Whatever the merit of this argument, it clearly reveals an honest determination in these writers not to be argued out of their integrity as artists. At the same time, their political sympathies give them a perspective from which they can see without bewilderment or dismay or aloofness the primary and universal experiences which man must suffer and endure. In certain expressions of their attitude, moreover, the possibility for a serious drama is implied: "So when, as often, their poems are gloomy," writes MacNeice as spokesman for the group, "the gloom is tragic rather than defeatist. Tragedy implies a hero, and in the works of these poets heroic values are once more being admitted."[52]

In view of the fact that the peculiarities of expression in modern poetry are in many ways a function of its moods and attitudes, it is not surprising that changes in attitude referred to above should be viewed as implying modifications in style. MacNeice states this relation between the two explicitly: "On the whole, modern poetry is becoming more lucid, and that because its subject is less esoteric."[53] "The primary characteristic of these poets," he writes of the younger group, "is that they are interested in a subject outside themselves—or at any rate in a subject which is not merely a subject for their poetry. This being so, it surprises many people that their manner should often appear esoteric—difficult syntax, difficult imagery, obscure allusions. The reasons for this are two—firstly, that, while reacting in the spirit from their predecessors—Eliot, Pound, the French Symbolists, Rilke—they have been much influenced by them in the letter (this is the manner in which they learned to write); secondly, that, being poets, and not propagandists or journalists, they approach their subject, though an outside subject, through themselves. They will get their poetry more in order when they have got themselves in order, which in its turn may depend on a re-ordering of their society; they must not, however, wait for this last, for their relation with it is circular and they themselves, by writing, may in a tiny measure contribute to it."[54]

It does not follow, however, that the qualities which give distinction to modern poetry are wholly jeopardized by a shift toward lucidity. Though the obscurity of modern verse is its most conspicuous and notorious characteristic, it is not an inseparable feature of it except under certain conditions. Such a poem as MacNeice's *Autumn Journal*, for instance, though wholly in the modern idiom, achieves clarity without loss of effectiveness and power. It is not often enough noticed that the revolution in twentieth-century poetry was inspired in part by the desire to restore energy and concentration to language. Many of the poets of this era have felt that this quality was lost even in the best Victorian poetry, and looked on the Georgian poets as a final fading out of the new force brought to poetry by the Romantics. The various influences from which they drew, Continental as well as English, older literatures as well as new, were not cultivated merely out of a desire for novelty, and in the end the experiments have had the effect of bringing freshness, toughness, and brilliance to diction. The career of Yeats, in the change from the dreamy lushness of his earliest poetry to the brilliance and sharpness and greater objectivity of his later writings, illustrates in the prolonged activity of but one man something of the drift of poetry generally in the present century. Though obscurity is often the result of a desire for concentration in these poets, it is not necessarily an adjunct of all the characteristic methods which they have developed. And it is significant that they should recently have come to express admiration for poets who are preeminently famous for their lucidity and perspicuity. Spender names among the poets whose style is most suitable to our times not only the late Elizabethans but Pope and Dryden.[55] And MacNeice's admiration for Dryden calls attention precisely to virtues in his style which he believes modern poetry wishes in its own way to attain:

Our diction should be masculine but not exhibitionist. After the feminine writing of most of the nineteenth century (with the exception of the lighter Byron, parts of Wordsworth and Browning) and after the neuter writing of the Georgians we are working back towards the normal virile efficiency of Dryden or Chaucer. It is significant that Eliot, for all his flux, his 'free associations,' his dream-jumps, his generally passive attitude, should so much admire the writing of Dryden. As it was significant that Hopkins, with his tortured soul and tortured language, should have expressed the same admiration, even saying, 'my style tends always more towards Dryden. What is there in Dryden? Much, but above all this: he is the most masculine of our poets; his style and his rhythms lay the strongest stress of all our literature on the naked thew and sinew of the English language . . . .'[56]

If such expressions of intention are taken at their face value, then, setting aside the question of native talent and ability for writing plays, it may be concluded that modern poets have gone a considerable way toward meeting the conditions of a new verse drama, which will reflect the circumstances of the present day and at the same time make use of the most powerful characteristic features of modern verse. Concerning the possibility of this consummation, however, certain recent critics have raised serious doubts because of a feeling of skepticism toward the verse medium which these poets wish to use. This is different in its nature from the objection, common since the later years of the nineteenth century, that dramatic verse has been exhausted; it is a skepticism of a more fundamental sort grounded on the radical assumption that verse itself has become "exhausted." The absorption of our age in science, the complex intellectual conditions of the present day, have produced, it is maintained, a general condition within which poetry cannot really flourish. It is noted as one indication of this condition that poetry is being addressed to an ever more restricted audience, the poets often writing within the context of a very private world, and that the genius which once went into poetry now expends itself in such remarkable prose constructions as the novels of Proust and of James Joyce. "Prose is showing itself, it seems to me," writes Edmund Wilson, who has given a vigorous presentation of this view, "quite equal to that work of the imagination and the intellect—that recreation for man of his hard and doubtful life in this world in man's own terms of harmony and reason—which caused men to call Homer 'divine.' "[57] Verse, Wilson points out, was at one time used for many functions and for many subjects now reserved for prose—storytelling, philosophy, agriculture, even medicine—and the ever decreasing range of functions for verse does not necessarily indicate a more sophisticated understanding of verse but a shrinking of its uses.

To illustrate how the modern prose novel, which he admires as the characteristic literary art of our day, has usurped the function of the poet, Wilson presents in *Triple Thinkers* a comparison of passages from Virgil and Flaubert. The passages from Flaubert are all from the author's comment, none from the dialogue, and this is to be expected, for it is the peculiar advantage of the novelist that he is at liberty to introduce at will suggestions of mood or sentiment supplementary to the talk of his characters or the direct exposition of the action. The dramatist cannot do this, and to approximate the same effect he must depend on various devices and expedients—some of which have been already discussed in this chapter—which are for the most part limited or inflexible. The only device which has so far shown itself capable of endowing drama with depth and magnitude and infusing into the limited compass of a play the kind of richness which Wilson regards as the property of the modern novel is that employed by such masters of tragedy as Sophocles and Shakespeare—that is, writing dialogue as a poet. If poetry is on the decline, therefore, poetic drama must be thought of as particularly out of the question. Wilson considers at some length the decline of verse; verse drama he dismisses in a rhetorical question:

Nor does it follow that, because we are coming to use poetry for fewer and fewer literary purposes, our critical taste is becoming more and more refined, so that we are beginning to perceive for the first time the true, pure and exalted function of poetry: that is, simply, as Valéry says, to produce a 'state'—as Eliot says, to afford a 'superior amusement.' It is much more likely that for some reason or other, verse as a technique of literary expression is being abandoned by humanity altogether—perhaps because it is a more primitive, and hence a more barbarous technique than prose. Is it possible to believe, for example, that Eliot's hope of having verse reinstated on the stage—even verse of the new kind which he proposes—is likely ever to be realized?[58]

The implications of the view that poetry is gradually receding

into oblivion are too significant and the arguments on which it is
based too plausible to permit considering the theory as trivial. Its
existence in modern criticism, whatever its merits, is by itself a
comment on the status of poetry. Yet there is justification for regarding it with something of the scientific detachment and absence
of alarm which is maintained toward theories that the sun is gradually cooling or that it is shrinking and will one day explode. For
good poetry continues to be written; what is more to the point, our
age has witnessed one of the major revolutions in the art and something of a renascence, and some of this poetry has not only commanded high critical admiration but has left a deep mark generally
on the literature of our times. Under the circumstances, it is not surprising that the poets do not appear to consider this critical pessimism concerning poetry as conclusive. Spender, for example, is not
convinced that the modern novel has supplanted poetry or is an
adequate substitute for it: ". . . the poetic novel has been evolved
as an endeavor on the part of the novelists to perform a task that
poets either are not able to perform or have neglected. D. H.
Lawrence was a writer who essentially was a poet and who might
have written great poetry from the materials in his novels. Virginia
Woolf's novel 'The Waves' is in great part scarcely distinguishable
from free verse. 'Ulysses' is a gigantic example of an abortive epic.
In all these works we feel the raw materials of poetry; and the
solution—the poetic novel—is never |satisfactory; there is often
energy and great inspiration, but the final concentration of poetry
is absent." [59] The poets are not unaware of what the critics have
said about their work or of the difficulties which under present
circumstances they must overcome; nevertheless, they manifest an
attitude toward the possibilities of poetry which is often the antithesis of defeatist. MacNeice, for example, writes: "As light verse
offers the poet needed change from the intensity of the lyric, so
drama offers him needed change from the single voice. In the lyric
the poet speaks with one voice only. In the drama he can do justice
to the many different people within him." "Poets . . . . should be
encouraged to write dramatic verse as they should be encouraged to
write narrative verse or occasional verse. It is particularly likely
that they may find a good medium in radio plays. Also verse may
be more suitable than prose for a commentary on certain types of
films . . . ." [60] Such an expression of confidence and of a desire to

extend the range of poetry and reach a wider audience does not constitute a refutation of the arguments on which the theory of the decay of poetry is based. It is further evidence, however, that poets have been showing a determination to alter precisely those circumstances which are a starting point for the skepticism concerning the further general usefulness and the potential vigor of poetry.

In the light of the issues raised by the development of poetry in the present age, it becomes understandable why the drama should appeal to the modern poet as a form which makes possible "the final concentration of poetry" and at the same time holds out a promise for the liberation of poetry from its present esoteric position. Something more than the perennial fascination which the play has exercised on writers since the sixteenth century, more than the search for novelty, of which, as Johnson phrased it, the common satiety of life sends us all in quest, prompts the modern poet to seek an outlet in drama. By its very nature, the form discourages indulgence in private despair or bewilderment and encourages a forceful and clearly-resolved artistic incorporation of the poet's insights and convictions. And while it imposes on him a discipline which his facility and experimentation with language requires, it imposes on him as well a responsibility for communication not encouraged by modern lyrical traditions, and thus holds out the promise that by this means the poet may resume a more active role in society. The general reputation of Eliot as one of the most recondite of contemporary poets renders his thinking on these matters of particular interest:

To return to the question of obscurity: when all exceptions have been made, and after admitting the possible existence of minor "difficult" poets whose public must always be small, I believe that the poet naturally prefers to write for as large and miscellaneous an audience as possible, and that it is the half-educated, and ill-educated, rather than the uneducated, who stand in his way: I myself should like an audience which could neither read nor write. The most useful poetry, socially, would be one which could cut across all the present stratifications of public taste—stratifications which are perhaps a sign of social disintegration. The ideal medium for poetry, to my mind, and the most direct means of social "usefulness" for poetry, is the theatre.[61]

Such views, consciously arrived at or felt unawares, have had an influence in turning certain poets toward the drama as one hope for modern poetry.

V

Eliot's first excursion into the drama was *Sweeney Agonistes*: *Fragments of an Aristophanic Melodrama* (1932), consisting of two parts, "Fragment of a Prologue" and "Fragment of an Agon," the latter of which had appeared several years before in *The Criterion* under the title, "Wanna Go Home, Baby?" It is an adaptation of the music-hall medium, brilliant and ingenious, barren of many of the characteristic marks of Eliot's best writing, and depending for its effect largely on the continuous contrast between the medium and the projection within which the play is drawn. It is an indication of the authority of Eliot in modern letters, and perhaps also a mark of our passion for literary novelties, that he could present for serious consideration a dramatic fragment with no apparent formal scheme, or at most one remotely hinted at, and receive for this incomplete portion of a laboratory experiment the kind of praise and attention which should greet a satisfactory completed effort. Probably the best commentary on this attempt to give artistic importance to the music-hall stage is the fact that it is, after all, a fragment. *The Rock* (1934) is referred to by Eliot as a revue; the title page describes it as a pageant. It was written expressly to promote the "Forty-Five Churches Fund," and hence is didactic in aim. It is based on a scenario, not by Eliot, which represents the efforts of workmen to complete a church against discouragement and opposition, with flash-backs into church history. Except for a few chants and songs by workmen, the scenes are in prose, interspersed with extended choruses done in verse. These are often impressive, but the looseness of the pageant form and the discrete separation of the choruses from the episodes cannot be regarded as more than a compromise answer to the way in which poetry must function in modern drama, since the effectiveness of the play proper does not depend on verse at all. With this work, Eliot abandoned his experiments with the popular music-hall and revue idiom. [62]

The most successful theatrically of Eliot's plays is *Murder in the Cathedral* (1935), which was given favorable reception in England and in this country. It deals with the martyrdom of Archbishop Thomas Becket, beginning with his arrival from France on December 2, 1170, and ending in his murder on December 29. The action is reduced to the utmost simplicity. The first part contains opening speeches by the chorus, the three Priests, and the Herald, and is centered in the scene with Becket and the four Tempters, over each of whom Becket triumphs. The Interlude which follows is in prose and is entirely given over to Becket's Christmas sermon, his last, which develops the theme of martyrdom. The second and final part contains, in addition to the choruses, a scene with the four Knights in which Becket defends himself against their accusations, the scene in the cathedral in which Becket is murdered, the speeches of justification by the Knights, and the final speeches of the Priests and the chorus.

There is little suggestion of such intrigue as the plotting of a play usually depends on. The subordinate characters receive no individual differentiation and are rather types or symbols—the Priests, the Tempters, the Knights, the Herald. The play possesses none of the customary traces of the historical play, it is in no sense a costume piece, and even the effect of remoteness in time is largely eliminated by the language. One effect of this process of simplification and abstraction is that Becket is made to stand out in relief, and though by the same process some of the artistic circumstances which enable a dramatist to produce an imposing character like Lear or Oedipus are also missing, Becket nevertheless is impressive as a type of figure pushed by circumstances to the lonely position of having to resolve a grave conflict within himself and ultimately with reference to principles which transcend prudence, politics, and social utility. The central action of the play lies within Becket himself, and the culminating point of the play is Becket's decision to accept martyrdom, or rather his final understanding of the proper reasons by which his decision might be justified, and its true meaning. This is the point around which the play is organized, and the murder, though the scene is effectively contrived, is not the final catastrophe concluding a closely related series of episodes in an intrigue, but the efficient cause of Becket's martyrdom. The function of the episodes is not so much to contribute to a catastrophe as to explore the issue of martyrdom. In consequence, Becket ceases to dominate the play as a character after the sermon. Becket's return to England and its possible consequences are viewed from several possible points of view: that of the women of Canterbury, who constitute the chorus, of the three Priests, of the Knights, of the Tempters, and of Becket, and each scene, each chorus, helps to establish a distinction.

This scheme of organization and emphasis determines largely the handling of the diction. Leaving aside for the moment certain portions of the choruses, the language is lucid and direct, but there is a great variety of rhythms and styles, ranging all the way from reminiscences of medieval drama to the clichés and sophistries of a political address. Whatever one's final judgment of these changes in style might be, there is method to them. The particular style in which any given speech is written is determined not solely by considerations of the character of the speaker, since character is often reduced almost to allegorical limits, nor by any principle of consistency or verisimilitude, but rather by a principle of appropriateness to the kinds of sentiments which the speech contains. The simple women of Canterbury, though inured to the hardships of nature and to the harsh contingencies of their poor lives, express a dread of the horrible and extraordinary evil which they fear will come on them; but the language of the choruses has a complexity and sophistication which bear no relation to the speakers. The Priests express their sense of joy at the return of a needed spiritual guide and fear for the strength of the church in his possible loss: their speeches have a simple dignity, even a trace of pedantry—

> I see nothing quite conclusive in the art of temporal government,
> But violence, duplicity and frequent malversation

—and at times a trace of Biblical flavor—"Yet our lord is returned. Our lord has come back to his own again."

The originality of Eliot's treatment of the language appears most sharply in the speeches of the Tempters and of the Knights. Each of the Tempters is a spokesman for some worldly solution of Becket's problem—return to the gaiety and pleasure of his early career, return to temporal power and the administration of good rule, alliance with the barons against the power of the king, and effective use of his ecclesiastical power to gain the permanent glory of martyrdom. These Tempters are direct descendants of the vices of the medieval moralities—promoters for an evil decision on the part of the chief character. Hence echoes from medieval verse can be heard in their tricks of speech—occasional jingling rhymes, clipped syntax, and alliteration:

> Mirth merrymaking, melting strength in sweetness,
> Fiddling to feebleness, doomed to disdain . . .

King is in France, squabbling in Anjou;
Round him waiting hungry sons.

The Fourth Tempter begins his discourse in much the same style.
He is the Tempter whom Becket did not expect. He expresses Becket's own hardly conscious desire for martyrdom and is therefore
the most dangerous, for, since he urges uncompromising spiritual
power and ultimate martyrdom as the greatest triumph over his
enemies, his, too, is a worldly solution and therefore unworthy.
His speeches at first have the same general quality as those of the
others, but as he approaches the crux of his argument the rhythms
and diction of his speech take on the longer cadences and the more
dignified diction of Becket's own utterances—

And between sleep and waking, early in the morning,
When the bird cries, have thought of further scorning.
That nothing lasts, but the wheel turns,
The nest is rifled, and the bird mourns.

And in his final speech he duplicates Becket's own words almost
exactly:

You know and do not know, what it is to act or suffer.
You know and do not know, that acting is suffering,
And suffering action. Neither does the actor suffer
Nor the patient act. But both are fixed
In an eternal action, an eternal patience
To which all must consent that it may be willed
And which all must suffer that they may will it,
That the pattern may subsist, that the wheel may turn and still
Be forever still.

By means of the style, through the changes in the poetical idiom
of the Fourth Tempter's speech from an original identity with that
of the other Tempters to a final identity with that of Becket, the
worldly aspect of Becket's yet-unexpressed desire for martyrdom is
revealed. Thus the latent difficulties of Becket's problem are suggested, and the ground prepared for the final resolution of the issues
in Becket's speech which closes the first scene, and in the sermon
which follows.

A similar ingenuity is shown in the speeches of the Knights. In
their first talk with Becket their speeches have the hard resolute accents suggestive of men of action, a quality intensified by the use of
couplet rhyme:

Saving your order! let your order save you—

As I do not think it is like to do.
Saving your ambition is what you mean,
Saving your pride, envy and spleen.

When they enter, slightly tipsy, to commit the murder within the
church, the desecration of their act is presumably implied in the
contrast between the background of the church ceremony and the
suggestion of ritualistic chant in the closing lines of the preceding
chorus, and the verses spoken by the Knights, which combine the
idiom of the more animated Protestant hymn and the negro
spiritual:

Are you washed in the blood of the Lamb?
Are you marked with the mark of the beast?
Come down Daniel to the lions' den,
Come down Daniel and join in the feast.

After the murder each of the Knights makes a speech to the audience
in justification of the act. Nothing else in the play has produced more
consistent comment; the prose speeches are generally regarded as
very clever, but often condemned as being in too violent a contrast
to the rest of the play. Yet they follow the principle which seems to
govern the other effects; i.e., of selecting the style with reference to
the quality of the sentiments and the impression they are to leave,
and without reference to any particular level of diction which may
be assumed as the norm for the play or for any particular character.
The Knights are crude men of action whose capacities are circumscribed by the conventional patterns of thought and behavior
and the common sophistries and hypocrisies which rule the lives of
unthinking, respectable people. They are in contrast with the
women of the chorus who, as simple people, have a deep perception
of the elemental and primitive forces which men must know and
endure, and with Becket, who understands his act in terms which
transcend the political, the useful, and the respectable. In contrast
to Becket's own justification of his act, Eliot has selected for the
Knights the language of the politician taking his constitutents into
his confidence after a questionable act, or the round-table speaker
defending things as they are:

I should like first to recur to a point that was very well put by our leader,
Reginald Fitz Urse: that you are Englishmen, and therefore your sym-
pathies are always with the under dog. It is the English spirit of fair play.
Now the worthy Archbishop, whose good qualities I very much admired,

has throughout been presented as the under dog. But is this really the case? . . .

No other medium available could so well have underscored the utilitarian, unoriginal, sophistical commonplaces which mirror the attitude of the Knights. The choice is consistent with the principle of using the style which will give the proper coloring to the ideas at any given moment in their relationship to the dialectical oppositions which form so large a part in the development of the play.

It might be assumed that the style which would best convey the mystery of martyrdom, the transcendant view of the problem which Becket adopts, would be some modification of the metaphysical style which the religious poets of the seventeenth century employed to advantage for similar themes. That there are but faint traces only of this style in Becket's speeches may be due to the way in which the problem is construed for him: against the conflicting and tangential attitudes which surround him, he is shown trying to purify his mind of improper motives and of presenting a just choice among false alternatives. Accordingly, his speeches at times show something of the puzzling paradoxes of the sharp logician, as in the speech beginning, "They know and do not know, what it is to act and suffer," and at times are phrased in a way reminiscent of the heroic couplet with its qualities of antithesis and paradox in the service of some dialectical exploration; for example,

> The last temptation is the greatest treason:
> To do the right deed for the wrong reason.

Or in a more modified form,

> The purple bullfinch in the lilac tree,
> The tiltyard skill, the strategy of chess,
> Love in the garden, singing to the instrument,
> Were all things equally desirable.

The sermon itself is couched in a style beautifully lucid and logical: yet the principal idea is a paradox—the mystery of martyrdom resembles the other mysteries of the church in that "we can rejoice and mourn at once for the same reason." In his concluding speeches Becket speaks with directness and force, as befits a man who has won through to a strong resolve and merely awaits the moment of consummation.

If this particular manner of handling the diction makes for great brilliance, it also limits somewhat the possibilities for sensuous

imagery or for effects of great concentration or for the extension of
the unique action to a wide sphere of emotional apprehension. It
is principally in the chorus that such functions are carried out, and
in this respect there is some similarity between the role of the chorus
in this play and in *The Rock*, where the choruses carry the poetic
freight almost exclusively, though the relations between chorus and
episode are much more intimately bound together in *Murder in the
Cathedral*. The chorus consists of the women of Canterbury, and their
attitude contributes in a way already noticed to the direct development of the play; but the choruses constitute nearly one-fourth in
bulk of the whole work, a disproportionate amount for a purpose
intended to be so limited. The women frequently call attention to
their simplicity, and many of the images derive from their life of
toil close to nature; yet the choruses are developed beyond these
limits and are not strictly "in character." In one instance, Chorus,
Priests, and Tempters combine in alternate lines in a chorus which
has for its theme the imminence of death.

The prominent characteristic features of the choruses are the
appearance of patterned repetitions and the recurrence of certain
themes. Some of the repeated lines take on the character of refrains; for instance,

> Seven years and the summer is over
> Seven years since the Archbishop left us.

> Living and partly living

> Kings rule and barons rule.

Some of the repetitions employ common images, notably that of the
wheel. The use of these same refrains or images by the Priests or
Becket as well as by the chorus helps to tie the sentiments of the
chorus with those of the more active participants in the play. There
are also certain themes which recur in the choruses: anticipation of
some awful doom too great for mortal strength, the annual return
of the seasons, the hard contingencies of the lives of the simple folk,
and the imminence of death are the principal ones. Usually one or
the other of these themes will predominate in any given chorus—
for instance, the combined chorus on death already referred to and
a remarkable chorus beginning "I have smelt them, the death-
bringers," in which the sense of impending evil is expressed in a
piling up of animal imagery and references to violence and cor-

ruption. Often the principal themes are intertwined, as in the following excerpt from the first chorus which, in its entirety, virtually announces all the leading motifs:

> Now I fear disturbance of the quiet seasons:
> Winter shall come bringing death from the sea,
> Ruinous spring shall beat at our doors,
> Root and shoot shall eat our eyes and our ears,
> Disastrous summer shall burn up the beds of our streams
> And the poor shall wait for another decaying October.

The wheel images undergo several transmutations, being at times related to the notion of cyclical seasonal change, the idea of change in recurrence, and the problem of man's will and the will of God. In the main, the diction in the choruses stresses suggestions of a dark or violent nature, not only in elaborate figures but in the insistence on such words as "bitter," "grey," "stifling," and the like. The final chorus brings together many of the major themes again, now related in a pervading spirit of submission to God's will and thanksgiving.

The chorus is a complex affair, not used in precisely the manner of its Greek originals. It establishes the deep undertones which are suggested by the central episodes; it develops a rich texture against which the other parts of the play are displayed. The devices by which the two are interrelated are ingenious and for the most part so successful that it does not become apparent at once that in reality the problem of diction is solved on two planes simultaneously. It is unlikely that as great a sense of harmony in the two kinds of treatment would have resulted had it not been that in different ways the chorus and the active participants stress not the action but the philosophical problem which it raises, and contribute to the dialectical exploration of the theme which determines largely the development of the play.

The Family Reunion (1939), the last so far of Eliot's plays, represents a turn in a new direction. The time is the present, the persons come from the English upper class, and the scene is laid in a country house in the north of England. This familiar combination of elements is given a wholly new character principally by two circumstances: the issue is the currently unusual one of a family "curse" and of evil and expiation, and verse is used throughout. As the play opens, Harry, Lord Monchensey, is expected home at

Wishwood for the first time in eight years. The occasion is the birthday of his mother, Amy, and the entire family is to be present.
Harry has not been home since his marriage, which was unpopular
with his family and unsatisfactory for him. A year before the play
opens, his wife had died by drowning on a trip across the Atlantic,
and the circumstances suggest accident or suicide. Harry arrives,
moody and uncertain, and fails to find the security and peace of
mind he hoped for at Wishwood. He tells his family that he pushed
his wife overboard, and the information is assumed by most of them
to be the fabrication of a deranged mind. He finds understanding
only in his Aunt Agatha and a distant cousin, Mary. He discovers
that his own father had at one time contemplated killing his own
wife, perhaps through an affection for Agatha, and this discovery,
and the clearing of his mind through conversations with Mary and
Agatha, leads him to the decision that he must leave. His departure
is a grave disappointment to his mother, who had pinned all her
hopes on his taking over Wishwood, and the play ends in her death.

This simple outline denudes the play of its subtleties, but it helps
to show how without them it possesses all the materials for a realistic play. And the characters also have the conventional features,
taken on the surface, of such a play—there is the sensitive young
man confronted with a grave problem, the strong-willed mother
who wishes to hold her son, the understanding older relative, the
sympathetic young woman, and the assortment of well-meaning
but stupid relatives and friends who cannot, or will not, see beyond
the teas, hunting, army experience, and terror of the wrong kind of
publicity which rule their lives. Only, the trouble which Harry
faces goes beyond the ethical or social considerations which usually
determine the problems in modern realistic drama, and the distinction which divides the characters is not simply greater or less
wisdom and capacity for sympathy, not the difference between the
intelligent and the commonplace, but between those who fear to
lose their happiness in facing reality, and those who consider facing
reality an obligation which brings terror with it but eventually
understanding. Harry makes the distinction early in the play:

                              You are all people
To whom nothing has happened, at most a continual impact
Of external events. You have gone through life in sleep,
Never woken to the nightmare. I tell you, life would be unendurable
If you were wide awake.

And this distinction is insisted on over and over throughout the play. The perceptive characters are thus concerned with the question of reality, of the family curse, of the problem of evil, retribution, and expiation. Their function in the play is to understand Harry and to help Harry understand.

To project all this beyond the limitations of realism, Eliot has imposed upon the play conventions and devices derived from various sources. He uses the type of soliloquy O'Neil introduced in *Strange Interlude*, which permits a character to speak out his thoughts without reference to the presence of others on the scene. This convention he uses only for the unperceptive characters. These also constitute the chorus, which is used to express collectively the common puzzlement and fears of this group. The difference between the two devices is brought out stylistically; the individual soliloquies are realistically phrased, the choruses are written with a concern only for the most vivid projection of the collective state of mind. For the perceptive characters, Eliot occasionally employs an extension of a device used by Tchekov, in which two characters indulge in mutual self-revelation, not through the kind of argumentative *éclaircissement* usual in Ibsen, but by a series of speeches which seem to have no conversational connection with one another. Eliot indicates this condition stylistically by a greater precision of rhythms and more numerous artifices of diction. From Greek drama he took over not only the chorus—which is not used here in a Greek way—but the Eumenides, suggested by the similarities between this play and the story of Orestes. Harry has been obsessed by the sense that "they" are pursuing him, but he sees them first in Wishwood, probably because in some remote way his own sense of guilt is related to his father's. To have used these Greek antiquities in a theatrical way as a symbol which tied this story to that of Orestes would have been one thing, though the device would then have been too literary in its inspiration and cast false lights over the particular attitude toward the problem of retribution which distinguishes this play from Greek treatments of the Orestes story. It might also have been possible to treat them as a figment of Harry's disordered mind (if it may be considered disordered), though such a use would seem precious by comparison with more familiar contemporary psychological symbols. But neither is wholly the case, because Agatha and Mary see the Eumenides independently as well as Harry on the two occasions when they appear in the play, and it later transpires that the chauffeur, Downing, has seen them at odd times himself. It may be that their seeing them is a mark of their understanding of Harry, but why the Eumenides should appear in this play at all is—judging from reviews—likely to remain one of the minor points for critics to puzzle over.

Set down in this fashion these devices sound forced, and in fact they are not welded into a harmonious scheme in the play. But only by the application of conventions of a rigid order and by insistence on them as such could the materials of a drawing-room play be rendered capable of poetic treatment, and only by such treatment could the psychic and religious features of the play acquire depth and dignity in such a context. These artifices help establish conditions which make a non-realistic diction possible, and the frequent brilliance of the verse nullifies to some extent the effect of disharmony in the contrivances.

The play opens with a speech by Amy which is rhythmical in a free way, with sufficient figurative suggestiveness and formality of construction and idiom to abolish expectation of verisimilitude:

Not yet! I will ring for you. It is still quite light.
I have nothing to do but watch the days draw out,
Now that I sit in the house from October to June.
And the swallow comes too soon and the spring will be over
And the cuckoo will be gone before I am out again.
O Sun, that was once so warm, O Light that was taken for granted
When I was young and strong, and sun and light unsought for
And the night unfeared and the day expected
And clocks could be trusted, tomorrow assured
And time would not stop in the dark!

This mood is dispelled, however, by the chattering of the sisters and brothers-in-law that follows, which, though written in verse, has a commonplaceness of phrasing and diction that renders their speeches quite indistinguishable from similar conversations in a typical drawing-room play. This sharp distinction suggests the scheme of separate levels of diction which is used throughout. Principally, the differentiations in the diction follow the separation of characters into the two groups already noted. The speeches of the characters who live in a sham reality and who cannot cope with the central problem of consciousness and evil and retribution are, though in verse, in effect the commonplace prose of commonplace people. This is true of their thoughts revealed in soliloquy as well as of their conversation. It is not the case, however, when they speak in the choruses, the function of which appears to be to provide insight into the quality of their minds by means of poetic language and thus to afford a comparison with the other characters on terms artistically equal. Reviewers have objected to this sudden shift from realistic conversational style to poetic use of words in the unperceptive characters, but, though it is not possible to deny the effect of disjunction thus produced, the change is usually preceded either by individual soliloquies by these characters or by a speech which is given frankly poetical treatment, so that it is a matter of passing through one artifice to an even more deliberate one.

Though the choruses introduce an additional principle of selection in the matter of diction, the broad one already described otherwise operates generally throughout, Thus the three characters who face reality and who probe beneath the surface appearances of Harry's problem regularly speak with a greater formality of rhythm and greater richness of diction than the others; and in the moments when Mary or Agatha reaches a high point of identity or understanding with Harry, the patterns become more precise, the language more oblique, and the device of dialogue breaks down and takes on something of the nature of responsive chant:

> The cold spring now is the time
> For the ache in the moving root
> The agony in the dark
> The slow flow throbbing the trunk
> The pain of the breaking bud.
> These are the ones that suffer least:
> The aconite under the snow
> And the snowdrop crying for a moment in the wood.

In two instances the shift from these sustained flights to the level which might be thought of as the norm for these characters is indicated by the phrase, "What have we been saying?" as though to call attention to the demarcation between the two styles. In the more formal style also are Agatha's speeches when she is at her most profound, and the reciprocal recitation between Mary and Agatha which ends the play. This final scene is given a ritualistic quality by the circumstance of having the two circle the birthday cake of the dead Amy as they speak, blowing out a few candles at each speech, the concluding lines being spoken in darkness. Perhaps the purpose of this business is to provide a ceremonial setting for the religious coloring of the final speech. It indicates further the prodigal variety of devices used in the play.

Like *Murder in the Cathedral*, this play reveals great ingenuity in the matter of diction and a multiplicity of styles; but the principle which determines the style to be employed is not the same, and though the effects in the earlier play are broader, the results are on the whole not so complex, depending as they do on a simpler and more consistent set of conventions. The merits of the solution of the problem of diction in *The Family Reunion* are difficult to estimate, however, for there are considerations which complicate the question of its success. The choruses are uniformly striking, conveying their impression by means of elaborated metaphors and similes, or of sustained series of concrete instances, which is one of Eliot's most characteristic devices:

And the past is about to happen, and the future was long since settled.
And the wings of the future darken the past, the beak and claws have
    desecrated
History. Shamed
The first cry in the bedroom, the noise in the nursery, mutilated
The family album, rendered ludicrous
The tenants' dinner, the family pic-nic on the moors. Have torn
The roof from the house, or perhaps it was never there.
And the bird sits on the broken chimney. I am afraid.

But the choruses are a relatively simple affair: in formally poetic terms they define the apprehensions and limitations of the commonplace and timid mind—no new task for Eliot. But for the characters who are at the focus of the problem of the play, the task was more difficult and seems less successfully accomplished. At what might be termed the first level of discourse for these characters, the projection of terror and of difficulty of understanding and communication are often effectively expressed, though the insistence on the latter is carried to the point of wearisome iteration. In speeches at the second level, the development is usually through the use of figurative symbols that bear obliquely on the problem, sometimes treated in a surrealistic manner:

> The eye is on this house
> The eye covers it
> There are three together
> May the three be separated

May the knot that was tied
Become unknotted
May the crossed bones
In the filled-up well
Be at last straightened
May the weasel and the otter
Be about their proper business
The eye of the day time
And the eye of the night time
Be diverted from this house
Till the knot is unknotted
The cross is uncrossed
And the crooked is made straight.

It is questionable whether the subtlety and difficulty of such passages, the abrupt transition to an order of symbolism that is quite remote from any of the concrete relations which obtain within the play, are quite what is demanded by drama. Supplementing this kind of treatment is a more intellectual phrasing of the abstruse issues by means of unexpected antitheses and cryptic paradoxes:

Accident is design
And design is accident
In a cloud of unknowing.
O God, man, the things that are going to happen
Have already happened.

There is a great deal of this, and the total result is that of labored profundity and smart sententiousness. The effect which these aphoristic utterances produce is analogous to the exhausting epigram-hunting on the part of certain characters in conventional drawing-room plays.

If Eliot's contrivances seem cumbersome and his treatment of language at times eccentric and strained, the problem he faced in *The Family Reunion* was formidable and allowed of no simple solution. The scene, characters, and setting, which suggest the contemporary realistic play, become amenable to poetic treatment only through a process of radical distortion and conversion by means of formalizing dramatic devices. And since, in addition, the philosophical and religious preoccupations of the play are unfamiliar in the modern context, only by a conspicuous insistence on these devices as conventions and artifices could the disparity be overcome between the nature of the materials superficially considered and the poetic means through which they are translated to an unfamiliar plane of meaning. [63] Under the circumstances, the need of adapting the language to these various devices and of making use of it to express the spiritual horror and theological subtleties of the play placed it under considerable strain, and a general impression of disharmony is the result. The diction sometimes fails to equal the profundities involved, or approaches success by passing beyond the limits of the dramatic framework.

VI

Of the younger poets, the most prolific in the drama has been W. H. Auden. His two earliest attempts, *Paid on Both Sides*, which is called a charade, and *The Dance of Death* are both slight and immature, though not without interesting flashes and plenty of evidence of real inventiveness. In particular, *The Dance of Death* shows a disposition to improvise devices from almost any source and to combine a variety of styles within a single work. In this respect it anticipates his next play, *The Dog beneath the Skin* (1935), which he wrote in collaboration with Christopher Isherwood, with whom he also wrote *The Ascent of F6* (1937) and *On the Frontier* (1938). These three plays are more ambitious in scope and show greater care in the craftsmanship—less inclination to throw things together in a slap-dash fashion—than the earlier works; but there is no essential difference between the earlier and later group in the approach to the problem nor in the lines of solution adopted. There is less, however, of the obscurity for which Auden is well known: *Paid on Both Sides* is frequently difficult as a result of shorthand syntax and unexpected transitions in the imagery not only in the "set" speeches but in the conversation; *The Dance of Death* has little difficulty in the style but is often puzzling with respect to the particular symbolism to be attached to a given episode or character—or even as to whether any symbolism is intended. The plays with Isherwood present fewer problems of interpretation on either score. They are also more fully developed as plays.

The Dog beneath the Skin is probably the most thoroughgoing attempt to adapt popular stage and motion-picture genres to the ends of the serious modern poet; one can detect traces from such diverse sources as Gilbert and Sullivan, Noel Coward, Cole Porter, and the Marx Brothers. But the general character of the work is determined rather by the later forms of German expressionistic drama, indebtedness to which Isherwood has freely acknowledged.[64] The play is concerned principally with the wanderings of Alan Norman in search of the lost Sir Frances Crewe, the reward of success to be marriage with the sister, Iris Crewe. This is in no sense a plot, but rather a device to bring together scenes from all over Europe and from the typical English village of Pressan Ambo, where the play begins and ends. The result is a critical and satirical survey of the delusions, sins, follies, and psychoses of post-war Europe. This design permits the widest possible variety in styles. Whether verse or prose is to be used, and if verse what sort of verse, is determined by the satirical or critical needs of the moment and the degree of fantasy with which any given episode is conceived; and, since the scheme of the play sets no limits to the kind of refraction which might be employed, there is a corresponding latitude in the matter of style and diction. Accordingly there is everything from doggerel to the stately measures of the choruses. The tendency of the modern poet to range freely among all possibilities, to subject old styles to new purposes, so that a jazz song takes on serious overtones and a Caroline lyric emerges with an unexpected ironic edge, is here illustrated to the full. What gives direction to all this variety is the choruses, which appear almost invariably before each scene. Written for the most part in a uniform style and with uniform seriousness and dignity of tone, the choruses establish the themes which the episodes treat with a diversity of devices. A typical chorus is that which introduces the "Paradise Park" episode:

Happy the hare at morning, for she cannot read
The Hunter's waking thoughts. Lucky the leaf
Unable to predict the fall. Lucky indeed
The rampant suffering suffocating jelly
Burgeoning in pools, lapping the grits of the desert,
The elementary sensual cures,
The hibernations and the growth of hair assuage:
Or best of all the mineral stars disintegrating quietly into light.
But what shall men do, who can whistle tunes by heart,
Know to the bar when death shall cut him short, like the cry of
    the shearwater?
We will show you what he has done.
How comely are his palaces of refuge and the tabernacles of his peace,
The new books upon the morning table, the lawns and the
    afternoon terraces!

Here are the playing-fields where he may forget his ignorance
To operate within a gentleman's agreement: twenty-two sins have here
    a certain licence.
Here are the thickets where accosted lovers combatant
May warm each other with their wicked hands,
Here are the avenues for incantation and workshops for the
    cunning engravers.
The galleries are full of music, the pianist is storming the keys, the great
    cellist is crucified over his instrument,
That none may hear the ejaculations of the sentinels
Nor the sigh of the most numerous and the most poor; the thud of
    their falling bodies
Who with their lives have banished hence the serpent and the
    faceless insect.

The choruses are often impressive, and there are flashes of incisive
brilliance in the episodes; and it is not impugning these merits to
insist that on these terms the problem of verse drama can be readily
solved—provided one's ingenuity in devising novel devices of presentation holds out, and provided one's satirical and critical vein is
all that demands satisfaction through dramatic creation.

    The last two plays represent a departure from these methods.
The Ascent of F6 is developed around a plot. Michael Ransom, a
person of great depth of mind and capacity for action, but infected
with philosophical melancholy, is asked to lead an expedition to
climb a mountain known as F6, a project which he had always
wanted to undertake. He at first refuses, because the purpose of the
expedition is political, but an appeal from his mother wins him
over. Each of Ransom's party but one dies on the ascent under
various circumstances, and Ransom is the only one to reach the top,
at the cost of his own life. The expedition takes on symbolical importance in relation to Ransom's search for the answer to his
philosophical questionings. This aspect of the play is emphasized
in the scene during which he at first refuses to lead the expedition
and then accepts, in the episode at the mountain monastery, where
the philosophic issues are made explicit in the conversation with
the Abbot but are endowed with an air of mystery through the use
of a magic crystal possessed by the monks, and in the final scene of
Ransom's death, in which the issues are translated into a dream-
state symbolism. On the periphery of this central focus, the attitude
of a number of other persons toward this expedition is developed.
For the members of the expedition, the ascent is a catalyst which

brings out their inner natures. The event is also seen in its relation to the dirty and foolish game of international politics and the hypocritical sentiments with which unscrupulous people endow it, and shows up the meaner persons who are indirectly measured against Ransom's largeness. The radio broadcast is ingeniously used in this connection. The ascent is also seen reflected against the cramped lives of the lower middle-classes by means of a series of conversations between Mr. and Mrs. A. before each scene.

The play is written principally in prose, the only consistent exception being the conversations of Mr. and Mrs. A, which are for the most part in a loose tetrameter couplet. For the rest, verse appears in a few selected instances. It appears first in the scene during which the project of climbing F6 is broached by Ransom's brother, refused, and then, on being seconded by his mother, accepted: prose is used in this scene until the intimate conversation between Ransom and his mother, which is in verse. The elimination at that point of the realistic framework within which the rest of the scene is written is accomplished by the mechanical device of darkening the rest of the stage and concentrating the lighting on Ransom and his mother, thus defining a distinct playing area which excludes for the moment those who lie outside the intimate sphere suggested by the dialogue and justifies the more intense style in which it is written. Each of the three appearances of Ransom's mother receives special treatment. On the second, she is alone on a darkened stage in "a sudden penumbra of light," and the scene ends in a song the words of which suggest a poem for children. She appears again in the final scene as the veiled figure at the top of the mountain. This final scene, in which all pretences of verisimilitude are abandoned for expressionistic methods, is introduced by a dignified speech in verse by a chorus, and verse is used occasionally during the scene. Verse is used also in Ransom's speech on the death of Gunn, which leaves him alone for the final stage of the ascent to the top. It is a Hamletesque soliloquy in blank verse. Verse is thus reserved for moments of the highest psychological or emotional intensity, or merely as one of the auxiliary devices of an expressionistic method. Except for the last scene, the removal of the realistic barriers to verse is accomplished by isolation—with the aid of mechanical devices of lighting in one and the impression of Ransom's complete physical and emotional separation on the mountain peak in the other.

On the Frontier is a play of the same order in the sense that it is chiefly in prose with verse used sparingly for special effects. It deals with the road to war between two contiguous rival European countries. The play is developed in a series of alternating episodes, one dealing with the affairs of a powerful and cynical financier and manufacturer, Valerian, and the other with the attitudes of two typical families, the Thorvald family of Westland and the Vrodny-Hussek family of Ostnia. In the family episodes the two groups are represented simultaneously, each occupying one half of the stage. They are unaware of each other's presence except for the two young people, Anne Vrodny and Eric Thorvald, who are represented as vaguely conscious of a mutual yearning toward each other.

Verse is used for two distinct purposes. There are four before-the-curtain sketches which may be thought of as choral in their function, reflecting a leftist or popular-front point of view. They represent, in order, factory workers, political prisoners, dancers and two leftists, and soldiers of both sides. Their songs contain suggestions of the blues, the popular song, and the ballad. Verse is also used in two episodes during which Anna and Eric speak together, the first time before the declaration of war, and the second at their death in the scene which closes the play. The mere elimination of the tacit barrier between the two rooms is a sufficient destruction of the conventional considerations which govern the language for the rest of the play, but the introduction of the verse is further assisted by the device used in *The Ascent of F6* of dissociating the two characters from the others by a ring of light on a darkened stage. This device illustrates again the necessity for the arbitrary introduction of unmistakably conventional devices which can succeed in forcing a break from the presumptions of realism in order to make verse possible in the course of the action, as distinct from such dramatically discrete elements as interludes between the acts or choruses. In this instance, the ring of light takes on a symbolical meaning as well, the spot where the young lovers can communicate, a separation from the darkness where they lose one another. Verse is useful here not only to give to the sentiments of the young people a greater poignancy, but also to distinguish their hope and idealism from the hard, benighted confusion which runs through the play:

> *Anna.*   In sorrow and death
> We tasted love.

> Eric.   But in the lucky guarded future
> Others like us shall meet, the frontier gone,
> And find the real world happy.
> Anna.   The place of love, the good place.
> O hold me in your arms.
> The darkness closes in
>
> . . . . .
>
> Both.   Dry their imperfect dust,
> The wind blows it back and forth.
> They die to make man just
> And worthy of the earth.

The device is effective in a theatrical way; it is striking, ingenious, and makes an immediate attack on the emotions. But it illustrates the difficulty of the merely occasional use of verse. The critical intelligence of Auden and Isherwood has already been too much for it; in the context of the almost unrelieved anatomizing and irony which precedes, this sudden affirmation of faith and hope seems like the pathetic and misguided immaturity of the adolescent youngsters, Anna and Eric, rather than the concluding sentiment of the play. It is, in fact, a general weakness of these plays that any positive affirmation, like that of Crewe and Norman at the end of *The Dog beneath the Skin*, or the appearance of Karl Marx in *The Dance of Death*, or the final scene between Anna and Eric, seems unexpected and improvised, and the language seems rhetorical either because it fails to reach the intense symbolization of the critical or ironical passages or because, by almost seeming to disregard them, it appears also to fail to have resolved them. It is symptomatic that there is a greater impression of vitality in such a performance as *The Dog beneath the Skin* where inventive ingenuity and satire are of the essence and the helter-skelter untidiness is not inappropriate, than in the two later plays where control over the form would also imply control over the intellectual issues which are implied and incorporated in the dramatic framework and where critical irony by itself is not quite enough.

This is not a criticism which could be applied to Spender's *Trial of a Judge* (1938), where the issues are precisely and clearly opposed and expressed. It is one of the most lucid and one of the most clearly-designed plays among recent examples of verse drama, and the term is more proper to it than to those of Auden's plays in which verse is an incidental instrument to be used for a few special effects.

Spender's play, moreover, gives the appearance of conforming more nearly to older notions of tragedy than most serious modern drama does. The play is concerned with a distinguished judge who tries certain Nazis for the brutal murder of a Jewish communist. The Judge believes in an abstract justice superior to the state, and sentences them to death according to law. He then presides over the trial of certain communists who wounded a policeman when they were bullied for distributing pamphlets, and finds them guilty under a new law which requires the death penalty for carrying firearms. His sense of humanity is outraged by the first crime, and his sense of fairness is outraged by the demands made on him by the law in the second. Yet his friend Hummeldorf, an official of the state, urges him to reprieve the Nazis in order to placate the new leader who has become very powerful. Moved by arguments of desperate expediency to save the state, the Judge consents to the reprieve and withdraws his demand for clemency for the communists. But seeing the arrogant violence his act has encouraged he renounces the death sentence for the communists, only, however, to discover that his power has been taken from him, and that he is on trial by the political gangsters. In the end, he is imprisoned and finally executed, questioning whether his courage at the right moment might have stemmed the tide of lawlessness and subordination of truth and justice to the service of a state that idealizes violence. However, the Judge is not, in reality, this tragic figure who by failing to be true to himself unleashed forces of evil and brought about his own destruction; as the communist prisoners tell him, he would have accomplished nothing by such courage, for he would have been quite useless to them, an antiquated liberal, whose very death will not breed new opposition as will theirs and is therefore a useless martyrdom. It is, in fact, the communists who have the last word: "We shall be free. We shall find peace." It thus appears that the resemblances of the Judge to the older type of tragic hero are superficial, and that the clarity of design in this play is accomplished by using the Judge as a central point around which are developed the progress of the Nazi revolution and the clashing views concerning the individual, the law, and the state. Up to a point the whole interest of the play is in the conduct of the Judge, but after his decision to reprieve the communists, the emphasis shifts, until in Act V the play resolves itself into a display of ideologies.

This emphasis affects the art of the play in several ways. It calls for great simplification of character, so that in the end the opposition of ideas will not suffer greatly from the individual qualities of their spokesmen. Only the broadest qualities of character are allowed to associate themselves with the different views—the intellectual honesty and humanity of the Judge, the brutality of the Black Troopers, the defiant confidence of the Communists, etc. The human tragedy in the person of the Judge is thus largely eliminated. In a sense, however, this is one of the conditions which enables verse to be written about this contemporary theme, since demands of verisimilitude need not be made on symbols and cartoon-like figures. Another circumstance which supports the verse treatment is the large use made of expressionistic methods. The play begins just after the Judge has pronounced sentence on the fascists, but the whole first act is conceived of as "a dream in the Judge's mind." With the stage decor and the acting designed to suggest this conception, little further preparation is needed for the verse which is used during the act. The second act, which is given over to a discussion between the Judge's wife, Hummeldorf, and the Judge, begins in prose, but frequently moves into verse as the opposition becomes more pointed and the expression more emphatic, until the concluding portion is entirely in verse. Act III is in verse. In large measure it is taken up by the argument between Black Troopers and Communists, and the staging is formally treated, opposing groups functioning as choruses with an occasional individual speech on a rostrum. Act IV is pure expressionism, a dream in Hummeldorf's mind. The final act becomes chiefly a concentrated opposition of the main views developed in the play; it is entirely in verse, which now hardly needs the expressionistic formalization in the staging to establish a proper setting for it. The use of expressionistic methods makes possible something more than a purely forensic exploration of the themes, and the simplification of character and the formalized staging make possible a harmony between the dream-state scenes and the rest. Granted the aim, the handling of the means is intelligent and judicious.

Since the scheme of the play eliminates the importance of the personal emotion, the function of the language becomes to endow the ideas with the proper emphasis and coloring and to give vividness to the descriptions of the general situation. To this end individual speeches are often successful, particularly those of the Judge:

> My mind no more dwells in printed codes
> Ordered to peaceful judgments like a poem,
> But in a cold dark vault, under a court
> Where justice is murdered: and in cells
> I see the trampled bodies of the dead
> And hear the living shriek: and those
> Who are the most disfigured, I yet recognize
> As the most just: and from this vault
> Run corridors through tall perspectives
> Of future years until they break their shafts
> Into gaseous air amongst the scalding ruins
> Of cities.

But the method of simplification tends also to reduce the thought to a common denominator, so that the clichés of the ideology often appear. Sometimes these are made telling through the force of some metaphor:

> Your world, comrade, is built upon a lie
> Which is the suffering of the many that the enlightened few
> May pick truths out of chaos
> Then claim 'beauty is truth, truth beauty' to justify
> The injustice of the total lie
> By saying it pressed those diamonds
> From years of dark and terror.

But more often phrases such as "the spoiled children of the rich" or "the masses" have the effect of undermining the strength of some passage with the flavor of party oratory:

> That is the signal for our attack!
> When liberal justice whines of violence
> Power flies to those with the right of might.

To state the case in an extreme way, *Trial of a Judge* is not so much a drama as an argument in play form, with the methods of expressionism as the vehicle which makes possible symbolical treatment and verse dialogue. The choruses themselves, used in recent verse drama for a variety of purposes, here stress this quality of the play, particularly in Act III with the opposing lines of Communists and Nazis confronting each other. The best things in the play, aside from some eloquent speeches of the Judge, result from the figurative brilliance, the pointed edge, which Spender gives to the oppositions in the controversy. The concluding line, "We shall be free. We shall find peace," is a call to action, not the artistic resolution of a tragic poem.

There are a few other recent verse plays which deserve attention in any survey. For example, C. Day Lewis's *Noah and the Waters* illustrates in its fusion of the medieval morality play and symbolical ballet the freedom with which modern poets select for their experiments, and MacNeice's *Out of the Picture* is perhaps the most finished example in recent verse drama of the expressionistic variety-show kind of performance. Although there has been nothing in America comparable to the drama which Eliot and the younger group of poets in England have written, the latter chiefly in connection with the Group Theatre of London, isolated instances deserve to be taken seriously; for example, the early work of Alfred Kreymborg and a play by Delmore Schwartz, *Shenandoah*. Consideration of these or other perhaps equally worthy examples would not add greatly to the understanding of the problems which confront the modern poetic dramatist and of the ways he has chosen to meet them, or modify the general picture of the accomplishment of our times in the form.

Seen in retrospect, the present age does not appear to have established any clear tradition or general style for the writing of poetic tragedy in the sense that the Elizabethan age did from *Gorboduc* to Marlowe. Each attempt seems to end in itself. Davidson, an early precursor of the modern effort, was unable to fix on any single procedure that would satisfy him for more than one or two tries. Yeats developed an original and often beautiful form of his own, but it had little resemblance in the end to what he apparently had in mind at the outset, and, except for a slight influence, it seems to have died with him. The latest development appears more vital because it is not centered in the work of one man, and it gives the impression of being a growing movement, until a glance at the dates shows that the entire output of this "movement" lies between 1932, the date of *Sweeney Agonistes*, and 1939, the date of *The Family Reunion*. Compared with the steady and vigorous development of the realistic drama, the verse experiments appear tentative and sporadic.

What gives the plays of the most recent poet-dramatists in England the appearance of a vigorous and continuous movement is that most of their work has in common a use of the devices and methods of expressionism, a style already well established in the modern theatre. The plays of Eliot, though not properly speaking expressionistic, are characterized by the use of a variety of verse forms and an ingenious use of several idioms within the same play and by unusual stage contrivances, so that his methods appear in many ways analogous to those of the younger group. Expressionism offers a number of advantages to the modern poet who wishes to write plays. It provides a simple solution to the problem of establishing a dramatic world appropriate to verse dialogue, and one, moreover, which makes use of devices already well tried in the theatre and familiar even in popular commercial drama. It provides ingenious schemes for the symbolical as well as direct exploration of ideas, and thus gives the poet some assurance that he will not lose himself in the archaic dramatic attitudes and clichés of another day. It lends itself, moreover, to the ironies, ambivalences, and unexpected associations of modern poetry. At the same time, expressionism is distinctly limited as a vehicle for poetic drama. It tends to encourage emphasis on the ideas as such, since it is possible to construct an expressionistic play which does not have an "action," with the result that the stylistic quality of the play is often controlled by the needs of argument and rhetorical effect. It tends to reduce character to an emblem and thus to intellectualize the matter of the play too much. By depending a good deal on technical devices and novelties, it tends to overstimulate theatrical ingenuity and cleverness. And in the end, the poet discovers that it is a mixed boon, since, while it provides a recognized dramatic convention which enables him to exercise his craft as he cannot in other current dramatic styles, it defrauds him as well, because verse and a poetically ordered diction need be no more than an auxiliary device among various others used in combination. In the expressionistic plays of Denis Johnston and Sean O'Casey, for example, the moments of impassioned or florid language do them no great credit as poets, but the fine writing can be made to pass in the general scheme of things. Spender came to the conclusion that expressionism is a symptom of the need or desire for a poetic drama but does not provide the means for a proper fulfillment of the need: "it is, really," he writes, speaking of the verse used in the average expressionistic play, "like the whole apparatus of the expressionistic stage, a hastily constructed improvisation to fill the need for a calmer, more permanent form, and that form, which should take the place of the expressionistic experiments, is the poetic drama . . . . I believe that the writers of poetic drama will learn to do without improvisation as they build up a form which aims at a calm realism." [65] Since Spender does not explain what this "calm realism" is to be or how it will be managed to make possible the use of verse, the statement may be regarded more as a sign of discouragement at the experiments with expressionism rather than as a prospectus for a new solution. It might, in fact, be conjectured whether the abrupt cessation of the most vigorous and promising experiments since the nineteenth century was as much a consequence of the war as of the realization on the part of the poets that they had not, after all, found the right answer.

There is a sense, however, in which the verse dramatists of the thirties in England have achieved a kind of success, and one which has its importance. Certain conclusions about poetry in general and about poetic drama in particular have become so generally current in our age as to be sometimes assumed as axiomatic and to be often entertained as a matter of course. It is one effect of the work of these poets that they have challenged some of these current critical assumptions and brought them into question, in part by their critical writings and in part by their modest accomplishments in the drama. To the problem posed by the failure of the nineteenth-century dramatists in verse and the widespread adoption of the realistic convention, they brought a fresh interest and a new importance not only by searching among the methods of the current drama for their means, but by relating the whole question of poetic drama to the more general problem of the character of modern poetry and the position which it occupies. Their answer to those who have maintained that no one would write verse drama again for performance who had considered the matter seriously has been to consider the matter seriously and then to write a number of plays not one of which is uninteresting or devoid of vitality, and to find theatres where their plays have had an interested hearing. Their answer to those who have maintained that the intellectual temper of the times in which we live is inimical to the creation of poetic drama, particularly poetic tragedy, has been to search the grounds of their own despair and to look there for the matter of the plays. Small and in many ways inconclusive as their accomplishments have been, they have also cast serious doubt on the current assumption that language is "exhausted," by the simple expedient of writing plays in which words are used with originality and at times with great vividness and power.

The dramatic work of the modern poets has had the effect of rendering plausible again a truism which had fallen into neglect, that as long as drama is essentially dependent on the spoken word, it can achieve its maximum power and richness only when the fullest resources of language are made available to the dramatist for whatever artistic needs he may wish to make them serve. The history of the drama shows that the special means by which this is to be achieved cannot be the same for any age, and that in any event success does not come readily. The drama of our own age indicates that we have not yet solved the problem for ourselves. And there is, of course, no telling what might happen to drama. It might succumb to the technical advances of the theatre and become a distant cousin of the motion picture, in which spectacle is of the essence and speech a secondary and even dispensable matter. It might, under the pressure of events, submit to the demands of the pulpit or the party tract. But if these are not the sole alternatives, it is not expedient to be condescending to the dramatic efforts of the poets of our age or disregard what they have said. They have been trying to say, in effect, that simply because salvation once came to the theatre by taking the business of serious playwriting out of the hands of men whose chief merit was that they were poets, we have perhaps not been wholly wise in concluding that the theatre will henceforth prosper only by keeping them out and discouraging their efforts. And in their plays they have given some evidence that perhaps we have been overhasty in concluding that a poetic drama can never again make its appearance—in a form which we cannot foresee, but which will be suitable to its theatre and to its time.

NOTES

CHAPTER I

1. The premises about drama which underlie this study show an obvious dependence on Aristotle's *Poetics*. However, the theoretical discussions should not be looked upon as an interpretation of, or commentary on, Aristotle. Opinion continues to differ as to the meaning of the *Poetics*, and the question of whether the present study represents a legitimate way of understanding that treatise or a proper extension of its principles should not be made to stand in the way of considering the present analysis on its own terms.

2. T. H. Dickinson, *Playwrights of the New American Theater* (New York, 1925), p. 251.

3. Mortimer Adler, *Art and Prudence* (New York, 1937), p. 644, note 164.

4. Levin Schücking, *The Meaning of Hamlet* (London, 1937), p. 52.

5. Granville-Barker has an excellent analysis of those qualities of Shakespeare's verse which are dramatic in the sense that the verse is adapted to the exigencies of the actor's speaking of the lines, the accentuation of vital words and phrases, and the building up of emotional heightening. See *On Dramatic Method* (London, 1931), pp. 67–112.

CHAPTER II

Note: I have modernized the spelling and made changes in punctuation in the quotations from Elizabethan plays. In some instances, therefore, I do not reproduce the text exactly as it is to be found in the editions to which I refer for the line numbering. All editors of this drama do not adopt a uniform practice, some reproducing an early text even to typographical peculiarities and others modernizing thoroughly, so that a strict following of the editions I have used would have introduced a lack of stylistic consistency in the chapter and needlessly set off certain lines as more archaic in flavor than others.

1. William Archer, *The Old Drama and the New* (Boston, 1923), p. 5.

2. T. S. Eliot, *Elizabethan Essays* (London, 1934), p. 10.

3. Muriel Bradbrook, *Themes and Conventions in Elizabethan Drama* (Cambridge, 1935), pp. 1–2.

4. *Ibid.*, p. 6.

5. *Ibid.*, pp. 30–31. Italics mine.

6. *Ibid.*, p. 59.

7. *Ibid.*, pp. 37–38. Levin Schücking, whose *Character Problems in Shakespeare's Plays* shows some affinities with this method, occasionally refers to Shakespeare's art as "primitive" in much the same way as Archer applies the term to the minor Elizabethans. A composite view of the fruits of this school of criticism may be seen in Elizabeth Drew's *Discovering Drama*, in the chapter, "The Elizabethans."

8. U. M. Ellis-Fermor, *Jacobean Drama* (London, 1936), p. 30.

9. *Ibid.*, pp. 42–43; also, pp. 48–49.

10. *Ibid.*, p. 31; also, p. 227.

11. See, for example, the leading article in the (London) *Times Literary Supplement*, July 3, 1937.

12. Briefly discussed in their relation to drama and diction in Wolfgang Clemen, *Shakespeares Bilder* (Bonn, 1936), pp. 306ff. For other general influences on style see *Ibid.*, pp. 278–85.

13. See W. G. Crane, *Wit and Rhetoric in the Renaissance* (New York, 1937), and Hardin Craig, *The Enchanted Glass* (New York, 1936), Chapter III.

14. W. G. Crane, *Op. cit.*, pp. 204–5.

15. Scaliger, *Poetics*, Book I (trans. F. M. Padelford; New York, 1905), p. 3.

16. David Klein, *Literary Criticism from the Elizabethan Dramatists* (New York, 1910), pp. 5–9.

17. Puttenham, *Arte of English Poesie* (ed. Arber; Westminster, 1895), p. 148.

18. Illustrative references in F. W. Bateson, *English Poetry and the English Language* (Oxford, 1934), pp. 34–37.

19. Richard Stanyhurst, Dedication to his translation of *The Aeneid* (1582), in Gregory Smith, *Elizabethan Critical Essays* (Oxford, 1904), I, 137.

20. In Smith, *Elizabethan Critical Essays*, II, 288–92.

21. The influence of these "falls of princes" narratives on Elizabethan tragedy has been discussed in Willard Farnham, *The Medieval Heritage of Elizabethan Tragedy* (Berkeley, 1936) and Howard Baker, *Induction to Tragedy* (University, La., 1939), These books press a little too vigorously the thesis that Seneca's plays were a relatively unimportant influence on the development of Elizabethan tragedy.

22. Quoted by T. M. Parrott in the notes to his edition of *The Plays of George Chapman* (London, 1910), I, 607.

23. On the origin and characteristics of early English blank verse, see Tucker Brooke, "Marlowe's versification and style," *Studies in Philology*, XIX (1922), 186ff.; Howard Baker, *Induction to Tragedy*, pp. 48–105; and John Bakeless, *The Tragicall History of Christopher Marlowe* (Cambridge, Mass., 1942), II, 173–204.

24. Howard Baker seems to reverse this emphasis: "The formula of the balanced line is, for Marlowe, a point of departure and a point of return. It seems consequently to be the norm of his rhetoric" (*Op. cit.*, p. 196). Baker later notes that "Marlowe also made positive strides in the development of eloquent and articulate metaphors" (*Ibid.*, p. 98). I am inclined rather to accept Tucker Brooke's view that the rhetorical devices under consideration are not really a very vital feature of Marlowe's verse (*Op. cit.*, p. 196). T. S. Eliot stresses as Marlowe's chief accomplishment in the handling of verse his introduction into blank verse of "the melody of Spenser" and the integration of individual lines into a larger unit: "He gets a new driving power by reinforcing the sentence period against the line period" (*Elizabethan Essays*, p. 27). *Gorboduc* shows some interesting anticipations of this kind of verse paragraphing; for example, Marcella's lament over the death of Porex at the end of 4.2.

25. My analysis is confined to Part I only of *Tamburlaine*. Part II impresses me as a relatively confused and less unified performance. Though it deals with the same characters and a similar series of military triumphs, and is characterized by the same grandiloquence, it does not deal with the same issues as Part I, at least not in the same way, and it does not reveal the same harmony of elements. A different view of these two plays is discussed by Roy Battenhouse, *Marlowe's Tamburlaine: a Study in Renaissance Moral Philosophy* (Nashville, 1941).

26. Howard Baker discusses the effect of these metrical tragedies on early Elizabethan tragedy, and particularly on Kyd, in the chapter "The Heroic Medium" in his *Induction to Tragedy*. Though his comments on Kyd show discernment, I believe he claims too much for the influence of this limited poetic tradition on Elizabethan tragedy generally.

27. The additions to *The Spanish Tragedy* by an unknown writer—generally assumed until recently to have been Ben Jonson on the basis of a note in Henslowe's Diary—suggest some interesting inferences on collaboration and revision in Elizabethan drama, and raise some suspicions on the method of establishing authorship of plays or portions of plays on the basis of imagery. There is hardly more than a trace in the additions of the patterned schemes which survive in Kyd's verse from the early experiments with dramatic blank verse; but in the free handling of rhythms to express Hieronimo's distraction, the later dramatist is following Kyd's practice, though his lines show greater flexibility and ease. What is particularly striking, however, is the use in the additions of Kyd's figurative schemes. The light-dark images appear and with much the same function; for instance, in Hieronimo's incomprehension

> That such a black deed of mischief should be done
> On one so pure and spotless as our son.   (2.5.79–80)

And in the extension of this imagery a few lines further when Hieronimo
pleads for death:

> Be gracious to me, thou infective night,
> And drop this deed of murder down on me.
> Gird in my waste of grief with thy large darkness,
> And let me not survive to see.the light
> May put me in mind I had a son.   (2.5.92–96)

Moreover, allusions to heaven and the underworld are introduced in much
the same way as in the original; for instance, in the expression of Hieronimo's reflection that perhaps heaven has its own way of punishing the
guilty ones:

> Well, heaven is heaven still,
> And there is Nemesis and Furies,
> And things called whips,
> And they sometimes do meet with murderers.   (3.2.40–43)

28. There have been a number of important studies of Shakespeare's
plays which depend on a consideration of their imagery. A convenient
survey of these is to be found in U. M. Ellis-Fermor's *Some Recent Research
in Shakespeare's Imagery* (London, 1937). Caroline Spurgeon was the first,
apparently, to make a study of Shakespeare's imagery on an elaborate and
systematic scale. The full results of her researches appeared in *Shakespeare's Imagery and What It Tells Us* (1935), in which she classifies Shakespeare's favorite categories of imagery as well as those of his principal contemporaries. She uses this information to discover the qualities of Shakespeare's mind, and suggests the possibility of using the method to settle
questions of authorship (on this point see note 27). As concerns Shakespeare's art, the most suggestive feature of her study is the demonstration
that in each of the plays there appears to run one or more series of related
images which derive from a single category of impressions or experiences.
Except for a few isolated hints, she does not associate the imagery directly
with the dynamic relations which function in the dramatic action. G. Wilson Knight—notably in *The Wheel of Fire* (1930), *The Imperial Theme*
(1931), *The Shakespearean Tempest* (1932)—also relies on a detailed consideration of the imagery in Shakespeare's plays, though not in the same
way as Spurgeon. One gets the impression that Knight regards the action
of the plays as a crude and, at best, a conventionally useful business which
served the dramatist merely as a framework. He treats the plays as a great
mystical-religious vision which was given body through myths, and whose
language is the imagery seen as a consistent body of symbols, dissociated
from the plot and distinct from any relation to character regarded psychologically or ethically. Moreover, Knight views the entire corpus of
plays as the complete statement of the vision, and hence, in spite of illumi-

nating comments on particular plays, seems to regard any generalization about a particular play as isolated and unresolved unless seen in the context of all the rest. Wolfgang Clemen, in *Shakespeares Bilder, ihre Entwicklung und ihre Funktionen im dramatischen Werk* (1936) discusses the development of Shakespeare's use of imagery chronologically. He analyzes the technical construction of the most important types of images, calls attention to the development of an increasing closeness between the image and the thing to which it is applied, and reveals a gradual shift from explicit figurative constructions to implicit ones during the course of Shakespeare's career. Clemen demonstrates the association of images with individual characters and important "themes," but he does not, except for incidental observations, carry the analysis to the point of associating the images to the form of any individual play regarded as a dramatic whole.

29. Caroline Spurgeon in *Shakespeare's Imagery*, pp. 310–15, has called attention to the use of images suggesting light and darkness in *Romeo and Juliet.*

30. This pun acquires additional interest from the use of religious figures in association with ideas of love: Romeo refers to his love for Rosaline as "the devout religion of mine eye" (1.2.93); the first meeting with Juliet is signalized by the elaborate playing on the conceit of the pilgrim, the kiss, and the shrine; in the balcony scene Juliet is a "bright angel" and "dear saint," and she refers to Romeo as "the god of my idolatry"; and in the same scene in which the pun appears (3.3), the doom of banishment is referred to as hell and purgatory since heaven is where Juliet is.

31. A. C. Bradley, *Shakespearean Tragedy* (2d ed., London, 1914), p. 266.

32. The discussions in the Greek and Trojan camps respectively in *Troilus and Cressida* (1.2, 2.2) contain excellent expressions of the issues centering in the political and ethical aspects of the law of nature. The following quotations will give some notion of the flavor of contemporary discussions of these issues and hence of the implications latent in the term "nature." The analogy between the laws of nature (or reason) in the ethical sphere and the physical, which was frequently drawn, is illustrated in the following from Hooker's *Of the Laws of Ecclesiastical Polity*, Book I, Chapter VIII: "Laws of reason have these marks to be known by. Such as keep them resemble most lively in their voluntary actions that very manner of working which nature herself doth necessarily observe in the course of the whole world. The works of nature are all behoveful, beautiful, without superfluity or defect; even so theirs, if they be framed according to that which the law of reason teacheth." The notion of the confusion occurring when the principle of order and mutual dependence is broken is expressed by Elyot in *The Governour*, though the context is primarily political: "Moreover, take away order from all things, what should then

remain? Certes, nothing finally, except some man would imagine eftsoons Chaos, which of some is expounded a confused mixture. Also where there is any lack of order needs must be perpetual conflict: and in things subject to Nature nothing of himself only may be nourished; but when he hath destroyed that wherewith he doth participate by the order of his creation, he himself of necessity must then perish, whereof ensueth universal dissolution" (Everyman's, p. 3). Order in this context has also the implication of subordination. The following, from a popular rhetorical work, Thomas Wilson's *Arte of Rhetorique*, deals with the relation between the law of nature and the restraints imposed by custom, and alludes also to the problem of parents and children: "And therefore though nature hath not stirred some, yet through experience that man hath concerning his commodity, many have turned the law of nature into an ordinary custom, and followed the same as though they were bound to it by a law. Afterward, the wisdom of Princes, and the fear of God's threat, which was uttered by his word, forced man by a law, both to allow things confirmed by nature, and to bear with old custom or else they should not only suffer in body temporal punishment, but also lose their souls forever. Nature is a right that phantasy hath not framed, but God hath graffed and given man power thereunto, whereof these are derived: religion and acknowledging of God, natural love to our children . . . ." (Oxford, 1909, p. 32). There are fewer expressions of the antirationalistic conception of the law of nature than of the rationalistic. Montaigne's *Essays*, however, offer examples: "I have (as elsewhere I noted) taken for my regard this ancient precept, very rawly and simply: That 'we cannot err in following Nature:' and that the sovereign document is, for a man to conform himself to her. I have not (as Socrates) by the power and virtue of reason, corrected my natural complexions, nor by Art hindered mine inclination. Look how I came into the world, so I go on: I strive with nothing" (Florio's translation, Everyman's III, 316). See also Theodore Spencer, *Shakespeare and the Nature of Man* (New York, 1945), pp. 139–46.

33. *Wheel of Fire*, p. 176.

34. The extraordinary number of animal images has been several times commented on. Bradley suggests that their presence in *Lear* and *Timon* is related to "the idea that this bestial degradation will end in a furious struggle of all with all in which the race will perish" (*Shakespearean Tragedy*, p. 246). Caroline Spurgeon notices them also and connects them with the images of physical strain and torsion (*Shakespeare's Imagery*, pp. 338–43). Knight associates the animal images with his view of the play as an "imaginative vision emergent from a pure naturalism" (*Wheel of Fire*, p. 225).

35. *Shakespeare's Imagery*, pp. 338–43.

36. Even in this play, however, Chapman was unable to preserve con-

sistency between the ideas and the persons who express them. Parrott calls attention in his notes to the Byron plays to a number of discrepancies of this sort (*The Plays of George Chapman*, I, 604, 605, 607, 613).

37. Examples are collected in F. L. Lucas' general introduction to his edition of *The Complete Works of John Webster* (London, 1927), I, 15.

38. *Ibid.*, I, 17.

39. *Ibid.*, I, 25–26.

40. *The Works of Cyril Tourneur* (edited by Allardyce Nicoll; London, 1929), p. 6.

41. For a characteristic statement of this not uncommon view see Felix Schelling, *Elizabethan Drama* (New York, 1908), II, 333-35.

42. T. S. Eliot, *Elizabethan Essays*, p. 139.

CHAPTER III

1. The history of this drama and the considerable contemporary theory concerning it are only incidental to the present discussion. The standard historical studies are those of George H. Nettleton, *English Drama of the Restoration and Eighteenth Century* (New York and London, 1914), and Allardyce Nicoll, *A History of Restoration Drama* (Cambridge, 1923; revised ed., 1928). Critical appreciation supplemented by historical treatment is to be found in Bonamy Dobrée, *Restoration Tragedy, 1660-1720* (Oxford, 1929) and Cecil Deane, *Dramatic Theory and the Rhymed Heroic Play* (Oxford and London, 1931). Clarence Green's *The Neo-Classic Theory of Tragedy in England during the Eighteenth Century* (Cambridge, 1934), though not very rigorous in its analysis, gives a general account of some of the principal critical questions and of the diversity of opinions concerning them. Critical theory is also taken into account in the work of Deane mentioned above.

2. Dobrée says concerning the place of action in the drama of the Restoration: "If, in expelling psychological subtlety, it reduced character too much to a cipher, at least it gave plot the foremost place (except where pretty verbiage got a stranglehold), a place which it yields to character to the detriment of the drama; for character is only the secondary symbol, meant to give life to the poet's main symbol, which is the plot" (*Restoration Tragedy*, p. 181). I believe Dobrée has been misled by the theoretical speculations of Dryden's age. The dramatists and critics often seem to be saying that the action is their primary concern. I do not believe, however, that it actually was.

3. Compared with a writer like Otway, Dryden's scenes of passion may be less numerous and extensive, but I do not believe Dobrée is justified in saying, "Clearly it is idle to blame Dryden for not painting the passions, since that was not what he was trying to do" (*Restoration Tragedy*, p. 93).

4. The following is quoted from Deane's comparison of heroic drama and French heroic romance: ". . . . both share that intricacy of design which was the age's substitute for amplitude, and which imperilled, while it changed the course of many arts . . . . Furthermore, interminable discussions hamper the course of their action; this may be partly derived from some mistaken notion of epic stateliness, which would also account for the notable absence of humor in both forms" (*Dramatic Theory and the Rhymed Heroic Play*, p. 9).

5. A convenient account of this controversy may be found in Deane, *op. cit.*, pp. 161–83.

6. I believe Dobrée exaggerates the distinction which he draws between the "antithetical couplet" and the "dramatic couplet" (*Restoration Tragedy*, pp. 48–50). Except for certain minor differences necessitated by the dialogue and, in the plays of Dryden especially, the occasional breaking of the couplet pattern for the sake of variety and ease, the couplet in the drama and in the other verse of the times seems to me to be essentially the same. Superficial manipulation of the mechanics of rhythm and rhyme should not be too greatly stressed where the handling of the language and the molding of the larger units out of the distichs is so very much alike.

7. Deane comments on this feature of the plays: "The fashion of the characters' arguing out all the possible issues during a critical phase of the action, and finally adopting the course presented by the winning argument, was probably inherited from the French heroic romances, in which these debates figure largely, as we have seen. The antithetical balance and precision of the regular distich, as Dryden perceived, made the latter the ideal vehicle for such abstract disputations, and eventually they became part of the regular stock-in-trade of the heroic play; so much so that they were gleefully seized upon by parodists" (*Op. cit.*, pp. 170–71).

8. The excellent use which was made of couplet verse in satire is scarcely ever reflected in the heroic plays. Occasionally, however, the satirical vein breaks through furtively, as in the following reply of the Emperor in *Aureng-Zebe* to Nourmahal's insistence on her virtue:

Such virtue is the plague of human life—
A virtuous woman, but a cursed wife.
In vain of pompous chastity y'are proud;
Virtue's adultery of the tongue, when loud.
I with less pain a prostitute could bear
Than the shrill sound of "virtue! virtue!" hear.
In unchaste wives
There's yet a kind of compensating ease;
Vice keeps 'em humble, gives 'em care to please.
But against clamorous virtue, what defence?

It stops our mouths and gives your noise pretence.   (2.256–66)

9. Byron, who was a great admirer of Otway, expressed violent distaste for Belvidera, though he did not appreciate how damaging his sentiments were for the play as a whole: "I am aware of what you say of Otway and am a great admirer of his,—all except that maudlin bitch of chaste lewdness and blubbering curiosity, Belvidera, whom I utterly despise, abhor, and detest . . . ." (Letter to Murray in *Letters and Journals* [ed. Prothero, London, 1898–1902], V, 89).

10. Prologue to *Aureng-Zebe*, ll. 21–22.

CHAPTER IV

1. A good brief account of the general theatrical conditions of the time and of the reasons for the decline is that of Allardyce Nicoll, *A History of Early Nineteenth Century Drama, 1800-1850* (Cambridge, 1930). The work of E. B. Watson, *Sheridan to Robertson* (Cambridge, 1926), contains a great deal of interesting information.

2. J. G. Lockhart, *Memoirs of the Life of Sir Walter Scott* (Boston, 1881), II, 63.

3. *The Dramatic and Poetical Works of Joanna Baillie* (2d ed., London, 1853), p. 6.

4. *Ibid.*, p. 10.

5. *Ibid.*, p. 10.

6. The Inns of Court and academic drama of the sixteenth century is not comparable, but the activity of the group centering in the Countess of Pembroke in translating and adapting Garnier was carried on in an even more purist spirit than the work of some of the nineteenth-century "closet" dramatists. The two tragedies of Fulke Greville also were not intended for performance on any stage.

7. Edward Bulwer-Lytton, *Dramas and Poems* (Boston, n.d.), p. 104.

8. *Ibid.*, p. 175, note.

9. St. John Ervine, "Shelley as a Dramatist," in *Essays by Divers Hands* (London, 1936), n.s., XV, 90–106.

10. See E. S. Bates, *A Study of Shelley's Drama The Cenci* (New York, 1908), pp. 47–48, and Ervine, *Op. cit.*, pp. 78–82.

11. Some of the influences are dealt with briefly by Bates, *Op. cit.*, pp. 54–55. Bates notes also the effect of Greek drama in the extended speeches and in the fact that "it is rare for more than two persons to be on the stage at once" (p. 57).

12. The letter is quoted in Mrs. Shelley's note to the play.

13. See Bates's comparison with others of Shelley's works (*Op .cit.*, pp. 65–80).

14. For a general discussion of Byron's plays see Samuel Chew, *The Dramas of Lord Byron: a Critical Study* (Göttingen and Baltimore, 1915).

15. *Letters and Journals* (ed. by R. E. Prothero; London, 1898–1902), V, 230–31.

16. *Letters and Journals*, V. 268.

17. *Ibid.*, V, 218.

18. *Ibid.*, III, 399.

19. Chew, *The Dramas of Lord Byron*, pp. 38–40.

20. *Letters and Journals*, V, 217.

21. *Ibid.*, V, 347.

22. *The Works of Lord Byron: Poetry* (ed. by E. H. Coleridge; London, 1899–1903), V, 199.

23. Frederick Faverty, "The Source of the Jules-Phene Episode in *Pippa Passes*," *Studies in Philology*, XXXVIII (1941), 97–105.

24. The most convenient source of information about the plays and about Browning's dramatic career is William De Vane's *Browning Handbook*. There is also Thomas Lounsbury's *The Early Literary Career of Robert Browning* (New York, 1911), which is more elaborate on the critical side.

25. The Shakespearean influence is the only one which has been studied in detail. G. R. Elliot, "Shakespeare's Significance for Browning," *Anglia*, XXXII, 90–162, is often uncritical. See also De Vane, pp. 88, 170; Lounsbury, pp. 68–71. Other influences are touched on in De Vane, pp. 91, 123, and in the article by Faverty previously cited.

26. Lounsbury's study is interesting in this connection, though at times moral rather than esthetic considerations predominate. Three long articles deserve mention: Caroline Sparrow, "Browning's Dramas," *Modern Language Notes*, XXII (1907), 65–71, 97–103; Arthur Du Bois, "Robert Browning, Dramatist," *Studies in Philology* XXXIII (1936), 626–55; and H. B. Charlton, "Browning as Dramatist," *Bulletin of the John Rylands Library*, XXIII (1939), 37–67. These analyses, though very different in detail, have in common the conviction that, given Browning's basic ideas, his peculiar way of regarding man, it must necessarily follow that Browning would not succeed as a dramatist in the conventional sense.

27. For a recent tilt, see J. M. Purcell, "The Dramatic Failure of *Pippa Passes*," *Studies in Philology*, XXXVI (1939), 77–87; and J. M. Ariail, "Is *Pippa Passes* a Dramatic Failure?" *Studies in Philology*, XXXVII (1940), 120–29. See also G. H. Clark in *Sewanee Review*, XVIII (1920), 213–17.

28. In illustration of this point, there is the lyric sung by Mertoun while he is climbing in at Mildred's window at midnight. It begins, with an immediate assault on idiom,

There's a woman like a dew-drop, she's so purer than the purest, and continues with a description of her beauties that piles up a violent juxtaposition of adjectives—

. . . while her tresses, sunnier than the wild-grape cluster,

Gush in golden-tinted plenty down her neck's rose-misted marble.

It also contains such harsh phrases as "the lark's heart's outbreak tuneless."

CHAPTER V

1. William Archer, *The Old Drama and the New* (Boston, 1923), p. 269.

2. Thomas Dickinson, *Playwrights of the New American Theater* (New York, 1925), p. 128.

3. *Ibid.*, p. 152.

4. William Butler Yeats, *The Cutting of an Agate* (New York, 1912), p. 73.

5. G. B. Shaw, "Cymbelline Refinished: a Variation," *London Mercury* XXXVII (1938), 375. Much of the present day rejection of plot and action as a primary requisite of drama is accompanied by a non-Aristotelian understanding of the terms; for example: "What we might have learned from Ibsen was that our fashionable dramatic material was worn out so far as cultivated modern people are concerned: that what really interests such people on the stage is not what we call action—meaning two well known rather short-sighted actors pretending to fight a duel without their glasses, or a handsome leading man chasing a beauteous leading lady round the stage with threats, obviously not feasible, of immediate rapine— but stories of lives, discussions of conduct, discovery of pitfalls—in short illumination of life" (Quoted from Shaw by Andrew Malone in *The Irish Drama* [London, 1929], p. 24).

6. Allardyce Nicoll, *British Drama* (New York, 1925), p. 345. Some of the premises and some of the conclusions in this statement seem to me disputable. For instance, "Nothing really happens in *Ghosts*." Nothing? A middle-aged woman comes to the realization that her life has been a hypocritical sham, a new orphanage burns down without insurance, a life-long friendship is broken, a mother learns that her son has congenital syphilis, and, while the son visibly corrodes under her eyes, the mother is faced with the decision of whether to permit her son to live out his life as a repulsive imbecile or kill him with poison then and there! Much less "happens" in *Oedipus* at the other end of Nicoll's scale. The last sentence quoted seems to me to do almost as well for *Hamlet* as for *Ghosts*. The phrase "quiet room" might have to be modified, but if it will do for Mrs. Alving's home it could, with a little stretching, be made to do also for the castle at Elsinore.

7. Joseph Wood Krutch has dealt with this problem in a series of articles, "The Meaning of Modern Drama," *The Nation*, CXXXXI (1935), 269ff.,

291ff., 320ff., 351ff. He touches on it again in *The American Drama since 1918* (New York, 1939).

8. Note Yeats's remarks on these characteristics of the native Irishman in *Plays and Controversies* (London, 1923), pp. 13, 168.

9. The impression which these scenic advances once made is hard to exaggerate. "With the opening of the new century there came a renascence that carried forward the imaginative potentialities of design to points undreamed of in the previous history of the stage. The growth of this movement is by many considered the most important event in the history of the modern theater. The artists of mass and design and color came to the stage with new enthusiasm. They had a new world to work in. Design had become dramatic. Movement had entered into design. The reverberations of daily discoveries extended not only throughout the theater but into the studios as well" (Dickinson, *Playwrights of the New American Theater*), pp. 41–42.

10. Much has been written on the question of just what expressionism is and what its historical antecedents were. An illustration will indicate the difficulty of using the term with precision. Krutch says in his *American Drama* of Lawson's *Processional*, "The method was again the method of expressionism . . . ." Lawson himself says in the Preface to that play, "I have endeavored to create a method which shall express the American scene in native idiom, a method as far removed from the older realism as from the facile mood of Expressionism." Both, however, recognize in *Processional* the departure from realism, the dramatist's dissatisfaction with the limitations of realism, and his desire for a more imaginative style. Lawson's Preface to *Processional* is explicit on these points: "And indeed the average drawing-room play has about reached this point of absolute nullity—three walls with footlights on the fourth side, lifeless dialogue and improbable enunciation—these have become a fixed standard. Color and movement are weeded out in the interest of a realism which has nothing to do with reality." On the development of expressionistic drama on the continent see Richard Samuel and R. Hinton Thomas, *Expressionism in German Life, Literature, and the Theatre, 1910-1924* (Cambridge, 1939).

11. Krutch, *American Drama*, p. 245.

12. Louis MacNeice, *Modern Poetry* (Oxford, 1938), p. 194.

13. Archer, *The Old Drama and the New*, p. 387.

14. *TLS* (May 26, 1921), p. 329.

15. Dickinson, *Playwrights of the New American Theater*, pp. 291–92.

16. Archibald MacLeish, "Foreword," *The Fall of the City* (New York, 1937), p. x. An utterly false simplicity is given the problem. Even on the radio, MacLeish has found it necessary to alter "the physical reality of the

scene" by essentially expressionistic devices in order to make it harmonize with the "artifice of verse."

17. Priscilla Thouless, *Modern Poetic Drama* (Oxford, 1934) provides a survey of the work of the principal modern writers of verse drama up to Yeats, but it is somewhat superficial on the critical side. There is also Sister Mary Beatrice Schiller's *Trends in Modern Poetic Drama in English, 1900-1938* (Urbana, 1939), an abstract of a thesis.

18. Maxwell Anderson, *The Essence of Tragedy and Other Footnotes and Papers* (Washington, D. C., 1939), p. 37. The essay from which this is quoted, "Poetry in the Theatre," appears also as a preface to *Winterset*. It is the source of all the critical material quoted from Anderson in this discussion.

19. For a critical but in general sympathetic estimate see J. W. Krutch, *The Nation*, CXXXXII (1936), 484–85, and his discussion of Anderson in *The American Drama*. For an unsympathetic review see Edmund Wilson, "Prize-winning Blank Verse," *New Republic*, XCI (1937), 193–94.

20. Yeats, *Plays and Controversies*, p. 140.

21. Yeats, *Cutting of an Agate*, pp. 30–31. See also *Plays and Controversies*, pp. 13, 168.

22. Yeats, *Plays and Controversies*, p. 121.

23. *Ibid.*, pp. 156–57; also pp. 158, 200–201.

24. Yeats, *Cutting of an Agate*, pp. 42–43.

25. *Ibid.*, pp. 40–41.

26. Yeats, *Plays and Controversies*, pp. 46–47.

27. Yeats, *Cutting of an Agate*, p. 41.

28. Yeats, *Plays and Controversies*, p. 13.

29. *Ibid.*, pp. 119–20.

30. *Ibid.*, p. 176.

31. Yeats, *Cutting of an Agate*, pp. 77–78.

32. *Ibid.*, p. 8.

33. Yeats, *Wheels and Butterflies* (New York, 1935), p. 121.

34. Yeats, *Plays and Controversies*, p. 206.

35. Yeats, *Cutting of an Agate*, pp. 110–11.

36. *Ibid.*, pp. 95–96.

37. *Ibid.*, pp. 113–14.

38. *Ibid.*, pp. 58–60.

39. Yeats, *Plays and Controversies*, p. 217.

40. *Ibid.*, pp. 212–13.

41. *Ibid.*, p. 22; also, pp. 136, 332.

42. Yeats, *Wheels and Butterflies*, pp. 61, 62.

43. Though Yeats felt himself forced into such methods by the circumstances under which he wrote, he seems also to have wanted to establish as

close a bond as he could between his work and the great drama of the past. Thus, he applied to the drama of the past a theory of character which conforms to his own treatment of it but which does not describe very accurately the way character functions in older tragedy. The objection that older tragedy was imperfect in introducing lyric flights into a form which represented character in action he resolved by practically eliminating character from tragedy: "In poetical drama there is, it is held, an antithesis between character and lyric poetry, for lyric poetry—however much it move you when read out of a book—can, as these critics think, but encumber the action. Yet when we go back a few centuries and enter the great periods of drama, character grows less and sometimes disappears, and there is much lyric feeling, and at times a lyric measure will be wrought into the dialogue, a flowing measure that had well-befitted music, or that more lumbering one of the sonnet. Suddenly it strikes us that character is continuously present in comedy alone, and that there is much tragedy, that of Corneille, that of Racine, that of Greece and Rome, where its place is taken by passions and motives, one person being jealous, another full of love or remorse or pride or anger. In writers of tragi-comedy (and Shakespeare is always a writer of tragi-comedy) there is indeed character, but we notice that it is in the moments of comedy that character is defined, in Hamlet's gaiety let us say; while amid the great moments, when Timon orders his tomb, when Hamlet cries to Horatio 'absent thee from felicity awhile,' when Anthony names 'Of many thousand kisses the poor last,' all is lyricism, unmixed passion, 'the integrity of fire.' Nor does character ever attain to complete definition in these lamps ready for the taper, no matter how circumstantial and gradual the opening of events, as it does in Falstaff who has no passionate purpose to fulfill, or as it does in Henry the Fifth whose poetry, never touched by lyric heat, is oratorical"(*Cutting of an Agate*, pp. 199–200; also, pp. 204, 207). This comes close to effecting again the separation of dramatist and poet, which has caused much controversy and confusion in Shakespeare criticism. There is a distinction between the way character is represented in comedy and in tragedy, but is it rather a matter of the accidents operating determinately in one and the essence in the other, a distinction of which Aristotle seems to have been aware.

44. Quoted by Louis MacNeice in *The Poetry of W. B. Yeats* (New York, 1941), p. 195.

45. The two principal followers of Yeats were Sturge Moore and Gordon Bottomley. They adopted the device of the curtain bearers in some of their plays, and even where they did not use that device they contrived plays short and slight in form, and lyrical in treatment, and, particularly in the case of Bottomley, used various methods of formalization suggestive of those of Yeats in his adaptation of the Noh plays. Their work is charac-

terized by meticulous and thoughtful craftsmanship, and they would be worth studying in detail except that this would add little to the critical analysis. The plays of Bottomley had some vogue for a while among theatre societies and experimental groups in this country and in England. His earlier plays are on heroic English themes, concentrated and pas-sionate, and written in good blank verse. He became interested in Yeats's experiments with the Noh form, and aware that "poetry is belittled and misused and maimed in the Theatre," hoped to aid in the creation of "a chamber drama to set beside our most precious heritage of chamber music" (see notes to *Scenes and Plays* [New York, 1929]). The work of Lascelles Abercrombie, though it does not lie strictly within the scheme of these experiments, also deserves notice. It is particularly effective in the short plays which deal with tense situations among rustic characters.

46. Stephen Spender, *The Destructive Element* (Boston and New York, 1936), p. 11.

47. *Ibid.*, pp. 190–91. In *The Modern Temper*, J. W. Krutch argues that our thinking about man renders impossible the writing of tragedy.

48. See James Sweeney, "East Coker: a Reading," *Southern Review*, VI (1941), 771–91.

49. MacNeice, *Modern Poetry*, pp. 174–76.

50. C. Day Lewis, *Collected Poems, 1929-1933* (New York, 1935), p. 219.

51. Spender, *The Destructive Element*, pp. 227–29, 235. See also MacNeice, *Modern Poetry*, pp. 200–201.

52. MacNeice, *Modern Poetry*, p. 16.

53. *Ibid.*, p. 177.

54. *Ibid.*, pp. 17–18.

55. Stephen Spender, "The Artistic Future of Poetry," *New Republic*, LXXVIII (1934), 269.

56. MacNeice, *Modern Poetry*, p. 152.

57. Edmund Wilson, *The Triple Thinkers* (New York, 1938), pp. 40–41.

58. Edmund Wilson, *Axel's Castle* (New York, 1931), p. 120.

59. Spender, "The Artistic Future of Poetry," *loc. cit.*, p. 268.

60. MacNeice, *Modern Poetry*, pp. 193, 196.

61. T. S. Eliot, *The Use of Poetry* (Cambridge, Mass., 1932), pp. 145-46. Also, p. 148.

62. For criticism of the attempt to transform music-hall practice into serious drama see M. D. Zabel, "Poetry for the Theatre," *Poetry*, XXXXV (1934), 152–56, and Stephen Spender, "Poetry and Expressionism," *New Statesman and Nation*, XV (1938), 408.

63. Eliot has complained that English drama has failed to establish a satisfactory and consistent attitude toward conventions. "The great vice of English drama from Kyd to Galsworthy has been that its aim of realism

was unlimited. In one play, *Everyman*, and perhaps in that one play only, we have a drama within the limitations of art . . . ." His general criticism of Elizabethan drama is that there is "no firm principle of what is to be postulated as a convention and what is not" (*Elizabethan Essays*, pp. 9-11, 16-17).

64. Christopher Isherwood, "German Literature in England," *New Republic*, XCVIII (1939), 255.

65. Spender, "Poetry and Expressionism," *New Statesman and Nation*, XV (1938), 408-9.

INDEX